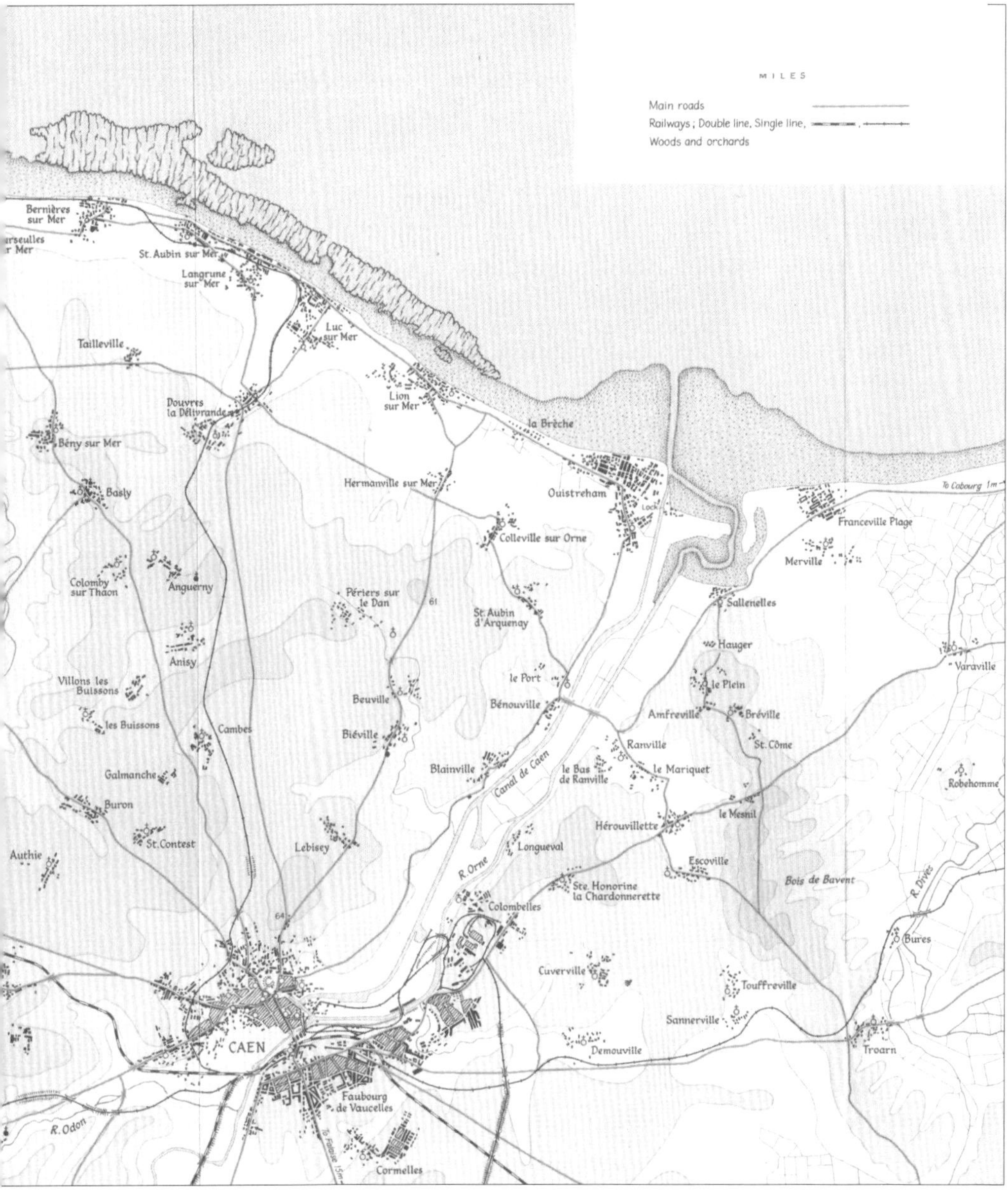

MILES

Main roads
Railways; Double line, Single line,
Woods and orchards

Bernières sur Mer
...rseulles ...r Mer
St. Aubin sur Mer
Langrune sur Mer
Luc sur Mer
Tailleville
Lion sur Mer
Douvres la Délivrande
la Brèche
Bény sur Mer
Basly
Hermanville sur Mer
Ouistreham
Lock
To Cabourg 1m
Franceville Plage
Colleville sur Orne
Merville
Colomby sur Thaon
Anguerny
Périers sur le Dan
61
St. Aubin d'Arquenay
Sallenelles
Anisy
Hauger
Varaville
Villons les Buissons
le Port
le Plein
Beuville
Bénouville
Amfreville
Bréville
les Buissons
Cambes
Biéville
Ranville
St. Côme
Galmanche
Blainville
Canal de Caen
le Bas de Ranville
le Mariquet
Robehomme
Buron
le Mesnil
St. Contest
Hérouvillette
Authie
Lebisey
Longueval
Escoville
R. Orne
Bois de Bavent
R. Dives
Ste. Honorine la Chardonnerette
Colombelles
64
Bures
Cuverville
Touffreville
Sannerville
CAEN
Demouville
Troarn
Faubourg de Vaucelles
R. Odon
To Falaise 15m
Cormelles

SWORD

Limited Signed Edition

SWORD

ALSO BY MAX HASTINGS

REPORTAGE

America 1968: The Fire this Time
Ulster 1969: The Struggle for Civil Rights in Northern Ireland
The Battle for the Falklands (with Simon Jenkins)

BIOGRAPHY

Montrose: The King's Champion
Yoni: Hero of Entebbe

AUTOBIOGRAPHY

Did You Really Shoot the Television?
Going to the Wars
Editor

HISTORY

Bomber Command
The Battle of Britain (with Len Deighton)
Das Reich
Overlord: D-Day and the Battle for Normandy
Victory in Europe
The Korean War
Warriors: Extraordinary Tales from the Battlefield
Armageddon: The Battle for Germany 1944–45
Nemesis: The Battle for Japan 1944–45
Finest Years: Churchill as Warlord 1940–45
All Hell Let Loose: The World at War 1939–45
Catastrophe: Europe Goes to War 1914
The Secret War: Spies, Codes and Guerrillas 1939–1945
Vietnam: An Epic Tragedy 1945–1975
Chastise: The Dambusters Story 1943
Operation Pedestal: The Fleet That Battled to Malta 1942
Abyss: World on the Brink – The Cuban Missile Crisis 1962
Operation Biting: The 1942 Parachute Assault to Capture Hitler's Radar

COUNTRYSIDE WRITING

Outside Days
Scattered Shots
Country Fair

ANTHOLOGY (EDITED)

The Oxford Book of Military Anecdotes
Soldiers: Great Stories of War and Peace

MAX HASTINGS

SWORD

D-DAY TRIAL BY BATTLE

William Collins
An imprint of HarperCollins*Publishers*
1 London Bridge Street
London SE1 9GF

WilliamCollinsBooks.com

HarperCollins*Publishers*
Macken House, 39/40 Mayor Street Upper
Dublin 1, D01 C9W8, Ireland

First published in Great Britain in 2025 by William Collins

1

A catalogue record for this book is available from the British Library

HB ISBN 978-0-00-869975-8
TPB ISBN 978-0-00-869976-5

Maps by Martin Brown

Set in Minion Pro
Printed and bound in the UK using 100% renewable electricity at CPI Group (UK) Ltd

In memory of Nigel McNair Scott (1945–2023),
my oldest friend, who never failed to read my books,
even the not-so-good ones

A day's trial by battle often reveals more
of the essential nature of an army
than a generation of peace

US historian Russell Weigley

Contents

Illustrations

First plate section

Richard Gale (*Imperial War Museum/H039075*)
Montgomery (*Imperial War Museum/H35682*)
Rennie (*Imperial War Museum/BU1518*)
A north-south reconnaissance image (*Imperial War Museum/ MH1997*)
Aerial view of Merville Battery (*Courtesy Airborne Assault Museum*)
Gliders and tugs (*piemags/Alamy Stock Photo*)
Lord Lovat (*piemags/Alamy Stock Photo*)
Bill Millin (*piemags/Alamy Stock Photo*)
A German panoramic shot (*Bundesarchiv*)
Men of 9 Para (*Imperial War Museum/55349*)
An upward view from Norman soil (*Courtesy Airborne Assault Museum*)
Otway (*Courtesy Airborne Assault Museum*)
Parry (*Courtesy Airborne Assault Museum*)
Jefferson (*Courtesy Airborne Assault Museum*)
Albert Richards (*Walker Art Gallery/Liverpool Museums*)
Richards' painting (*Withdrawing from the Battery after the Battery's Guns Had Been Destroyed., 1944. Albert Richards. Tate, presented by the War Artists Advisory Committee 1946. © Tate, Photo: Tate*)

British paratrooper with a disconsolate German prisoner (*Courtesy Airborne Assault Museum*)
John Gwinnet (*Courtesy Airborne Assault Museum*)
Paul Greenway (*Courtesy Airborne Assault Museum*)
Paras dug in on the Caen road (*piemags/Alamy Stock Photo*)
An aerial of the Caen Canal (*Courtesy Airborne Assault Museum*)
S/Sgt Jim Wallwork (*Courtesy Airborne Assault Museum*)
Howard in the midst of a cluster of his men (*Courtesy Airborne Assault Museum*)

Second plate section

The first view of Sword (*National Army Museum, London*)
Guy Hattu's vivid memoir (*Elsa Frontier, graphic designer/Tallandier*)
Advancing through Ouistreham (*Imperial War Museum/MH_002349*)
A typical Sword Scene (*Imperial War Museum/B5091*)
'Banger' King (*Courtesy of Adam Shuch des-Forge*)
Infantry move inland (*Imperial War Museum/MH2011*)
Aerial view showing choas (*NARA. This image was produced through a partnership with the National Collection of Aerial Photography*)
Tanks crowding the shoreline (*Imperial War Museum/B5111*)
Medics tending a casualty (*Imperial War Museum/B5095*)
Hussars' tanks (*National Archives/DEFE 2/419*)
Men of K.P. Smith's brigade headquarters group (*Imperial War Museum/B5092*)
A famous image of commandos disembarking (*Imperial War Museum/B5103*)
The beach (*Imperial War Museum/MH2021*)

Third plate section

Introduction

The year 2025 marks the eightieth anniversary of VE-Day, end of the Second World War in Europe. This is the last of such major commemorations to be attended by a handful of survivors of the old guard who were themselves participants in the greatest conflict in human history. I have written several big books addressing the macro-story of the struggle. This one is, instead, like my recent *Operation Biting*, a micro-study of the experience of a relatively small number of men, on a single day that was almost certainly the most memorable of their lives even if they were fortunate enough to survive long beyond it. What follows is the tale of a baptism of fire; of how thirty-five thousand British soldiers, few of whom had ever before heard a shot fired in anger, played a critical role in D-Day, most spectacular battlefield event of the Second World War in the West, when they landed on Sword beach and in the soon-to-be-adjoining 6th Airborne Division perimeter. Rather than reprising the 'big picture' of 6 June 1944, except where context is necessary, it focuses upon the impact of the novelty of extreme violence on the British Sword invaders. It fills in many pieces of the jigsaw on which I embarked several books ago, in exploring the countless strands of the Operation Overlord story.

Participants in the previous global struggle, once they had joined the colours and completed training, were thereafter deployed in a theatre of war – for British soldiers, overwhelmingly the Western Front – where they remained until incapacity, death or the 1918 Armistice imposed a closure. In World War II the same was true for Russians and Germans. Likewise the sufferings of occupied and victim societies, in both Europe and Asia, continued uninterrupted until their liberation. Churchill's people, however, enjoyed a relatively privileged experience. They were not occupied, though they sometimes thought themselves to be so – by three million Americans whom they hosted in 1943–44. They had enough to eat, even if rations offered few taste treats. Once the Luftwaffe blitz ended in 1941, until Hitler's V-weapons began to descend on South-East England in June 1944, they were chiefly at risk from road accidents in the blackout, which for long periods killed more civilians than did enemy action.

As for the eventual 2.92 million men of the British Army – a peak attained only briefly in June 1945 – while a minority served in the Mediterranean and Far East, more than half spent the four years between Dunkirk and D-Day training in England, unimaginably bored. Historians of the war devote most of their attention to action, which is understandable. In this book, however, before we hear the sounds and view the spectacle of the invaders' collision with Hitler's Atlantic Wall, I shall try to explain something of men's lives and thoughts during the long years of inaction, before that battle was joined. They knew that the world around them was in flames, but day upon day and month after month, clad in itchy serge battledress, they themselves endured kit inspections, route marches and weapon training, leavened only by more food than was conceded to civilians and by the occasional moderate bliss of a weekend pass out of camp.

When my narrative turns to the 'longest day', the invasion of North-West Europe, I focus exclusively upon events at the extreme eastern end of the fifty-mile D-Day front. Sword was the codename of one of the two beaches assaulted by British troops, the other being Gold, further west. Between them lay Juno, objective of a Canadian division, and beyond all three Omaha and Utah, the US Army's appointed landing places. The three easterly names were chosen by Montgomery, with fish in mind but little sensitivity, since Juno was initially dubbed Jelly. The prime minister intervened, however, to insist that a more dignified codeword should be adopted for the Canadian beach, on which men were plainly destined to die. Those who landed on Sword and its adjoining paratroop drop zone were drawn from the 3rd Infantry and 6th Airborne divisions, together with commandos of the 1st and 4th Special Service Brigades. These formations had in common that the overwhelming majority of their men had never experienced sustained action – even most of those wearing green berets had met the enemy merely as raiders.

In World War I, after the Western Front stabilized in November 1914 commanders adopted the practice of committing units newly arrived in France to serve a few weeks in a relatively quiet trench sector, to accustom them to the least intolerable aspects of war, before subjecting them to its extremities. On D-Day, by contrast, the men of 3 Div and the Airborne were precipitated direct from Britain, where they had spent four years playing at battle, headlong into its most hellish circumstances. In some cases the first shots which these civilians masquerading as soldiers heard fired in anger were also the last.

Many found it almost as shocking to inflict injury or death as to suffer it. A few miles inland from the beach, a British commando NCO was confronted by a fifteen-year-old Wehrmacht prisoner from Graz, whom he had just shot in the stomach with his Bren gun and who was now screaming in agony. The corporal asked a Viennese Jewish interpreter the German word for 'sorry' – '*verzeihung*' – which he then kept repeating to his victim, explaining that he had never shot anyone before. Next day this penitent novice in the craft of killing, one among thousands who had entered Normandy that morning, was himself killed.

How did these virgin soldiers bear themselves? What manner of warriors did they show themselves to be? The modern legend of D-Day, strongly influenced by Steven Spielberg's movie *Saving Private Ryan* and his TV mini-series *Band of Brothers*, purveys a sense that 6 June was a pre-eminently American story, which is not so. British and Canadian losses on D-Day were at least half those of the US Army, and contributed at least as much to the overall triumph. Richard Gale's 6th Airborne Division suffered 17 per cent casualties and achieved a critical success, such as Arnhem's more famous Operation Market Garden, four months later, did not.

In my 1984 book *Overlord*, which explored the Normandy campaign from both sides, I wrote much about the German and American experiences. I shall not revisit their stories, nor my word-portraits of the command personalities, only recalling the doings of Rommel's soldiers insofar as this is necessary to frame what happened to the British. My main purpose is to address relatively little people, in a detail that was unattainable in my earlier broad-brush books.

Many published memoirs by old soldiers of all ranks bear scant relation to the record of events in which they participated. My understanding nonetheless benefits, I hope, from recollection of the many interviews with Normandy veterans which I carried out between 1981 and 1983, and then again in the early twenty-first century, when they were still hale and hearty. Oral history is unreliable on points of fact, but at its best conveys an incomparable sense of time and place, to lend colour and shade to a historian's narrative. Among those associated with Sword whom I met were Patrick Hennessey of the 13th/18th Hussars; Arthur Heal, an engineer who played a significant role in the 1st Suffolks' controversial assault on the Hillman strongpoint; German artillery officer Rudolf Schaaf and Werner Kortenhaus of 21st Panzer Division. I also recall a rough-shooting party in West Berkshire at which one of my fellow guests – the chairman of Lloyd's as it happened – wore a faded camouflaged smock. I asked him where he had got it. He responded laconically: 'with 6th Airborne on D-Day'. This was Sir Havelock 'Hal' Hudson, former adjutant of 9 Para, who on 6 June was severely wounded in the storming of the Germans' Merville Battery, above Sword beach. Such men were ever after revered by their contemporaries, and it seems right that it was so.

Many of those who landed from the air were delivered to the battlefield by glider. In our own, morbidly risk-averse era, we should retain a sense of awe that thousands entrusted their lives to these craft constructed of plywood and canvas, weighing seven tons fully loaded and frail as gigantic child's toys. It defied probability that hundreds of such weird artefacts, unique to that brief season as tools of war, completed passages to France and offloaded cargoes of men and guns to engage the enemy.

An important point about all battles, notably including the Sword invasion sector on 6 June, is understood by few people who have not attended a war. Memoirs, reports and war diaries chronicle what happened, but say little or nothing about what did not. They narrate violent incidents as if these took place in a continuous succession. Yet between conspicuous dramas most men on D-Day spent many minutes, and sometimes hours, doing nothing. They were awaiting decisions, orders, clearance of mines and wreckage, preparations for attacks. These intervals of inactivity, mostly enforced by circumstances rather than by choice, contributed critically to the relatively slow advances inland. Even some commandos, who moved fast, experienced pauses on their lines of march.

Moreover, many units or sub-units stopped and went to ground as soon as they came under fire, in accordance with human instinct. Some quickly thereafter rose again and pressed on, but others reported themselves as 'pinned down' for relatively long periods while they awaited support from tanks or artillery, or merely hugged cover until they could be induced by their officers to renew an advance, at mortal peril. None of this represents abnormal behaviour, but an understanding of it is indispensable to grasping the way the story played out.

D-Day was not, as our parents' and grandparents' generations of British, Canadian and American people fondly believed, the decisive event of World War II. Few modern historians dispute the claims upon that title of Stalingrad and other Eastern Front battles. But Operation Neptune/Overlord was the pre-eminent landmark of Britain's struggle, because it represented the moment of resurrection, almost of rehabilitation, after all the defeats and humiliations which Churchill's forces and, indeed, nation had suffered since 1940.

El Alamein, in November 1942, in which were engaged only a tiny fraction of the forces then in collision on the Eastern Front or later in North-West Europe, remained the only battle of the war that a British imperial army won alone, unaided by US forces. But the landings on 6 June constituted a stupendous feat of planning, logistics, training, air and maritime organization – and courage – in which the British, for the last time in the war, played the dominant part, and in which we, their descendants, should continue to take just pride. I began to write *Sword* posing the same question that fills my mind when I embark upon every new book: what can I tell my readers about war, and about this aspect of this war in particular, which they do not know already? In what follows, I hope to provide some fair answers, not least to the whodunnit – or rather, whonotdunnit – of 3rd Division's failure to fulfil Montgomery's proclaimed purpose of reaching Caen on D-Day. No responsible historian claims that their work represents 'the truth'. Sources are corrupted. Timings are often guesstimates. Even after eighty-one years judgements and conclusions must remain tentative. The best to which chroniclers like me can aspire is to offer fragments of truth, stabs at reality.

In 1994, as editor of the *Daily Telegraph*, I commissioned our defence editor John Keegan to write a fiftieth anniversary study of Arnhem. In this he cast strictures – justly, I thought – upon the 1944 performance of some elements of 1st Airborne Division. A storm of shot and shell descended on Keegan from veterans. Figuratively battered and bruised, he came into my office and told me he would never write about Arnhem again as long as Gen. Sir John Hackett, a brigade commander in the battle, was still alive. My generation of writers must wryly confess that it has become easier to attempt brutally frank assessments of World War II events now that participants are no longer among us, to leap at our throats as once they did, when they believed that 'young whippersnappers' were traducing in print the honour or prowess of their regiments.

One droll twenty-first-century reflection: D-Day was among the last great military events of history for which the narrative addresses the doings almost exclusively of men. That word recurs 561 times in the text that follows, while the word 'women' is used just four. The latter were important members of the supporting cast for the invasion back in England, but in Normandy on 6 June they served almost wholly as spectators and victims, such as was the unwilling fate of hundreds of millions of their gender through the Second World War. By contrast, when the stories are written of the wars of the present and future, women will feature prominently as armed participants, in a fashion that was almost unimaginable to those who fought in 1944.

In this narrative I seek to explore above all human behaviour, rather than to detail each battlefield event in strict chronological succession. Thus, for instance, I mingle the sensations of men as they landed, heedless of the fact that some individuals cited may have experienced them minutes or even an hour or two apart. Stephen Fisher has recently published an impressively minute record of exactly what took place on, off, above and beyond Sword on the morning of 6 June. I am here, instead, attempting mostly to explore hows, whys and wherefores.

What I can assuredly testify about the text which follows is that, as with every such work that I have researched and published since my first book on World War II appeared in 1979, in the two years of writing *Sword* I have learned much that still comes new and fascinating to me, as I hope it will appear likewise to readers, about the conduct of humankind at war.

MAX HASTINGS

Chilton Foliat, West Berkshire, and Datai, Langkawi, Malaysia

February 2025

Glossary

AVRE Armoured Vehicle Royal Engineers – a 'funny' tank, most often a Churchill, fitted with specialized equipment such as a minesweeping flail, 'scissors' bridge, bombard or fascine. On D-Day 'funnies' were manned partly by Royal Engineers, partly by armoured regiments

Bangalore torpedo A device invented in 1912 for blowing gaps in barbed wire, by locking together five-foot sections of explosive-filled tubing, then thrusting them beneath entanglements before detonation

'Blighty one' A slang term carried over from 1914–18, signifying a soldier's dream wound – severe enough to require repatriation to Britain while not inflicting lasting damage upon organs or limbs. Few men on battlefields were fortunate enough to secure these ideal passports home

CO Commanding officer (**2ic** – his second-in-command)

COPP Combined Operations Pilotage Parties – beach reconnaissance teams which operated in wetsuits

CSM & **RSM** Company Sergeant-Major and Regimental Sergeant-Major

DD Duplex-Drive Sherman tank modified to land from the sea, fitted with flotation screens and propellers. It was originally intended that the entire 27th Armoured Brigade should be equipped with DDs, but insufficient modified tanks proved to be available and thus only two squadrons of one regiment fought from them in the Sword sector

D-Day The day appointed for the execution of any military operation, though since WWII the term has been inseparably identified with the invasion of Normandy on 6 June 1944

Decorations Army officers were awarded **MCs** – Military Crosses – for conspicuous single acts of bravery, recipients being almost unfailingly deserving. The **DSO** – Distinguished Service Order – was most frequently awarded to unit commanding officers, sometimes to majors, for impressive leadership, though not all recipients' awards received unanimous applause from their subordinates. Other Ranks were eligible for the **DCM** – Distinguished Conduct Medal – comparable to an officer's DSO, or **MM** – Military Medal – equivalent to an MC. Almost all generals commanding divisions or corps were sooner or later awarded **KCB**s – Knighthoods of the Bath – unless they fell foul of their commanders-in-chief

Firefly One troop in each squadron of many British armoured regiments was armed with a 17-pdr gun, which packed a much more deadly punch against enemy armour than did the usual 75mms fitted to most Shermans

FOB Naval gunnery Forward Observer Bombardment, accompanying infantry, radioing target orders to offshore warships

FOO Artillery Forward Observation Officer who accompanied each infantry battalion, radioing target orders to army gun batteries

Grenades All WWII armies used explosive grenades in huge numbers both in defence and attack. The standard British version was the Mills bomb, introduced in 1915 and afterwards modified into the 36 Grenade, which remained in service until 1972–2021 with the Indian Army. A good man could throw a 36 15–25 yards, and on its detonation fragments might be lethal up to 100 yards, though fortunate soldiers often survived within ten yards. Before going into action men unscrewed the bases of their grenades and inserted primers attached by fuses to detonators. Ahead of use a soldier pulled the ring of the safety pin which restrained a lever that guarded a spring-loaded striker, which banged down onto the primer while the lever flew free. In 1940, a man had seven seconds thereafter before his bomb exploded, but this was shortened to four seconds when it was found that the longer interval allowed the enemy to throw grenades back before they exploded. Butter-fingered soldiers not infrequently killed themselves or their comrades by dropping grenades after pulling the pins, or throwing them short. The Germans meanwhile employed so-called stick grenades, M24s detonated by a pull-cord in the wooden handles, which could be thrown further, but were clumsier to carry.

Heer German word for army, thus the men defending Normandy – except the Waffen SS – were properly referred to as the Heer, whereas the term **Wehrmacht** embraced Hitler's entire armed forces

H-Hour The time appointed for the execution of any military operation, which of course had special significance on 6 June 1944

LCA Landing-Craft Assault – a wooden vessel 13½ tons loaded, capacity 36 men, used to transfer assault troops from ships to shore

LCT Landing-Craft Tank – 286 tons unladen, capacity 4–5 tanks

LSI Landing-Ship Infantry – a larger assault vessel, fitted with gangways descending parallel on each quarter of the bows, to be lowered onto beaches

LST Landing-Ship Tank – a large transport vessel, 1,475 tons unladen, carrying 20 Sherman tanks or 70–120 vehicles. The RN used 59 of them for Neptune, though not in the initial assault phase

LZ Landing Zone for airborne troops

MG34 & **42** The two commonest models of belt-fed German machine-gun, known to every Allied soldier as Spandaus, and superior to any comparable weapons in British hands, because of their higher rate of fire and handiness. Some German strongpoints on D-Day, however, were armed with old French or Czech automatic weapons

NAAFI Navy, Army and Air Force Institutes, the company which since 1920 has run canteens for the armed forces

NCO Non-Commissioned Officer, most commonly a sergeant, corporal or lance-corporal, chief among whom were sergeant-majors, designated as Warrant Officers

NEPTUNE Codename for the initial landings in Normandy, today less familiar than **OVERLORD**, codename for the entire air/land/sea operation to liberate North-West Europe

'O' Group Assembly of officers by a CO in the field, to give orders for an imminent operation

PIAT Projector, Infantry, Anti-Tank – a crude spring-loaded weapon which propelled an armour-piercing bomb up to fifty yards on a good day

RV Rendezvous or agreed meeting point in a military operation

SHAEF Supreme Headquarters Allied Expeditionary Force

Acronyms are inescapable in such a narrative as this, but the list above is designedly limited.

Some regiments were customarily identified by British soldiers through acronyms – for instance, the King's Shropshire Light Infantry were known as the KSLI, the King's Own Scottish Borderers as the KOSB, the East Riding Yeomanry as the ERY, and so on. Below, however, wherever possible I favour referring to such units as Shropshires, Borderers or East Ridings, to minimize acronyms.

All timings in the text are given by the twenty-four-hour clock, thus 9 a.m. is 0900, and so on.

1

Garrisoning Britain

1 'WAR SEEMS TO BE MOSTLY HANGING AROUND'

In June 1940, following the fall of France, the men of the defeated British Army found themselves languishing at home, almost bereft of arms, vehicles and equipment. They had no notion of when, where or even whether they would fight again. During the years that followed tens of thousands of them, along with new recruits in proportion, were dispatched to the Mediterranean or Far East, to participate in Britain's little campaigns against the Italians, Germans or Japanese. More than half of all the King's soldiers, however, including the 3rd Infantry Division which, under Sir Bernard Montgomery's command, had served as part of the British Expeditionary Force on the continent, lingered in their beleaguered island.

At first they formed a garrison, deployed to defend Churchill's people against threatened Nazi invasion. Major Charles Boycott of the 1st Suffolks cherished the memory of a visit to his unit by the prime minister in the summer of 1940. Churchill stuck a mischievous thumb in the wet concrete of one of their new pill-boxes, inscribing his initials WSC. Later in those dark days, Britain's leader delivered one of his greatest BBC broadcasts, to the people of occupied France on 21 October. 'Goodnight, then,' said Churchill, bidding farewell to his broken-spirited wireless audience across the Channel. 'Sleep to gather strength for the morning, for the morning will come. Brightly will it shine on the brave and true, and kindly on all who suffer for the cause, and gloriously upon the tombs of heroes. Thus shall shine the dawn.'

Yet almost four apparently interminable years were to pass, before Churchill's great vision of liberation started to be fulfilled, and Charles Boycott, still serving with 3rd Division, became one of the men who landed on Sword beach. Another such officer was Major John Rex, a forty-year-old World War I veteran, who between 1919 and 1939 had been a civilian – an accountant. Rex wrote bleakly of his own fatalism after Dunkirk: 'The future! There seemed no future.' Their days were devoted to marching, range-firing, exercising for the mystical event which, as early as June 1941, began to be spoken of as 'the Second Front'. This was to be the invasion of Europe, focus of debate, frustration, argument and apprehensive excitement from the humblest pubs in Britain to the conference chambers of the Allied warlords. The 'First Front' was, of course, the struggle which began that same June, between the rival masses of Russia and Germany.

An officer cadet who passed out of Sandhurst in 1943, aged nineteen, was thrilled to find himself joining a tank unit in time to participate in the main event of the Western war. He wrote in the third person: 'For the past two years the invasion had dominated his life. The rest of the war – in Africa, Burma, the Pacific – was a sideshow … He had no idea when the invasion was going to be, but now at least he would make it.' Keith Douglas, another such youthful addition to the army, was more equivocal in his mingled apprehension and curiosity. He sent a verse to a woman friend during his training:

And when I prepare to die behind my gun
I shall not glow with fervour like a sun
Then, whatever will restrain
the coward reasoning closely in my brain
I think it will be that I am mad to see
the whole performance and what the end will be.

This last ambition – for personal survival – represented a privilege to which all humankind aspired. Though the likes of Douglas had unwillingly donned battledress 'for the duration', and subsequently played minuscule warrior parts as best they could, their distant vision was not of winning martial glory, but instead of completing an unwelcome duty, so that they could return to their 'real' lives in offices and factories, homes and schools, on beaches where they might build sandcastles with the children they dreamed of fathering. This was an outcome which more than a few would be denied, including Keith Douglas. Another aspiring poet, Sidney Keyes, wrote likewise before he was killed in 1943, aged twenty-one: 'I am the man who looked for peace and found/My own eyes barbed/I am the man who groped for words and found/An arrow in my hand.'

Many British people between 1940 and 1944 noticed that the happiest men in army uniforms were the Home Guard, elderly dugouts in whom part-time local duty instilled a sense of purpose, and of comradeship, absent from most of their civilian lives. By contrast it is hard to overstate the frustration suffered by British soldiers of the garrison army during those years between the expulsion from France and the return to it. They had been plucked from mostly humdrum but at least sheltered civilian lives, jobs and families, in which they enjoyed the supreme luxury of personal choice, to experience season after season of sun, rain, snow and mud in hutted encampments or on wasteland training areas, often in the company of men with whom they had little sympathy, rehearsing the skills of battle yet denied the chance to practise them. Early in 1942 Ron Lane's colonel paraded his battalion of 3 Div and announced enthusiastically: 'This division has been chosen to spearhead the invasion of France. Just when that will be, we do not know. So we have a new role to play and a lot of new things to learn.' One of Lane's comrades in the tracked carrier platoon said: 'Looks as if we are booked for a hot number!' For weeks and even months, the supposed imminence of action lent urgency and excitement to their training. But as the months stretched into years, how could not disillusionment set in? Tobruk and Alamein, Stalingrad and Kursk, Sicily and Salerno came and went, yet in England men repeated the same routines, fatigues, exercises, drills. 'War seems to be mostly hanging around,' said a rueful 1941 commando officer in Evelyn Waugh's contemporary fictional portrait of those days.

Wartime armies are fundamentally uncivilized institutions, because their business is to organize and condition men towards doing an unnatural thing – killing each other in the most uncomfortable imaginable circumstances. 'Training,' wrote Len Waller, 'was designed to transform sloppy civilians into soldiers. It wasn't done by kindness, either. We were marched and yelled at up and down the barrack square. We were cursed, humiliated, degraded and worked until we were fit to drop. At the end of each day we were allowed to relax by sitting beside our beds polishing and burnishing a bewildering array of equipment.' The armed forces communicated in a strange language of acronyms, which spilled over into civilian Britain: Tommy Handley's vastly popular BBC radio show was called *ITMA – It's That Man Again*. A generation including King George VI learned to laugh at his admonition NCTWWASBE – 'Never Clean The Window With A Soft-Boiled Egg'. They bid farewell to each other with one of the show's catchphrases 'TTFN' – 'Ta-Ta For Now'. Such were, indeed, the last letters spelled out to loved ones by many men posted overseas, some saying TT not merely 'for now'.

Ghosts from India haunted British barracks. When seventeen-year-old Patrick Hennessey joined the 13th/18th Hussars direct from his tank training at Bovington, he met a friendliness that pleasantly surprised him, but old soldiers spoke a language which the Londoner found hard to interpret, 'ungrammatical English laced with infusions of pidgin Hindi. "Got any *muckin* for this *rooti*?" meant "Have you any butter for this bread?", or "Shove some *pani* in me *piala*" would be an invitation to "put some water into a man's cup". A "*bundook*" was a rifle and "*Kitna budgi hi?*" meant "What's the time?"' The 1st Norfolks' Major Humphrey Wilson once sought to communicate with a cluster of foreigners, then turned away and said to a comrade in real or assumed disgust: 'Eric, these bloody fools can't even speak their own language!' Wilson, who had served for years in India, was addressing Frenchmen in Urdu.

Liverpudlian Royal Engineer George Duncan returned from the continent in 1940 on an Isle of Man ferry which he boarded from the Dunkirk mole. In the ensuing four years, he was shuffled around Britain at three-monthly intervals, nowhere permitted to settle. Richard Todd, a doctor's son from West Devon born in 1919, went to Sandhurst in 1940 to transform himself from a budding actor into an army officer, and was asleep one night when the college received a near-miss from a Luftwaffe bomb. Five cadets were killed and Todd suffered puncture wounds. Next he spent two years defending Iceland, and many months bombarding the authorities with applications to join the Commandos or Airborne Forces. He wrote despairingly: 'In the summer of 1943 my three years' army service had had little impact on the course of the war ... I had never seen a shot fired in battle

... I had been wounded in my pyjamas and stuck on a scree slope ... I was beginning to feel a fraud.'

Another soldier wrote of how army life made him feel a lesser creature: 'To thrive on a few encouraging words from an unthinking oaf in authority, to delight in a cup of bad tea and a cigarette snatched between parades, to laugh inordinately at clumsy humour or to be moved almost to tears by another's misfortunes – these were not the natural preoccupations of a mature and fairly experienced mind, yet in all those years they were mine. I was wholly lost in that life, following it with all I had of capacity to experience.' The novelist Anthony Powell, who served as an elderly subaltern with an infantry division training in a remote corner of the British island, wrote of 'that terrible, recurrent army dejection, the sensation that no one cares a halfpenny whether you live or die'. The routines of all units were periodically punctuated by suicides.

Military service ennobled a few men, but immersed and sometimes submerged many more. John Phillips, a graphic artist transformed into an artillery driver, wrote to his wife Peggie after a leave: 'Uniform does something to you. I hope it isn't permanent. In that hotel room I felt quite shy with you ... not quite myself.' A soldier penned a 1940 magazine article about leave, and how dreams of it filled the waking hours of himself and his comrades. But 'when we did at last get our forty-eight [hour passes] ... we realized the revolutionary truth. There is no such thing as leave ... War follows you around ... On the platform of the London terminus it is waiting there to meet you, and as you round the bend of the village street you come face to face with it again. You encounter it in the eyes of your civilian friends. The burr-burr of the telephone in the empty room of the girl who has gone away convinces you.' There was an enduring popular fallacy that mess tea and cocoa were laced with some substance which curbed soldiers' interest in sex. Len Waller decided there must be something in this after spending a week's compassionate leave at home. His wife said she had been 'very disappointed in my prowess as a lover'.

Many of the young of that generation knew nothing of such things, however. In 1939 Stan Bridgen was an eighteen-year-old trainee accountant who lived at home with his parents in Balham. He confessed: 'I was very immature and inexperienced, for I had never had a girlfriend, never travelled more than sixty miles from my home and had a very limited social life because I spent a lot of time studying.' The biggest excitement in Bridgen's peacetime life was playing rugby on Saturdays. By 1942, he was nonetheless a subaltern in the Royal Artillery. Londoner Reg Blake, who would helm a landing-craft into Sword beach, joined the Royal Marines when he reached eighteen, after selling his beloved bike to a friend for three pounds. He shook hands with his father in farewell – 'None of this modern hugging and kissing in those days!', but there were tears in both their eyes. Blake hated abandoning at home a tweed sports jacket in which he took pride. He never wore it again, however, because after a few months' military service he filled out so much.

Finlay Campbell, a stiffly proud young Scot conscripted in 1941 and thereafter a signaller, felt almost permanently dejected: 'I did not like being shouted at.' Appalled by barrack-room language, 'I was surrounded by Englishmen who had barely heard of Scotland and regarded me as a foreigner.' Campbell seriously considered desertion. Some men were, of course, merely relieved to find themselves enjoying 'cushy billets' in England, spared from shot and shell. Those whose peacetime lives had been impoverished and deprived in the pre-war years of the economic depression were sufficiently content to find themselves housed, fed and clothed, with no responsibility save to obey orders. Motor mechanic Albert Griffiths had been summoned to the army in 1939, then married his girlfriend Edna on his twenty-first birthday. They were, he wrote long after, 'two kids, a two-shillings-a-day soldier and his twenty-year-old bride, without a care in the world or a troubled thought for the future, sublimely happy at being married' and thus – let us be frank – to have legitimate access to sex.

Officers and their loved ones were not excluded from such yearnings. When Lt. Robin Dunn was posted to North Africa in 1941, he told his girlfriend that he doubted whether they should get married before he sailed, because he might not come back. She demurred, and they agreed on an immediate wedding: 'Judy thought that if the worst happened, she would prefer to be a widow rather than someone whose fiancé had been killed.' By the time Dunn returned wounded from North Africa, destined for Sword beach, he was father of a daughter.

Albert Griffiths later looked back on his week-long honeymoon as one of the happiest periods of his life. Though he served briefly in the chaos of 1940 France, afterwards he experienced three blissful wartime Christmases at home with Edna and their baby son, while attached to armoured units that went nowhere. He rejected offers of promotion, to diminish his chances of being posted overseas – of engaging the enemy. His haven of tranquillity was rudely assaulted in 1943, however, when his mother warned him that his adored wife had changed her name to Jean and was cavorting with Americans. Griffiths secured compassionate leave to hasten home for a showdown with his spouse, and 'left her in no doubt what would become of her, if she stepped out of line again ... I was very naïve and unworldly wise.' Somehow their marriage staggered on, as did many difficult wartime near-disunions, afflicted by the loneliness of one or both partners. Griffiths shouldered uneventful and relatively comfortable service until he landed on Sword beach in 1944, his condition rendered more tolerable because, in pre-war civilian life, he had so little.

Divisional commander Percy Hobart wrote to his wife: 'I've just been looking through the Compassionate file for Feb. Dozens of cases of pitiful trouble. Officers and men. Dependent invalid mothers: ruined small businesses: arrears of rent: bombed homes: sick wives and families with no home: hopeless loads of overdue instalments for rent or furniture on the instalment system: divorces: unfaithfulness: wife and children gone and not known where etc. etc.'

Most garrison soldiers yearned inexpressibly for useful activity – a chance to play a role that might advance themselves as well as their country up the path towards ending this interminable nightmare; to bring closer the defeat of the enemy, which alone could enable them to return to their real lives and jobs, their women and children, cosiness and comforts. Major John Howard of the Ox & Bucks Light Infantry, who on D-Day would undertake one of the invaders' most dramatic roles, struggled for years beforehand to assuage his company's boredom, the weary repetitiveness of its daily routines, which in 1942–43 seriously corroded its morale. One of his men, Private Wally Parr, had joined the army at sixteen in February 1941 and been chafing ever since: 'Never doing a damn thing that really mattered. Putting up barbed wire, taking it down again the next day, moving it … never fired a rifle.' Many commanding officers addressed this problem by setting their young men incessant physical challenges designed to tire them out. Howard's battalion was once sent for two months' cliff-climbing in Devonshire, then ordered to march 130 miles back to their barracks at Bulford. A young officer succumbed to such ecstasies of indifference during a lecture on how best to combat German tanks that he occupied the session creating an enchanting satirical

study in his SO 223 army notebook. This was Rex Whistler, whom a German tank would kill in Normandy.

Only seven officers and 230 other ranks of the East Riding Yeomanry, few of them from its fighting squadrons, mustered back in England after Dunkirk. They were 'tired, disillusioned and dispirited' in the words of a survivor, but provided a nucleus around which the regiment slowly reformed. The Yeomanry, a nationwide volunteer cavalry force with units recruited within county boundaries and loyalties, which trained at weekends, was a throwback to the Napoleonic Wars. The novelist Walter Scott, himself an old Yeoman, wrote sentimentally in 1826: 'It kept up a spirit of harmony between the proprietors of land and the occupiers, and made them known to and almost beloved by each other; and it gave to the young men a sort of military and high-spirited character which always does honour to a country.'

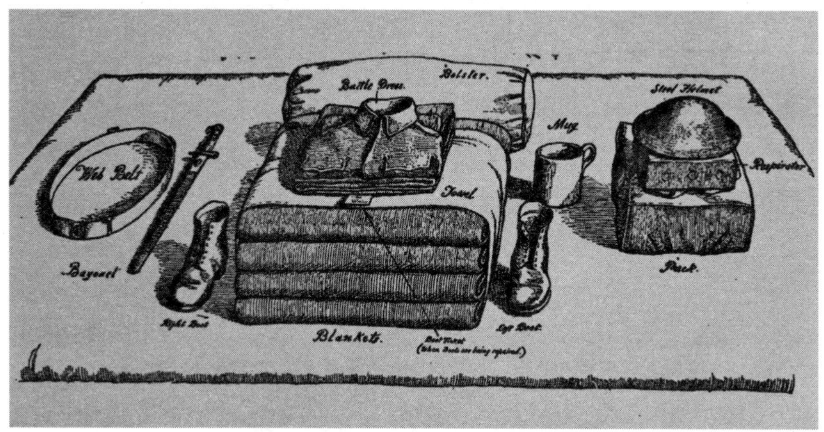

Whistler's sketch of a bed kit lay-out

Even in the twentieth century, many of the Yeomanry's officers were landowners and foxhunters; some of the other ranks tenants on their estates. Its character and traditions sustained a useful cohesion when they went to war. After its regiments were obliged to abandon their horses in favour of tanks in 1941, however, sceptics felt that for all the courage they often displayed on the battlefield, in the armoured role they lacked the professionalism of the Royal Tank Regiment. Be that as it may, the Yeomanry had played a significant role in the North African desert campaigns and would do likewise in North-West Europe, their proficiency increasing. Among themselves, however, even in 1944 they often referred to their tanks as 'horses', crews as 'jockeys'.

In the years before D-Day the East Ridings, like every Home Forces unit, found themselves repeatedly and apparently mindlessly transferred from camp to camp, county to county. Their ranks were combed to provide drafts of skilled specialists – drivers, signallers, gunners – for units fighting overseas. A popular and respected colonel quit in 1943, having insisted upon a transfer to 'a more active theatre of war'. His regiment would eventually land on Sword, but only after four years in limbo.

Those not serving in operational areas were granted a week's leave every three months, plus a day for travelling, and one additional forty-eight-hour pass. Planning for these yearned-for events became an obsession. A soldier wrote to his wife in an attempt to plan a transitory hour together near Waterloo Station when moving from a camp in Kent to another on Salisbury Plain: 'I can't get a room for you on Thursday. It's New Year's Eve and everywhere is full. We could have dinner together. You could come by a train which leaves Victoria at 5.18 and catch one back which arrives at 10.15 … If you stayed the night we should only have ½ an hour together … it's all a bit risky because one never knows what ghastly thing will turn up. I asked the sergeant if he thought I'd get away by 6.30 on Thursday and he said he'll fix it (but he might not be about that day). If I am not on the platform go to the hotel – it's called the Royal Star – about 10 minutes' walk from the station. I've booked a table for dinner at 7. Start if I don't turn up and if I'm not there by 8.15 … take the train back.'

2 OFFICERS AND 'OTHER RANKS'

Then there was leadership, a vital component of morale. When the war began the British Army had 14,000 Regular and 19,000 Territorial officers. Thereafter, almost a quarter of a million more men were commissioned. Almost all unit commanding officers, lieutenant-colonels, were pre-war regulars, aged around forty, though later, under the stress of battle casualties, this could sometimes fall to twenty-five. The overwhelming majority of their subordinates, however, were civilians in uniform. A disproportionate one-third of officers had attended public rather than state schools, a reminder that class remained alive and well in wartime Britain.

A minority treated their men with easy familiarity. Private Len Waller was impressed as well as delighted that off duty his company commander allowed him to listen to the classical music which he loved in the officers' quarters. On 24 April 1944 a long-serving forty-year-old major in the East Yorks, the exuberant, unaffectedly eccentric yet fatherly Charles 'Banger' King, wrote to his batman's mother: 'Thank you for your kindness in doing my washing. As a bachelor I haven't any family worries, but I feel that it's up to me to get as many of my company through this business as I can. The men take the place of a family in my estimation. I have never cared very much what the higher authorities think (which is probably why I'm only a major) and you can be sure that I won't lead your son or any of my company into any damn suicide act. We are a very happy company – and quite efficient too, which is the best protection your son could have.' If King's words were sentimental, their obvious sincerity seems moving. When he received a small legacy, he used some of the money to buy his entire company a drink.

Men respected and indeed loved considerate and courageous officers such as King. They deplored cowardly ones but hated those, of which every unit had at least a small quota, who appeared eager to win medals or promotions on the back of their soldiers' sacrifices. One of Montgomery's divisional commanders in Normandy, G.I. Thomas, became known to his subordinates as 'Butcher' Thomas or von Thoma, because of his supposed indifference to their casualties.

Most officers sustained a distance from their men. Soldiers in many units complained that they seldom glimpsed their CO, and some did not even know his name. Gen. Sir Ronald Adam, the adjutant-general who proved the most imaginative British military administrator of World War II, believed officer training units did too little to teach leadership, seeking instead to produce 'the perfect private soldier', schooled to prize obedience – compliance – above thinking for himself. Huw Wheldon of 6th Airborne Division, despite being commissioned, harboured a distaste for his caste, 'the silly snobbishness about the whole system of officerdom in the British army ... Young gents with nonsense-caps and bad taste & coarse manners and offensive habits & tiresome ways ... sparrow-gents ... They want a new sort of material, but an old sort of officer, with the result that they pick very largely on clerk types who say "endeavour" instead of "try" and "require" instead of "want" ... These English semi-people are no good.'

Wheldon himself sprang from a literate and musical Welsh family – he complained to his battalion chaplain about the low standard of hymn-singing on church parades. He was among many who endured mountainous boredom between 1940 and D-Day, writing glumly: 'In khaki men have nothing except faces. Faces over tea & beer with cigarettes stuck into them. A species, like monkeys or sparrows.' Wheldon incurred suspicion for his alleged 'Bolshie' sentiments, for calling Churchill a mountebank 'which he certainly is in my opinion', and deriding his commanding officer's mindless perusals of *Tatler* and the *Daily Sketch*.

Many officers of the wartime army discovered that their default condition, especially on the battlefield, was anxiety. A lieutenant in his late thirties who had been commissioned in 1940 wrote: 'The proliferating responsibilities of an infantry officer, simple in themselves, yet, if properly carried out, formidable in their minutiae, impose a strain in wartime even on those to whom they are a lifelong professional habit; the excruciating boredom of exclusively male society is particularly irksome in areas at once remote from war, yet oppressed by war conditions. Like a million others, I missed my wife, wearied of the officers and men around me, grew to loathe a post wanting even the consolation that one was required to be brave.'

A soldier of the Home Army who went absent without leave to visit his wife after she gave birth prematurely was marched back to barracks by military police and hauled before his crudely insensitive young company commander who said on hearing the story: 'Well! Two pounds! [weight] She'll probably be some sort of imbecile.' Only when a senior officer intervened was the father granted four days' compassionate leave and disciplinary charges against him withdrawn.

Every officer had his batman or personal servant, which today seems a gross anachronism. Yet there were good military reasons for maintaining the practice. On the battlefield, along with duties of command came endless responsibilities that did not trouble private soldiers: reconnoitring ground, supervising weapons and defences, attending and conducting 'orders groups', monitoring wireless traffic, censoring men's mail, inspecting weapons and feet. Few conscientious officers in contact with the enemy achieved more than two or three hours' sleep a night. It was far more useful to the war effort to assign a private soldier to clean kit for 'his' officer, dig a slit trench, cook the rations, fix a bivouac, than to demand that the platoon or company commander did so, in obeisance to democratic correctness.

A class of cadets under instruction in 1936 were told by their commandant: 'The qualities required by an officer are courage, physical fitness and brains – in that order!' Not much changed in the following decade. Huw Wheldon wrote to his father deploring his new CO: 'Another utterly incredible appointment – a pig-eyed lout of a chap with the legs of a mastodon & the thoroughly credible reputation of having the brains of a hen.' Wheldon eventually transferred to 1st Royal Ulster Rifles, a unit of 6th Airborne Division, and by 1944 was second-in-command of a company, with a reputation for having the loudest voice in his brigade. Despite the strictures above, the British Army's officers, like their men, were a mingling of the good, the bad and the ugly, such as characterizes all mankind.

Infantry bore the brunt of ground fighting, and there were never enough of them, because an overwhelming majority of those in uniform fulfilled support functions, far from the sharp end. For these latter, though classified as soldiers, in the memorable words of John Ellis, 'the war was merely foreign travel tempered by excessive regimentation'. Rifle companies would dominate the confrontation with the German coastal defences on D-Day itself, until tanks secured space to manoeuvre. Less than a third of the men in a 15,000-strong infantry division were combatants. But as David French has written, 'Their significance was out of all proportion to their numbers, for if they were unwilling or unable to advance in the face of the enemy, the whole army stalled.'

It was difficult for the 'teeth arms' to secure their rightful share of the nation's brightest and best. Almost no one, on being conscripted, chose to wear boots and berets, far less to carry a rifle – they sought instead to join the Royal Navy or RAF. John Phillips again: 'Getting involved in this army business does seem an awful waste of time. If I can come out of it a stronger and better person, that'll be something. But it is very maddening to be a protected, trained animal with no ideas or responsibilities, just fed at regular intervals, allowed out at regular intervals, while you' – his wife Peggie – 'have to do everything worth doing, keep the home going on next to nothing, look after the well-being of the children.'

Des Chamberlain, once he found himself unwillingly drafted into the army, hastened to become a signals craftsman: 'The general fear was to end up in the infantry – without a trade, that was it.' Chamberlain would land on Sword beach, but only behind the assault troops, at the wheel of a six-ton truck. The 3rd Division on D-Day boasted 2,603 vehicles including motorbikes, and in consequence much of its manpower, its most technically skilled personnel, were committed to mechanical support functions, rather than to shooting at Germans.

Among all the branches of the army, while signallers received the longest period of training, ten months, infantrymen received the shortest, ten weeks. They were taught only the arts deemed necessary to march, shoot and die. Towards the end of the war when manpower shortages turned desperate, some redundant RAF and navy personnel were compulsorily transferred to the army. Officers immediately noticed how much more physically impressive were these recruits than veteran infantrymen, who stood on average half an inch shorter than sailors, airmen or soldiers serving in specialist roles.

The nation's keenest, strongest and best men volunteered for the armed forces early in the war. Many of those who came later were less impressive. Of 710,000 recruits who joined up after July 1942 only 6 per cent were deemed fit to be officers, and about the same proportion were classified as NCO material. By July 1944, this percentage had fallen to 4.2 per cent. Just a quarter of all

British soldiers had some secondary education, and nearly a third were categorized as possessing below average intelligence. A large number of those nominated to undertake specialist technical training were rejected at the outset, or failed the subsequent courses.

All through those dreary years the army continued to be reinforced by new recruits, as schoolboys turned eighteen and became eligible for service. Foreign volunteers also swelled the ranks – Poles, Czechs, Frenchmen who had survived extraordinary odysseys in order to play their parts. Hubert Faure was born in south-western France in 1914, son of a court bailiff. He served in a tank unit in the 1940 campaign, then fled through Spain where he was consigned to the notorious Miranda de Ebro prison camp, in which inmates were obliged to shout '*Viva Franco!*' at roll-call every morning. He escaped to England in May 1943, and promptly joined a French naval detachment of the British Commandos, led by Commandant Philippe Kieffer, training at Achnacarry.

Guy Hattu reached England after a journey halfway around the world that began when he was demobilized from the French army in Dakar in December 1941. He travelled first to visit an uncle in Rio, then to England where he applied vainly to join de Gaulle and parachute into France as a secret agent. He wrote to a cousin: 'We shall meet again one day, either in Paradise or in France – our France.' After a spell writing radio scripts for the BBC's French Service, he wearied of the Gaullists and their factional struggles, joining the Commandos in March 1943. He became known in his troop as one of 'the three *Guys*' – pronounced 'Geese' in French. The others were Guy Vourc'h and a painter named Guy de Montlaur, who had reached England in November 1940 after a nightmare ten-day voyage in a fishing boat which he and friends clubbed together to buy for 42,000 francs. Meanwhile Maurice

Chauvet had sailed a dinghy from Morocco; been picked up by a Spanish vessel; imprisoned in Algeciras for eighteen months before reaching Britain.

At the commando training centre he enlisted alongside two hundred others who had endured similar travails before earning their green berets. Men like these seem to merit high respect, after voluntarily submitting to such ordeals in order to join the struggle for freedom. Hattu wrote to his uncle in Brazil that he was thankful to have 'plunged himself into military servitude, with all its absurdities … It is only through battle that we can win the right to enjoy once again the freedom which we are threatened with losing.' He was made a sergeant, for a time refusing a commission. In August 1943 he wrote to a friend: 'It is in the front line that a Christian must serve today, on behalf of all those who have flinched, committed treachery or turned away.' In November, Hattu wrote to his mother in France: 'I am proud of not having abandoned the struggle, of having come to England at a time when all seemed lost, of having come here for the sake of honour and fidelity to my beliefs, to fight as a Frenchman alongside the British.'

Yet while Hattu and his commando comrades were confident that sooner or later they would join battle, every formation of the Home Army meanwhile experienced disappointments and anti-climaxes. Early in 1943, 3rd Division was dispatched north to the wilds of Galloway, where its men trained to invade Sicily, and even received two weeks' embarkation leave in anticipation of action. Then, instead, a Canadian formation was assigned to the Mediterranean. The 3rd Division returned to routine exercises. Morale fluctuated, but could be precarious. A tank troop commander wrote of those days: 'The men were discontented, sometimes almost mutinous. On the one hand there was the CO's constant demand for efficiency, on the other constant fatigues for cookhouse, salvage and hut-sweeping, which took two-thirds of them away from their tanks and training.'

Relations between Allied troops crowded into camps the length of Britain were seldom harmonious. Tensions occasionally erupted into violence, especially between British and French-Canadians, who simply did not like each other. 'There is apparently a lot of fighting going on at dances,' wrote a rifleman. The Canadians had a reputation for wild behaviour, not always confined to hostilities against the British. Rumour held that the Fort Garry Horse had killed their cook, as a gesture of disappointment about his culinary shortcomings. As for the Americans, most thoughtful British people acknowledged their pivotal contribution to the Allied war effort but also resented and even feared their wealth, increasing dominance … and energy. Major John Rex wrote with rueful awe: 'They were go-getters, those Americans, they would get their teeth into anything, worked hard, would never admit anything was beyond them.' He was impressed – and a little scared – by the comparison between Yankee dynamism and the relatively sluggish tempo at which his own impoverished, weary nation conducted the war.

By the time D-Day came, a quarter of all adult British men under fifty were in uniform. Yet even after the invasion, a million of the King's soldiers remained in camps, barracks and technical facilities at home. Meanwhile a further five million male civilians, in occupations ranging from boiler-making and lighthouse-keeping to teaching and doctoring, continued to serve in 'reserved occupations', a status for which some became eligible only after attaining a certain age. An unmarried soldier was paid a guinea a week – three shillings a day, fractionally increased in April 1944. This was far less than the pay of a comparable civilian, especially one working in munitions. A private who returned from the battlefield totally disabled gained a pension of £2 a week, plus ten shillings for his wife and 7/6d for each child. Just under half the army was married. If a man over forty was killed, his widow got a pension of thirty-two shillings a week for herself, and eleven shillings for each child. If the man was under forty and childless, this was reduced to a mere pound a week.

In every week of 1944 three million air letters, 4.5 million items of surface mail and half a million brief airgraphs – 'blueys' – passed through army postal services, a reflection of the ruptures and loneliness to which the war subjected families. Colonels may sound lofty figures, but they suffered as much as their men. 'Darling, I am horribly homesick!' wrote forty-four-year-old Jim Eadie of the Staffordshire Yeomanry to his adored wife Naidita. After protracted battlefield service in the Mediterranean, he brought his regiment back to England to prepare for D-Day; enjoyed a brief leave at home; then was obliged to start invasion training in Suffolk.

Eadie was an archetypal Yeomanry officer, an amateur soldier from a smart Staffordshire county family which owned a brewery, in which he himself had worked since 1920 and where in 1939 he was serving as a director. A school and Cambridge athlete, he was a keen follower of the Meynell Hunt. Naidita, born in Chile to a British father and French mother, had married Jim in 1930 when both were thirty. They had four children of which he met the youngest, Alastair, for the first time aged four, on returning from North Africa. At their home in Derbyshire, Naidita cared not only for her own brood, but also for two young cousins. In January 1944 her husband wrote: 'I can never tell you how much I loved my leave. I realise more and more the heroic efforts you have made during these past 4 ½ years, and my love and gratitude are unbounded. I found my family utterly adorable. You have done wonders with them and for them. I couldn't talk to you as I always wanted. This war and the uncertainty of the future dried something up inside me. But one day I will be able to tell you so much more.'

A medical officer serving in the Middle East observed that 'the fidelity of nearly all wives could stand a separation of two years but in the third and subsequent years an increasing proportion of wives lapsed'. As for the men, one wife told her husband, after a written confession of infidelity, that she would overlook what happened abroad, so long as it was not repeated in England. Marital troubles were by no means confined to the lower ranks. The officer commanding 27th Armoured Brigade, Erroll Prior-Palmer, forty-one in 1944, wrote no wartime letters home, because he had no loved one with whom to correspond. In 1940, his wife Kay had left home in pursuit of a relationship with the painter Raoul Millais, raffish grandson of the Pre-Raphaelite. That year in Britain, 26,574 illegitimate births were recorded. Five years later the annual figure had risen to 64,743, and this did not include many babies born to married women by a man other than her husband.

Who could be surprised, given the stresses imposed by sacrifice, uncertainty and often tragedy? Every wife dreaded finding mail returned, with an official stamp: 'It is regretted that this item could not be delivered because the addressee is deceased.' John Phillips's wife wrote to him in December 1943 about the family holiday preparation: 'We went to see Father Christmas at Selfridges … [Linda and Vanessa] are very excited about Christmas. It is the first time Linda has understood anything about it. I think it will be the last Christmas without our Daddy … Here's hoping.' Her dream went unfulfilled. Her husband in North Africa was by then newly dead. When Jack D'Arcy went to show off his new naval uniform to former colleagues in the Bournemouth bank at which he had worked as a teller before the war, one of the girls burst into floods of tears: her husband had just been killed at sea.

As the war advanced, a trickle and then a thin stream of men who had fought in the desert or Italy returned to England. They reported that most Italians were laughably incompetent, but that the Germans were very, very good. Arthur Pearman was a twenty-one-year-old tank crewman, son of a regular soldier, who had served in Palestine and then North Africa without working up much enthusiasm for the war. He quoted a doggerel:

> Oh they fitted us up with Shermans and sent us into the blue,
> We saw the bloody desert from Benghazi to Matruh.
> We chased the bloody Eyeties and we made the bastards run,
> But we dropped a great big clanger when we met the bloody Hun!

Pearman was disgusted – 'permanently browned-off' – to be posted back to England after surviving a year in the Mediterranean, to join a regiment earmarked to land on Sword. As the verse suggests, he and his mates had developed a healthy respect for the fighting power of the German soldier. They knew, as most of their new comrades in England did not, what they would be getting into. Nineteen-year-old Patrick Hennessey asked his sergeant-major, who had seen action in 1940, 'What's it like in battle, sir?' He got the reply: 'Bloody noisy, mate!'

Private Lionel Roebuck left a reserved occupation in a Holmfirth electric motor factory to join the East Yorkshires aged eighteen, in hopes of 'ultimate adventure'. As the war dragged on, he divided his leisure hours between a correspondence course to complete his engineering apprenticeship and giggling nocturnal rendezvous with NAAFI girls in his battalion's Motor Transport park.

Keith Wakelam worked in a naval ordnance depot in Birmingham, which was a reserved civilian occupation he could have retained through the war. His father, a retired music hall entertainer, urged him to do just that. But in 1939, when everybody else was joining up, he felt that he should do the same and trained as an army signaller: 'It had by then dawned on everybody that it was going to be a long war, and there was general gloom.' He volunteered for the commandos.

Here was one of the worst consequences of Home Forces' long inactivity: some of the best and bravest men in their ranks quit their units to don green or maroon berets with the Commandos or Airborne formations, in hopes – often disappointed – of an earlier induction to violent action. Emlyn 'Taffy' Jones joined the former from boredom with his tank unit: 'I thought, "There's a bloody war going on out there, what the hell am I doing?" I could see the war passing me by.' Bill Bidmead was chivvied around the army for eighteen months, growing ever more disillusioned, not least by cooks who sold their units' rations on the black market: 'I was nineteen years old and it didn't look as if I was ever going to have a crack at the Hun.' Near to despair he, too, volunteered to become a commando.

This was the last war in history in which most of the British upper class felt able to employ themselves as they chose. Some opted for heroics, others for relative tranquillity, and the nation's warlords accommodated both. Between Dunkirk and D-Day, many 'toffs' who had donned khaki occupied more time playing than training. John Hislop, a celebrated pre-war amateur jockey, served with the smart Phantom reconnaissance regiment. He found time to ride in several steeplechases, in one of which he was badly injured. Though he spent the subsequent year unfit for military duties, this turned out not to matter: his unit did nothing in particular before he rejoined it in time to enjoy an adventure in France in the summer of 1944.

Some people who should have known better adopted a notably unworldly approach to the titanic clash which, after apparently interminable delay, was now finally approaching. On 4 March 1944 the Archbishop of Canterbury, William Temple, wrote testily to the King's private secretary, Tommy Lascelles, urging that the generals should hurry up and choose a date for the invasion of Europe. The primate was concerned this might clash with Easter or Palm Sunday, and he wished to arrange a day of prayer at a suitable interval before the event. Lascelles observed drily: 'He is, in some ways, most curiously out of touch with realities.' More than a few men of the King's armies nonetheless shared the archbishop's impatience to bring on the action, main event of the Second World War in the West.

2

Montgomery's Fantasy

At Christmas 1943, an officer instructed by his colonel to lay on a special dinner for the men of their armoured regiment in Suffolk went to commune with the unit's fatherly quartermaster, who pursed his lips and nodded. 'It'd better be slap-up,' he said. 'For some poor benders it'll be the last.' And so indeed it proved, though happily no man knew for whom the bell would toll. The tempo of war in the West, so slow for so long, especially in Russian eyes, quickened dramatically at the turn of 1943–44. It became apparent that British and American armies would soon land on the continent. Churchill's island could not indefinitely bear the weight of the five million American, British, Canadian, French and Polish soldiers who now crowded camps and barracks from the south coast to the Scottish Highlands, together with their guns, tanks, vehicles and equipment. A vast amount had changed since Dunkirk, surrender at Singapore and bloody fiasco on the beach at Dieppe, all for the better. The armies assembling had, with the injection of American might and industrial genius, achieved mass such as Britain never dreamed of in 1940, together with weapons, vehicles and air power on a titanic scale.

Many men's training switched from the general to the particular. Formations were earmarked for explicit roles in the landings from the sea, known to naval commanders as Operation Neptune

– the subsequent codeword Overlord embraced the development of the advance across Normandy and then North-West Europe. Some units would form spearheads – airborne troops and a mingling of infantry, engineers and tank crews, designated as 'breaching parties', which must crack the crust of the German coastal defences. Others, notably the armoured divisions, would land later, passing through the first-comers, or whatever survived of them, to exploit inland.

One of the few advantages Hitler's forces possessed in 1944 was that they were already deployed on the continent of Europe. The Allies faced a huge challenge simply to get there, which became the preoccupation of those who would travel first in arms to France, and of their commanders, almost to the exclusion of what might happen later. It was a phenomenon of Neptune that the requirement to stage an amphibious landing before engaging the German army obliged the Allies to devote vast resources to ships, aircraft, weapons, special equipment which would merely transfer Eisenhower's army onto the Normandy battlefield. Most of this prodigiously expensive hardware would become redundant once the Overlord land battle developed.

There was little doubt in anyone's mind that both the invasion and subsequent campaign would be bloody, on a scale unmatched by any previous British or American wartime experience. Of the one French, one Polish, twenty-three American, seventeen British and Canadian divisions concentrated in Britain before D-Day, seven had seen previous war service in the Mediterranean, though each of the other, unblooded formations contained a sprinkling of individuals who had done so. Keith Douglas, newly returned from Tunisia, wrote to his former Oxford tutor Edmund Blunden in April, expressing the 'bolshieness' – resentment – felt by many veterans of the desert campaign and Italy, who were now to be required to fight once more while so many men in England –

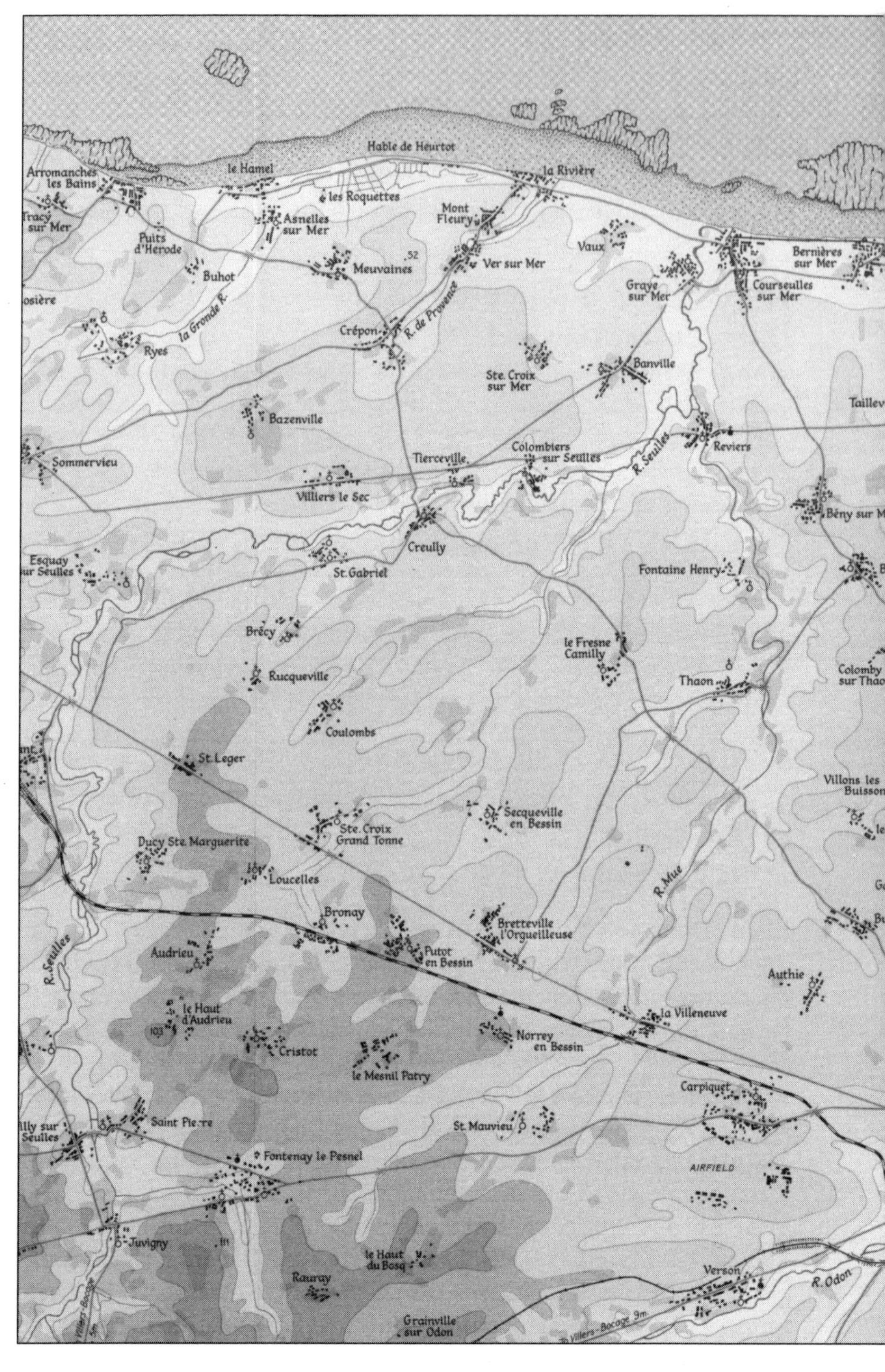

Hable de Heurtot
Arromanches les Bains
le Hamel
la Rivière
les Roquettes
Tracy sur Mer
Asnelles sur Mer
Mont Fleury
Puits d'Herode
Meuvaines
52
Ver sur Mer
Vaux
Bernières sur Mer
Buhot
Graye sur Mer
Courseulles sur Mer
la Gronde R.
R. de Provence
Crépon
Ryes
Ste. Croix sur Mer
Banville
Bazenville
Reviers
R. Seulles
Sommervieu
Tierceville
Colombiers sur Seulles
Villiers le Sec
Creully
Esquay
St. Gabriel
Fontaine Henry
Brécy
le Fresne Camilly
Rucqueville
Thaon
Coulombs
St. Leger
Secqueville en Bessin
Ste. Croix Grand Tonne
Ducy Ste. Marguerite
Loucelles
R. Mue
Bronay
Bretteville l'Orgueilleuse
Putot en Bessin
Audrieu
R. Seulles
Authie
le Haut d'Audrieu
103
la Villeneuve
Cristot
Norrey en Bessin
le Mesnil Patry
Carpiquet
Saint Pierre
St. Mauvieu
Fontenay le Pesnel
AIRFIELD
Juvigny
111
le Haut du Bosq
Rauray
Verson
R. Odon
Grainville sur Odon
To Villers-Bocage 9m

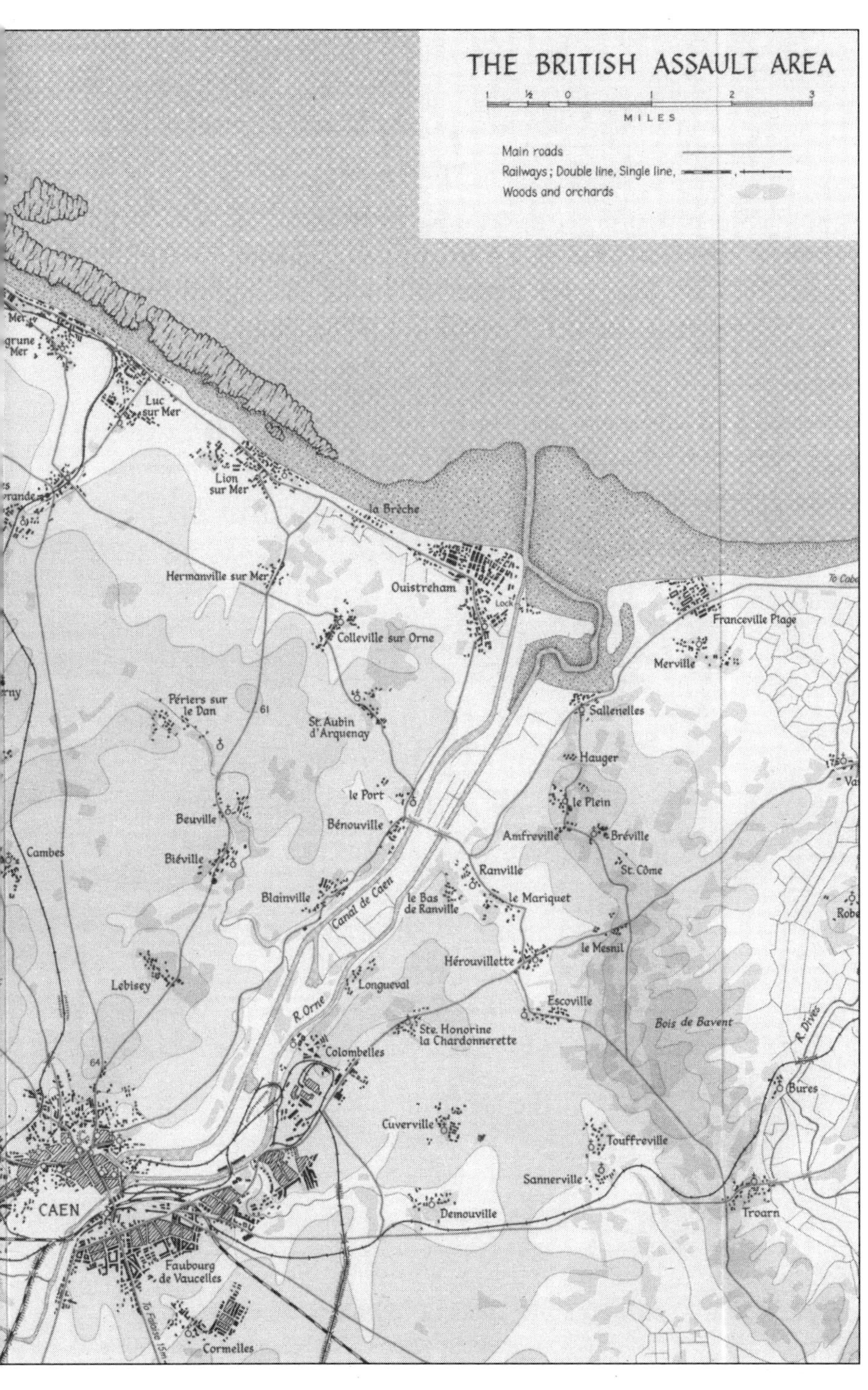
THE BRITISH ASSAULT AREA
MILES
Main roads
Railways; Double line, Single line,
Woods and orchards
Luc sur Mer
Lion sur Mer
la Brèche
Hermanville sur Mer
Ouistreham
Lock
Colleville sur Orne
Franceville Plage
Merville
Sallenelles
Périers sur le Dan
St. Aubin d'Arquenay
Hauger
le Port
le Plein
Beuville
Bénouville
Amfreville
Bréville
Cambes
Biéville
Ranville
St. Côme
Blainville
Canal de Caen
le Bas de Ranville
le Mariquet
le Mesnil
Hérouvillette
Lebisey
Longueval
Escoville
R. Orne
Ste. Honorine la Chardonnerette
Bois de Bavent
R. Dives
Colombelles
Bures
Cuverville
Touffreville
Sannerville
CAEN
Demouville
Troarn
Faubourg de Vaucelles
Cormelles
To Cabourg
To Falaise

including 3rd Division – had been shielded from enemy fire: 'I am not much perturbed at the thought of never seeing England again, because a country which can allow her army to be used to the last gasp and paid like skivvies isn't worth fighting for. For me, it is simply a case of fighting against the Nazi regime. After that, unless there is a revolution in England, I hope to depart for sunnier and less hypocritical climates.'

By contrast, there was real enthusiasm among some of those who were as yet unbloodied. One such wrote in old age: 'In 1944 the war could still be regarded, if not as an adventure, at least as a kind of self-proving ground by those who had not been in action. The end was in sight, we were plainly going to win. As a twenty-year-old subaltern, my chief anxiety was that it might be over before I got there.' Naval officer Jack D'Arcy had likewise enjoyed an astonishingly unfrightening and even domesticated war for four years, skippering small craft on combined operations exercises, mostly in the Highlands of Scotland, where his wife Betty was able to live with him. Until June 1944, D'Arcy's experiences in naval uniform had yielded only an album of happy family snaps. Now, however, he was placed in command of a Beach Control Group destined for Sword, where he would face mortal peril.

General Sir Bernard Montgomery, the victor of Alamein now appointed Allied land force commander for D-Day, made a decisive contribution in January 1944, within days of his return to England from Italy. The invasion planners who had laboured for a year under COSSAC – the acronym for Chief of Staff to the Supreme Allied Commander, which came to mean not one man, though Lt. Gen. Sir Frederick Morgan filled the titular role, but instead his huge staff – proposed that an initial three divisions should assault Hitler's Atlantic Wall on a front of twenty-five miles. 'Monty' immediately dismissed this concept, saying – assuredly rightly – that to land on such a narrow front would make it dangerously easy for the Germans to concentrate forces against it. He insisted, with full support from Gen. Dwight Eisenhower, who now took up his own post as Allied Supreme Commander, that a five-division beach assault was essential, spanning fifty miles of coastline. After serious difficulties raised by sailors and airmen were overcome, Montgomery's will prevailed. Indeed, the reinforced fighting strength of the initial landing force was equivalent to more than six divisions, plus three airborne formations.

The invasion front was broadened to include what was now designated Sword beach, reaching from the small village of La Brèche in the east to Luc-sur-Mer in the west. Beyond the latter to the west lay a five-mile stretch of rocky shallows, unsuitable for landing-craft, so that there would be a gap between the Sword assault force and the Canadians tasked to attack on their right, which would need to be closed inland. The 3rd Infantry Division, supported by 27th Independent Armoured Brigade, together with four Commandos of 1st Special Service Brigade and one from 4th SS Brigade, was to assume responsibility for seizing Sword. Wide coastal marshes surrounded the estuary of the River Orne, to the left of the invaders: these would provide important security for 3 Div's eastern flank. As for the countryside a mile or two inland, also east of the Orne, Montgomery proposed to land a large parachute and glider force – 6th Airborne Division – to protect the amphibious invaders and extend their foothold.

Montgomery's authorized biographer Nigel Hamilton wrote: 'It is to Monty's credit that, however much fame turned his head and inflated an already insufferable ego, he retained his grip and grasp of the essential factors that would determine the coming battle.' This seems just, though the range of his enemies and critics in high places also deserves notice. The Brigade of Guards disliked him, for instance, partly because he was conspicuously not a gentleman, and partly because he, who considered himself instead the supreme player, had no time for them, as perceived dilettantes. Before D-Day he sought to sack the general commanding the Guards Armoured Division, Allan Adair, believing with good reason that he was not up to his job. But Adair had powerful friends, starting with King George VI, and Montgomery's putsch failed, leaving a sour legacy on both sides.

One key issue would remain a bone of contention not merely among Allied commanders, but to posterity: whether it was credible, feasible, attainable to secure on D-Day the key road-junction city of Caen, nine miles south of Sword. At the first formal meeting between Montgomery and the planning staff, at St Paul's School in west London on 3 January 1944, Maj. Gen. Charles West, COSSAC's senior planner, rejected the new C-in-C's claims that his forces could immediately push deep inland: 'I told Monty he couldn't take Caen the first day. He was very optimistic. After all it is nearly 12 miles from some of the beaches. It would take troops a day to move that far. Only large airborne forces could have taken [Caen].' This last proposition was wildly implausible: if the lightly-armed 6th Airborne had landed beyond the city, it would almost certainly have suffered the same fate as did 1st Airborne at Arnhem three months later – to be crushed by nearby German panzers, before relieving British tanks and infantry could reach it from the sea.

West nonetheless clung to his belief in the original COSSAC plan, for a mere three-divisional assault, which anticipated penetrations three to five miles inland on D-Day, then getting Caen on D+3. But an infantryman of 3 Div noted ruefully, and with only modest exaggeration, after the war: 'You can do with a platoon on D-Day, what you cannot do with a battalion on D+1 or a division on D+3', by which time German reinforcements would be massing on the battlefield.

Montgomery knew that the prime minister, a formidably influential member of the Neptune-Overlord high command though he wore no generals' badges of rank, was fearful of stalemate developing around an Allied coastal enclave in Normandy. Churchill told commanders at a briefing in April: 'Remember that this is an invasion and not the creation of a fortified beachhead.' Montgomery spoke of 'pushing forward fairly powerful armoured force thrusts on the afternoon of D-Day … Even a few armoured cars 20 miles inside the German lines would create confusion and delay.' Churchill sought speed, speed, speed from the landing forces, and his Army Group commander repeatedly promised this. Monty said on 7 April: 'The enemy build-up can become considerable from D+4 onwards; obviously therefore we must put all our energies into the fight and get such a good situation in the first few days that the enemy can do nothing against us.'

Once the cocky little commander-in-chief's five-division proposal had been accepted, immense effort was committed to marshal the resources, and to refine the plans, to bring it to fulfilment. One of many misunderstandings about shipping requirements was that commanders and planners made initial calculations based upon the carrying capacity of landing-craft, and especially of LSTs – tank landing-ships. Yet this was not at all the same as these vessels' beach unloading capacity, which was substantially smaller. Thus much more tonnage proved necessary to land the invasion force than had at first been estimated. On 1 May 1944, the US Navy's all-powerful tyrant Admiral Ernest King, who viewed the Pacific as the only theatre of war that should rightfully matter to Americans, had at his disposal across the world 31,123 landing-ships and landing-craft, of which he had allocated just 2,493 to Neptune. The British could do little to make good the shortfall, since they were then building only 150 such vessels a month. The delay of D-Day until June, from its earlier planned May date, was imposed overwhelmingly by the need to overcome King's stubbornness and secure an increased allocation of shipping to convey the invasion forces to Normandy.

Later in this narrative we shall explore the difficulties faced by 3rd Division on the afternoon of D-Day, as its follow-up units sought to push inland in the wake of the spearheads. For now it suffices to say that, whatever commanders said then and historians have argued since, the minds of the men who spent the winter and spring of 1943–44 preparing and training to land on Sword beach, or to make the airborne assault beyond the Orne, were overwhelmingly fixed on the challenge of getting ashore; of seizing their initial objectives. Norman Scarfe, an officer of 3 Div who later became its historian, wrote: 'Try as you would, during the days of preparation you could never project your mind beyond the great assault.' The adjutant of the 13th/18th Hussars thought likewise: 'D-Day was our horizon and rightly or wrongly we didn't look much beyond it.' During the early months of 1944, tens of thousands of men exercised with ever-increasing intensity for the tasks they were to fulfil in the first hours after they attacked, though as yet they were told nothing of the location of their points of descent upon the continent of Europe.

The Germans had meanwhile been labouring furiously, under the direction of the legendary Field-Marshal Erwin Rommel, to transform Hitler's bombast about an 'Atlantic Wall' into something like a reality. The able and experienced Gen. Fritz Bayerlein, commanding the Panzer Lehr Division in France, asserted: 'We considered the repulse at Dieppe as proof that we could repel any invasion.' Wherever on the Channel coast the Allies landed, they faced formidable defences into which twenty-three million tons of concrete had been poured; there were beach obstacles, minefields, wire entanglements, strongpoints equipped with artillery, mortars and machine-guns. 12 SS Panzer Division, stationed east of Caen, was especially eager to fight. In the last week of May, sixty of its key officers were ordered to report to their divisional headquarters, where to their astonishment they found gathered their wives, summoned from Germany. Fritz Witt their general said: 'You can all go to Paris for two days, then say goodbye at the Gare de L'Est!' Walter Kruger, one of those fortunate men, gave his wife all his personal possessions to take home to Germany, 'since we were obviously "for it"'.

Rommel argued presciently: 'It is more important to have one panzer division in the assaulted sector on D-Day, than to have three there by D+3.' He reasoned that in the first days the Allies would not get sufficient tanks ashore to launch a deep thrust inland, and thus the defenders could dismiss that immediate threat. Hitler disagreed, as did Gerd von Rundstedt, his C-in-C in the West, instead ordaining that the most powerful panzer formations be held back from the coast, to be deployed only at Berlin's discretion. The Führer nonetheless continued to pay the price of accepting punishing setbacks to the struggle on the Eastern Front in order to send some key formations to reinforce his armies in the West. Montgomery's intelligence chief, Brigadier Bill Williams, described this as accepting 'more and more Stalingrads in the hope of achieving one Dunkirk'.

Never in history had such sustained intelligence effort focused upon a single prospective battlefield as was now applied by the Allies to Normandy. Ultra – the output of Bletchley Park's code-breakers – was immensely valuable in forming Montgomery's picture of the defences, but decrypts of German army traffic were never comprehensive, and often failed to deliver in 'real time', a limitation that would persist throughout the North-West Europe campaign. In February 1944 Bill Williams thought the Allies might have to fight only six German divisions on D-Day itself. By May he had come to expect eight, two of them armoured. It is hard to overstate the possible impact on Sword beach, especially, if Rommel had got his way and been permitted to deploy 12 SS Panzer, probably the best German tank formation in France, in a position from which it could have counter-attacked the invaders north of Caen – notably 3 Div – on 6 June.

As it was 21st Panzer Division, leaguered just south of the city, became the only major armoured force the British or Americans would meet that day. The Allies knew the formation was there; that it was almost certain to intervene on D-Day. Even at H-Hour, however, they had not pinpointed its exact locations. As for the static coastal defence formations in Normandy, one morning in May Rommel visited the 1716th Artillery Regiment in its positions around Ouistreham, behind what was destined to become Sword beach. He told a circle of officers: 'If they come, they'll come here.' Lt. Rudolf Schaaf did not really believe him. He was one of many posted to France because unfit to serve in the East again, after being twice wounded. His men did as little work as possible, beyond erecting 'Rommel's asparagus' – anti-glider poles – in Norman fields. Every German in France knew how perilous was their predicament: the weakness of the Luftwaffe and German navy; the reliance of the defenders on thousands of Ukrainians, Poles and suchlike, clad in Heer uniforms, to compensate for manpower shortages; the deficiencies in weapons, equipment and mobility. For instance, it was a source of embarrassment to the proud young Nazis of 12 SS Panzer, leaguered thirty miles further east, that each day their letters had to be collected and incoming mail delivered by horses and carts.

The flanks of every army in every war are its most vulnerable and exposed places, and these needed to be secured in the first hours of D-Day. The plan developed by Montgomery's staff demanded that Richard Gale's parachutists deploy on the left of the invasion beaches, even as the two US airborne formations did likewise on the right, at the base of the Cherbourg Peninsula. The Americans would drop twice as many paratroopers, but their British counterparts in the east would be reinforced within hours by the four Commandos of 1st Special Service Brigade, which would speed-march inland from Sword to join 6th Airborne.

Gen. Sir Miles Dempsey later described his February private meetings at St Paul's School with Montgomery and Omar Bradley, to formulate strategy for the Allied drive inland from the beaches: 'We crawled around on the floor spreading out the maps ... Monty stressed that after the immediate [enemy reinforcements] had been brought in, all German reserves would arrive at the battlefront from the East and South-East ... They would have to pass across the British front around Caen. It was to be my job to make sure they didn't move across, that they were kept fully occupied fighting us in the Caen sector. Monty also stressed that whatever happened my left flank had to be kept absolutely secure. The eastern wall along the Orne must be held, otherwise the whole bridgehead could be rolled up from that flank.'

Yet the new, much more ambitious, 1944 plan had important implications for Montgomery's initial objectives, above all the swift capture of Caen. Although an assault by five divisions – which swelled to six, plus the three Airborne formations – would oblige the defenders to spread themselves thin, it would do the same for the attackers. As some planners protested, it lacked concentration at a decisive point. Montgomery dismissed this objection. Yet if he was serious about capturing Caen on the first day, 3rd Division was not remotely strong enough to seem likely to achieve this, even with the formidable reinforcement of 27th Armoured Brigade's 190 tanks. Moreover, in an astonishing moment of naivety, indeed madness, the Allied commanders revived discussion about the possibility of dropping a second

British airborne division, the 1st, on or around Caen to check German panzers which sought to intervene against the beachhead. Fortunately for the Allied cause this proposal foundered, for lack of aircraft to carry them.

When Montgomery conducted his high command briefing for D-Day at St Paul's School on 15 May, Churchill emphasized his bitter disappointment that at Anzio in February the Allies had landed 160,000 men and 25,000 vehicles to achieve a penetration which, three months later, did not exceed twelve miles. At St Paul's, in the presence of the entire Allied senior leadership, the prime minister made plain his own determination, ambition, expectation, that in France the armies should push inland far more aggressively. And Montgomery once again promised this.

Until the very day of the invasion, Allied intelligence estimates continued to change. On 22 May John Crocker's I Corps was warned by 21st Army Group to expect 'immediate local counter-attacks by reserves and tanks of 21st Panzer near the coast and by the 352nd Infantry Division'. The German armoured formation had been recreated from scratch in May 1943 after its forebear surrendered in Tunisia. It was thought that 21 Pz might muster as many as 240 tanks, forty assault guns and possibly a few heavy Tigers, a formidable force, though in reality it had less than half that number of Mk IV tanks, together with forty assault guns and no Tigers. The formation's total manpower strength was sixteen thousand, of whom 4,500 were fighting soldiers.

Montgomery's staff thought that by evening on 5 June, 12 SS Pz might also intervene against the Sword penetration. There were believed to be tank-killing 88mm guns – four of them, along with other less potent artillery – on the Périers ridge, three miles inland. The aforementioned 352nd Division did not, in the event, engage 3 Div on D-Day. There appears to have been some failure of liaison between I Corps and 3 Div about 21 Pz's location – most

British subordinate commanders believed the formation's regiments were deployed between ten and thirty miles inland – within a few hours of the beaches but not as close as they really were.

Before D-Day, Montgomery's preoccupation with his grand tour of Britain and jeep-top addresses to soldiers caused him to show an amazing lack of interest in the intelligence and planning for the battle beyond the beaches. With specific reference to Sword, he never quizzed Crocker about what the corps commander might do in various contingencies. Montgomery himself, if charged with this, would probably have blustered that he issued general directives about plans and objectives then left his subordinates to implement them. It nonetheless seems a historic truth about his record as a commander both in the Mediterranean and North-West Europe that again and again he planned a set-piece battle then failed to think through the follow-up – exploitation of success. Although he would never admit as much, it seems likely he felt unable to make further plans for the development of the invasion after the landings because he deemed it impossible to do so until the outcome of D-Day – the exact land holdings in possession of the Allies at nightfall on 6 June – became apparent.

That shrewd American historian Carlo D'Este has written of Montgomery's commitment to secure Caen on the first day: 'This was the fragile reed upon which the entire campaign in the eastern sector was to be built: all future actions … were predicated upon the successful capture either of Caen itself or of the Orne-Odon crossing in the west.' Thus, 3rd Division's landing on Sword beach assumed a pivotal role in Neptune/Overlord.

3

Paras

To the young men who flew the planes of 1944, and who leaped out of them, powered flight was a mid-twentieth-century commonplace. But to the older generals, admirals, air marshals directing Neptune/Overlord, there was still something miraculous about air power and the immense distance it had travelled technologically in the mere four decades since the Wright Brothers first staggered into the sky. Twenty thousand British and US Airborne troops were to lead the way for the invaders of Normandy, in the early morning darkness of 6 June, to exploit their principal selling point: surprise.

Maj. Gen. Richard Gale's one Canadian and five British battalions, together with support troops, in the initial drop – the division's third brigade was to descend by glider on the evening of D-Day – would occupy high ground east of the Orne river, north-east of Caen. Moreover, three elements of 6th Airborne would be committed to special tasks. A gliderborne *coup de main* force would land ahead of everybody else, British or American, to seize the two parallel bridges across the Caen Canal and Orne, five hundred yards apart, then defend them until relieved from the sea. A parachute and glider battalion would meanwhile assault and destroy a battery of German artillery mounted in concrete casemates at Merville, from which its guns commanded Sword beach. Further east, parachute engineers were made responsible for destroying the five bridges over the Dives river, the only routes by which German defenders might counter-attack through the marshes.

At St Paul's on 7 April Montgomery rang alarm bells with First Sea Lord Admiral Sir Andrew Cunningham by mentioning possible new amphibious and airborne insertions on the continent after D-Day, 'to prevent the battle from becoming static'. He spoke of withdrawing the Airborne troops as soon as they had secured their objectives and been relieved from the sea. This was loose talk such as Montgomery had employed before El Alamein, when he stated his determination to 'hit Rommel for six', whereas in truth the Afrika Korps was hit for no more than say, three. Now his optimistic words filtered down Gale's paratroopers. Some of those who would precipitate themselves into the night sky over Normandy cherished a delusion that their first combat mission of the war should be completed within hours or, at worst, days. Cunningham did not believe a word of this. He wrote that withdrawing Airborne forces when they had secured their immediate objectives was 'a thing practically never done in the Mediterranean'. Sure enough, on the Normandy battlefield Gale's men, like their American counterparts, proved indispensable elite infantry: their survivors would not be taken out of the line until September.

Lt. Gen. John Crocker, the I Corps commander charged with responsibility for 3rd Division and 6th Airborne on D-Day, as well as for the adjoining Canadian landing formation, wrote later: 'No troops were ever given a more momentous task than the men who landed by sea and air in the early hours of D-Day to seize high ground on the eastern flank of the Allied invasion.' Crocker himself was regarded as a competent professional, albeit taciturn and undemonstrative. After enlisting as a private soldier in 1915, he won a

DSO and MC as a subaltern on the Western Front, then left the army to train as a solicitor. He soon decided he preferred soldiering, however, and returned to uniform in 1920. He saw action briefly in France in 1940, and rose to a corps command in Tunisia, before returning home to take over I Corps for the invasion. Crocker never became a celebrity. But the fact that he retained his post until 1945, unlike several of his peers, argues that Montgomery and head of the army Gen. Sir Alan Brooke trusted him.

Richard Gale, 6th Airborne's commander, was likewise no high-flier. Born in London in 1896, he was reared in Australia by peripatetic parents. He always wanted to be a soldier but was rejected for service in 1914 because he was deemed to have a weak chest. Through the early months of World War I he devilled as a City clerk and exercised fiercely to make himself fit for the army. This did not spare him from being presented with a white feather by a woman who one day accosted him in his business suit on a London street. In 1915 Gale finally secured entry to Sandhurst, and after commissioning spent two years as a machine-gun officer in France – a role John Crocker also fulfilled. There followed long inter-war years in India, five of them spent instructing on automatic weapons. In 1936, he came home from the subcontinent as a forty-year-old captain. Yet somebody in the War Office, where he spent the ensuing years, recognized quality in 'Windy' Gale. In 1940 he was selected to command the embryo parachute brigade, which evolved into an airborne division. By February 1944, when he was told of his formation's key role in the invasion, this big, bluff, ebullient leader had made himself liked and respected by both officers and men, though he had never commanded a large force in battle. One of his paratroopers described him enthusiastically as 'a real man's man, a soldier's soldier'.

In the Mediterranean, British airborne units had fought on the ground with courage and determination. It was less assured, however, that mass parachute and glider drops could deliver results proportionate to their immense demands on resources, especially aircraft. Operations in support of the Sicilian invasion had been shambolic, through no fault of the Parachute Regiment. Its battalions could never escape the handicaps that they were lightly-armed and lacked mobility. They were shock troops ill-fitted to endure long battles, especially if the enemy deployed armour against them.

Gale, though a passionate believer in airborne warfare, recognized that parachute-landed troops were always scattered, sometimes disastrously so, and especially when dropped in darkness, as must be the Normandy invasion formations. He pushed the exploitation on an unprecedented scale of gliders, each of which could deliver an entire platoon. He never doubted that D-Day would be a bloody business for his seven thousand men: 'I budgeted for a 20 per cent loss in the drop and initial fighting', and indeed the division's casualties came close to his estimate. But this would be a price worth paying if 6th Airborne could secure its D-Day objectives before 3rd Division began to land from the sea.

Gliders could bring in some vehicles and heavy weapons to support the parachutists. By 1944 the army's principal type was the Horsa, built of laminated plywood and fabric laid upon a wooden frame. It was fitted with the same controls as a powered aircraft except that, absent engines, it had no need of complex instruments. It flew to the battlefield attached by a 300ft hemp rope to a towing aircraft, before being released over a landing zone by pulling a red-knobbed lever in the glider's cockpit.

A fully-laden Horsa weighed seven tons, had a wingspan of eighty-eight feet, and in free flight steadied at 80 mph, rising to a maximum of 190 mph in a dive. It carried thirty-odd men or a jeep and gun or trailer, while its larger brother the Hamilcar could take a light tank and had a fully-laden weight of seventeen tons.

The army secured authority to train its own NCO pilots to fly the gliders because when they landed the fliers were expected to fight alongside their passengers. The men who joined the Glider Pilot Regiment, as it became, revelled in the opportunity to take to the air, denied to their kind by the RAF since most lacked secondary education.

The first time Staff-Sergeant Jim Wallwork saw a Horsa, he thought it resembled 'a big, black crow'. Another pilot, Vic Miller, wrote of the experience of being airborne: 'It was awe-inspiring gliding almost silently past the swirling masses of white … It is the free flight that is the most exhilarating part … just a clean gentle roar of air past the big perspex canopy rising to a sharper whistle whenever we increased airspeed to go into a turn or dive. Beautiful smooth landings were possible … for the vision forward and downward was perfect.' A glider pilot had to learn to match the movements of his tug plane, sometimes for great distances: before the Sicilian invasion, thirty Horsas were ferried 1,400 miles from Britain to North Africa, of which three fell into the sea.

It was prudent to sustain a course above or below the tug to avoid the slipstream. If a pilot failed to play follow-my-leader, the trip could get very rough indeed: at worst, the tow rope broke, confronting glider and passengers with a landing on rough terrain or 'in the drink'. In bumpy weather a glider heaved, lurched and rolled, while its tow rope tautened and slackened alarmingly. One soldier likened passage in a Horsa to being 'yanked across the sky in a very old railway carriage'. For passengers, the motion was chronically sick-making. It seems amazing that tens of thousands of British and American soldiers accustomed themselves to regard these impossibly flimsy craft as acceptable conveyances, until they descended to attempt controlled crashes on the battlefield. In the Sicilian landings sixty-nine gliders fell in the sea and the Glider Pilot Regiment lost fifty-seven pilots, some of them killed by friendly fire from the Royal Navy. By 1945, 3,655 Horsas had been manufactured, and most of them flew in action before collapsing into mangled framing and plywood.

Whatever the persistent doubts at the top of the army about airborne assault, the spirit of Gale's soldiers was terrific, based upon years of arduous training and the thrill of knowing themselves a volunteer elite. The biggest men in each battalion were appointed to carry its medium machine-guns and three-inch mortars, back-breaking loads. Malcolm Hill, who commanded 7 Para's Vickers, was dubbed Garth, after the strip cartoon giant, and regarded as 'a sort of superman'. An early 1944 War Office report on the invasion forces, based on censors' readings of men's correspondence, asserted that morale was 'excellent, particularly in the case of 6 Airborne Division'. One of its officers, Richard Todd, observed: 'Our confidence was boundless. We were quite sure that we could take and hold anything.' While Gale's men were no more eager to die than were their comrades of 3rd Division, they were perhaps more willing to embrace courses of action likely to precipitate their deaths.

In the last months before D-Day, officers of Gale's division who had been selected to carry out special tasks in the first minutes and hours paid discreet visits to Broadmore, a requisitioned country house near Netheravon in Wiltshire. This was 6th Airborne's intelligence headquarters, nicknamed 'the Madhouse' because its name was close to that of a notorious secure facility for deranged criminals. Within the closely guarded walls, Major John Howard of the Airlanding Brigade studied photos and a model of his personal objectives on 6 June: the twin bridges over the Caen Canal and River Orne, the only plausible road links across the water obstacles that lay between Sword beach and the designated Airborne perimeter.

Howard commanded D Company of the 2nd Ox & Bucks Light Infantry, which for the invasion was attached to Brigadier Nigel Poett's 5th Parachute Brigade. He and 150 men – his own soldiers reinforced with two extra platoons and a thirty-strong engineer party – were to land by glider, overrun the bridges and hold them until they were joined from the sea, optimistically around midday, by commandos of 1st Special Service Brigade, and thereafter by infantry of 3 Div. 'Provided the bulk of your force lands safely,' ran Poett's orders to Howard, issued on 2 May 1944, 'you should have little difficulty in overcoming the known opposition on the bridges', which would consist of low-grade troops. 'Your difficulties will arise in holding off an enemy counter-attack until you are relieved.' A German thrust, possibly supported by armour, was plausible at any time from 0100 on D-Day, forty-five minutes after the Ox & Bucks attacked. Poett himself would be flying close behind the major, in one of six RAF Albemarles carrying Pathfinders charged with marking landing zones for 6th Airborne.

Howard, thirty-one years old, was anything but a conventional product of the officer class. From a humble background, his only childhood passion had been the Boy Scouts, in which he distinguished himself. He left school at fourteen and in 1932 joined the army for the same reason many others did – lack of a prospect of anything better. When he completed his enlistment six years later he became a policeman, and at the outbreak of war was pounding a beat on the streets of Oxford. Recalled to the colours, he applied to be an officer – and was rejected, instead becoming a regimental sergeant-major. When finally permitted a commission, he found himself facing condescension, or so he thought it, from socially smarter comrades. Yet he showed himself a fine leader, fiercely competitive and a physical fitness obsessive: he chivvied and goaded his men to win almost every sporting event staged by his battalion. Unusually for a soldier, he was a near-teetotaller, happily married to Joy, who still lived in Oxford with their two children. By 1944 he was not merely a company commander, but the one chosen to lead the first operation of D-Day, and among its most vital. There was an irony here because Gale's paratroopers looked down on their gliderborne comrades as 'chairborne airborne' – not real sky soldiers. However, if John Howard's mission failed, the entire division would be at risk.

The planners focused immense ingenuity upon devising means of securing the objectives fast, before the Germans could detonate the explosives they would surely have laid beneath the bridges, for which the electrical switch was thought to be located in a pillbox at the eastern end of the Caen Canal crossing. Paratroopers need many minutes – often hours – to concentrate before mounting an attack. Thus this task must be entrusted to gliderborne infantry, landing in dense clusters to execute a lightning *coup de main*, before the defenders could gather their wits. Howard's force had been appointed to launch the first assault of D-Day because only absolute surprise, an attack coming literally out of a clear sky, offered any chance of success.

The major himself made the detailed plan. He appointed three men in his own leading glider to storm the eastern enemy pillbox guarding the bridge, which should be immediately before them when they 'pranged'. They would push grenades through the firing slits then riddle the interior before any German occupant could detonate the demolition charges. Simultaneously twenty-six-year-old Lt. Den Brotheridge would lead his platoon in a dash across the bridge to secure its western end. One minute behind Jim Wallwork's glider, David Wood's platoon was scheduled to reinforce them. A further minute later would come men led by 'Sandy' Smith, a Cambridge cricket and rugby star. Smith said: 'We were eager. We were fit. And we were totally innocent. My idea was that everyone was going to be incredibly brave with drums beating and bands playing and I was going to be bravest among the brave.'

The simultaneous assault on the Orne was to be led by Captain Brian Priday, Howard's second-in-command, with the platoons of Tony Hooper, 'Tod' Sweeney and Dennis Fox in three gliders. Engineers and vital munitions were dispersed between the six planes because the planners knew that it would be wildly unrealistic to imagine Howard's entire force arriving where and when it was supposed to – Richard Gale told the major to expect to fight his little battle with no more than half his take-off strength. Glider loads were allocated so that each element of the company should be armed and equipped to fulfil the mission even if some Horsas went missing.

They were scheduled to hit the bridges less than twenty minutes after midnight, almost five hours before dawn. They trained relentlessly and had their share of accidents. In a careless moment with a Sten gun, nineteen-year-old David Wood shot Den Brotheridge in the leg, interrupting his fellow lieutenant's career as a passionate football player, but happily without impairing his fitness to join the assault. A month before D-Day, Howard took D Company to a new training area. In South Devon planners had identified two parallel bridges over a river and a canal that could masquerade as their objectives in Normandy. For six days they assaulted these crossings by day and night. Then they returned to Hampshire after a rumbustious final night out in Exeter. On 26 May they moved into a transit camp at Tarrant Rushton, near Blandford in Dorset, where they met their Horsa pilots, survivors of the Sicilian bloodbath. Three days later Howard briefed his officers, and on 30 May the entire company. Private Wally Parr was among those who recklessly breached security to tell his wife Irene what the job was. He added that he guessed they would go when the moon looked right, which meant early June. Happily

Parr, like every other humble soldier, had no inkling where the objectives lay. Until the last night, John Howard alone knew their exact location.

The pilot selected to lead the descent on the canal was twenty-four-year-old Jim Wallwork, a cheerful young man who radiated confidence in his own ability, and in the operation. There was a moment of alarm in the last days beforehand, when photographs showed the Germans sinking anti-glider poles into the field in which they were to land. Nothing to worry about, shrugged Wallwork insouciantly: the poles were a bonus. They would check the Horsas' landing speed and, with luck, shear off the wings.

Even as Howard and his men trained to assault the bridges another of Gale's officers, twenty-nine-year-old Lt. Col. Terence Otway was likewise visiting Broadmore House, to view a model of a different objective, deemed equally vital, which he and his parachute battalion had been tasked to seize a few hours later on D-Day: the Merville Battery, four guns believed to be 150mm heavies, sunk in deep concrete emplacements behind the coast east of the Orne. The crews had no view of the shoreline, screened by undergrowth on their immediate front, but they were linked by telephone to the coastal bunker of their forward observation officer, who could see the entire Sword beach. This German's fire orders could, it seemed, wreak havoc if not suppressed before the amphibious force began to land.

A platoon commander who saw the Merville briefing exhibit only days before the assault thought that it was 'the most wonderful model I had ever seen, about 1.5m square with each building beautifully constructed out of plaster-of-paris'. It included correctly coloured wire entanglements, machine-gun positions, trees and bushes, chewed-up earth and constantly updated bomb craters. To the soldiers who saw it for the first time the battery 'looked so formidable that everybody laughed'.

Otway, CO of 9 Para, was a slight figure, highly-strung, irascible, with a toothy grin, born in Cairo in 1914, son of an Irish officer who died while he was still in school. He himself served for three years on the North-West Frontier of India with the Royal Ulster Rifles, and almost quit the army in frustration about his slow advancement. He nonetheless had a reputation for brains, passing out of Staff College fourth of two hundred students. He would need to be clever on 6 June: his brigadier, James Hill, warned him that his allotted D-Day role was 'a stinker'. And so it was.

Throughout the spring of 1944, during Otway's regular visits to Broadmore he brooded over the model of the Merville. At West Woodhay in Berkshire, the colonel persuaded the War Office to pay £15,000 compensation to destroy growing crops, so that engineers could construct a mock-up of the German battery on terrain similar to that which 9 Para would encounter in Normandy. In those early months he and his men rehearsed their role with live ammunition, five times by day and four by night. CSM Dusty Miller said: 'We ate, drank and slept the bloody battery!' Every two weeks, to sustain their fitness the entire unit ran ten miles in two hours, wearing full battle kit. One young officer said, almost euphorically: 'It was a marvellous battalion – I was never so happy in my entire army service. We were all wildly together. I've never known it before and have never known it again.'

The colonel planned the attack with imagination and finesse. The main body of paratroopers would land more than a mile south-east of their objective, but Major George Smith and two warrant officers, famously the toughest men in the battalion, would first reconnoitre. They would drop earlier, closer to Merville, and explore routes through the German wire and minefields, while the rifle companies marched in darkness to the forming-up area. Just before the battalion launched its ground assault, gliders would insert a *coup de main* party to crash direct onto the battery, within the wire, just as John Howard's men intended to land beside the river bridges. Ignoring the bruised egos of more senior claimants on this command, Otway entrusted the company carrying out the vital role to 'GB', Captain Robert Gordon-Brown, a former architect whom he judged to have the right combination of coolness, brains and dash.

The training and preparations of Otway's battalion were as good as could be contrived, yet exposed to yawning vulnerabilities. Most significant, no gliders were made available to 9 Para in Berkshire, so that in rehearsals the *coup de main* parties simply ran forward through darkness to the guns, starting from the points inside the battery where they were supposed to land. This same wildly optimistic hypothesis dominated the battalion's expectations: Otway was to launch his assault at the head of six hundred men, who were assumed to have assembled in the right corner of Normandy, at the appointed early hour of D-Day.

As for the other elements of 6th Airborne, which were tasked to seize the high ground east of the Orne, amid all the fevered preparations Huw Wheldon spent his leisure hours reading Gibbon and Macaulay. He wrote to his mother: 'One sits in the middle of all this boiling up, these increasingly urgent moves, in a strangely dispassionate mood. There is an unreality about everything, as if the invasive colours and moving distances of early spring were making the very lorries insubstantial, giving a vague and faery quality even to logistics.' He wrote with a spasm of passionate romanticism to his friend Ben Leeper: 'England indescribably lovely with her parklands and beech trees & little hills; the whole countryside a pressing testimony to the proprieties, and even to the virtues of peace.'

4
The Seafarers

1 COMMANDOS

Britain's wartime commando legend, which endures into the twenty-first century, is founded upon a reality that the soldiers and Royal Marines who wore green berets were exceptionally fit, tough, motivated. On battlefields they proved themselves bolder fighters than the average infantryman. But through the years of relative inertia on the home front the force wildly outgrew its utility, as did the SAS and Airborne Forces, inflicting a drain on the rest of the army by recruiting thousands of its best men, who would have been more useful – and have participated in much more fighting – serving with infantry regiments in active theatres of war. Before D-Day, only the four Commandos posted to the Mediterranean saw significant action. A further four such units were deployed in the Far East. The eight based in Britain fired their weapons in anger only in a handful of raids lasting a matter of hours, of which St Nazaire in June 1942 and Dieppe in the same August were the most conspicuous and bloody.

The 1940 Churchillian inspiration to create the force became justified more by the morale-boosting publicity they generated, when their existence was revealed and then trumpeted to the public, than by their military achievements. In July 1943 commandos under the orders of Mountbatten's Combined Operations Command started to launch small-scale raids on the coast of France, to gather information about its defences. These ventures suffered all manner of mishaps – boats breaking down, heavy surf, clashes with German E-Boats. One canoe party abandoned attempts to land after being caught in a German searchlight beam. Its officer swallowed a bromide tablet in mistake for Benzedrine and promptly collapsed, having to be paddled home by his sergeant. Another group was rescued in mid-Channel by an RAF amphibian aircraft. In September a ten-strong group landed and lingered two nights ashore, their only tangible booty a pack of postcards showing the coastline, which a local fisherman exchanged for chocolate. They dispatched towards England five pigeons bearing messages, but peregrine falcons swooped on these hapless couriers. Attempts to secure German prisoners were persistently unsuccessful.

Another September party landed in France by parachute – fifty volunteers from each Commando took the Ringway jump course. Like all jumpers, once on the ground they suffered a protracted delay before assembling ready to move. They cut samples of German barbed wire, then roped themselves down a cliff, miraculously undetected by the enemy. One man said without pride: 'It was like Brighton beach; the noise we made would alert sentries in England, but not the Germans.' Two boats awaited them, but one engine refused to start, obliging its passengers to paddle half a mile – 'it seemed a long way' – to an offshore rendezvous with a torpedo-boat, the skipper of which scolded them roundly. 'We hadn't done a thing apart from getting soaked.' On Christmas Eve a group of nine mostly French commandos set out for the enemy shore, all of whom drowned. Another Anglo-French party scaled two-hundred-foot cliffs but strayed into a minefield where two men were killed and the rest wounded. Several more French commandos drowned or perished of exposure during raids on the Dutch coast.

So-called COPP parties of frogmen performed useful reconnaissance work on prospective invasion beaches, working under Admiralty direction. These missions required not merely iron constitutions, but steel nerves, crawling in darkness on the shoreline to make measurements with weighted lines, marking details with indelible pencils on white slates. One such pair, George Lane and Roy Woodbridge, were captured in May near Abbeville as they paddled back out to sea. Lane – in reality a Hungarian named Lanyi – was taken to be interviewed personally by Rommel, who exchanged pleasantries with him and was no doubt responsible for decreeing that he and his companion should not be executed. All the above tiny operations reflected splendidly on the courage of their participants, but only the COPP parties contributed much to the war effort, never mind to the invasion of North-West Europe.

The 1st Special Service Brigade, as four Commandos now earmarked to land at the eastern end of Sword beach were designated, was commanded by thirty-two-year-old Lord Lovat, a supreme exemplar of a vanishing species, the warrior 'toff'. The chief of clan Fraser, a pre-war Scots Guards officer, was distinguished by unshakeable courage, film star looks and an arrogance that would have won the respect of Lord Cardigan of the Light Brigade. In his memoirs, Lovat writes with contempt of almost all those with whom he served – notably including the novelist Evelyn Waugh – save his own followers, whom he adored. And they, strangely enough, in a Britain on the cusp of socialism, adored him. Harry Drew, who landed on D-Day expecting the worst, touched the brigadier's belt on the beach so that if he was killed 'at least they could say that Private Drew died fighting alongside Lord Lovat'. To modern eyes, the chieftain totters between meriting ridicule and repugnance.

Lovat the soldier railed against his Marine Commando counterparts, whose men were not volunteers like his own, and whose colonels were allegedly 'not so amiable. Their outlook was, understandably, stiffer and more hidebound than our own. Great traditions lay behind them. We had none. They could drill and counter-march better than most of the regular army, with bands in white solar topees ... But few of these Marines had ... seen action ... None had Commando battle experience or knew what close fighting was about. I found the patronizing "old pro" attitude to "upstarts" very hard to swallow.'

The Royal Marines, meanwhile, had their own doubts about Lovat and his followers. Col. John Moulton, commanding 48 RM Cdo, wrote between gritted teeth: 'Marines felt, and usually tried not to say, that while there was much to admire and envy in the well-publicized efforts and records of the Army commandos, not all of it was above criticism and some of it was positively amateurish.' Only one officer in 4 Commando was a regular soldier, for instance, and sometimes lack of professional expertise proved a handicap. It was assuredly a nonsense, to have created rival forces of Royal Marine and Army commandos.

As for Lovat himself, his panache and coolness under fire were legendary, but his personal experience of battle amounted to just three days in raiding action against the Germans, one of them at Dieppe. He nonetheless radiated sublime confidence that he knew best, endlessly rehearsing the mantra that in war, 'the worst casualties are caused by incompetence, not the enemy'. When promoted to command 1st Special Service Brigade he demanded impatiently of Robert Laycock, who had by then succeeded Mountbatten as chief of Combined Operations: 'Do I have to wear red tabs on my battledress?' The CCO responded drily: 'Yes, you must wear the red flannel of inefficiency against which you have railed repeatedly and denounced so often!'

By 1944, when some Royal Marine commandos were brigaded with his own men for the invasion, and another so-called Special Service brigade of Marines was earmarked to land further west, it would have better served Allied forces had both forces been broken up, their personnel transferred to infantry units, now that the pinprick raiding phase of the war was ended. Alan Brooke, head of the army, never wavered in his view that every infantry division should have had a 'battle patrol' to fulfil 'any commando work that might be asked of it' and that it was a waste of resources to have allowed the commandos to become a 'private army'. On 27 January Montgomery's chief of staff, Freddie de Guingand, wrote to Laycock at Combined Ops, requesting that no further large-scale raids should be directed against the French coast, because they encouraged the Germans to strengthen their defences. Only Ushant and the Dutch seaboard remained licensed raiding territories, since nobody was likely to invade them.

During the North-West Europe campaign the Commandos, each four hundred and sixty strong, would often display courage and dash, but lacked the firepower of line infantry, and worked uneasily with the latter, for they had been schooled to scorn them. However, propaganda had made commandos popular heroes, matching the SAS in the twenty-first century. It was deemed politically impossible to wind them up.

For D-Day on Sword, Lovat's men were tasked to land behind the lead infantry, then to divide: No. 4 Commando, with a French contingent, attached for political reasons, was to clear Ouistreham from the west, while the rest of the brigade hastened inland to cross the Caen Canal and Orne river bridges and reinforce Gale's 6th Airborne. Lovat wrote that the Germans' concrete bunkers imposed upon them a defensive outlook, which the attackers must exploit: 'The view inside a pill-box remains restricted while those without can see more clearly. I intended to make full advantage of this fact. After dealing with immediate defences we faced a running fight across country. Three hours to get through to the bridges appeared on the short side.'

Lovat's disdain for almost all combatants save those under his own orders extended to generals. When Gen. Sir Miles Dempsey, Second Army's commander, ultimately responsible for Sword beach on D-Day, inspected 1st SS Brigade, the visitor was rash enough to try a hard-pulling 'chaser' which Lovat liked to ride when acting as an umpire on exercises. To the brigadier's delight, the horse bucked Dempsey off. After Montgomery's final briefing for the invasion, his lordship observed disdainfully: 'I had a feeling that I had been listening to a headmaster taking a backward class.'

As D-Day came closer, the commandos' sufferings on exercises intensified. Frenchman Guy Hattu never forgot a night during which, in an icy gale, he and his troop lingered for fifty minutes in water up to their necks. Their commandant Philippe Kieffer, an iron man, was the only one among them who suffered no medical consequences, though himself forty-five years old. When the Frenchmen began to study maps and aerial photos of their intended objectives, they were impressed by the precision of the intelligence, and by the immense labours of the British and French agents who had assembled it. Hattu wrote: 'We knew that in this casemate were fifty German soldiers, in that one about fifteen; of which regiment, and on what date they had deployed; whether this or that unit was composed of old or young soldiers, and whether they were fanatics or war-weary. We passed the first fortnight of May 1944 in a fevered atmosphere. Since the previous summer, everybody in England asserted that the landing would take place in the spring ... The whole of southern England was transformed into a vast military encampment. We were on tenterhooks for the least morsel of news, but the British, as always, contained their impatience behind a mask of imperturbable calm.'

A significant difference between ordinary soldiers and elite units was that many infantrymen instinctively went to ground when they came under fire: only the most highly-trained and motivated, commandos and paratroopers notable among them, sustained an advance even when taking substantial losses. Moreover, such men also understood, as most novices to battle found difficult to accept, that it was safer to keep moving than to remain in an area registered by enemy artillery or mortars. Terry Skelly had joined the army at sixteen, giving his age as eighteen, and within months became a corporal. Then he was accepted and commissioned by the commandos. 'As an ex-infantryman trained that the battle drill under enemy fire was "down, crawl, observe and return fire" it was interesting to be taught that as soon as you go to ground you have lost the moral advantage and that the correct drill was to charge towards the direction from which fire was coming, firing from the hip at places likely to conceal the enemy,' wrote Skelly. 'We found that by employing such tactics we had fewer casualties than orthodox units that would get pinned down and present worthwhile machine-gun, mortar and artillery targets.'

In the last weeks before D-Day, Lovat's units trained on beaches between Worthing and Eastbourne, and made themselves responsible for all manner of mischief. No. 6 Cdo had brought home from Tunisia several German uniforms and some of its men caused a sensation by wearing these on the streets of Brighton. David Haig Thomas, commando liaison officer with James Hill's 3rd Parachute Brigade, was a former Cambridge oarsman, naturalist, explorer, author of a memoir entitled *I Leap Before I Look*. One day in May he amused himself by climbing the outside of the tower of Winchester Cathedral. Lovat applauded: 'He had the supreme gift of making soldiering fun.' The 1st SS Brigade staged one invasion rehearsal on the south coast between Angmering and Littlehampton. Their commander said: 'I asked for a blinder with no holds barred, and signalled that we must show Home Forces what commando speed was all about.' Under the eyes of Sir Frederick Morgan, Laycock and Montgomery's chief of staff de Guingand, the commandos put on their exercise with Lovat delivering a running commentary through a loudhailer. Once ashore, his men used inflatable dinghies to cross water obstacles, then commandeered thirty parked army vehicles for a dash inland. This display of initiative amused some red-tabbed spectators but infuriated rather more.

Not every humble ranker appreciated the flamboyance of senior commandos. Cardiff-born Ray Hatton joined the cavalry in 1938 as a barely literate boy soldier and in 1940 had participated in mounted anti-invasion patrols armed with a sword. He adored army life and was one of many who sobbed when their horses were taken away, especially his own Molly. Hatton volunteered for the commandos in 1942 from boredom with Home Forces, and survived a bullet wound in the thigh during training at Inveraray. He was among those unimpressed by his own 6 Cdo's CO, the notoriously foul-mouthed Derek Mills-Roberts: 'A madman ... he wasn't liked at all.' Yet Lovat thought Mills-Roberts wonderful, probably because he possessed the virtues that 'Shimi' – his nickname derived from the Gaelic name for the clan chief – esteemed above all others: courage and iron will.

Despite the scepticism about commandos expressed above, on D-Day the wearers of green berets, like their maroon-bereted comrades of the Parachute Regiment, displayed a speed of action and initiative that sometimes went unmatched by the infantry rank and file. Moreover on Sword beach the Highland chieftain was granted a stardom that he craved. Lord Lovat fulfilled an anachronistic destiny as an authentic blue-blooded hero.

2 ARMOUR

Maj. Gen. Sir Percy Hobart, a celebrated though controversial – among 'brasshats' – pioneer of tank warfare, was rescued by Churchill in 1941 from service as a lance-corporal in the Home Guard. The prime minister rebuked the then head of the army for opposing Hobart's recall by saying that it was not only a school's good boys who helped to win wars, but 'the sneaks and stinkers as well'. 'Hobo' first trained 11th Armoured Division, then in 1943 was given command of the new 79th Armoured, a formation of specialized tanks forged explicitly to fulfil assault roles on D-Day. These became known as 'the Funnies'. When Hobart inspected one unit of his new formation, the 13th/18th Royal Hussars which prided itself on being a crack cavalry regiment, he was led down serried ranks of immaculately polished Valentine tanks. 'Very nice,' he said. 'Now start them up.' To the general's disgust, only seven drivers achieved this successfully. A rueful Hussars officer described Hobart as 'oldish … and of an uncertain temper'. There was far to travel before the Home Army would be fit to invade anything.

Yet travel it did. In the course of 1943–44, whole regiments of 'funnies' were created: 'Crocodile' flame-throwers; flailing 'Crab' mine-clearers; AVREs – Armoured Vehicles Royal Engineers – to lay bridges, bombard strongpoints, fill ditches with fascines. It was an example of the fantastic detail of intelligence study that a stretch of clay, in which tanks might bog down, was identified on Sword beach at Luc-sur-Mer by a British officer who pored over the 1938 *Bulletin de la Société préhistorique française* Vol. XXXV. In response Hobart devised 'Bobbins', rolled-up pathways which unreeled under a tank as it advanced, creating a track for its successors, and they were duly allocated to the soft Sword sector. Infantrymen on invasion exercises grew accustomed to seeing an array of weird military artefacts, 'funnies' foremost among them: 'If an elephant had appeared with wings and a gun on top,' said signaller Finlay Campbell, 'I would have just assumed that it was one more cog in the assault.'

In the summer of 1943, three regiments of gun tanks were grouped to form 27th Independent Armoured Brigade, supporting 3rd Division for D-Day. Their commander sought to revive flagging morale, to dispel men's weariness with repetitious routine, by gathering his officers and telling them they had been chosen to fulfil one of the most thrilling and challenging roles in the approaching invasion of Europe – 'the biggest test of physical and mental courage in their lives'. The 13th/18th Hussars, seconded from 79th Division, together with the East Riding Yeomanry and North Staffordshire Yeomanry, mustered between them 190 tanks, far more than Rommel's 21st Panzer Division. The Staffordshires had been recalled from the Middle East, where they fought through the desert campaigns, to lend experience to the brigade, which they did to great effect. Their colonel, Jim Eadie, wrote in his diary on quitting Tunisia: 'I am very lucky to have such super chaps left, after all we have been through.' Meanwhile the Hussars were to spearhead the assault in a revolutionary fashion – fighting from amphibious Shermans that would land on Sword beach just ahead of the leading infantry. There were initial hopes that the whole brigade could do likewise, but insufficient converted Shermans proved to be available.

Swimming tanks had been conceived during World War I by a Hungarian-born engineer, Nicholas Straussler. Churchill in 1940 demanded that the British Army, beyond defending the homeland against threatened German assault, should start to plan for a new descent on the continent. When the War Office ordered the first landing-craft, it also resurrected Straussler and his proposal. Tanks were to be rendered seaworthy by fitting canvas flotation screens around their hulls, held upright by struts and compressed air. In the water the tanks would be driven by propellers, but the tracks also revolved, to sustain traction as they approached the beach. The first trials of 'Duplex-Drive' tanks were held in a north London reservoir, followed by later 1941 experiments in Portsmouth Harbour.

Crewing a DD, wherein the driver operated his controls from a seat eleven feet below the top of the flotation screen, was never less than daunting. The navy fancifully characterized the tank as 'a canvas boat with a 30-ton keel'. The first 450 modified Valentines were ordered by the War Office in June 1942. By 1944 it was understood that Shermans would fulfil the role far more effectively, and the DDs which landed on D-Day were modifications of this latter American design. The crews of 27th Armoured Brigade, all of whom were taught to drive DDs – though on 6 June only two squadrons of Hussars used them – found the amphibious training tough. The East Riding Yeomanry's technical adjutant, Captain Ernest Clark, was in civilian life a well-known West End actor who added lustre to its concert party performances. Now he and his men had to learn to erect and dismantle the big, ungainly engine air-intake tubes which towered over the tank hulls.

They were shown how to charge and change the compressed-air bottles for inflating the canvas flotation screens encircling the tank hulls. They were sent to Gosport to practise escape from sunken DDs using ATEAs – specially-designed amphibious tank escape apparatus. The naval chief petty officer instructor said cheerfully to one crewman, 'Rather you than me, mate!', and indeed no DD crew which sank in action used ATEAs successfully. Since drivers could see nothing when the screens were raised, commanders learned to steer by ordering through the intercom, 'Left a bit – not too fast – straighten up – steady as you are.'

A troop sergeant was court-martialled and lost his stripes for alleged reckless driving which caused his tank to founder, with loss of life. The unit's RSM was likewise sacked after failing the amphibious course. On an exercise in Dorset's Studland Bay six tanks sank and a seventh had to be abandoned: six crewmen drowned. The Americans, during similar rehearsals, lost sixteen Shermans. Several men requested transfers out of units committed to man DDs, and some such pleas were acceded to. COs felt that nothing could be worse than to confront the huge challenge of the assault with unwilling comrades: '*And he that has no stomach for this fight/Let him depart, his passport shall be made*'. It seems hugely to the credit of the DD crews that the overwhelming majority persevered, accepting the prospect of mortal peril even before they engaged the enemy.

Erroll Prior-Palmer who commanded 27th Armoured Brigade was, in the words of his biographer, 'respected but not always liked'. One of his colonels wrote: 'I can never like him as a man, though he is a capable soldier' – which was the only thing that mattered in the spring of 1944. Among his considerable virtues, 'PP' possessed a gift for noting and remembering people's names, an important tool in sustaining loyalty. But he was a harsh disciplinarian, who regarded amateur soldiers without enthusiasm. Many Yeomanry officers were country gentlemen, who sustained throughout the war the attitudes of their estates, and of the hunting field.

Not all units were 'bands of brothers'. Late in 1943, the East Ridings' officers became bitterly alienated from their CO. Feeling exploded after a long night exercise when the tank crews faced an even longer drive home. The colonel, Tom Williamson, quit his turret, boarded a staff car and was driven away to bed, leaving his men to follow beneath driving rain. A group of officers protested to the brigadier about the shameful example they had thus been set. Yet Prior-Palmer – against the opinion of Percy Hobart – felt discipline must trump sentiment or even justice. He backed the colonel and sacked two of the 'mutineers' from the regiment. Feelings in the officers' mess were still running high in the approach to D-Day, but the unloved Williamson retained command until the end of the war. Moreover he must have done something right, for he was awarded two DSOs.

In the last months before the invasion, there was a rush to make units up to strength, ensure they were fully armed and equipped. The East Ridings were reinforced, implausibly, with a draft of men from the Highland Light Infantry. Their B Squadron received a new commanding officer, sent to join them because he had gained battle experience in the Mediterranean. Worn-out vehicles were replaced. As the end of May neared, men spent days waterproofing the seams and apertures of tanks, jeeps and trucks with a special black 'Compound 219' made of putty and grease, becoming indescribably filthy in the process. To everyone's astonishment, it worked supremely well on the Day if it had been thoroughly applied, which required 186 man-hours per tank. They were thus prepared to face the sea. But there was no 'Compound 219' to preserve them from the shot and shell of the enemy.

3 PBI

Infantryman Len Waller thought wonderingly in 1945: 'How ever did we win?' He had found the exercises before D-Day 'highly disorganized affairs, and we couldn't help thinking that if real war was anything like this it was God help us. Whenever we were supposed to meet up with somebody or other you could bet they wouldn't be there … We stumbled for miles across fields in the wrong direction; at nightfall we were told that "the enemy" had captured our blankets. But the worried expressions on the faces of the senior officers confirmed our suspicions that the enemy were in our midst.'

Foot-soldiers characterized themselves as PBI – 'Poor Bloody Infantry' – an acronym that seemed especially apposite as D-Day approached. It was obvious that the first men ashore – on Sword beach, the 2nd East Yorks and 1st South Lancs of 8th Brigade – would pay heavily for the honour of leading the British Army's return to the continent. If some officers were eager for glory, most of their men, understandably, cared more about their own survival. The infantry made up less than a quarter of all fighting troops – a designation that included tank crews, gunners, engineers – but in North-West Europe accounted for 71 per cent of casualties, which helps to explain why 89 per cent of deserters were members of rifle companies.

It is an exaggeration, nonetheless helpful to understanding mid-twentieth-century battles, to suggest that the principal usefulness of the six or seven riflemen of a ten-man infantry section was to serve as escorts for their Bren light machine-gun pair, who represented the important firepower, just as on the German side the same was true of the crews of their MG34s and 42s, known to the British as Spandaus. Meanwhile most officers recognized that their companies were convoying forward the artillery FOOs – forward observation officers communicating by radio with gun batteries a mile or two to the rear – without whom the infantry were unlikely to accomplish much. If a company's FOO went down, an attack often stalled until he was replaced.

In the course of the NW Europe campaign, a foot-soldier who landed on 6 June was more likely to be hit than not, and faced a one-in-ten chance of dying, rising to one-in-four if he was an officer. Many became so convinced that death must be their fate that they learned to welcome mere wounds, especially a coveted

'Blighty one'. A major who sought to reassure a man weeping after suffering a slight wound, telling him he would soon be safe, was quickly disabused of the illusion that the victim was unhappy: 'It's the relief, sir. It's such a relief.'

Sir Alan Brooke wrote irascibly to a fellow general in 1942, shortly before the Dieppe raid: 'I agree with you that we are not anything like as tough as we were in the last war. There has been far too much luxury, safety first, red triangle etc. in this country. Our one idea is to look after our comforts and avoid being hurt in any way.' Much about the army had improved two years later, but its commanders – and Britain's prime minister – remained fearful that its soldiers were still no match for Hitler's Heer.

The historian David French has written: 'Montgomery's operational techniques were chosen to exploit the strengths and weaknesses of the army he commanded.' This meant that, unlike Churchill, the commander-in-chief did not look to every man to prove himself a hero. The invasion formations that landed on D-Day were suffused with a yearning for post-war social change, which only reactionary officers condemned as 'bolshevism'. Even many of those with commissions shared the mindset of Keith Douglas: D-Day and the campaign to follow represented essential but profoundly distasteful tasks that must be fulfilled. Thereafter, however, their dream of the future focused not upon martial glory but upon lives as civilians once more, no longer at the absolute mercy of the enemy's violence and the army's tyranny.

Huw Wheldon deplored the rush of religious services before D-Day: 'I am tired of being dedicated to the 2nd Front ... All this stuff about our crusading spirit is desperately false – I think dishonest in fact. At the best the whole war is a poor thing, but alas necessary – I don't think that any soldier would fight more feebly if he stayed on that level. What we fight for is, I am sure, as right as what we fight against is wrong. This fact can be quietly accepted ... I feel that chaplains & their like might keep quiet about our so-called determination and our love for this and that until such time as the demand for an emotional expression of that sort comes from the men themselves ... It makes me furious.'

Efforts were made to weed out men conspicuously unsuited to battle, of which almost every unit possessed its quota. Nonetheless, there was never a realistic prospect of transforming entire infantry formations, such as 3 Div, into elites matching 6th Airborne and the Commandos. An experienced battalion commander wrote in 1944: 'The average platoon includes three or four heroes, three or four irreconcilables and the rest respond in direct relationship to the quality of their leaders.' A colonel in Sicily, Lionel Wigram, reported likewise that every platoon contains 'six gutful men who will go anywhere and do anything, twelve "sheep" who will follow a short distance behind if they are well led, and from four to six ineffective men who have not got what it takes ever to be really effective soldiers'. When Montgomery read this report, the brilliant Wigram was sacked from battalion command for his frankness.

The Shropshires – 2nd KSLI of 3 Div's 185th Brigade – had spent the early war years in a posting exotic even by the standards of the empire: Curaçao in the Dutch East Indies, six hundred miles from the nearest other British troops. They returned home in March 1942 wholly ignorant of modern war, requiring the removal of many men whose age or health disqualified them from further service. They lacked modern weapons and equipment. Yet in the ensuing two years, though shuffled seven times from camp to camp around England, they were progressively remade into a credible fighting unit and in July 1943 appointed a new CO, Jack Maurice, a thirty-eight-year-old bachelor of notable charm and man-management skills, whose only identified weakness was that he became visibly nervous under the eye of generals.

The 1st Norfolks were another typical 3rd Division battalion, part of an old county regiment which suffered grievously in the first years of the war. The battalion sailed home from India in 1940, and had since escaped action. In 1943, however, its men began to train for the invasion. Major Humphrey Wilson said: 'We were all wondering how we should react under fire intended to kill us.' Yet the battalion history said: 'We longed to get on with it', and by early 1944 for most men this was probably true.

Training for the invasion force, much of it with live ammunition, turned ever more dangerous – and was intended to be so. In exercises with artillery, for instance, men were ordered to dig in, then guns dropped shells across their front, of which the closest was found to have fallen just eighteen yards beyond the nearest trench. There was a pathos about the thousands of British, American and Canadian soldiers who died in England or off its coasts in 1944, preparing themselves to participate in Operation Overlord, before the Germans fired their first shots in defence of Normandy.

In every unit somebody, or several somebodies, fell victim to accidents. In Charlie Chilton's battalion a subaltern drowned during a river crossing and one of Chilton's mates was killed by a carelessly-thrown grenade. A battle-school pupil described how a Guards ensign, 'a fresh-faced boy in a tailored battledress', was appointed gunner in a tracked carrier, leaping forward across rough ground in a mock assault. The young man fired the carrier's Bren, 'but something went wrong. Suddenly the ensign wasn't to be seen any more. The gun went on firing, out of sight and curiously muffled, all thirty rounds in the magazine. The driver stopped and waved his arms: "The gun must have slipped inside when we went over a bump." The ensign's finger was jammed against the trigger. When they lifted out the corpse, its battledress had dark damp patches, which gave it a rust colour; there were

COMMANDERS: (top) Richard Gale addresses men of his 6th Airborne Division before they jump into Normandy on 6 June 1944. (Bottom left) Montgomery inspects infantry of 3 Div during exercises in Scotland with – left to right behind him – Maurice of the KSLI, Rennie and K.P. Smith. (Bottom right) Rennie, shortly before he was killed.

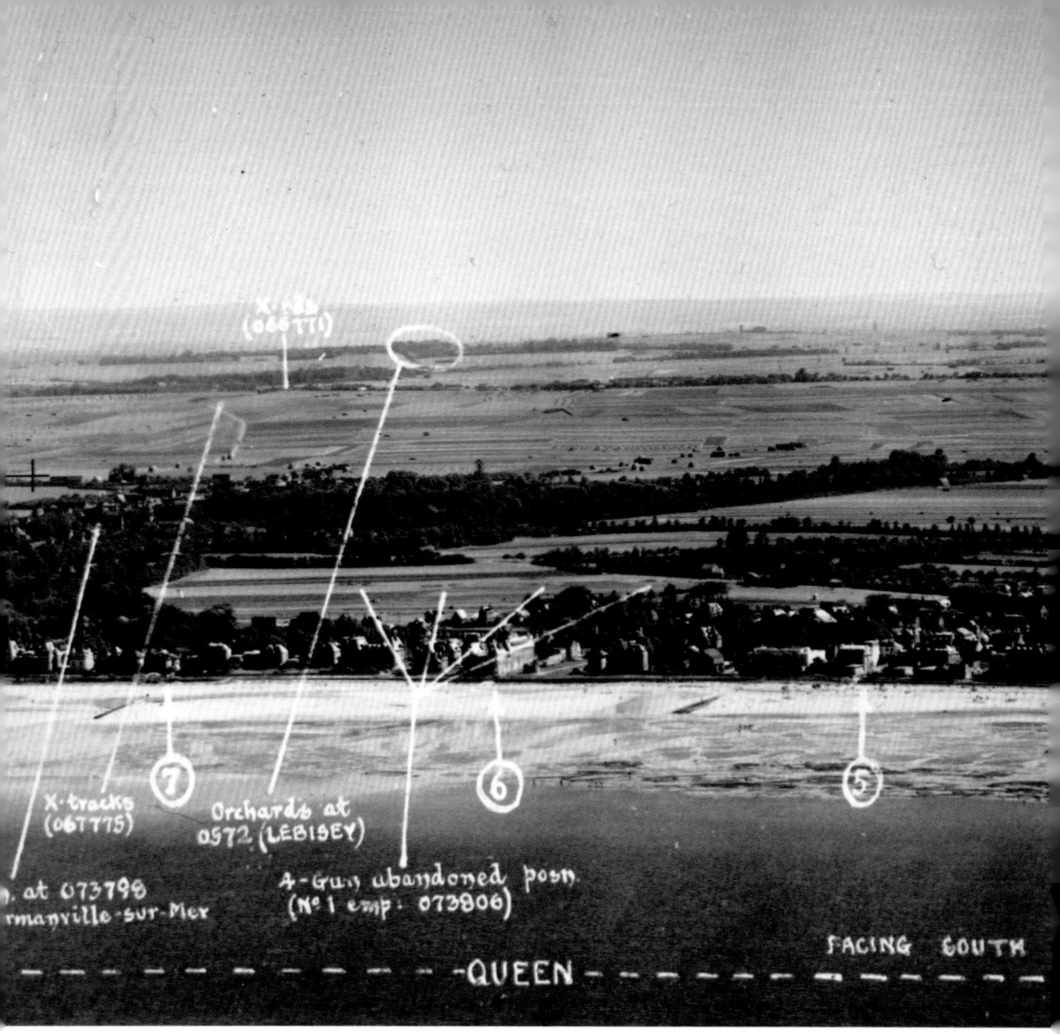

(Top left) A north-south reconnaissance image of the SWORD landing area, before the Germans laid beach obstacles, and showing the open ground inland, towards distant Caen. (Below left) Aerial view of the Merville Battery showing a profusion of bomb craters, few of them near the guns at bottom right. (Below right) Gliders and tugs massed at an English airfield before D-Day.

(Above) Lord Lovat after one of his finest hours, the August 1942 commando assault at Dieppe. (Right) Bill Millin, Lovat's personal piper, performs to green berets about to embark for Normandy.

(Top) A German panoramic shot of the Allied Normandy invasion fleet, taken from east of the Orne river. (Below left) Men of 9 Para, in exuberant mood after they thought the worst was over. (Right) An upward view from Norman soil repeated many hundreds of times on D-Day, much to the dismay of the defenders beneath.

(Top, left to right) Otway, Parry, Jefferson and (left) war artist Albert Richards with (below) one of the paintings he made of the Merville Battery.

(Right) British paratrooper with a disconsolate German prisoner and (below) padre John Gwinnett who drove twice through German-occupied territory to recover men wounded in the Merville assault, with Paul Greenway who probed the German minefield by hand. (Bottom) Paras dug in on the Caen road.

(Top) An aerial of the Caen Canal, showing the dazzling skill with which three glider pilots landed the assault groups within yards of its bridge, Howard's being closest. (Below) Howard in the midst of a cluster of his men a few days after the Caen Canal triumph.

S/Sgt Jim Wallwork, pilot of Howard's glider.

raw red gashes where its eyes had been.' The instructor addressed the young man's comrades reproachfully: 'You've got to master your weapons.'

Some paratroopers died in jump accidents, and the entire complement of one aircraft in flight perished when a weapons container, released from higher altitude, descended on it. A carrier overturned after a mine explosion, and seven men of the Ox & Bucks were killed in a glider accident at Netheravon. Norman Scarfe, historian of 3 Div, wrote affectionately of a captain who was killed at the Moffat battle school early in 1944: 'An unfortunate shooting accident deprived the Division of an individual who would have wrought considerable havoc among the Germans.' A naval rating was fatally mangled when caught in the winch of a landing-ship as its ramp was being raised, and an officer of the Hussars was decapitated by a closing tank turret lid. Just weeks before D-Day it was discovered that the gelignite used to fill Bangalore torpedoes for breaking wire entanglements would explode if hit by a rifle bullet. As late as 4 June, three sappers were killed when handling the old charges. Thousands of Bangalores had to be emptied, then refilled with a more stable explosive.

The Norfolks spent many months with the rest of their parent division, training in the Scottish Lowlands. Several units were dispatched for a fortnight's street-fighting practice in Luftwaffe-devastated Glasgow tenement areas. In February 1944 they joined divisional amphibious rehearsals in the Moray Firth, east of Inverness, for which the Tarbat peninsula was evacuated of its civilian population. On the 26th, 3rd Division planning staff moved up from London into new quarters at nearby Aberlour House, where they set about implementing and disseminating the formal orders – though not the location details – which had now been issued by Second Army to Tom Rennie, their formation commander since Christmas Day 1943: 'Task for 3 Brit Inf Div to secure the high ground NORTH of CAEN and, if possible, CAEN itself; to relieve 6 Airborne Div on the bridges over the CANAL de CAEN and the R. ORNE at BENOUVILLE and RANVILLE'. In accordance with the British Army's centuries-old addiction to equating war with sport, the two bridges were codenamed RUGGER and CRICKET. Exhaustion of imagination appears to have afflicted other chosen codewords for objectives inland from Sword, which included Marigold, Snowdrop, Guinness, Vermouth, Gluepot, Crowbar, Milk and Tea. It may be that the planners deemed it as implausible that any of the above locations would be reached on D-Day as indeed proved to be the case.

Of the three British and Canadian beaches Juno was the narrowest at 9,800 yards while Gold was 19,000 yards and Sword 13,000, or seven miles on the invaders' maps. But this last number was seriously misleading: the real landing front was five miles narrower. On Sword's right or westerly flank, offshore shallows rendered a long stretch of coastline unnavigable. And from the outset, with memories of the disastrous Dieppe raid, the decision was made not to attack frontally at Riva-Bella/Ouistreham, largest town on the Neptune front, but instead to concentrate the assault on the hamlet of La Brèche and coast west of it – little more than a mile of beach, codenamed on British maps Queen White and Red. Other sectors marked Oboe, Roger and Peter played no part in the initial landings. Shortage of shipping prompted another decision, to land just one infantry brigade in the first wave, two battalions 'up', the third following, with their tank support and accompanying engineer 'funnies'. Even had more landing-craft been available, on such a narrow front it would have been difficult to sustain COSSAC's original idea of landing two brigades 'up'.

For staff officers, constant changes and refinements of the plans required labour almost around the clock. Rennie had expected that his formation would take ashore 3,200 vehicles of all types. In

May he was abruptly informed that the pressure on shipping meant his battalions must make do with 2,500. Any German commander would have been green with envy of the latter figure, but the British had been infected with American expectations of vehicle wealth. Staffs became almost submerged in logistical problems and loading tables. Major John Rex wrote: 'We toiled far into the night setting down who, what and when was to go into each craft or ship. Everything had to be measured and weighed, a nightmare of checking and rechecking … When a vehicle turned out to be 25 feet long instead of the advertised 23, something else had to be left out.' Planners sought to consider every contingency and opportunity: at a 6 May meeting of 6th Airborne support services, it was agreed the senior officer of supply services should nominate personnel capable of driving farm horses, such as they hoped to requisition from the Norman countryside.

Gunner officer Norman Scarfe wrote later: 'A new spirit was born in the early hours of 6th June 1944, that was conceived on the shores of Scotland the previous autumn and carried securely through a wild northern winter. With all infants, we are told, the early period is the most impressionable … so it was with the Division.' This was a fanciful vision. The Moray Firth exercises were variously codenamed Smash, Grab, Crown, Anchor and Leapyear. They embraced 3 Div, 27th Armoured Brigade together with 1st Special Service Brigade, and took place in persistently vile weather.

The outcome was far from an unqualified success. Two squadrons of the 13th/18th Hussars still lacked their DD tanks. Many landing-craft skippers proved incompetent – one LCT broke its back offshore on encountering a massive wave. An engineer corporal was killed practising beach clearance with live mines. Men bucketing offshore in waterlogged landing-craft resorted to the catchphrase 'Roll on death!' so often that it became a cliché.

On 5 February Montgomery visited them, arriving late and doing little to boost the morale of thousands of men who had shivered for hours in icy conditions awaiting the great man. Inspecting 2nd KSLI, Montgomery asked Rennie his opinion of its colonel, Jack Maurice. The general replied that their brigadier thought well of Maurice but that he personally had his doubts. Derek Mills-Roberts, CO of 6 Commando, brought back to Lovat from Scotland a report of 3 Division's infantry as 'hesitant and badly-led troops'.

There is an old military saw: 'The art of war is the choice of men.' The officers of 185th Brigade, responsible for thrusting inland from the beaches towards Caen after their predecessors had broken through, decided that their brigadier, Ken Pearce Smith, was no good. It was Smith's misfortune that Montgomery was of the same opinion, having sacked him from a brigade command a few months earlier, ahead of the Sicilian invasion. Following this, it seems remarkable that Home Forces had seen fit to appoint to such an important new role a man who had been badly gassed in 1918, spent most of the earlier World War II years on Malta, frequently bombed but never in ground action, ahead of the invasion that would be under Montgomery's direction.

Nor were relations between soldiers and sailors universally friendly. During one landing exercise a naval rating urged his mates in an LCA: 'Get the pongos off quickly!' A huge army driver, taking umbrage at being dismissed as a 'pongo', seized the matelot, lifted him off his feet and slammed him against a bulkhead, shouting: 'Say that word again and I'll spread your head!' Lord Lovat described the Moray Firth rehearsal as 'disastrous' and claimed it fed wider fears: 'I had my own doubts about the Second Front. Despite superior technical resources in men and equipment, and increased air strength, the general standard of efficiency – both British and American – left much to be desired … Few regiments had faced a German tank, nor, in cold hindsight, had General [Sir Bernard] Paget [C-in-C Home Forces] been the best of trainers.'

Despite such strictures, some officers and men found consolations in the Moray Firth shambles. The adjutant of the Hussars, twenty-four-year-old Julius Neave, wrote: 'The chaos on the beach itself ... was quite unbelievable, but this strangely enough was an asset for on [D-Day] itself chaos reigned and our experience had taught us that it was the normal thing.' Neave was also impressed by the brutality with which naval officers openly lambasted each other at an exercise post-mortem conference held in Inverness: he felt that the sailors' honesty 'showed up the vagueness of the Army to a remarkable degree'. On 14 April, the whole of 3 Division headed southwards from Scotland, an apparently interminable road journey in warm weather, the columns of military vehicles passing Easter holidaymakers making the most of the weather, even during the war. For most of the invaders, there would be no more holidays until their next job was done.

5
The Eve

The invasion formations, in their new camps in southern England, were addressed by Montgomery for the last time before embarkation. It has become customary for historians to view cynically the little general and his relationship with the soldiers whom he commanded. It is probably true that his pre-D-Day speeches were better received by men of the Home Army, including 3 Div, than by Eighth Army veterans recalled from the Mediterranean to stiffen the spearheads, and deeply unhappy about the prospect of their renewed exposure to the whitest heat of war. Huw Wheldon of 6th Airborne Division observed that his own battalion's regular officers did not care for their commander-in-chief. But, said Wheldon, who was nobody's fool, many of the soldiers respected him: 'Monty really was a heroic figure, in the sense that people did project great hopes upon him, and a great many expectations, and what is more he didn't let them down. Nowadays it is fashionable to think of him as being very full of bombast – and so he was – but he certainly exercised a great hold over troops.'

The Australian war correspondent Alan Moorehead, a master of his craft, wrote of Montgomery creating before D-Day 'an atmosphere of adolescent innocence and simplicity … a community of simple emotion, a curiously childish monasticism'. Moorehead himself had spent almost four years reporting from

Mediterranean battlefields. He knew Montgomery well and his soldiers even better, and recorded of the army now preparing to invade Normandy: 'They were committed to the assault. Everything in their lives … had been shaped to that end. Nothing else was of any interest any longer. To run, to shoot, to kill. And not to be killed. All the usual decoration of life was stripped away from these children; the normal life of playing football and going out with girls and visiting the movies … Even the most intelligent showed no glimmer of irony or sarcasm or criticism in their faces. They were to run and shoot and kill, and here was the expert, the man who knew all about it.'

Monty, as he was universally known, stood almost daily atop a jeep at one of fifty assemblies around Britain between March and June, each attended by thousands of men, and said: 'I wanted to come here today so that we could get to know one another: so that I could have a look at you and you could have a look at me – if you think that's worth doing. We have to go off and do a job together very soon now, you and I, and we must have complete confidence in one another. And now that I have seen you, I have complete confidence … absolutely complete confidence. And you must have confidence in me.'

In the twenty-first century, we know of Montgomery's almost deranged conceit; his refusal to treat Americans with respect; his private peculiarities. We also acknowledge the divide between his belief in himself as a modern Caesar and the more limited commander whom historians characterize. Churchill memorably observed that it was regrettable that Britain's first general who appeared capable of defeating Germans should be 'a bounder of the 1st water'. In May 1944, however, the foxy little Montgomery was Britain's most celebrated soldier, fêted as the victor of Alamein and indeed of Britain's entire Mediterranean war. Many of the soldiers who crowded around his vehicle in those weeks before

D-Day, when he delivered his set speech four or five times a day, more than once to 3rd Division, became true believers because it was vital to their entire beings to feel confident not merely that he could win this battle but – much more important – that he would try to keep them alive. Ronald Lewin, who served under Montgomery in the desert and North Africa, and later became one of his best and most balanced biographers, wrote of this commander 'whose brilliant staff stuck to him like leeches and whose troops would have followed him to the end of the world'.

'We have been fighting the Germans a long time now,' he continued his oration, 'a very long time ... a great deal too long. I expect like me you are beginning to get a bit tired of it ... beginning to think it's about time we finished the thing off. And we can do it. No doubt about that. The well-trained British soldier will beat the German every time. We saw it in Africa. We chased him into the sea in Tunisia ... Then we went over to Sicily and chased him into the sea again ... I don't know if there are any more seas.' He got his laugh, then continued: 'The newspapers keep calling it the Second Front. I don't know why. I myself have been fighting the Germans on a number of fronts and I expect a good few of you have too. They should call it Front Number Six, or Front Number Seven.

'We don't want to forget the German is a good soldier ... a very good soldier indeed. But when I look around this morning and see the magnificent soldiers here, some of the finest soldiers I have seen in my lifetime ... I have no doubt in my mind about the outcome ... You and I will see this thing through together.' Moorehead observed that he had heard many generals make better speeches, but that which Montgomery addressed to his troops soon to assault the Atlantic Wall 'had magic. No mention of God. No mention of England. No hate. No question of revenge ... The whole performance succeeded because it was the expression of a wanted emotion.' Gunner officer Robin Dunn of 3 Div enthused: 'We felt that if we had to go to war, Monty was the man to go with.'

In mid-May thirty-one-year-old Major George Appleton, who was to command a Beach Group on Sword, enjoyed a luxurious last leave in London. He stayed at the Savoy, dined off lobster at the Écu de France, met a relation at the House of Commons and saw several shows. Perhaps he knew the lines of Robert Browning:

I shut my eyes and turned them on my heart.
As a man calls for wine before he fights,
I asked one draught of earlier, happier sights
Ere fitly I could hope to play my part.
Think first, fight afterwards – the soldier's art:
One taste of the old time sets all to rights.

Appleton spoke at length on the phone to his wife, at home in Liverpool with their small daughter. The major, unusually among the invaders, was an optimist about the likely scale of Allied casualties. A sternly religious man, he was confident that Neptune/Overlord would succeed.

Col. Jim Eadie of the Staffordshire Yeomanry, like most unit commanders, was weighed down by the life-and-death responsibilities of which he could tell his family nothing. He was troubled that he knew some of his officers less well than those with whom he had served in North Africa. 'I am having to call on all my reserves now,' he wrote to his wife. 'I have so few friends now, and am surrounded by people who do not give me the same confidence as those of past times.'

When the men of 3 Div boarded shipping for Exercise Fabius, which took place on 3 and 4 May, some believed they might be setting forth for the real invasion. In the event they staged landings on the coast at Littlehampton in Sussex, which proved almost as chaotic as those in Scotland. On 13 May it was the turn of Eisenhower, the Supreme Commander, to visit the formation and address thousands of its men. Everyone laughed when he said he knew what some of them thought of Americans, 'and he had the advantage of knowing what some of the Americans thought of them'. In the following week, King George VI came. An officer wrote: 'It must have seemed to him more than ever poignant as he, and they, contemplated the imminent event; very soon, now, it would resolve itself as the most glorious or most disastrous passage of arms ever attempted by the nation or by humanity.'

An officer of the Norfolks, sent to warehouses in the London docks to collect essential stores, encountered obstruction from dockers who were engaged in an industrial dispute, and cared absolutely nothing for the imminence of D-Day. Only belatedly did the soldier prevail: 'After much arguing and threats of armed force we were eventually able to offload the equipment.' There was disgust later, in France, when men broke open some ration boxes to find that the dockers had been there first; substituted bricks for missing food.

Beyond the vast importance of D-Day to the Allied cause, it represented for senior officers an extraordinary career opportunity. Few, especially among those landing on Sword beach or with 6th Airborne, had previously exercised higher commands on a battlefield. Personal ambition was not in the least an unworthy feature of their thoughts and speculations as they prepared for the invasion, but its presence should not be forgotten. To achieve recognition, commanders would be required to fulfil daunting responsibilities, to make instant decisions and tactical choices. Not only would the colonels, brigadiers and generals landing on D-Day face the same perils as their subordinates – indeed, a significant proportion of men holding all three ranks would be killed or wounded in Normandy, including a score in 3 Div – but in the privacy of their hearts they would also endure stresses and burdens that only the least sensitive could fail to be sobered by. Their apprehensions were not ill-founded: while some forged lasting reputations on D-Day and after, others found their careers broken.

Lt. Col. Terence Otway, whose 9 Para would assault the Merville Battery, was tortured by apprehension, only a hint of which he felt able to confide to his wife Stella. One of his officers later described two of Otway's men who grew convinced they were going to die in the assault – and indeed did: 'One sergeant became very bolshie, and a lieutenant behaved as if he had entered a different world from us.' On 3 June the colonel did not sleep at all; he merely roamed the battalion's camp while his men slept. He did better on the following night because he was exhausted. From the 4th onward he banned alcohol in the unit, but took a flask of whisky when he finally boarded his Dakota. Lt. Alan Jefferson felt a surge of melancholy: 'We knew that this was the last time 9 Para, as we knew it, would be together.' And so it proved.

At Cowdray Park in Sussex commandos played football and stump cricket. On the last day before embarkation, French priest René de Naurois held a mass for three hundred Catholics. Other men attended an interdenominational service presided over by a new padre who added himself to Lord Lovat's lengthy hate list by preaching 'a rotten sermon about death and destruction'. Within minutes of the subsequent blessing, the brigadier informed this man of the cloth that he would not be permitted to embark for the invasion. This caused the padre to atone for his sins by shooting himself. He was reported by Lovat as a 'battle casualty'.

The clan chieftain himself addressed the brigade on the eve of battle, mostly in English but also briefly in French for the benefit of Kieffer's men: '*Vous allez rentrer chez vous. Vous serrez les premiers militaires français à casser la gueule des salauds en France même. À chacun son Boche.*' Before departing for C18 Transit

Camp, Lovat breakfasted on his last day in the Park with his fellow territorial magnate Lord Cowdray, who had lost an arm in the 1940 French campaign: 'This was a special, almost festive occasion. A battle honour to be shared between old friends.'

Jim Eadie of the Staffordshires broke down at what he knew, but his wife did not, was their last meeting before D-Day. Afterwards he wrote apologetically to her: 'I was so ashamed of myself when we parted. Thank God you have courage enough for the two of us. It is far worse to be left behind and I so truly realise that you can control yourself when I cannot. I don't think I really lack courage, it is just some wave of feeling that quite overcomes me for the moment. You are right that this time it won't be for four years, but I have so much better a realization of what [the battlefield] means ... The ignorant are usually better than the experienced ones.'

Eadie, exhausted by two years of battlefield command in the Mediterranean, could have opted for a staff job on returning to England, but believed he owed it to himself, his family, his men and his country to take the regiment to France on D-Day. The colonel embodied the vision of G.K. Chesterton that 'the true soldier fights not because he hates what is in front of him, but because he loves what is behind him'. On 2 June, he sent a final letter to Naidita from the Staffordshire Yeomanry's concentration area: 'I write in a world ill at ease. There is a feeling of expectancy which hangs heavy on the air ... I can hear the click of bat on ball and just the drum of insects, and yet it seems there is another and larger drum waiting to roll forth its beat. And now yet another sound, a single fighter aircraft winging its way overhead, forerunner of thousands, a note the world would be happier without. It's gone again and now all is quiet; when shall it be quiet again? The only noises I want to hear are those of nature – the running of a burn, the plash as a trout rises, the calls of birds.'

That same day men of 8 Brigade, in their sealed camp near Lewes, attended a farewell performance by the vaudeville star Vic Oliver, then married to Sarah Churchill, daughter of the prime minister, somewhat to the latter's distaste. Only the few officers in each formation on an 'X list' knew their real destination. Yet Major Arthur Hyde of the East Ridings, when shown a map of the Caen area with key features given false place names, said laconically: 'They can't fool me. I know that racecourse' – nearby Carpiquet, destined to become scene of some of the bloodiest fighting of the campaign – 'which is the crookedest in France.' French commandos were likewise undeluded by the Russian or Polish names overlaid on their maps. Guy Hattu wrote: 'Several among us recognized the area. Some even had memories of, for instance, the casino now transformed into a blockhouse.'

Huw Wheldon wrote on 5 June to his father: 'I have just finished packing. I wonder whether any major crisis will ever find me ready. The soap I meant to get, the bootlaces I put off buying, the holster which should have been repaired … Yesterday's procrastinations are at last bearing fruit! Wheldon goes to war pitifully ragged …' He knew that this letter would not be read until he was committed to battle in France, and thus felt liberated from oppressive censorship: 'Free at last, at least to tell you that the last few weeks have been very very happy ones, working away at our operation orders (the whole thing has been very like working for an exam) – sunbathing and taking things easy.

'We are off very shortly, and the sounds of whistling and shouting, odd songs, the gang around the goal posts, reach into this tent. Everyone is amazingly happy. We have studied the whole thing so deeply that the natural apprehensions are submerged in a general feeling of elation based on this great preparation and on the knowledge that the job is well within our capacity. The staffs have indeed done their jobs well. We have much to be thankful for. I personally would not like to miss it.' He sent his parents his unused clothing ration coupons, observing, 'I don't fancy they will be much good in France.' The invaders were told to strip themselves of all personal documents except their army paybooks 'and any religious book we chose', as Finlay Campbell recalled. But he himself was among many who clung defiantly to family letters, to be reread obsessively under fire.

In the wired and guarded concentration areas, through the last days tannoys blared messages and instructions: 'Sergeant Jones report to Major … Look to your black-out … Black-out NOW!' Men prepared themselves for their trial by ordeal in many and various ways. Jack Levington, a former Berkshire policeman in 4 Commando, was among those who had all his hair shaved off. Those who had not yet seen the armoured 'funnies' were shown films of them, especially the Crocodile flamethrowers, which cheered them up. Then, to sober them down, they heard the rumours that lead assault companies were expected to suffer 50 per cent casualties. Men wearing German uniforms moved among them, to accustom the invaders to the garb of the enemy. They were issued with extra field dressings, and in many units also with brand-new clothing. To the disgust of some, conditioned by lifetimes of parsimony, the old stuff was burned. 'Write all the letters you like,' an officer told his company, 'but they won't be delivered until D+3.' He added: 'This is the final camp. The next one will be the beach.' A cheeky soldier piped up: 'Yes, sir. Could I be excused. I think I need the toilet!' They all howled with laughter, but in truth few were not afraid. One of Terence Otway's NCOs was killed by momentary carelessness with a weapon – or, more likely, by something else – in the last hours before 9 Para's take-off.

Some of the special equipment issued was controversial. One unit commanding officer raised moral objections, which were overruled, to using flamethrowers. James Cunningham, commanding 9th Brigade, was obsessed with seeing his men land with dry feet and had thus devised huge canvas waders, 'Cunningham's paddlers', which his men could wear over their equipment. Meanwhile the first attempt at kitting the infantrymen for landing burdened them with 95 lb apiece. Before 6 June this was reduced to 65 lb, but such a load still foreclosed upon nimbleness. Most infantrymen wore large packs, small packs, pouches filled with rifle clips, Sten or Bren magazines, one smoke and two explosive grenades apiece, a shovel and several mortar or PIAT anti-tank bombs. In addition they carried twenty-four-hour ration packs containing repellent dehydrated meat cubes, rather tastier oatmeal blocks, concentrated chocolate and concentrated tea, milk and sugar cubes which yielded a barely drinkable brew. There were also cigarettes, boiled sweets and 'Army form blank' – toilet paper – together with a miniature solid-fuel cooker.

A small number of men in every unit reported sick, some with genuine maladies. East Yorks infantrymen viewed with disdain a comrade who escaped embarkation: 'He was crafty, was Pepper … He said he wasn't going … [that] he had stomach pains, so they put him in an asylum because he'd been briefed about where we were going and what time and everything.' One of John Howard's men, committed to assault the Caen Canal bridge, bolted from his Horsa and disappeared just before take-off, claiming later that he had a premonition of his own death in a glider crash. A rifleman in Harry Jones's platoon of the Shropshires shot off his trigger finger.

Units approached the embarkation ports in trucks, tanks and vehicles from which markings had been erased. 'Taffy' Jones said: 'The scene that greeted us was fantastic; line upon line of craft of various sizes and overhead a ceiling of hundreds of barrage balloons, so awe-inspiring. So this was the last of *terra firma* and before boarding our landing-craft, for some unknown reason I kissed the ground.' Some men marched into Newhaven flying curious little balloons – contraceptives issued by medical officers to every invader, instead blown up and attached irreverently to rifle muzzles.

The tanks of the East Yorkshire Yeomanry drove 'through dense streets of half-cheering, half-bewildered people'. A Hussars officer wrote: 'Portsmouth was an incredible sight. Along all roads to it and every little suburban street were tanks and assault vehicles, bulldozers and infantry-carriers and vehicles of every sort. Every few yards there was a camp and the place was a display of military signs, while loudspeakers blared continuously.' Further west in the New Forest stood row upon row of steel anti-blast bays, each sheltering thirty-two tons of artillery ammunition.

The French commandos sang '*Sambre et Meuse*' and suchlike martial airs in the trucks that bore them towards Southampton, a journey interrupted for an hour in a roadside field where they were issued with grenades and explosives. One man had tattooed on his forehead the enigmatically bleak words *Pas de Chance*. Lovat's brigade boarded its shipping late on the afternoon of 5 June. Captain Tony Smith spoke of 'a grotesque gala atmosphere, more like a regatta than a page of history, with gay music from the ships' loudhailer and more than the usual quota of jocular farewells bandied between friends'. A very few men had done it all before: 'Slinger' Martin, 4 Commando's admin officer, had served in France in 1914. Cheers echoed from ship to ship. Lovat said: 'I never loved England so truly as at that moment.' It was 'a moment of release. The invasion build-up had grown interminable: a mounting tension, to some unbearable, that weighed like a millstone until we stepped at last into the boats.' Once settled below decks Col. Peter Young, a bachelor, immersed himself in a paperback he discovered in his cabin, entitled *Dr Marie Stopes' Marital Advice Bureau for Young Couples*.

Just after the East Riding Yeomanry had boarded their ships, to the indescribable humiliation of one of its young troop leaders, he was found to be suffering a plague of carbuncles on his rear end, and ordered to disembark. Naval surgeon-lieutenant Graham Airth noted laconically in his diary before the armada sailed, 'Delivered fresh blood to ships off Spithead.' An officer watching the loading of so many exotically-named 'funnies' – Crabs, Crocodiles, Snakes and their like – observed wryly that they 'turned each landing-craft into a sort of Noah's ark'.

Some tank crews aboard the big LSTs which carried their Shermans and Churchills endured as long as four days at sea, suffering much from sickness. The only interruptions of their boredom were twice-daily vehicle engine starts, and visits by a NAAFI launch which toured the anchorage, purveying sweets and small comforts. Twenty-eight-year-old Captain Islywn Davies of 3rd Recce Regiment agreed with Lovat that: 'We had been training a bit too long, and it really was time to go.' He ignored a telegram he received on the morning of their embarkation saying 'Grandfather dead, come home'. He also suppressed a telegram directed to one of his men, reporting that his daughter was ill in hospital, an intervention for which that soldier never forgave him. 'As we slipped quietly downriver out of Newhaven Quays I thought: "Here we go on the biggest adventure of our lives and no-one to wish us luck except a crowd of Wrens and dockyard maties". But, as we turned into the Channel, there on the grassy headland were thousands of people from Newhaven, all cheering and waving like mad. How big a secret was D-Day?!'

Major John Rex, who embarked further north, wrote: 'The face of the Thames was choppy, white horses everywhere and thick clouds overhead.' As a forty-year-old veteran, he saw the experience through a prism which included Dunkirk: 'That exodus in 1940 had been a shocking affair. The power of this return in 1944 was beyond reasonable simple thought.' He might have added that the Allied army now embarked seemed to belong to a wholly different age, in spirit, arms and equipment, from that which had returned from the continent four years earlier.

On 3 June a naval officer aboard one of the mass of ships congregating off the south coast wrote in bewilderment in his diary: 'Last night passed uneventfully. Why Jerry is leaving us alone I cannot imagine.' There was frustration at Eisenhower's twenty-four-hour holding order, announced on the night of 4 June. 'We had got all dressed up for the ball, but the band had got lost in a fog', in the words of paratrooper Richard Todd. He nonetheless reflected later: 'For most of us it was a frustrating postponement; for many, it was a twenty-four-hour extension to their lives.'

As one vessel cast off its moorings, an infantry officer was among scores of men lining the side who saw a WRNS driver leave her vehicle and walk to the edge of the quay where she hailed a commando seated atop a vehicle. Just before the gap between ship and shore widened forever, she stretched out a hand, which the soldier took, and shook. She said: 'Goodbye. Good luck.' The eyewitness, one of the Shropshires, said long afterwards he never forgot the moment: 'In that simple phrase we felt that she had said goodbye for everyone that each of us loved.'

One of the Frenchmen, Guy Hattu, wrote emotionally of the England receding behind his ship's stern: 'This country that we were quitting, and whose uniform we now wore with pride, had welcomed us generously and offered us unforgettable hospitality.' He and his countrymen found it droll to read, in a pamphlet issued to all the invaders, a British account of recent French history which concluded with the admonition: 'You are not conquerors but instead soldiers who come to free their allies who have been held captive.' Lovat once more broke into French before his Gallic contingent: '*Demain les Boches, on les aura!*' More pragmatically, on crowded ships men were told that anyone who wished to urinate should do so over the side. The heads – lavatories – were reserved for 'big jobs'.

As the armada set course for Normandy many men felt the atmosphere was merely that of another exercise. Below decks some of the Hussars played their beloved Housey-Housey – bingo. Adjutant Julius Neave recorded: 'One's chief fear was that of being afraid, and the uncertainty of one's own reaction to the battle.' As they broke open sealed packages of maps and orders, an infantry officer wrote: 'At last the names "in clear"! So Poland *was* Caen, Portugal *was* the Caen Canal, and they'd probably be in Caen this time tomorrow!' All the divisional briefing documents for Overlord appeared to assume that next day Rennie's forces would achieve a deep penetration inland. One such for the Hussars' tanks noted, for instance: 'South of Caen the going is good as far as BRETTEVILLE-SUR-LAIZE'. The same intelligence brief identified the preservation intact of Caen power station as a priority comparable in importance with the survival of the canal bridge and lock-gates just inland from the beach.

Some men displayed defiant ingenuity in telling loved ones where they were going. Keith Douglas, who would land with his armoured division behind the assault waves, defeated the censor by writing to a girlfriend: 'Well, fair stands the wind for ...?', knowing that she remembered the line from Drayton '*Fair stood the wind for France/When we our sails advance*'. There was irritation among those landing on Sword when they discovered that it lay near the intersection of four 1:50,000 maps, so that examples of all these – drawn from 170 million printed for the invasion forces – must be accommodated beneath the celluloid of a small mapcase.

Naval officer Alan Richardson was aboard a tank landing-craft laden with ammunition. In its tiny wardroom stood a vase of roses, presented to the skipper before they sailed by his wife, who lived nearby in Brighton. She said simply: 'Take a little bit of England with you.' Richardson wrote: 'In some strange way it didn't seem to us to be such a vast assembly of ships as so vividly described by those fortunate enough to be privy to the broader picture. Our world was this barely floating steel box of high explosives that we had to beach and unload on a hostile shore, and this tended to concentrate our minds rather forcefully on the immediate problems ahead.' They would have to 'dry out' on the beach while the tide fell, and rose again.

Many of the ships' captains, as well as their crews, were amateurs, and on some bridges it showed: Henry Rogers' LSR – Landing-Ship Repair – ran aground on the Goodwin Sands on 5 June and could be refloated only when high tide came. Thereafter its captain sustained a flow of facetious broadcast bombast which the ship's company disliked intensely. In the early hours of the 6th, he promised the crew, and especially those manning the armament, all the action they could want; he talked of 'fighting until all our guns are silenced, then ramming the enemy and boarding with cutlasses'.

In a running sea, tank commander Harry Morris was disgusted to be offered for dinner tinned steak-and-kidney pudding, from which he recoiled as the ship's motion grew more pronounced. RAF war correspondent Alan Melville said: 'It never got really dark that night; you were always able to make out grey shadows … and it was the last quiet night I was to enjoy for many weeks.' Wilf Todd of the East Yorks later wrote to his wife of those hours before the dawn: 'I prayed that night as I have never prayed in my life … My heart was beating like a trip-hammer.' Aboard every ship in the invasion armada millions of pounds, francs, dollars changed hands as thousands of passengers played cards or – on some American vessels – craps with the abandon of men who saw themselves facing a future to which mere money was irrelevant.

A naval officer wrote in his diary, 'The ship's got a really fine roll on her now. These landlubbers don't seem to understand that everything has to be tied down (and that includes one's wife!).' An officer of 79 Assault Squadron, who failed to heed this message, was crushed to death while sleeping under an AVRE tank, which had been imperfectly chained. The issue of live ammunition and explosives also posed frightful risks. Aboard *Glenearn* a corporal of the East Yorks laid on a mess table a Sten gun which he had just loaded, only for the weapon to clatter to the floor as the ship lurched in a heavy sea. It fired, hitting in the thigh a sergeant who bled to death during the pandemonium which followed.

Major George Appleton had written in his diary on 3 June, 'If anything untoward does happen to me, I could not wish it to be in better company than I'm in now.' He added, on the eve of battle: 'It is amazing to think that we are now on the verge of what the whole world has been waiting for, for years. Strange to think that this time tomorrow, 2130hrs, I may have "passed over", but I have complete faith in God that even if I should not survive, the invasion will be an unqualified success and that, after all, is the main thing. My wife, although dear to me, and those I love, is nothing compared with the misery that the Nazis and Japs have caused to countless people.' Very early next morning he read his self-appointed daily passage from the Bible, because he knew that at nightfall he would lack leisure to do so.

On British transports, there was no patriotic singing that matched Brigadier-General Theodore Roosevelt's lead on the voyage to American Omaha beach, when he called on his comrades to join him in 'Battle Hymn of the Republic'. Instead tannoy messages warned signallers, 'all batteries in the charging room to be collected *now*', to be fitted to wirelesses. At 0300, many ships broadcast from the bridge in words similar to those from the captain of *LCT825*: 'We have just heard that the postponement of Neptune has been cleared, and we are now putting the force into landing order. The show is *on*, and may I wish you all the best of luck!' Aboard those landing-craft carrying vehicles, engines were now run for five minutes in every hour, to keep them warm. L/Cpl. George Lane wrote: 'Looking around at the other chaps, they did not look like storming up any beach', mostly because of chronic seasickness. In the first light of dawn, infantrymen clambered clumsily into the little vessels that would take them the last lap to the shore. Geoff Duncan of the Norfolks said: 'Each of us was loaded down like a pack mule.' They wore 'assault jerkins' – canvas waistcoats with pouches on the outside and pockets on the inside for grenades, ammunition, Bren-gun magazines, emergency rations.

An NCO of the Norfolks, a veteran of Dunkirk, said with apparent relish as his men donned their webbing: 'This'll sort the men from the boys.' It was a foolish remark at that moment, when young infantrymen needed above all reassurance. But it was also a true one. No amount of training, exercises and preparation could reliably determine who, on the day of battle, would surge forward while others hung back. All that was certain, on Sword as on every battlefield, was that a handful of every unit's officers and men would head the charge; many more would follow their lead; while a cluster of less bold spirits hung behind, flinching before the wrath of the enemy. Yet that morning the rear would offer no more safety, and probably less, than did the van. Twenty-one-year-old Lt. Harry Jones of 2nd KSLI was especially haunted by the rumours that the enemy might pump burning oil onto the sea, as the British had planned to do back in 1940 in the event of a German invasion: 'The thought that I might end up like so many fighter pilots with badly burned, scarred faces really did worry me.'

The twenty-four-hour postponement on 5 June had obliged the major naval units to reverse course and steam north for twelve hours. Those that were to bombard Sword headed into the Irish Sea. There was the monitor *Roberts*, the battleships *Warspite* and *Ramillies*, the cruisers *Mauritius*, *Arethusa*, *Danae*, *Dragon* and *Frobisher*, together with their destroyer escorts. The following evening, however, found them once more at 'Piccadilly Circus', as the navy dubbed the sea space south of the Isle of Wight, where all Normandy convoy routes converged. At 2300, the force entered the easternmost swept lane, between lines of lighted buoys that marked paths through British minefields.

The Americans had declined to replicate the British commitment of midget submarines to provide inshore guidance for the armada. The absence of such markers caused the US 4th Division to land several hundred yards north of its intended destination, on Utah beach. Off Sword, by contrast, British minesweepers leading in the fleet were guided by a radio beacon, underwater signalling device and flashing light mounted on an eighteen-foot telescopic mast erected before dawn on the sea-swept hull of *X-23* by Jim Booth, one of the four men manning the midget submarine commanded by twenty-five-year-old Lt. George Honour.

Operation Gambit, as the beacon mission was codenamed, had been launched three days earlier. On the night of 3 June, trawlers had towed *X-23* and its sister vessel *X-20* towards the coast of Normandy. The two tiny craft cast off at 0415, then moved inshore on the surface, submerging before dawn: *X-20* took station at the western end of Gold beach. More than a few men rejected service in X-Craft, or withdrew after trying it, because they found the suffocating conditions intolerable. There was less than five foot of headroom; a permanent stench of diesel; not only were the crew unable to move freely, but conversation had to be kept to a minimum to conserve oxygen. They settled on the Channel bed.

At midday on Sunday the 4th, Honour and his companions brought their craft up to periscope depth, juggling controls and ballast tanks to hold its position against the tide and currents. They took repeated bearings on Ouistreham lighthouse and church towers on shore, checking and rechecking their exact position, grateful for unexpected assistance from an enemy light marking the entrance to the Orne estuary. Honour watched a crowd of Germans playing beachball on the shore: 'We were saying "Little do they know".' He studied a grazing cow intently, to relieve his own boredom.

They descended once more, then surfaced again at midnight to receive the depressing message 'Your aunt is riding a bicycle today'. This was the coded warning of a twenty-four-hour postponement. Back on the bottom, a mile from the German army, they played poker; tried to sleep; fretted about their diminishing oxygen supply. No one could smoke. Their gyro-compass failed, and likewise one pump.

At midnight on 5 June they rose again; learned by signal that this time there would be no postponement. At 0500, just before dawn, they surfaced yet again. The weather was miserable, the sea washed over their casing, and they could not launch their rubber boat. The men below passed up through the hatches tools for crewman Jim Booth, clad in a wetsuit and secured to the submarine by a lifeline, to erect the mast, a task he completed twenty minutes later. Booth also hoisted aloft a huge white ensign: Honour was sensitive to the risk that, even if he and his comrades survived H-Hour, with so much exuberant naval shelling *X-23* might be destroyed by friendly fire. The submarine immediately began to show a green light and to emit radio signals. Here were historic beacons, lighting the way for the fleet to approach Sword beach.

6

Operation Tonga

1 THE BRIDGES

The Airborne contingent took off a few hours before the host approaching by sea began its run-in to the beaches. Ahead of departure one colonel told his companies, 'We are History', and he was not wrong. The men of 7 Para drove to their embarkation airfield at Fairford in Gloucestershire where they were served stew and rice pudding, some of which reappeared in the aircraft not long afterwards. 9 Para's Lt. Alan Jefferson, a young man of passionate musical enthusiasms, carried as a luck charm a tuning fork, along with a paperback edition of *Hamlet*. He had been much teased in recent days, mostly jealously, since on 3 June his engagement to a pretty dancer had been announced in the *Daily Telegraph*.

Dennis Wheatley, the popular novelist and vinophile who in the uniform of an RAF wing-commander had worked on deception planning for D-Day, arrived at Harwell in Berkshire to wish luck to Richard Gale and his officers, and to share with them a prized bottle of hock. The general expressed fears that once in France he would be unable to get treacle, one of his favourite delicacies. The station commander promptly presented him with a tin. Gale, immensely popular with his men, addressed some of them for the last time: 'As for the op itself, only a bloody fool would think of going where we're going, so that's why I'm going there!' A paratrooper said: 'We cheered him to the skies.' Philip Burkinshaw of 12 Para was pestered until the last moment to wear a bulletproof breastplate made for him by his anxious father. The lieutenant observed wryly that had he succumbed to parental pleading and emulated Don Quixote, 'laden as I was already with half a hundredweight of weapons and equipment', after landing 'I would never have risen from the soil of Normandy.'

For D Company of the Ox & Bucks, the vanguard tasked to seize the vital inland bridges ahead of the main drop, those hours before take-off were, if possible, even more nerve-stretching than for 156,000 other British and American invaders destined to follow them next day by air and sea. John Howard played poker with the battalion's padre, to whom he lost the French francs with which they had all been issued. There was a last-minute crisis when lead glider pilot Jim Wallwork told Howard that, laden with all the company's special equipment including collapsible canvas boats, the Horsas would be overweight. Who, and what, might be left behind? Engineers? Their officer convinced the major that every sapper was indispensable. The boats? Two were crammed into each glider – in case the Germans blew the bridges before they could be overrun and it became necessary for Howard's men to paddle across the water and secure the crossing places until Bailey bridges could be brought up from the sea. One of the two craft in every glider was offloaded.

But still more weight needed to go. Howard reluctantly detailed two men from each Horsa to stand down. Some sobbed without embarrassment about being left behind, after spending so many months preparing for their hour of prospective glory. Yet another man looked like being removed from the order of the battle to make space in the gliders for a further afterthought – a doctor. But then a rifleman sprained his ankle playing football and was replaced by the medic.

The major assembled his company before take-off: 'It was an amazing sight,' he said later. 'The smaller chaps were visibly sagging at the knees under the amount of kit they had to carry.' He delivered a few final words of encouragement, then they boarded the gliders. Wally Parr lingered a few moments to chalk on the side of his own Horsa the name of his wife: 'LADY IRENE'. Den Brotheridge walked back to Sandy Smith's glider to shake his friend's hand, saying: 'See you on the bridge.'

The first Halifax towing aircraft took off at 2256, followed at one-minute intervals by the other five. The gliders were still so heavily loaded that, in the words of twenty-one-year-old pilot Roy Howard, 'we staggered into the air'. The little formation crossed the Channel at the usual towed speed of 145 mph, holding an altitude of seven thousand feet and conscious that hundreds of other aircraft would soon be filling the sky behind them. The soldiers sang 'Abby, Abby My Boy', 'Cow Cow Boogie' and 'It's a Long Way to Tipperary'. Many carried luck charms. John Howard's was a tiny red shoe, once property of his infant son Terry. Den Brotheridge was one of six men whose wives were pregnant. Few doubted that some of these impending offspring would be fatherless before the night was over, but most were doggedly confident that it would not be their own.

Back at Harwell, BBC correspondent Chester Wilmot, accompanying Richard Gale in the glider lift to be launched three hours later, quizzed some Pathfinders about their earlier lives. One had been a hod-carrier on building sites, another a Kent toolmaker; there were also an Edinburgh bricklayer, a Worcestershire foxhunt kennelman, a Dumfries lorry driver. There were also two pre-war regular soldiers, a deserter from the Irish army, an Austrian Jewish refugee. Three had been at Dunkirk in 1940, one had fought in Africa. They were led by a young lieutenant who, before the war, performed in the chorus line of a West End musical comedy.

Then Gale boarded his Horsa, piloted by Major Billy Griffiths. It took off for France, one among a fleet of seventy-two British gliders and a total of eleven hundred British and American aircraft aloft or soon to be so. Most of the Halifax and Stirling towing aircraft were obliged to linger over England for thirty minutes before joining their formations to cross the sea. At first, flying through cloud, the pilots and those closest behind them in the darkness could see only the lonely light on the tail of their own tug. Then, in mid-Channel, the overcast cleared somewhat, offering glimpses of dark, troubled waters below and shadowy shapes all around.

Many gliders began to pitch and soar, causing their passengers to fear that their tow ropes would break, a fate that indeed befell three which force-landed in England and another three that ditched in the sea, with fatal consequences for their occupants. Many Airborne soldiers, condemned to passivity until they landed, had too much time to take counsel of their fears: Would the enemy be waiting? Would the pilots find the drop zone? Would the fields be mined as well as staked? Alan Jefferson wrote: 'Each aircraft, which was its own island, contained miniature islands of soldiers, each thinking, wondering, tight inside and fearful of the outcome … We were all too introspective.' In Hal Hudson's C-47, men on their way to storm the Merville Battery sang Vera Lynn's old favourite 'There'll Always Be an England/ And England Shall Be Free'. The sophisticated Hudson found himself surprised to be moved by this.

The bridge assault company knew it was by no means assured that their bombers would tow them to the right place. Aloft during a rehearsal Horsa pilot Roy Howard had remonstrated furiously with his tug crew over the linking intercom: 'You've got the wrong airfield!' When the operation was first mooted, the airmen questioned whether, lacking ground beacons, they could land close enough to the two objectives to secure surprise. By experience, however, they found that given clear views of the waterways below, the bridges might indeed be successfully pinpointed – as now they were by most of the Horsa pilots.

This opening act of D-Day, first incision of the massive Allied penetration of the Atlantic Wall, took place at the battlefield's eastern extremity. Carlo D'Este has written that while post-war popular and especially movie attentions to 6 June emphasize events on the beaches, 'it was the battle for the foothold in the Orne bridgehead' – codenamed Operation Tonga – 'which largely determined the fate of Montgomery's master plan and the course of the struggle for Normandy which followed'. If a 6th Airborne perimeter could be seized and held, the Germans would be denied a launching-pad for a counter-attack to roll up the Allied D-Day beachhead from the east, whence most German reinforcements would come. D Company's glider assault on the bridges was to be Tonga's first tiny bloodletting, harbinger of assured carnage to come.

Over Cabourg, where the pilots successfully exploited a gap in the German flak defences, Roy Howard's tug navigator bid him farewell through the cable link: 'Good luck! Cast off when you like.' The pilots slipped their tows at five thousand feet, adopted a course first of 270 degrees, then of 187, and against stopwatches began to count down their descent inland. When they reached 1,500 feet, they shouted to the passengers to drag open the sliding side doors of the gliders. One pilot saw a German parachute flare burst in the air below him, then briefly entered a cloud from which he emerged to find himself back in welcome darkness. The Horsas' Halifax towing aircraft meanwhile sustained their southbound course for two minutes before delivering token bombloads aimed at a cement factory to divert German attention from the real purpose of their mission. The bombs missed, and indeed by the end of the Normandy campaign the cement works was Caen's almost only undamaged building.

Each of D Company's six gliders made its approach independently, invisible to one another. This was a wiser disposition than it might seem: even should a leader land in the wrong place, others might do better. Jim Wallwork, first in Horsa No. 91, focused on watching his compass, holding a bearing for three minutes and forty seconds until co-pilot John Ainsworth cried 'Now!' and Wallwork made a full right turn, peering intently through the cockpit perspex in search of a landmark. Behind him John Howard ordered silence among his men. Then Ainsworth called time on another right turn so that they headed north, parallel with the east bank of the Caen Canal and descending rapidly. Airspeed fell from 160 mph to nearer 100.

Roy Howard, flying one of the Orne gliders, said confidently to his co-pilot: 'It's all right now, Fred, I can see where we are.' They had staged so many rehearsals, studied the model and photos for so long that 'I had the strange feeling that I had been there before.' The pilot put on full flap for the last steep descent, with his Horsa at a forty-five-degree angle, losing height at a rate of two thousand feet a minute. On the final approach, however, try as he would Howard could not cut their overloaded craft's speed below 90 mph. 'What a load there was behind me! … We were falling like a spent rocket.' Another pilot described the approach to landing: 'The gentle hiss of the slipstream rose higher and higher … the ground rushed up faster and faster, the noise grew louder and louder.'

Wallwork and his comrades had made forty-three practice landings on runways, more than half of these in darkness. He was now aiming to set down in a field five hundred yards long, between the two waterways. Suddenly he glimpsed below the silver strands of canal and river, the vital western bridge a mile ahead, with a water tower conspicuous near its western end and a pillbox on the east bank. In those last seconds, Wallwork made himself the first hero of D-Day. Knowing that he was landing too fast, he called Ainsworth to release their braking parachute, which burst open with a jerk that drastically checked the Horsa. He called to Howard and his men: 'Prepare to prang!' so that they took up brace positions, with arms linked and feet lifted off the floor. The major could see 'great footballs' of sweat on the pilot's forehead and face.

As Wallwork pushed Horsa No. 91 into its controlled crash, Howard thought he saw incoming tracer rounds, but these proved to be streams of sparks shooting upwards as the rushing plane bounced on ground obstacles. Then there was a rending, conclusive concussion. The glider lurched to a halt, its nose shattered, at a speed that in a car collision would likely have been fatal to the occupants. After the thunder of the impact momentary silence fell, interrupted only by the moaning of the pilots, both battered and bleeding. On this, the 1,405th night of the German occupation of Normandy, Wallwork had achieved a miracle – landing Howard and his men in the wire entanglement just forty-seven yards from the pillbox on the east bank of the Caen Canal. One of the Germans at the bridge, Pte. Wilhelm Furtner, said later, as a prisoner, that for vital moments he supposed an RAF bomber had crash-landed beside the bridge.

The impact stunned Wallwork's passengers, who lingered for some seconds – which they themselves afterwards felt to have been minutes – before moving. Denis Edwards heard 'a God Almighty crash like a clap of loud thunder and my body seemed to be moving in several different directions at once … I was dazed and literally seeing stars. I thought: we must all be dead.' John

Howard had been thrown against the roof beams, ramming his helmet down over his ears. Then the attackers seized their senses and sprang into movement, smashing an exit from the wrecked hull. Platoon commander Den Brotheridge emerged from a gaping hole on the far side of the glider; ran around the tail and tersely demanded of John Howard: 'All right?' Yes, said the major: 'Carry on.' Brotheridge shouted, 'Able, Able!', to rally his men, and tossed a phosphorus smoke grenade towards the pillbox from which a machine-gun had opened fire. Another attacker pushed an explosive grenade through its slit, then Brotheridge ran across the bridge, still calling the watchwords for his men to follow him.

The nearest German sentry was just sixteen years old, a Berliner named Helmut Romer who had started his spell of duty at midnight, less than twenty minutes earlier. Romer bolted as he saw the blackened attackers racing towards him. He crossed the bridge westward shouting '*Fallschirmjäger!*' – 'Paratroopers!' A second sentry fired a flare from a Very pistol before Brotheridge emptied his Sten gun into him. The three attackers detailed to seize the east-side pillbox tossed their grenades through the slits, and the engineers began to check the bridge for explosives, severing wires wherever they found them. On the west side the conscripted foreigners in the enemy trenches sought flight, but their German NCOs opened fire with MG34s and Schmeisser machine-pistols. A bullet caught the neck of Brotheridge, who fell just beyond the bridge, while his men dashed past his prostrate form, firing from the hip and throwing grenades.

The sound effects of further collisions signalled the arrival of the other two canal-bound gliders. Sgt. Oliver Boland, piloting Horsa 92, released his braking parachute, then swerved to avoid 91, and shuddered to a halt, breaking the plane's back. Platoon commander David Wood was thrown clear, yet clambered to his feet uninjured. Boland claimed later to have said to the rest of his passengers: 'We're here, piss off and do what you're paid to do.' John Howard, who was lying prone to escape the attentions of a German rifleman, called to Wood 'Number Three task!', which meant clear the north-east trenches. The lieutenant sprang away followed by his platoon, just as the third glider, No. 93, landed at 0018 and collapsed with a shattering crash into a deep pond. Their doctor, John Vaughan, was hurled through the cockpit perspex and after hitting the ground remained concussed for thirty minutes. Lt. Sandy Smith, a former Cambridge rugger blue, was thrown into the water and broke his arm. Somehow scrambling out, he found that he had lost his weapon and was covered with mud. He seized a discarded Sten gun and ran to the bridge, quite rightly ignoring six men trapped in the half-submerged glider, one of whom drowned.

Seconds later David Wood, together with his sergeant and the platoon runner, were all hit by a single burst of enemy fire while clearing trenches. A corporal took over command. There were shouts of 'Baker!' and 'Charlie!', as these two platoons ran to their assigned positions. The attackers at first took no prisoners; simply cleared every trench and bunker with automatic weapons and grenades, killing the occupants. The sappers reported to Howard that no explosives were laid, but they had removed the cabling. The German officer responsible for defence of the bridges was an ardent Nazi named Major Hans Schmidt, who commanded an understrength company of grenadiers of the 716th Infantry Division. He had prepared both structures for demolition, but had not connected the charges, for fear of an accident or intervention by the 'terrorists' of the French Resistance.

Here was a dilemma which had troubled both sides ahead of 6 June: Germans and British alike agreed that the bridges represented a link prospectively vital to themselves as well as to the enemy. Both armies preferred, however, to see the crossings destroyed than to become available to their foes. Major Schmidt was foolish not to have placed the explosives beneath the bridge, but he would have been in dire trouble with his superiors – as well he knew – had the Orne and canal crossings been blown prematurely. Schmidt anyway assumed he could expect at least an hour's grace in which to take action, following even a British parachute landing in his vicinity. On the night of 5/6 June, the major was five miles from his post of duty, disporting himself with a girlfriend in the village of Franceville-Plage, close to the Orne estuary.

On the canal bridge one of Howard's men stooped by the prone Brotheridge, lying just beside the café on the western bank. The lieutenant's eyes were open, his lips moving, but he was obviously dying, first fatal battle casualty of D-Day. Sandy Smith had already encountered some surprises that morning, among them that not all his men aspired to be heroes. He found one cowering in a German foxhole, praying, while another pleaded a sprained ankle to retire from the action. Most of the others, however, performed superbly. D Company began to take up positions in the abandoned German trenches and pillboxes, to face the counter-attack which they knew must come. This first phase of the little battle had lasted barely ten minutes, but every briefing before they left England emphasized that the second stage – clinging to the bridge until seaborne invaders could relieve them – was just as vital, and potentially far more hazardous.

Howard's orders stated: 'You must expect a counter-attack at any time after H minus 4 … This attack may take the form of a battlegroup consisting of one [infantry company] in lorries, up to eight tanks and one or two guns … down one of the roads leading from WEST or SW, but a cross-country route cannot be ignored … It is vital that the crossing places be held … at all costs.'

Jim Wallwork helped his co-pilot John Ainsworth to escape from the wreckage of Horsa No. 91, then started to unload ammunition and carry it forward, heedless of his own blood-streaked face – for some minutes, he believed himself to have lost an eye. Sandy Smith was hit in the wrist and had suffered a badly wrenched knee. He kept going, but obviously could not do so for long. While D Company had triumphantly fulfilled its mission, three of John Howard's officers had become casualties. John Vaughan, their medic, gave David Wood a shot of morphine and confirmed that Den Brotheridge was moribund. Vaughan himself still felt considerably dazed: when he began to stumble along the road westward, he was halted by cries of 'Come back, doc – wrong way, unfriendly!' Desultory enemy fire was soon coming from houses in Bénouville, only a few steps beyond the bridge, where some panzergrenadiers had arrived.

Five hundred yards eastwards, above the Orne, Roy Howard and his passengers had been making their final approach when they glimpsed gunflashes below – the first exchanges of fire at the canal. They scraped over treetops, lifted the nose, then heard the rumble of Horsa No. 96's wheels as they thumped down and stopped, within yards of the river bridge. Howard shouted to Lt. Dennis Fox: 'You're in the right place, sir!' Yet when the platoon commander stumbled out of the wreck, he was dismayed to find himself unsupported. Of the other two gliders assigned to the Orne, Horsa No. 95 had overshot by four hundred yards. Meanwhile No. 94, which carried Brian Priday, designated commander of this attack, was ten miles away, in Roy Howard's sardonic words 'busy capturing a bridge on the wrong river'. Priday and his platoon had been landed beside the Dives, south-east of Cabourg. They rejoined the company twenty-four hours later, after a trek during which they lost four men.

Fox was amazed and vastly relieved, after leading his platoon racing for their objective, to find it unguarded: they took possession without firing a shot. Tod Sweeney's 5 platoon, from Horsa

No. 95, arrived panting to join them after doubling across the fields. Sweeney said: 'I still had that awful feeling as I went over the bridge that the thing might go up under our feet, blow up in our faces.' No such misfortune occurred, however, and when Sweeney met Fox, his fellow subaltern delivered a line which he had obviously rehearsed: 'Well, so far the exercise is going fine, but I can't find any bloody umpires!' Sweeney said: 'The strongest recollection I have is not of fear but of excitement.'

John Howard's signaller, Corporal Tappenden, now received a triumphant voice radio message from Fox: the Orne bridge was secure. The assault had been a dazzling success, for the British fatal loss of only two men. Seldom in the entire war did five of six assault gliders land in exactly the right place by day, far less by night: D Company's achievement owed at least as much to their pilots as to their own prowess. Major Howard felt a stab of guilt when Den Brotheridge died, an hour after being hit: he had personally persuaded his young friend to join the Airborne. Tappenden the signaller could for a time gain no acknowledgement of his success message – 'Ham and Jam!' – to 5 Para Brigade headquarters, because its own communications had gone missing in the drop. Howard sent Dennis Fox to lead a fighting patrol, probing nearby Bénouville. Then, at 0050, they saw parachutes of many hues descending. Men of 7 Para, their relief force, were in the air to the east of them. The big drop had begun. Tod Sweeney succumbed to a spasm of melancholy as he contemplated those dead, missing, wounded – and assuredly still to fall: 'A feeling of sadness crept over me, that our company which had trained together for two years would never be the same again … In our youthful innocence it had not occurred to me that we would not all somehow remain together until the end of the war.'

2 'GET ON, I SAY! GET ON!'

As the first aircraft of Gale's main force crossed the French coast the winds, 15–20 mph, were higher than would have been permitted for parachute training drops. Air Vice-Marshal Leslie Hollinghurst, commanding the RAF's 38 Group, newly-formed to provide transport aircraft for Tonga, himself flew as a passenger in one of six Albemarle bombers bearing the lead Pathfinders. Yet only one stick landed in the right place, and all their beacons were lost or damaged. Eisenhower's deputy, Air Marshal Sir Arthur Tedder, afterwards estimated that only a sixth of the entire British and American airborne force was dropped accurately.

Here was a poor start to a hugely important, boundlessly complex operation. The RAF had striven to prepare its pilots, adopting the most ingenious techniques. Aircrew were first shown a big model of the Orne valley. Then they viewed an instructional film, showing how the terrain below would look as they approached from the air. After several normal viewings, the same footage was then shown to them through a blue filter, to approximate the appearance of the ground in moonlight. To avoid chaos in the night sky, the entire fleet of troop-carrying aircraft flew a loop course over France. Each successive plane, after dropping its men, swung north-east near Caen, then for the flight home crossed the Channel coast east of Le Havre.

For both the RAF and USAAF the harsh fact persisted that the men appointed to fly transport aircraft were those at the bottom of their services' proficiency ratings – deemed unsuitable for fighter or bomber duties. On the night of 5/6 June, when suddenly their role became important, some displayed dangerous incompetence or carelessness, banking and weaving when they found themselves under fire. Though air chiefs later sought to excuse and even applaud the fliers' performance, soldiers damned some pilots as 'gun-shy'.

In the gliders, making their last flights, the wind roared against the flimsy fabric and plywood coverings. Pilots and some passengers glimpsed flashes to port from the detonation of bombs around German batteries south of Le Havre; streaks of red and yellow tracer from light flak. Then, in the words of Chester Wilmot, 'here below is the white curving strand of France and, mirrored in the dim moonlight, the twin ribbons of water we are looking for'. One of the pilots turned and called back to the soldiers, 'I'm letting go – hold tight.' Momentarily the glider seemed to stall, then to hover. The wind noise dropped to a murmur and 'we are floating in a sky of fathomless uncertainty – in suspense between peace and war … gliding so smoothly that the fire and turmoil of battle seem to belong to another world'. Wilmot, a thirty-three-year-old Australian who would later become one of the finest historians of the war of which he had already seen much, was supremely conscious of his responsibility as a chronicler of 6th Airborne's assault, a climactic experience.

An astonishing number of paratroopers had contrived to sleep in their aircraft, among them Richard Todd of 7 Para, who was wakened by the RAF dispatcher. Below he saw white-etched wave crests, then fields, then he jumped: 'The din was almost mind-numbing: aircraft engines, chattering machine-guns, the thudding of shells or mortars. And the night sparkled with tracer bullets.'

As one of Brigadier Nigel Poett's staff officers wrenched aside the jammed floor hatch of his aircraft, he slipped and fell away into the Channel, never to be seen again. Lt. John Sim of 12 Para wrote, 'The monotonous greyness of the sea broke into parallel white lines. I saw the waves rolling towards the dirty yellow beach, then the cliffs forming a step from the beach to the darker woods beyond. For some minutes I gazed down on a landscape clearly visible in the moonlight. The tracks of lanes, fields and hedgerows were etched in various tones of grey and black.' Then he jumped. 'There was the sudden stillness, the clean crisp rush of air behind the ears and round the body, sensations quickly following one after another, and I found myself floating lazily down, silently and, it seemed, alone … As I watched the field seesawing, a wire fence flashed to one side; the ground hit me and I rolled over. I was in Normandy and over Hitler's West Wall.'

Others felt less fortunate. James Hill, the thirty-three-year-old general's son commanding 3rd Parachute Brigade, was very tall and very bright, a dominant personality who scared most of his subordinates. Landing in water and deep mud gave him cause for special discomfort because he had secreted a supply of teabags in the waistband of his trousers. But he was also alarmed for his men, misdropped into similar unwelcoming places. Many containers of heavy weapons could not be located in the dark. Mortarmen and Vickers-gunners, who thus found themselves impotent, had to be designated as reserves, until arms became available for them.

In Lt. Jeremy Spencer's plane, one man baulked the jump, precipitating chaotic scenes in the fuselage and obliging his pilot to make three runs before his entire 'stick' was out. Unusually, Spencer reached the ground to discover he was not far from 11 Para's appointed drop zone. Yet he felt disoriented, because this was the first time in his life he had set foot on foreign soil: 'There was no emotion of fear, merely an intense curiosity and eagerness to do one's job.' Many men struggled to grasp the idea that, little more than an hour after quitting the England in which they had spent their entire previous lives, they were in German-occupied France.

Geoffrey Pine-Coffin, 7 Para's colonel, landed among tall trees and found it impossible to spot any landmarks until the brilliant eruption of a German flare illuminated Ranville church: its tower was easily recognized because separated by several yards from the original fourteenth-century building. One of his men, Richard Todd, thumped into a cornfield half a mile away, in pain after skinning his hand when he released his weapons container on its suspensive rope. He glimpsed dim figures, and reached his battalion RV sooner than most of Gale's men contrived. Philip Burkinshaw's bulky kitbag refused to obey its release clips and free itself from his waist. This threatened him with a broken leg or worse, but after seconds of fear as he descended he hit the ground intact, and within yards of half a dozen members of his platoon.

Near Bréville fifteen local people, including the mayor, had formed the habit over recent nights of taking refuge from Allied bombing in a ditch. Early on 6 June they again heard planes. The cows in the next field stampeded as shadowy figures began to descend from the sky. The mayor's English wife, Madame Magnenat, exulted to her husband: 'They've come!' He remained doubtful that this was, indeed, the invasion. Then, as his group left their ditch and threaded a cautious path to their home, Le Bois des Monts, they found themselves under fire from both sides. The early drizzle of falling paratroopers had become a cloudburst, rousing into violent action every German within range.

Later in the war, at the March 1945 Rhine crossing, airborne forces launched drops from aircraft at higher altitudes – between eight hundred and a thousand feet, to give jumpers more time to release their personal kitbags and control their descents – but in daylight this proved grievously mistaken: Germans on the ground thus enjoyed longer in which to shoot them as they fell. Every parachute unit required at least an hour before being ready to fight as a formed body – on 6 June, 12 Para took ninety minutes, then easily overran Le Bas de Ranville, where many missing men appeared during the hours which followed. Commanding officers kept their battalion buglers sounding calls, to rally strays. The colonel of 8 Para, deploying on the edge of the great wooded expanse of the Bois de Bavent, at first mustered only 230 men, but immediately began to patrol aggressively.

Several of 13 Para, tasked with seizing Ranville, got caught in trees as they were about to land – one survived in a lofty perch for twelve hours, suspended in his harness, before rescuers freed him. Three war dogs accompanied the battalion. One of these, terrified, broke loose from its handler in their Albemarle. A flier wrote: 'The crew had an awfully difficult job chasing it around the aircraft to get its parachute fastened to the static line and then to throw it out after the paratroopers.' This hapless beast was never seen again, but of the other two dogs one was wounded and the last survived the war.

Capt. Robert Kerr landed in the Dives but managed to flounder ashore. A French boy guided him and four others to Varaville, which they reached at 0330: 'Complete chaos seemed to reign in the village. Against a background of Brens, Spandaus and grenades could be heard the shouts of British and Canadians, Germans and Russians.' Kerr headed instead for Le Mesnil, still guided by the boy, who in turn was instructed by a middle-aged Englishwoman who lived nearby, originally a cockney from Camberwell. Yet when the paratroopers collided with more Germans, the child was killed by a stick grenade. Kerr's party grew to some twenty strong, falling in with farmers who led it through the Bois de Bavent. Eventually, 'all completely whacked' after a five-mile trek through countryside crawling with Germans, they reached 13 Para.

James Byrom spoke French and was thus deputed to knock on the front door of the first house they saw: 'At the sight of the motherly, middle-aged peasant the gulf of the years disappeared and I might have been back in 1939, an English tourist on a walking tour dropping in to ask for a glass of cider and some camembert:

"*Excusez-nous, madame. Nous sommes les parachutistes anglais faisant partie de Débarquement Allié.*" There was a moment of scrutiny, then the woman folded me in her arms. The tears streamed down her face, and in between kisses she was shouting for her husband, for lamps, for wine … We found ourselves – an evil-looking group of camouflaged cut-throats – surrounded and overwhelmed by the pent-up emotion of four years.' By contrast Bill Elvin and three others of 7 Para knocked on a farmhouse door to ask directions to be greeted by a man in spectacles and a moustache who shook his fist and told them to go away.

The writer Jonathan Raban once observed, in the context of his own father's experience of 1940s France: 'Warfare and tourism are less often linked than they should be. For my father, as for so many of his fellow soldiers, this was his first chance to experience the continuous cascade of new sensations that drenches the stranger when he sets foot in a foreign land.' So it was for many men of 6th Airborne that night of June 1944. Jeremy Spencer said: 'The welcome was astounding. French people were leaning out of windows shouting, laughing, singing and giving little bunches of flowers to the lads.'

And now it was time for the glider force to land. In scores of Horsas pilots pulled back control columns to level out from their dives, while passengers clutched sinking stomachs and bursting ears. Then, in Chester Wilmot's words, 'the glider is skimming the ground when out of the night another glider comes straight for us'. His Horsa lurched skywards again to pass over the interloper, then 'the soil of France rushes past beneath us, but the glider careers on with grinding brakes and creaking timbers, mowing down "Rommel's asparagus", snapping off five stout posts. There is an ominous sound of splitting wood and rending fabric and we brace ourselves for the shock … until with a violent swerve to starboard it finally comes to rest scarred but intact … We are two minutes late. Shouts and cheers echo down the glider, and a voice from the dark interior cries out, "This is it, chum. I told yer we wouldn't 'av ter swim!"'

Richard Gale contrived to doze until his aircraft encountered bumpy weather approaching the coast of France. This caused the intercom cable linking the Horsa to its tug to snap, so that they lost communication. Despite this momentary cause for alarm, minutes later Major Griffiths put down the glider almost exactly where the general wanted, close to Ranville. The only hitch was that his jeep got jammed in the fuselage until dawn, when somebody found time and tools to extract it. The general himself appeared briefly concussed. He stumbled over to Philip Burkinshaw of 12 Para and bellowed: 'Where the hell am I?' He was soon masterfully himself, however, his men hearing a familiar, booming voice: 'Don't you dare argue with me – I'm Richard Gale. Get on, I say, get on!'

As Chester Wilmot gazed upon the chaos of damaged and wrecked Horsas around him in the Norman cornfield, it appeared a scene of disaster. A pilot wrote after such a landing: 'I had but one thought, to get out of the glider before one of two things, or possibly both, happened, which was either another glider landing on top of us or crashing into us, which was highly probable, or enemy fire coming down on us.' The two men in the cockpit tore open their harness release pins, felt a blast of cool air enter the fuselage, then threw aside their shoulder straps and jumped out. The crews of those gliders carrying vehicles released four bolts connecting the tail to the main part of the fuselage to enable the jeep or gun – if it was not hopelessly jammed in the wreck – to be pushed out.

In the small hours of 6 June, forty-nine of the seventy-two aircraft tasked to land at the British LZ reached the right place with few casualties. Ten of eighteen anti-tank guns were moving to their appointed positions. One group of men harnessed a farm horse to a six-pounder stuck in a glider that had crashed into the Dives, though they were unable to extricate it. It was just after 0330. For some minutes there were no sounds of firing nearby, so that men could hear each other muttering and cursing, hacking holes in fuselages with axes, hauling out guns. Only as they approached Ranville church did shooting erupt nearby.

In the faint half-light the general's ADC, Ulsterman Tommy Haughton, was seen leading a chestnut horse that had been grazing on the landing zone. 'Take care of that animal, Tommy!' said Gale. 'It's a fine morning for a ride.' He was play-acting, of course, to sustain the steadiness of men within earshot. But it was a good act, which would be sustained through the battle that soon began. The horse, almost inevitably, perished under German mortaring.

A total of 368 aircraft and ninety-eight gliders participated in 6th Airborne's night landings, carrying 4,512 paratroopers of which all but two hundred reached Normandy. Fifty-nine gliders landed accurately on the landing zone, carrying 493 men, forty-four jeeps, fifty-five motorbikes, fifteen six-pounder anti-tank guns, two seventeen-pounders and one bulldozer. The RAF lost seven aircraft, and thirty-four glider pilots were killed. This outcome was a remarkable achievement and, given the wildly erratic parachute drop, emphasized the superiority of gliders as a means of delivering forces to the battlefield. The army Horsa pilots performed far more impressively than had the RAF's fliers charged with dropping paratroopers.

Gale's division landed into close countryside, small fields bordered by treelines and stretches of dense woodland. The village streets seemed oppressively narrow, with many high walls. Such terrain offered both defenders and attackers plentiful cover if they stayed motionless. But for British and Germans alike, all movement was perilous when every house and hedge might conceal an enemy machine-gun or sniper. It was a heart-stopping business hastening over unknown territory, and the best hopes of survival rested upon speed and exploiting cover. Many of the combatants on 6 June, and in the ensuing days, experienced shock collisions with their foes. While woodland restricted views, open ground offered fields of fire against all those who sought to cross them.

Major Tim Roseveare's pilot had taken such energetic evasive action that the thirty-year-old Royal Engineer, commanding the 3rd Parachute Squadron, almost fell out of the Dakota's open door. He hit the ground at 0030 to discover that his men were scattered and had been landed three miles short of their immediate objectives: five road bridges across the River Dives upon which the Germans were dependent, if they sought swiftly to launch a counter-attack against the Airborne bridgehead, and thereafter the Sword beachhead. Many men receiving orders for D-Day had been told that their own roles were critical to the success of the invasion, but in Roseveare's case this was truer than most. The marshes around the Dives extended between half a mile and two miles in width, east of the landing zone. They were impassable, save by those five bridges.

In the air the major's sixty-pound kitbag had failed to release from his body harness, causing him narrowly to avoid a broken ankle on landing, encumbered with tools and demolition gear. He cut himself free with his fighting knife, then struggled to disentangle the container from his harness. 'What a shambles!' he observed ruefully, after finding that blame for his misdelivery lay with a Pathfinder who had illuminated a beacon in the wrong place. He cheered up, however, on receiving a smart salute from his RSM, Bob Barr, who had dropped nearby. He recalled: 'Troops from every formation in the division were milling around trying to locate their rendezvous. Gliders were a hazard as they came in with a swish and a thump.'

The conduct of the scattered elements of the squadron that night represented a tribute to Airborne training, with its emphasis on personal initiative. Richard Todd wrote: '[It] was constantly dinned into us … that parachute and glider-borne forces will probably operate in groups and pockets behind enemy lines.' One of Roseveare's troops under Sgt. Poole, in civilian life a railway engine-driver, begged Gammon grenades from some passing Canadian paratroopers. Poole then used their explosive innards to improvise a charge with which he destroyed the metal lattice girder of the single-span bridge at Varaville, causing it to collapse into the Dives. Poole and the Canadians who had landed nearby then retreated to Le Mesnil, under fire from Germans who belatedly arrived on the scene.

By 0230 Roseveare had mustered forty-seven of his sappers, together with trollies laden with 500 lb of plastic explosive and forty-five 'General Wade' shaped charges. Lacking a vehicle, they set out on foot towards Troarn, seven miles away, where the largest bridge stood. For the first hour and more, passing Hérouvillette and Escoville the little column encountered no enemy: 'If there were Germans there they must have pulled their bedclothes a little higher – we had no wish to disturb them.'

At 0400 they met some men of 8 Para, together with a Medical Corps jeep and trailer which Roseveare commandeered. He dumped its cargo of medical supplies, which were eventually delivered to the brigade dressing-station at Le Mesnil, borne by sulky German prisoners. Instead the engineer loaded half a ton of explosives, seven men and a Bren gun. The major himself took the wheel of the jeep and forged through the darkness until, just short of a railway level-crossing, in the darkness he plunged the vehicle into a knife-rest barbed-wire entanglement set across the road, inviting a single shot from an enemy sentry who then fled. The jeep, however, enmeshed in the wire, required twenty minutes' hard labour to break free, using cutters providentially carried by an NCO. A torch beam was indispensable to work on the obstacle, and thus every second they were acutely conscious of their vulnerability. Roseveare said: 'I felt just like a pea waiting to be plucked out of the pod.'

Two scouts were sent ahead towards the next crossroads, on the edge of Troarn, but met a German on a bicycle. He protested noisily on being dragged off it, and was killed – foolishly – with a Sten-gun burst. The night's silence was banished. Roseveare hastily called his men back onto the vehicle and set off again, leaving behind one straggler. They careered through Troarn at their best speed, 35 mph, pursued by erratic German fire, including streams of tracer. 'There seemed to be a Boche in every doorway shooting like mad,' said Roseveare later. 'However the boys got to work with their Sten guns and Sapper Peachey did very good work as a rear-gunner with the Bren gun.' His sergeant said: 'The further we went, the more the fire was coming at us and the faster Roseveare drove the jeep … We were all so excited there was no real feeling of being frightened.' A German dragged out an MG34, dashed aside as they approached him, then belatedly fired at them as they receded.

When the trailer swerved wildly, however, Peachey fell off and it was unthinkable to stop to rescue him – the sapper was taken prisoner. Roseveare and his precious cargo careered down the steep descent from the village to reach the road bridge unscathed – and found it unguarded. Within less than five minutes they had laid their charges on the masonry crown of one of the arches. Just as the sun began to rise Sgt. Irving twisted the igniter to blow a six-foot gap. Knowing they had no chance of driving back through Troarn, they dumped the jeep up a woodland track and made their way back westwards on foot, fording or swimming several waterways. They snatched an hour of sleep among the trees of the

Bois de Bures. Resuming their march, they met an elderly Frenchman milking a cow, whom Roseveare informed that he was being liberated: 'He was not impressed. Perhaps he did not understand my accent.' They reached the 3 Brigade perimeter around noon, 'a very bedraggled and exhausted party, having been shot at by Germans, bombed by the RAF and unappreciated by the French'.

In the meantime one of Roseveare's troop leaders, Captain Tim Juckes, not realizing that his commanding officer had already blown the Troarn bridge, himself reached it later in the morning with more charges and widened the gap. One or other parties of British and Canadian engineers successfully wrecked all five of the crossings of the Dives. In the days that followed the enemy was able to restore them but they had been effectively denied to German passage when it mattered, on 6 June. Subsequently the sappers embarked on their usual tasks – clearing mines, building bunkers partly roofed with German anti-glider poles, fixing water supply and laying booby traps. The two Airborne sapper squadrons started D-Day with just short of three hundred men and ended it with almost a hundred casualties.

From all over Normandy, paratroopers who had been dropped wide trudged, crept, sometimes crawled or swam towards Gale's perimeter. Lost men were grateful to encounter signposts, enabling them to establish their locations. They were astonished that the Germans were so obliging as to have left these in place: in England, all local markers had been removed back in 1940, to confuse prospective invaders. Padre Whitfield Foy of 13 Para found himself four miles astray, and expressed to himself the unchristian hope that the eggs and bacon issued to returning operational aircrew might be burned on his own navigator's plate.

Some of the wanderers made it into the divisional perimeter, others did not. It is a reflection of the poor relations between the British and French Canadians that some members of the latter's parachute battalion afterwards asserted a bitter conviction that they had been deliberately dropped wide – exploited as human sacrifices – to confuse the Germans. A substantial number of Canadians became PoWs. Their colonel, George Bradbrooke, later spoke disconsolately about his battalion having been 'just one little pocket on the end of nowhere', even after he and some of his men assembled following their wild drop.

When Lt. Gen. Josef Reichert, commanding the German 711th Division, found British paratroopers descending around his headquarters conceit caused him to decide this was a personal *coup de main*, directed against himself. He ordered his staff, messengers, drivers and orderlies into combat kit, and muttered irritable regret that he had disbanded the headquarters defence platoon. Reichert sent out fighting patrols, which quickly captured two paratroopers who had landed within his immediate perimeter. He summoned the nearest combat unit, an engineer company, to come at once to take over local defence. Meanwhile his confused and jumpy HQ personnel made matters worse by firing on returning patrols, albeit without effect. Soon after 0300 the engineer company reached Reichert, who by then understood – as did few other senior Germans at that hour – that the Allied Airborne drops were securing the eastern flank for a seaborne landing.

At the Caen Canal bridge, Howard and his men watched the main fly-in as searchlights lit up parachutes, triggering more German tracer. The major said: 'It really was the most awe-inspiring sight. Above all, it meant that we are not alone.' But he knew it would take the men of 7 Para at least a half-hour, probably longer, to reach and reinforce him. Howard began to blow his whistle as a beacon signal to the new arrivals and, perhaps surprisingly, some parachutists heard and heeded it, as far as a mile or two away.

Brigadier Nigel Poett reached the bridge at 0052, without his signallers. With Howard he crossed to the canal's west bank, where there was still only desultory incoming fire. 'Well, everything seems all right, John,' said the brigadier. But every British soldier well knew that Germans would soon be coming, probably in strength. An hour after the drop started, only a hundred men had reached 7 Para's rendezvous, yet another hour later that number had doubled. The battalion CO was Geoffrey Pine-Coffin – 'Tall, lean and tough, with long-nosed, humorous features and quizzical, crinkled eyes … the quintessential military leader', in Richard Todd's words. A product of Eton and Trinity College, Cambridge, he affected cowboy boots on the battlefield and professed to be untroubled by his men's uninspired nickname for him: 'Woodenbox'. When his bugler blew a call, more scurrying figures converged on the rendezvous, some singly, some in groups. They had no mortars or medium machine-guns, but eventually set off for the canal at the double, leaving one man at the RV to await stragglers.

The next excitement at the bridges, around 0100, was caused by the arrival of Major Schmidt, hotfoot from his outing with a girlfriend in Franceville-Plage, to save the crossings for his Führer. He was driven in an open Mercedes, followed by a motorcyclist, and stopped momentarily by the woman's house to let her out. As they approached the Orne bridge, their vehicles took Tod Sweeney's men on the east side by surprise. The invaders thus failed to fire as the Mercedes approached but riddled the motorcycle and its rider, causing it to skid into the river. When the car reached the west bank, Sweeney himself let rip with his Sten gun, causing the Mercedes to run off the road into a field. Both the driver and Schmidt proved to be badly wounded, but their cargo of wine, lipstick, food and stockings became first booty of the invasion.

After Schmidt was carried to Captain Vaughan's aid post by the canal bridge, he had recovered sufficiently to shout that he had lost his honour and failed his Führer and wished to be shot. He also predicted the imminent repulse of the invaders. Under the influence of morphine, Schmidt calmed, and even thanked Vaughan for his attentions. The doctor could do nothing for the German driver, however, a sixteen-year-old who had lost a leg and died shortly afterwards. Sweeney found this brief but lethal exchange sobering. When he looked down on the dead German motorcyclist, 'the realization that we were in a bloody, serious fight suddenly struck home'. Howard took Schmidt's binoculars.

Minutes later, at 0130, on the west bank D Company heard the ominous clatter and squeal of tracked vehicles. Two appeared from Bénouville, advancing twenty-five yards apart, very slowly. These were not tanks, but half-tracks. They and their crews nonetheless had power to devastate the little British party, given a chance. They were followed on foot by an engineer company of the 716th Division, mostly Russians and Poles, led by Germans. Sandy Smith was directing the three British platoons deployed west of the canal, but he was increasingly troubled by pain from his wounds and would obviously soon have to quit the battle. Most of his men opened fire towards anyone they glimpsed moving behind the half-tracks, but knew they would be wasting ammunition to use it on the armour.

Sgt. Wagga Thornton was holding the company's only serviceable anti-tank weapon, a clumsy spring-loaded PIAT which threw a bomb thirty yards and required nerves of steel from its firer, who was seldom offered time to fire a second shot if he missed. Thornton later confessed his own terror: 'I was shaking like a leaf … The PIAT is a load of rubbish, really.' He took aim as the vehicle swung right from the village, towards the bridge, 'and bang, off it went'. The sergeant achieved a rare feat, hit his target plumb centre, causing the armoured vehicle to explode and burst into flames with a series of violently spectacular detonations of munitions.*

A wounded enemy soldier lay screaming by the wrecked vehicle, having lost both legs. One of Howard's men, displaying a compassion of which supplies would soon expire among the armies in Normandy, carried the soldier to Vaughan's aid post, where he died a few hours later. He proved to be the commanding officer of the panzer engineer company. The second enemy armoured vehicle turned and fled, to report that the British at the bridge had anti-tank weapons. The Germans decided that no further significant attack on Howard's men could be launched before dawn.

As the 7 Para column led by Pine-Coffin approached the bridge they saw pyrotechnics and heard a succession of explosions ahead, as the Ox & Bucks addressed the panzer engineers, causing them to fear that they were about to march directly into a battlefield. As it was, however, by the time they reached Howard's company, firing had ceased, the continuing detonations from the burning German armoured vehicle the only warlike sounds around the bridge. Still in darkness, Pine-Coffin greeted Howard and relieved him in local command.

Tod Sweeney wrote: 'The parachutists began to drift in, not in the properly formed units we had expected, but in small groups and much later than we had expected.' The men of 7 Para set about digging in just short of Bénouville and taking over some

* Some colourful accounts of this episode suggest the Germans committed two tanks, but probability is against this. Commandos described seeing a burned-out half-track at this point when they passed much later in the day.

enemy trenches. Richard Todd was told to establish Pine-Coffin's headquarters on a hill north-west of the crossing, just below the hamlet of Le Port. For a time then, 7 Para was left in peace, though German parachute flares kept bursting, as the enemy sought to pinpoint the invaders.

At 0230 a German motorcycle roared around the corner from the south, into the path of the newly-arrived paras and obviously oblivious of them. Major Nigel Taylor, their company commander, observed that his men had been 'waiting God knows how many years to kill Germans, and this was the first one they'd seen'. In a storm of fire the motorcycle was hurled into the air, landing on its rider and killing him, and also fatally injuring one of Taylor's men, who was trapped beneath it. Pine-Coffin pushed his men further forward into Bénouville.

Howard's D Company withdrew to positions between the two bridges, to become a local reserve. At 0500 Sandy Smith was in such pain from his wounds that he was obliged to seek morphine and retire from duty. He and his comrades had done their part, and more than their part.

Small excitements continued to interrupt the night, and then the dawn. Sgt. Thornton, who had destroyed the enemy armoured vehicle, was convinced there were still Germans in one of the deep dugouts and led his officer, Fox, to a rear bunkroom where they found three Germans fast asleep, their rifles stacked in a corner. They awakened one and shone a torch in his face, to meet the disbelieving response, unmistakable though in an alien language: 'Fuck off!' The man supposed himself the victim of a comrade's joke and had to be reawakened with his mates and led away. Thornton laughed heartily. Fox was bewildered: 'Here was I, a young officer, first bit of action, first German I had seen close up: and giving him an order and receiving such a devastating response – well it was a bit deflating.'

Thornton found that one German spoke a little English and persuaded Fox to try and interrogate him about the local garrison. The enemy soldier ignored the questions and demanded: 'Who are you? What are you doing here? What is going on?' He required persistent assurances before accepting that Fox was a British officer. He had heard nothing of the firefights, and only agreed to be removed to join the other captives after showing the lieutenant pictures of his family.

Even as the Ox & Bucks revelled in their first small but vital victory, just three miles away the ordeal of another Airborne unit had just begun. They, too, had been entrusted with a critical mission, which must be accomplished before the seaborne invaders landed.

7
Merville

In the wars of Napoleon British attempts to storm heavily-defended fortresses were assigned to so-called 'forlorn hopes', such as were the men who spearheaded Wellington's 1812 assault on the French-held fortress of Badajoz in Spain. Losses were murderous but the objectives were sometimes secured and survivors garlanded as heroes. In more recent times the British Army has contrived plenty of bloody follies, yet no doctrine was taught at Sandhurst or the Staff College which explicitly demanded suicidal conduct, on the Japanese model. Nonetheless, the 6 June 1944 assault on the Merville Battery, some four hours after John Howard's men overran the Normandy bridges, and when Maj. Gen. Richard Gale was already at Ranville, deserves to rank close to the storming of Badajoz as an operation which, from its inception, required the attackers to emulate a 'forlorn hope'.

The battery was composed of four six-foot-thick concreted casemates, sunk into high ground a mile east of Ouistreham and about the same distance south of the sea. Each position appeared to mount a 150mm heavy gun, with a range of eight miles. Such weapons, firing on Sword beach, could wreak devastation among the seaborne invaders. The Germans more especially expected the battery to protect the lock gates of the Caen Canal, through which they feared the Allies might dispatch assault craft. They surrounded the Merville with minefields and two thick belts of wire entanglements, the whole perimeter forming a rectangle seven hundred yards by five hundred, covered by machine-guns mounted in pillboxes. The artillery and its defences were manned by 130 men of the 176th Artillery, many of them Russians and Poles commanded by German officers and NCOs.

Back in England the invasion planners deemed it to be worth almost any sacrifice to silence the Merville before the first landing-craft lowered their ramps. Ideally the guns would be destroyed by air bombardment, but even the RAF's bomber chiefs did not dare to be optimistic about the prospects of pinpointing and penetrating the casemates from high altitude. Of a thousand bombs released in a March 1944 attack, just two landed on target, without effect. A renewed battering on the night of 19 May demolished only the nearby officers' mess, killing the battery commander Captain Karl-Heinrich Wolter, who was passing an energetic night there with his French girlfriend Denise. His men did not mourn him, observing contemptuously that Wolter was the sort of man who drank Calvados with cream on top. The battery passed into the custody of an Austrian, Lt. Raimund Steiner. On 25 May Friedrich Dollmann, commanding Seventh Army, visited and Steiner briefed him on the unit's many deficiencies, to be assured by the general that he should not distress himself: the Allies would not land in his area. Meanwhile on the other side of the Channel a renewed RAF air bombardment was scheduled for 0030 on 6 June.

The planners had always recognized that the best chance of overrunning the Merville was to crash-land gliders inside its perimeter, employing identical tactics to the Ox & Bucks descent on the Orne and Caen Canal. On the day, however, while everything went amazingly right at the bridges, everything went amazingly wrong at the battery. At 2249 the previous evening four

Horsa gliders took off from Harwell in Berkshire to deliver 9 Para's heavy weapons, explosives, equipment, jeeps and two anti-tank guns. In the cockpit of one of the tug aircraft was Jimmy Edwards, who later became a celebrated post-war radio and TV comedian. Nobody laughed, however, about his squadron's performance on 5/6 June. Two gliders came down in the Channel, and in all six of the eight Horsa pilots died. None of 9 Para's heavy weapons and equipment reached the appointed drop zone. At 2316 a further three Horsas left Brize Norton in Oxfordshire, carrying fifty-eight men of A Company commanded by Robert Gordon-Brown, their helmets painted with piratical skull and crossbones, to execute the *coup de main* assault.

This glider party had been somewhat cruelly mocked by the rest of 9 Para, who told them that since they had volunteered to become 'chairborne airborne' for the night, they should rightfully strip the parachutists' wings from their shoulders. One Horsa, numbered serial 28a, broke its tow rope soon after take-off but was fortunate enough to set down safely on an airfield at Odiham in Hampshire. From there its passengers hitched road rides to Portsmouth, where they boarded ships to Normandy to rejoin their mates on the battlefield. Of the two other troop-carrying gliders, one endured a nightmare passage during which its arresting tail parachute billowed open over the Channel, making the aircraft scarcely controllable.

Terence Otway and the main body of his battalion jumped into Normandy around the same time as the rest of 6th Airborne's parachutists. It was intended that his heavy weapons crews would mark the Merville with starshell fired from three-inch mortars. The mortars, however, were lost forever and thus the objective could not be illuminated. Moreover, the sky around the battery was shrouded in high-rising smoke and dust from the bomber attack, by ninety-nine Lancasters and Halifaxes. One Albemarle towing aircraft courageously circled four times, searching for the objective, before releasing its glider at 1,800 feet, to crash three miles from the battery. Most of the passengers survived, but rejoined their comrades only after the night battle ended. The other glider, which cast off at 1,200 feet, was shot up by a 20mm flak gun mounted atop the Merville – receiving three full clips of which the last caused the tail to catch fire – and landed in an orchard a mile south-eastwards at 0425, bursting into flames and killing seven men of Lt. Hugh Pond's platoon.

The Merville glider pilots lacked any conspicuous visual pointers such as were granted to John Howard's aircrew by the silver strands of the Orne and Caen Canal. Perhaps also the pilots lacked something of the skill and determination of Sgt. Jim Wallwork and his comrades. In any event, the *coup de main* decisively failed. The planners, however, had never dared to pin all their faith on the gliders. Simultaneous with the Horsa landings, the main body of 9 Para was scheduled to launch a direct ground assault on the Merville's perimeter, which they had been told must be pressed home at any cost. Otway and his men knew they faced a deadline: if no word of their success reached the navy by 0515, the cruiser *Arethusa* would launch a bombardment of the German guns. Win or lose, every British soldier needed to be clear of the perimeter before that witching hour.

The paratroop operation started well. Major Allen Parry, A Company's commander, after being airborne from Harwell for only eighty minutes, dropped from his RAF Albemarle at 0020 immediately following Major George Smith's little party, tasked to reconnoitre the battery while the main force gathered. They all landed accurately, a thousand yards south-east of the objective and only ten minutes ahead of RAF bombers which dropped 349 tons of explosives not on the Merville but on the neighbouring hamlet of Gonneville, which was devastated along with most of its inhabitants. Parry, Smith and their parties survived, crouching in a bomb crater, but if the Lancasters had been more accurate, the paratroopers would have been dead men. After the bombing, in Smith's words, 'We sat up. I realized how lucky we were to be alive. The others were getting to their feet, surprised to find their limbs still worked.' Dusty Miller said succinctly, 'Fuck.' It was recklessly irresponsible of the planners to have timed the recce party's arrival just ahead of the bombers and so close to their aiming point.

The beanpole-tall major was one of four sons of Canon Allen James Parry of St Peter's church, Upton Cross – and younger brother of George, chaplain of 7 Para, who was already ministering to British wounded three miles further south. Arrived on the ground, Parry first encountered two boisterous Canadians and was enraged by their noisiness. They had forgotten the night's password and lost their weapons on the dropping zone. Being himself over-burdened, he gave them his Sten gun. When he got to the rendezvous – the RV – his first task was to set up beacons for the rest of the battalion. He was greeted by his batman Pte. James Adsett, nineteen years old but formal to the point of both pomposity and cheek. Adsett said, 'Good evening, sir. What kept you, then?'

Parry climbed a tree from which he illuminated an upward-tilted Aldis signal lamp as a marker for incoming aircraft bearing the rest of the battalion, but he saw and heard far fewer than he should have done, because most planes were off course and missed his light. The major's Rebecca/Eureka electronic beacon failed, as did nearly all such sets. In the sky above, chaotic scenes characterized 9 Para's drop. Most of its men descended far from the objective. One stick of twenty landed thirty miles away, rejoining the unit four days later, carrying the paybooks of several Germans they had killed. Others never reappeared, landing in the inundations on three sides of the drop zone, estuarial marshes flooded by the Germans.

Then there was the flak, by now thoroughly awakened. Some Dakota pilots adopted such drastic evasive action approaching the DZ that their passengers were hurled in a jumble onto aircraft floors. Terence Otway found himself sharing the rage towards the RAF which suffused most of 6th Airborne Division. As his plane weaved and banked, the colonel shouted at his pilot, 'Hold your course, you bloody fool!' Some of his men fell on the floor, cursing. An ashen airman said: 'We've been hit in the tail!' 'You can still fly straight, can't you?' No, apparently they could not. Some crews mistook the Dives river for the Orne. The anti-aircraft fire which caused many pilots to fly erratically was not severe – of 373 aircraft which dropped British troops that night, only nine were lost to all causes, and six others damaged. The egregious Sir Trafford Leigh-Mallory, RAF air supremo for Neptune/Overlord, wrote later: 'The accuracy with which these forces were delivered to the allotted zones contributed greatly to the rapid success of their coups-de-main.' This was a travesty. Almost all the memorable flying achievements that night were performed by soldiers of the Glider Pilot Regiment, not by RAF aircrew. Most of the men of 6th Airborne were dropped by the fifteen squadrons of 38 Group and the newly-formed 46 Group, their aircrew painfully inexperienced to fulfil such a sensitive role.

The men of 9 Para were scattered across fifty square miles of France. Some of Otway's soldiers heading for the rendezvous found themselves encountering Germans and even bandying words with them. They had been warned to move discreetly – 'not to wage private war', but instead to focus single-mindedly on the battalion task. More than a few, however, were forced to fight for their lives. Lt. Jock Lepper, oldest man in the unit, led a group which for twenty-four hours defended a farmhouse at Le Mesnil, three miles south-west of the drop zone. Brothers Ron and Terry Jepp, two of twelve children of a Portsmouth family, were among the only four men of twenty in their respective sticks to reach the battalion rendezvous, soaking wet. Terry, a medic, lacked his medical stores and stretcher. Private Tony Mead landed in the top of a tree, where a branch painfully impaled him.

Otway, after exiting his aircraft, saw tracer tear through his canopy in the air, only to come down in a farmyard beside a German battalion headquarters, a thousand yards south of the designated dropping zone. Within seconds he met two of his men, together with Wilson his batman, a former professional boxer and also ex-gentleman's valet, who crashed through the farm's greenhouse. As bewildered Germans began to emerge one paratrooper, lacking a weapon, picked up a loose brick and hurled it, causing the enemy soldiers momentarily to take flight, thinking it a grenade. When more enemies poured out of the farmhouse door, however, Otway and the others hastily retreated and set out northwards for the battalion RV, wading through flooded areas and twice being obliged to swim.

Meanwhile the pilot of the colonel's aircraft, having bungled his first run over the supposed drop zone, returned repeatedly in attempts to make good. His twenty men finally all got out, but several landed in deep mud, and Otway's party heard their shouts and screams. They watched two splash into a marsh, impossibly laden, and tried unsuccessfully to pull them out. He said: 'I am afraid that many were lost like that.'

When at 0130 Otway entered the wood which was their appointed rendezvous, he was confronted by his second-in-command who said, 'Thank God you've come, sir. The drop's bloody chaos. There's hardly anyone here.' Much of 6th Airborne had been on the ground in Normandy for more than an hour, widely dispersed, and 9 Para's drop turned out to have been the division's worst-scattered element. Otway said, recalling the situation at the rendezvous: 'There was desultory firing going on, but otherwise everything was quiet except for the moans of a sapper with a broken leg.' The colonel commanded a force equipped with only twenty lengths of Bangalore torpedo, no radios, no explosives, one medium machine-gun, and two medical orderlies who were conscientious objectors. There was also a courageous twenty-four-year-old Liverpudlian war artist named Albert Richards who made sketches through the hours that followed. Five hundred-odd men were missing. They were 1.5 miles – at least a thirty-minute march – from their objective. The colonel had expected to face difficulties in attacking the Merville but not to have to overcome the German battery with less than a quarter of the battalion's strength. Otway's batman Joe Wilson liked to mimic a stage butler. He proffered a flask to his commanding officer in a characteristically theatrical gesture, saying: 'Shall we take our brandy now, sir?' But Otway himself said: 'I was a very worried man.' Indeed, he was in a rage, as many of those around him quickly realized. Alan Jefferson recalled: 'He looked very peculiar indeed – hardly human.'

The colonel said abruptly to the young lieutenant: 'You're commanding C Company!' Jefferson expostulated, only to be silenced by Otway: 'Well, don't stand there, go and take over your company!' Jefferson found himself at the head of just eight men, one of them a private soldier in tears: 'Oh Sir, I've lost my rifle and my helmet. What am I going to do?' Jefferson soothed him: 'Never mind, Love' – for that was the man's name – 'we'll find you another rifle, probably a German one.'

The only good news was that 9 Para's recce party – two sergeant-majors led by Major George Smith and dubbed the Trowbridges, in emulation of a Nelsonian frigate captain of that name – had been dropped in the right place to fulfil their vital functions. Smith's trio marched to the battery, where the recce officer left the two warrant officers at different spots outside the perimeter in case he himself was captured or killed as he crawled further forward. Smith penetrated the German wire and spent thirty minutes listening to the movements and conversation of the garrison; watched sentries smoke. Lt. Paul Greenway, charged with probing the minefield and marking paths, also arrived, though without his group's specialized equipment. He and six men instead lifted several mines by hand, then made rough marks in the grass to define two cleared paths. They also cut through the Merville's outer wire entanglement. These were notable and indeed remarkable achievements.

However by 0235, more than two hours after the battalion had started to jump, just 150 of its men were assembled at the RV, some of whom had arrived without weapons. 'What the hell am I going to do, Wilson?' the CO demanded of his batman in mock bewilderment. 'Only one thing to do, sir. No need to ask me.' Otway laughed. 'Yes, I know. Get the officers and NCOs. We'll move in five minutes.' Many of 9 Para afterwards testified to their colonel's obvious frustration and dismay that the RAF's failures should have set at naught all his weeks of meticulous planning. He was now obliged to mount the assault with just one man in five of his unit's strength on take-off. A sergeant murmured to a fellow NCO: 'Not many here, are there?' Then he felt ashamed of himself for sounding defeatist. Otway allowed a further fifteen minutes' grace, in vain hopes that more stragglers would appear, before ordering his depleted battalion to set out for the attack forming-up point, on the south-east side of the German perimeter, well to the rear of the gun emplacements.

Allen Parry had been bitterly disappointed not to fly with – indeed, to command – the gliderborne *coup de main* party, drawn from his own company. Probably because he was a quiet, easy-going character, deemed insufficiently forceful to lead the storming group, he was denied the role entrusted to John Howard at the bridges, which at the Merville had been assigned to Robert Gordon-Brown. Yet now Parry bore responsibility for the equally vital task of guiding the stormers across the intervening countryside to the battery.

Otway told off four parties, each composed of fifteen men, respectively to address the four German guns. Some of the paras were bemused that the colonel selected a CSM and a sergeant to lead two of these groups – once again, probably because he thought them more aggressive or even courageous than the available officers. With their meagre stock of Bangalores, they would attempt to blow only two gaps in the wire. All the colonel's elaborate earlier planning, for fire teams with medium machine-guns and PIATs to cover the assault, had to be discarded. Just one Vickers, and a single Bren, would support the stormers. Four men were sent to circle the German perimeter, then stage a diversion at its main gate on the north side. It must have occurred to the colonel, in those fraught minutes before the attack, that even if they were successful in penetrating the casemates, they lacked the specialized 'beehive' charges needed to disable the guns, which had been carried in the lost stores gliders. Despite such grim awareness – the possibility that the infantry attack might thus prove futile – he concluded he had no choice save to do his part, fulfil his battalion's mission, heedless of what later difficulties the morning might bring. At 0250, in a single column extending almost two hundred yards, they set out to cover the ground between the RV and the south-east corner of the Merville Battery perimeter, from which the colonel had decided to launch the attack.

Allen Parry and Joe Worth, the unit's intelligence officer mocked by the men for his alleged 'la-di-dah' voice, led the way.

The moon periodically emerged from behind clouds. They passed a German flak battery in silence, undetected. Otway said afterwards: 'The last half of the journey was hell, as we had to lie doggo when Jerry patrols passed and also climb in and out of RAF bomb craters.' A file of some twenty enemy trudged past the prone paras, chatting to each other and oblivious. A herd of cows stampeded through the column of burdened men. They passed dead animals and others moaning in agony, victims of the RAF's Lancasters. Repeated pauses were necessary to check compass bearings – it would never do to lose themselves now, with the sand in the hourglass running through fast. When one of Otway's officers, Hal Hudson, asked what was to be done with a cluster of French civilians whom they encountered, the overwrought colonel growled that they must be collaborators and told the

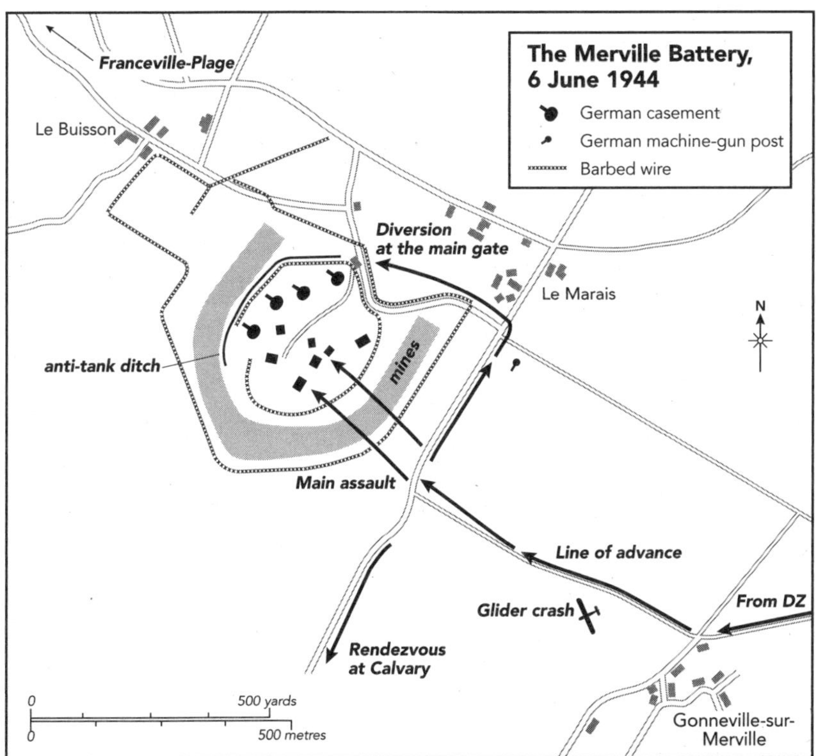

adjutant: 'Shoot them!' Instead, however, Hudson locked the men in a barn, warning they would be killed if they ventured out. Paul Greenway proffered his flask to the colonel, saying cheerfully, 'Have a nip' – perhaps to calm him down. Otway dismissed the offer.

The 2,400-yard march from the RV took ninety minutes. Once arrived, in a silence broken only by whispered orders and gestures – in the distance, plenty of shooting and explosions were audible – they deployed for the assault, then lingered several minutes in hopes of seeing the *coup de main* party crash inside the defences. Instead, however, they were obliged to watch in impotence as two gliders swooped low overhead while the paratroopers on the ground lacked any means of signalling to them or illuminating the battery. One Horsa disappeared from view and the other crashed thunderously behind them, at the forming-up point which they had vacated minutes earlier. As the plane burst into flames, in Otway's words, 'Dante's Inferno was let loose. The Germans began to shell us from neighbouring positions with complete disregard for their own troops.'

Major George Smith, who had led the reconnaissance party so gallantly, said the gliders' appearance 'started a frightful hullabal-loo in the battery, shouts and cries everywhere, deep guttural voices bawling out orders'. Before meeting the arriving battalion, he and his two companions noted the positions of four machine-guns firing tracer. Smith told Otway 'things are going well and it should be easy'. The major changed his mind, however, when the colonel told him that most of the battalion was missing: 'Looking back it seems incredible that everything was then arranged and organized on the spot, amidst what seemed the most awful chaos.' He was impressed by the way his CO gripped the situation and set about launching the attack. Otway dispatched sergeant-major Dusty Miller to discover the fate of survivors of the glider crash, who found themselves in immediate action against Germans of the 736th Infantry, two hundred yards behind the assault force: the ensuing firefight at least ensured that those enemy soldiers could not join the struggle for the Merville.

At the battery's northern gate, on the opposite side of the perimeter, the diversion party set up an impressive racket, shooting and shouting. Parry gave a final succinct briefing. Then, with clattering machine-gun fire coming from the defenders, Otway's men threw themselves into their head-on assault. At 0430, just half an hour short of dawn, his bugler sounded reveille. Alan Jefferson blew blasts from a little tin horn he liked to carry. There was a series of explosions as sappers detonated their few Bangalores under the entanglements. The first men launched themselves on top of the unbroken wire beyond, allowing those that followed to use them as stepping stones. Attackers shouted wildly as they ran forward, 'which we used to do in training, and did us good'. One foolish soldier fired his Sten gun at an exposed Teller mine, causing it to detonate beside a comrade, who lost an eye. Otway again: 'The German garrison concentrated its fire waist-high on the gaps in the entanglements; booby traps were going off all over the place and fierce hand-to-hand fighting was taking place inside the battery. I was just inside the wire and it was getting light, so I sent in most of the few reserves I had to assist in the hand-to-hand stuff.' Germans were shouting, '*Fallschirmjäger!*' Otway felt no personal fear of death but suffered a horror of mutilation. He claimed later that he was impelled to keep moving by reflecting upon what batman Joe Wilson would think, should his colonel falter.

Adjutant Hal Hudson was just short of a gap in the wire when he was blown off his feet and found that he could not get up again: his stomach had been torn open by fragments from a mortar bomb or grenade. Otway's smock was nicked by one German bullet, his waterbottle by another. Alan Jefferson, known to his disrespectful men as Twinkletoes because he had done some pre-war professional dancing, was thrown into a crater by a blast and lay bleeding 'like a sheep on its back'. Captain Harold Bestly was much more severely wounded.

Allen Parry momentarily thought himself kicked in the right leg which collapsed, tipping him into a bomb crater: he had been hit by a machine-gun bullet. His men rushed on past him, firing, grenading, finally bursting into German casemates where some defenders fled, others emerged to surrender, others again perished. George Smith said, 'A tornado of action swept into the battery. The sheer speed of the assault and determination of the men carried the day.'

More Germans, or Russians in Heer uniform, began to come out, throwing down their weapons. Some of Otway's men shouted 'Shoot the bastards!' but most of those who gave themselves up were spared. A further succession of attackers fell as they closed the battery: half of all men hit by machine-gun fire in Normandy died, and so it was at the Merville. In that brief assault the shrunken battalion suffered sixty-five casualties, including two company commanders. Days later 192 others of 9 Para were still listed as 'Missing', some of them drowned, many taken prisoner by the Germans.

Then some Germans raised a white flag, causing the last of the defenders' machine-guns to fall silent. Allen Parry wound his whistle lanyard around his wound as a tourniquet and hobbled towards a casemate, seeing dead and wounded men, British and German, on all sides while his own survivors marshalled prisoners. Parry approached one of the Merville's guns, which proved, like its counterparts in the three neighbouring emplacements, to be an elderly World War I Czech-built 100mm field piece, mounted on a carriage with wooden wheels. He felt sickened that so many men had died for this anti-climax: such weapons posed a far lesser threat to Sword than would have done the 150mm guns which they had been told to expect. Then a German shell exploded outside the casemate and something struck Parry's wrist. Momentarily he feared he had lost his hand, before discovering that it had merely been gashed by a flying splinter.

The successful attackers now faced a critical problem: how to disable the guns in the absence of most of the sappers and all their special charges. Paratroopers were taught little or nothing about how to spike field guns. Parry told his sergeant to improvise from the sticks of plastic explosive with which they were supposed to arm anti-vehicle Gammon grenades. When detonated, these small charges provoked 'a good bang' in the breech of each German artillery piece. Otway said: 'I heard four explosions clear and distinct – the battery guns going up.' This was what the colonel wished and indeed desperately needed to hear. In truth, however, 9 Para's survivors failed to disable the Merville's guns effectively. They had won their desperate struggle against the odds, but Otway was at a loss about what to do next. He had little time in which to resolve the dilemma.

It was 0500, and the battle had lasted just twenty minutes. As dawn broke, the attackers looked around them. The Merville was a building site, scene of immense recent German excavations, dug by scores of French labourers. Jefferson wrote: 'The whole place was an eerie mess of mounds and holes, the earth sticky from recent rain and not a trace of green anywhere. It was a desert of brown and grey filth, organized by some giant maker of mud-pies in the craziest of ups and downs.' The doctor examined the lieutenant, saying cheerfully, 'You're my first real wartime casualty. This isn't much of a wound!' Bert Richards the war artist sketched him where he lay. When Richards told Jefferson not to move, Jefferson responded incontestably 'I can't!'

Twenty-two defenders died in the battle for the battery and 9 Para took the same number of prisoners. Otway dispatched the agreed success signal, firing a Very light for the benefit of an overhead Allied spotter pilot. This went unseen, however. The signals officer, James Loring, released a pigeon bearing the same triumphant message which circled twice before disappearing, apparently in the direction of Germany. In the absence of a radioed acknowledgement from the navy of its receipt of Otway's success signal, he felt obliged to withdraw his men before the barrage fell upon them. In the event this never happened, because even without having received 9 Para's success messages, the cruiser *Arethusa* declined to open fire in the absence of confirmation that no British troops were in the battery. It was reassurance enough for the navy that no fire from the Merville was unleashed towards the invasion fleet.

As Allen Parry limped out of a casemate he glimpsed a body prostrate, face down on the ground: it proved to be that of Lt. Mike Dowling, who had been first man to reach the guns. Dowling had been accustomed to exchange jokes with his close friend Alan Jefferson, about which of them would be first to step on a schu-mine. Dennis Slade, the battalion's assistant adjutant, reported the life-threatening condition of Hal Hudson. Otway heard that the battalion RSM, Ulsterman Bill Cunningham, 'had taken on three Germans by himself'. The colonel continued: 'I saw what I thought was a dog tied up outside a pillbox but an officer with a shattered leg shouted: "Don't touch that, you bloody fool, it's a booby trap!"' In truth it was the German battery's grotesque stuffed terrier mascot. Otway riposted irritably to Jefferson, the man who had shouted: 'Don't call your commanding officer a bloody fool!'

The colonel, acutely conscious of the imminence of the scheduled bombardment, ordered his men to start their withdrawal, without exploring several bunkers in which Germans still hid.

Sixty-five of Otway's battalion, about half the number with which he had begun the attack, remained standing and unwounded. He made the prisoners walk back across the minefield ahead of his men. When some showed signs of reluctance, the colonel fired a Sten-gun burst just short of their feet. The survivors of 9 Para withdrew five hundred yards, to a roadside Calvary, seeing no choice but to leave three badly wounded men where they lay, to become prisoners. An elderly German doctor, who was assisting both sides' wounded, went back towards the casemates to fetch more medical supplies and was killed by a shell fired by one of his compatriots.

Some stragglers drifted in from the drop. Sergeant-Major Dusty Miller spotted one such and demanded in his best warrant officer's voice: 'Where've *you* been then?' The soldier responded complacently: 'I've got here, sir. I've made it.' Miller said accusingly: 'You're late. It's all over. So get fell in, you idle, useless man. Get on, shift yourself!' Otway gave the same order to his entire unit. Their next priority, the colonel believed, was to join Gale's divisional perimeter, more than a mile southwards.

Allen Parry noticed outside a cottage a child's soapbox car, mounted on pram wheels. He lowered himself awkwardly onto this, and began to use his good leg and a rifle to propel himself along with the retiring paratroopers. Then his own Sgt. Taylor attached a toggle rope and towed the major, who surprised his comrades by becoming voluble and noisy under the influence of morphia. Alan Jefferson was only superficially wounded by shrapnel fragments, but was also suffering acute pain from an arm injured in the drop. He said of the mood among the survivors: 'There was a feeling of elation, because we believed we'd destroyed the battery.'

In reality the Germans quickly reoccupied the Merville – many defenders had taken refuge, unnoticed by 9 Para. Next day they faced a renewed assault by British Commandos: Lord Lovat hailed the need for this as a fresh example of Airborne inadequacy. Yet his own men were no more able to spike the battery's guns than had been Otway's, and Major John Pooley, leader of the attackers, was killed. The Germans appear to have been able to restore the Merville to service, allegedly firing on the British until the German army's wholesale withdrawal from Normandy on 17 August. Evidence is contradictory about what shells landing on Sword were delivered by which German artillery, on 6 June and in the days that followed. When the British had gone, the surviving defenders gathered in the casemates and inspected the guns, which they claimed to have found still operational. The battery sergeant-major, Johannes Buskotte, demanded in bewilderment: 'Why did they come, then? … If they had broken the sights or taken them away, the guns would have been useless! What did they come for?' The German evidence seems convincing, and was first published by Alan Jefferson in 1987, that 9 Para had been unable effectively to disable the Merville Battery before its withdrawal.

Terence Otway and some of his men remained until their deaths highly sensitive about the question of whether the Merville was, or was not, silenced. They believed that to suggest their attack was ineffectual diminished both the battalion's achievement and their comrades' sacrifice. That view seems mistaken. Otway and his men, facing huge handicaps, performed a notable feat of arms, which achieved a limited but useful purpose. Before the first infantry landed on Sword, the British could be confident the Merville Battery posed no important threat. The drop and assault had been no more and no less of a shambles than are most battles. The Airborne troops displayed the initiative and will for sacrifice that distinguished the performance of many of Gale's division that day and in the weeks to come. The general wrote of the Merville assault: 'It was an enterprise as miraculous as it was gallant.' Allen Parry said triumphantly to a comrade: 'A jolly good battle, what?!' And indeed, it sort of was. Soon after dawn Otway's survivors were bombed by the USAAF, fortunately with no more effect than the earlier heavy bomber assaults had made on the Germans.

When the Allied naval bombardment opened, minutes after dawn, one of John Howard's men on the Caen Canal bridge said: 'Hear that, sir? That's the Navy! Cor, what next? They're firing jeeps.' Thousands of Airborne soldiers who had failed to reach their units likewise heard the thunder. Pathfinder Arthur Boardman had landed at 0018, but within a few hours been captured by a German patrol: 'The Allies would just be landing on the beaches and here was I being taken prisoner, something I would never have believed – killed in action "yes" but not a PoW.' He was fortunate because he survived. Eight captured paratroopers were summarily executed by a German warrant officer, in accordance with Hitler's notorious 'Commando order'. Many other men still at large were making haste across country, suffering from run-ins with bramble bushes, 'to date the greatest enemy we had encountered', in the words of a subaltern of 7 Para.

Others were more fortunate. Richard Todd, on high ground above the Caen Canal, could see the coast and vast armada offshore: 'From our grandstand position, the sights and sounds were breathtaking. The ground shook beneath us, and I felt sorry for the poor sods I could visualize in those German bunkers.' Yet there was good reason to feel much sorrier for the invaders from the sea, who were about to experience an ordeal by fire little diminished by the storm of shells unleashed from the Allied fleet.

8

Grappling the Atlantic Wall

1 INSHORE

At midnight on 5 June the invading armada went to action stations, with watertight doors closed. Each element, preceded by minesweepers since last light on the previous evening, approached the coast of France in double lines of darkened ships that seemed to stretch almost back to England. The 3rd Division and commandos of 1st and 4th Special Service Brigades, which were destined for Sword, occupied 250 vessels including the LCAs – assault landing-craft – borne across the Channel on the davits of the big transports. For HMS *Largs* there was a sense of déjà vu about Neptune: the headquarters ship had fulfilled the same function for operations Torch and Husky, the North African and Sicilian landings. Biggest among the landing vessels were *Dacres*, *Glenearn*, *Cutlass*, *Battleaxe*, *Broadsword*, *Astrid*, *Maid of Orleans*, around ten thousand tons, escorted by the destroyers *Goathland* and *Locust*. The troops aboard those transports had spent the night in somewhat less discomfort than those sailing in the smaller LSIs and LSTs, but now they were required to endure ninety minutes bucketing in the flat-bottomed cockleshells that would carry them to the shore, twenty-odd men apiece.

Thus began the final passage of what had often seemed an interminable journey, to reverse the humiliation of the British Army which had quit France in 1940. The democracies were about to launch a death-grapple in North-West Europe with the forces of Nazism. Men peering ahead into the darkness that still shrouded the enemy coast saw desultory tracer, which had been sustained for hours, now replaced by almost continuous flashes and explosions as 6th Airborne Division engaged enemy troops at the Merville Battery, Caen Canal and on fifty impromptu Norman battlefields, while Allied aircraft pursued their appointed purposes.

Montgomery had briefed his armies before their units embarked: 'By dusk on D-1 the enemy will be certain that the NEPTUNE area is to be assaulted in strength. By the evening of D-Day he will know the width of frontage and the approximate number of our assaulting divisions.' Yet, disastrously for German arms, the first part of this warning proved unfounded. The birthday of Lucy, Rommel's wife, fell on 6 June. The field-marshal had driven home to Herrlingen near Ulm to join a family celebration, trusting in the adverse German forecast for the Channel, which seemed to make an Allied assault impossible. Allied captures of far-flung Kriegsmarine Atlantic and Arctic weather ships and stations, much earlier in the war, thus exercised a critical influence on events in June 1944, by crippling the enemy's predictive capability. In Rommel's absence, the command machinery in Normandy functioned with a sluggishness that mocked the vaunted efficiency of the Wehrmacht.

Gen. Wilhelm Richter, commanding the 716th Division, addressed a conference at his headquarters in Caen only a few hours before the landings, to outline the weekly training programme. Officers discussed the problem of preventing beach obstacles from being carried away by rough weather. Richter said he had been warned that the invasion was likely to come between the 3rd and the 10th, but added that he was wary of treating this intelligence too seriously, since the same alert messages had been issued at every full moon and moonless period since April. The meeting broke up at 1900 on 5 June. The Germans failed to respond effectively to what should have been the electrifying interception of twenty minutes of *messages personnels* – coded invasion action messages – broadcast by the BBC's French Service to the Resistance at 2115 in a breach of security by SOE, amazingly authorized by SHAEF. At 2200 Rommel's headquarters issued a Most Urgent signal, for all units to be ready for instant action, yet for some reason this was transmitted only to German forces in the Pas-de-Calais and not to Fifteenth Army in Normandy. Shortly after midnight, hearing reports of the airborne landings LXXXIV Corps called all its forces to the highest state of alert, but stated that it still did not expect large-scale landings.

Nonetheless, by the small hours of 6 June, every man of 21st Panzer Division, most of them a mere fifteen miles south of Sword beach, was poised in expectation of receiving the order to advance its hundred-odd tanks and thousand vehicles. Nineteen-year-old Werner Kortenhaus, who crewed a Panzer IV, said: 'Even with the heavy labour and poor food, morale was pretty good … We became a good team. I and most of my friends gave no thought to politics, though we were already sceptical about how the war would turn out for Germany … But we assumed that we would be able to repulse an invasion from the sea. Indeed, we took that for granted. People find this weird, but we tank men were burning at the thought of getting into some action. Of course we had no idea what that would mean. No idea at all.'

Kortenhaus awakened the Frenchwoman who did his laundry and insisted on collecting it. She protested that the clothes were still wet, but he said he must take them anyway. The teenage soldier might have spared his impatience. As 3rd Division approached Sword, the order for 21st Panzer to move was still hours away. As late as 0600 Seventh Army told Army Group B that while the large scale of the airborne landings was evident, '... purpose of coastal bombardment not yet apparent. It could be a diversionary attack in conjunction with attacks to come later at other points. Air and sea reconnaissance have brought no further news since daybreak.'

The British were granted eight to ten further priceless hours, which they did not and could not expect, before heavyweight enemy armour began to engage them on the Normandy battlefield. The Germans responded far less energetically than they should have done, given the evidence available through radar and intelligence sources of vast Allied air and naval movements. Here was a manifestation of one of the most important realities of the European war: whatever the professional battlefield skills of the German army, the wider Allied war machine functioned incomparably better than did that of Hitler. In Normandy the coastal defences were indeed awakened, weapons readied. In the absence of Rommel, however, and with prohibitive restrictions imposed by Hitler, no order had yet been given to commence the movements of reinforcements from inland towards the threatened sector of coastline. In consequence, such formations as 12 SS Pz were denied the chance to exploit the morning overcast on 6 June, when Allied aircraft would have struggled to operate effectively against them. British deception operations deserved much of the credit for confusing the enemy about the significance of D-Day, but German command incompetence made a notable additional contribution.

Aboard the transports in mid-Channel there was a ferment of activity as tens of thousands of men dressed and armed – almost literally steeled themselves – for the ordeal to come. Some were eager; others appeared reluctant to ascend to the upper decks from the warm embrace of the bigger vessels' nether regions. The naval bombardment squadron which was to anchor before Sword was led by the cruiser *Mauritius*, with the destroyer *Stord* a thousand yards to port, *Svenner* following. The Royal Navy had sent to sea that day almost every major warship in home waters that could float and shoot … and was deemed sufficiently expendable to be risked within close range of enemy-held France. Every ship was now streaming flags, ensigns and pennants, earnests of their crews' absolute commitment to the day's purpose. Behind the leaders of Bombarding Force D came the monitor *Roberts*, built in 1941 explicitly for inshore support with its shallow draught and twin fifteen-inch guns, together with the old battleships *Warspite* and *Ramillies*, cruisers *Arethusa*, *Danae*, *Dragon* and *Frobisher*, accompanied by more escorts. At 0340, from the ships' upperworks crews saw to southward the flashes of explosions and flickers of fire reflected off clouds, as the RAF's final air assault began.

These attacks, addressing targets close behind the beaches, created an impressive spectacle, and did more harm to the enemy's bunkers and their occupants than had the preceding weeks of pummelling from the air. But Hitler's Todt Organization, constructor of the Atlantic Wall, had done its work well. A few Germans, relatively exposed in trenches, became the first of many defenders to die that morning. But the 114 Lancasters which aimed 580 tons of bombs at batteries around Ouistreham killed greater numbers of French people in Caen, Montebourg, Valognes, Pont l'Abbé – and in Ouistreham itself – than they did defenders.

This largest town on the invasion front lay at the eastern end of Sword. A monument stood on its shore, recalling an attempted British landing there on 12 July 1792. Naval surgeon-lieutenant Graham Airth, when told where his ship would be landing its embarked troops, consulted an old tourist guidebook. This listed among Ouistreham's charms, '*Casino 10 Juin–15 Sept*', and the principal hotel's bill of fare: '*Porc aux huitres chauffées ... Homards à l'américaine ... Soufflé au Grand Marnier ... Poulet vallée d'Auge*'. Airth noted facetiously, perhaps even tastelessly, that the promise of such delights caused him to gaze on the assault troops, clambering clumsily into their landing-craft, and 'to wish I was going in there with them'. The doctor might jest. His own neck would be far less exposed in the next few hours than would be those of the assault troops.

The Germans now mounted their most significant naval sortie of D-Day. Three big T-boats raced forth from Le Havre, seven miles eastwards, to launch sixteen torpedoes against the warships approaching Sword, from a range of around four miles. The RAF had just begun laying smokefloats on the eastern flank to protect the fleet from German shore-gunners' eyes. The attackers, each the size of a small destroyer, burst from the dense, drifting black cloud at twenty-eight knots, led by the 1,400-ton craft of Heinrich Hoffmann.

Miraculously, the torpedoes missed all the important targets, including *Largs*, which went full astern. The Germans achieved just one hit, on the Norwegian *Svenner*, part of the easterly anti-submarine screen. She was an 1,800-ton fleet destroyer with a crew of two hundred. Her captain, thirty-year-old Tore Holthe from Trondheim, ordered full ahead and full port-rudder as he glimpsed the bubbling track lancing through the water towards his ship. *Svenner* was doomed, however, buckling as soon as the torpedo struck amidships. She sank at 0525, a sight never forgotten by tens of thousands who witnessed it. One said: 'It was rather appalling. The ship just cracked in half, and the two ends folded together as if it were a pocket knife closing.' Thirty-two men, including almost the entire engine-room watch and two British liaison officers, died before the Norwegian vessel had fired a single shot in action. Captain Eric Bush on HMS *Goathland* said, 'No one on our bridge spoke, which seems strange now, though it was not at the time. We just steamed on into battle.' They had always known that ships must be lost, many men perish, on this day of days. All that seemed important lay ahead, on the shoreline of France. The broken warship, its fate a steam-by casualty in the vastness of the landings, lingered on the bottom for hours with its ends rearing from the sea in a huge V-sign. All three German boats, despite being engaged by the secondary armament of *Ramillies*, escaped back into the British smokescreen and thence to their haven at Le Havre.

There was then a brief interval of silence before, just short of 0530 and 120 minutes before H-Hour, a flash of light shot forth from a warship turret, followed by many more of the same, rippling across the sea along with thunderous detonations, as the warships commenced their symphony of gunfire. A telegraphist aboard *Ramillies* wrote: 'I had never seen so many ships at one time and of course never experienced such a sustained bombardment as we were throwing, with broadside after broadside. Soon the flashes of those great guns were lost in the haze of smoke that had long hidden the ships from view.' In the LCAs the shells passing overhead seemed to infantryman Peter Brown 'so close you felt you could almost touch them and sounded like a bus passing by. God knows what it must have been like on the receiving end.' Before *Ramillies* sailed home from Normandy her gun barrels would be shot out, unfit for further service.

Surviving defenders told British interrogators after their capture that continuous 'drum fire', such as the bombarding vessels delivered, 'inspired … a feeling of utter helplessness, which in the case of inexperienced recruits caused fainting or indeed complete paralysis'. Two hours of incessant shelling sufficed to destroy the fighting spirit of many men. The naval bombardment was certainly more effective than earlier air attacks in suppressing the coastal defences. Because the leading assault troops met such heavy opposition, they formed an understandable view that the naval guns had failed. But later intelligence analysis concluded, credibly, that the bombardment had wrecked perhaps 15 per cent of the defences, especially those positions that were not encased in concrete. This made a significant contribution to the landings, not to be dismissed.

Thirty minutes before H-Hour, 224 heavy bombers of the USAAF dropped 3,494 bombs behind Sword beach, with little effect on the defences since cloud obliged them to deliver the ordnance by radar guidance, from a height of 16,000 feet. Likewise, radar-directed bombing of the bridges linking Caen to the battlefield inflicted widespread devastation, but not upon the crossings that were the targets.

The invasion planners did not anticipate that bombs and shells would penetrate the huge concrete coastal bunkers. They did expect, however, that many of the defenders would be stunned, even paralysed, by blast. Yet a Canadian officer who later conducted a close study of the impact of the naval bombardment on neighbouring Juno beach concluded that it had done 'no serious damage to the defences', and the same was true on Sword. Most of Rommel's coastal forces began to fire their weapons, whether machine-guns, mortars or artillery, as soon as the invaders approached the shore, and continued to use them until their positions were overrun. To be sure, many of the Russians and East Europeans in Heer uniform who manned the coastal positions had no desire to be there, no enthusiasm for Hitler. Under the command of German officers and NCOs, however, most were obliged to wait minutes, or even hours, before being delivered either by death or an opportunity to surrender.

Ouistreham's Hôtel de Normandie had been purchased six months earlier by Raoul and Odette Mousset, in a moment of fanciful optimism and perhaps also at a literally firesale price, though this is not recorded. Raoul chanced to have been in Caen the previous night, but on seeing bombs fall he raced his truck back towards the coast. He was checked on the road by a German, to whom he explained that his wife was in their hotel. The soldier shrugged: 'It isn't there any more. It's gone.' At 0400 the building had received a direct hit. Odette miraculously escaped, to take refuge with some twenty others among trees on the outskirts of the town, from which she watched the ruins of the hotel burn. Then a naval shell landed in their group, killing thirteen. Odette survived but was badly wounded. She spent the ensuing eleven months in an English hospital.

Seven miles out at sea the leading elements of 8th Infantry Brigade, A & B companies of the East Yorks, which would land on the left – designated Queen Red – with A & C companies of the South Lancs on the right – Queen White – mustered on the decks of their ships beside landing-craft at the lowering position on their davits. Every step of this vast naval and military ball had been rehearsed, but they knew that hereafter its movements would become entirely unpredictable. At low water, four hundred yards of sand and shingle lay between sea and shore, shrinking to a mere thirty yards at high tide, with the entire front exposed to artillery, mortars and machine-guns. Above high-water mark ran two parallel lateral roads, one immediately beyond the sand and scattered beach houses, the second two hundred yards inland.

The first troops were scheduled to disembark at the mid-point of the tide rise. On the beach was set a double row of German stakes and ramp-type steel obstacles, thirty to sixty yards apart, laced with explosive contact charges to wreck landing-craft. Smaller 'hedgerow' obstacles, six feet high, were laid seven yards apart. It would be the task of 5 Assault Regiment, Royal Engineers, aided by Royal Marine frogmen, to render the explosives harmless while AVREs – engineer tanks – towed away the obstacles under German fire.

In the bigger vessels carrying armour, men shifted their personal kits into the hulls of the tanks, released the chains and chocks which had restrained the steel brutes through the overnight passage, then clambered into their fighting seats. Those East Yorkshires and South Lancs still on the landing-ships, awaiting their turn to descend into the second wave of LCAs, cheered the lead companies, huddles of armed humanity crowded crouched in the little boats' wells, some white faces visible beneath Roman tortoises of steel helmets. A Sherman commander of the Hussars' C Squadron, which would land direct onto the beach forty-five minutes behind the DDs, looked down with pity on the infantry in their LCAs: 'Many of them looked very sick and cold and knew they would be wet before long.' The men of the four initial assault companies were conscious of being tiny components of a collective might, though in the wry words of an officer, 'it did not go so far towards removing the purely personal sense of mortality'. They knew, with chilling certainty, that within an hour or two a good number of their company must perish and turn cold. Each man could ask only that he himself might not be among the human sacrifices indispensable to the success of Neptune and, indeed, of every operation of war.

The infantry elements of 3rd Division were to be borne to the shore in sixty-nine craft, drawn from eight flotillas. Tom Rennie exercised divisional command from *Largs*, a former French passenger vessel, while forty-six-year-old Edward 'Copper' Cass, the tough and battle-experienced Yorkshireman commanding 8th Brigade, would crossdeck to a landing-craft from the destroyer *Goathland* once his men had established a beachhead. James

Cunningham, commanding 9 Brigade which would land behind the vanguard, had crossed the Channel in a former Yangtze gunboat, HMS *Firefly*, and now transferred to a landing-craft commanded by a Thames barge skipper who affected a bowler hat.

After lingering offshore while each flotilla completed loading, the LCAs formed into ordered arrays, then at 0600 set forth on the ninety-minute passage towards the beach. Aboard one of the East Yorkshires' craft, roaring petrol pressure-cookers heated a breakfast of greasy bacon, tinned sausage and fried bread, 'but few had any appetite', according to Private Lionel Roebuck. In most boats far more food was disgorged than consumed: a vivid memory of every seaborne invader that morning was of vomit, and yet more vomit.

The landing vessels' shallow draught, essential to their purpose, rendered them unstable on the billow. Lt. Teddy Gueritz, one of Sword's naval beachmasters, started his day's work ill-disposed towards the army because a soldier threw up over his blue battle-dress, on which the stench lingered throughout the hours that followed. Bill Bidmead and comrades of 4 Commando likewise parted with their breakfasts. Lt. Jack Pearse was among several East Yorks who had skipped eating that morning but 'got shot of last night's meal into the scuppers rather than chance our heads over the side'. At least, he added ruefully, 'another retching half-hour keeps one's mind off the war'. In the words of a comrade, however, 'Many usually tough and cheery fellows were reduced to the death-wish by seasickness … The smells … and sounds … were enough to turn the strongest stomach.'

General Sir Claude Auchinleck, C-in-C in North Africa two years earlier, had offered a £25 prize for any soldier who composed a new song to rival, in Hitler's war, what 'Tipperary' had done for British morale in the Kaiser's. There were few entrants and no winners. Most of the singing in the LCAs that morning was anyway half-hearted, among men preoccupied with their digestions, though one of Lovat's commando troops bawled out 'Jerusalem'. Major Charles King of the East Yorks used his landing-craft's tannoy to read from Henry V's Agincourt speech as his company approached Sword: 'On, on, you noble English!' If the gesture was absurdly melodramatic, it moved some men then, and many more later, when they heard of it. Moreover Banger King was no mere peddler of bombast, but a much-loved and courageous officer who distinguished himself repeatedly in the hours and days ahead.

An able seaman aboard *Largs* found time to write to his wife: 'Connie my dearest, Hello darling here I am with a few lines hoping they find you in the best of health as it leaves me at present. Before I start I just want to say I love you so very much. I can make this letter a little more interesting than usual, as we have been given permission to let you know something of what is happening. I am just off the coast of Normandy, taking part in the invasion of Europe. We are doing remarkably well, when you take into consideration the opposition we are up against …'

The 22nd Dragoon Guards issued rum to the crews of their minesweeping flail tanks, then when a German shell smashed into an LCT, the men were told to close down their hatches, an order disobeyed by Captain Charles Munday, who suffered a haunting fear of being trapped by fire. The bugler of the East Yorks sounded a general salute as his LCA passed *Largs*. Commander Angus McKinnon stood in a Highland bonnet, playing his bagpipes on the bridge of the destroyer *Undaunted* as craft ploughed past. Never more vividly, on any battlefield of the twentieth century, did so many warriors recognize themselves as participants in a great historic event, and thus set about creating tableaux and uttering words worthy to be recounted in its future chronicles.

Once the bombardment opened, the invaders' objectives were laid bare to the Germans, and thus Allied wireless silence could be broken. A young signals officer named Lt. Whiteman, whom nobody has ever heard of, achieved a sort of miracle off Sword that morning by getting the gunners of three artillery field regiments 'on net' – in contact with their forward observers – and keeping them that way. This essential preliminary function required putting seventy-six radio out-stations in communication with each other. While Rennie's orders for 3 Div occupied a mere fifteen pages plus appendices, the signals instructions for Sword's gunners – wavelengths, codewords, procedures and suchlike – filled thirty-eight pages of foolscap.

At 0615 Erroll Prior-Palmer of 27th Armoured Brigade conferred with the navy's commander Edmund Currey aboard the landing-craft which was floating headquarters of Group 1, Assault Force S3, about his amphibious tanks. Given the rough sea state, the brigadier and the senior naval officer agreed that these should be launched five thousand yards out from the beach, not seven thousand as planned – less than three miles rather than four. At 0630 the signal was sent to all the vessels carrying the DDs of A and B squadrons of the 13th/18th Hussars: 'FLOATER 5000'. 'PP''s landing-craft then closed to within three miles of the beach for the supremely anxious experience of watching the tanks literally sink or swim, in a disturbed sea and under ever more intense enemy fire from the shore.

At 0640 the first of the Shermans lurched to the end of its LST's ramp, then plunged over. It was an impressive, even terrifying spectacle, to see thirty-five tons of steel duck underwater then, almost miraculously, rise again. As propellers engaged, these hybrids began to creep sluggishly towards land. How fortunate it was, for the confidence of the crews, that they had repeatedly rehearsed off the south coast of England. Against all landlubbers' logic they knew that, with a good deal of assistance from the Deity, the passage might be made.

The DD offload was not accident-free, however. On one vessel the lead tank struck a metal projection, tearing its canvas. The exasperated Hussars' squadron commander demanded the damaged DD be ditched in the sea, the other tanks launched, but the craft's skipper made the instant, prudent decision instead to abort the offshore launch and land all his five Shermans direct onto the beach. On a neighbouring vessel, the fourth tank of five struck a supporting chain, severing it and buckling the ramp. Once in the water the propellers of Sgt. Sweetapple's tank refused to engage. Thus as the powerless amphibian wallowed, with seas breaking over its flotation screen, the crew abandoned it, taking to a dinghy in which they survived. Meanwhile Sgt. Rattle's canvas was torn by either a wave or enemy fire, so that he and his men were likewise obliged to bail out of their Sherman. The rest of the DDs sustained their perilous passage for an hour – an apparent eternity, in such circumstances – before touching sand, 'and it was a miracle that most of us did', in the words of one vastly relieved crewman.

At 0655 the first wave of landing-craft, heading for the shore just west of Ouistreham, passed submarine *X-23* at its post off the coast. George Honour and his three comrades stood on the midget's casing, watching the LCAs and DDs – 'those poor wretched tanks' – approach under fire: 'As they passed us, we cheered them and they cheered us. That was our job done, then.' The tiny submarine's function fulfilled, Honour cut its mooring rope because he and his men were too exhausted to haul up the anchor. *X-23* made its passage home on the surface, latterly under tow.

From the sea, those infantrymen who were not anaesthetized by sickness saw on the shoreline, wreathed in smoke, a dreary row of villas and boarding houses, thickening eastwards into the communities of Riva Bella and Ouistreham, the latter with its lighthouse and church tower, while to the west lay Lion-sur-Mer. A cluster of houses midway between was marked on their map as La Brèche: 'the breach', hub of the Sword assault. Men who knew a little French – not many – thought hopefully: how appropriate!

The Royal Artillery's self-propelled 105mm howitzers, three regiments of them, began to fire from their landing-craft when still a mile out from the beach, delivering two hundred shells a minute. A chain of hands in the wells of the gunners' LCTs passed rounds up to the guns, while the cardboard tubes that had held them were tossed overside, to bob in the vessels' wake. Between each shot the guns lifted their aiming points by a hundred yards, then five minutes before H-Hour raised their sights to four hundred. On the turrets of three of the Hussar DD tanks ahead of them stood gunner FOOs, observing fire even as the Shermans ran in: one such officer drowned aboard a tank that foundered. A second gunner was rescued from a stricken DD and continued to report his battery's fall of shot from a landing-craft that picked him up. Rocket-ships were firing flights of projectiles electrically and often wildly, while the steel decks grew red-hot beneath the launchers. One of their skippers was devoted to the novels of Marcel Proust. When he opened his orders he shrank from the realization that the town of Cabourg – the *fin de siècle* Balbec of Proust's great lyrical narrative – lay only a few miles east of their battlefield. He prayed his own missiles might not fly astray, towards that literary shrine. By a fortunate chance for the town, though not for the Norwegians, Cabourg had been the appointed target of *Svenner*, no longer a part of the bombardment squadron.

Minutes before H-Hour, the landing-craft carrying the howitzers turned back out to sea, to wait their turn to offload once the infantry and tanks were ashore. First, however, came the moment for Percy Hobart's supremely imaginative armoured creations to prove their worth.

2 FINEST HOUR OF THE 'FUNNIES'

Sword constituted an almost private theatre of war, from which the action on more westerly beaches was invisible, though to the east, when the smokescreen at sea lifted, the invaders could see for many miles the long curve of the coast, occupied by German gunners. Even as the British bombardment harrowed the shore directly ahead, the defenders – the same men whom the previous morning George Honour in *X-23* had watched through his periscope playing innocent beachball – unleashed shells, mortar bombs, machine-gun fire at the approaching flotillas, intensifying into a cacophony not to be stilled for many hours. The din, interspersed with shouts and screams, became a dominant memory of that morning for all those who survived it.

Several swimming tanks adopted zigzag courses to ease the effect of finding themselves beam-on to breaking waves. To the fury of Hussar crews, some landing-craft skippers of the AVRE flotilla, 'apparently driven by maniacs', raced past them, often dangerously close. Captain Noel Denny recorded that his DD stood up to the buffeting of the sea 'far beyond my expectations', until he was rammed by an LCT, eight hundred yards out. His tank sank immediately and only Denny survived, to be rescued after thirty minutes adrift in his Mae West. Elsewhere the regiment's second-in-command, the portly Major Lord Feversham, found himself aboard a craft on which the engine failed so that he and four tanks wallowed uncomfortably offshore, until towed into the beach several hours later. Sgt. Harry Morris's DD was slowly sinking, as successive waves descended on the Sherman's turret faster than its bilge pump could drain the inflow. Over the inter-

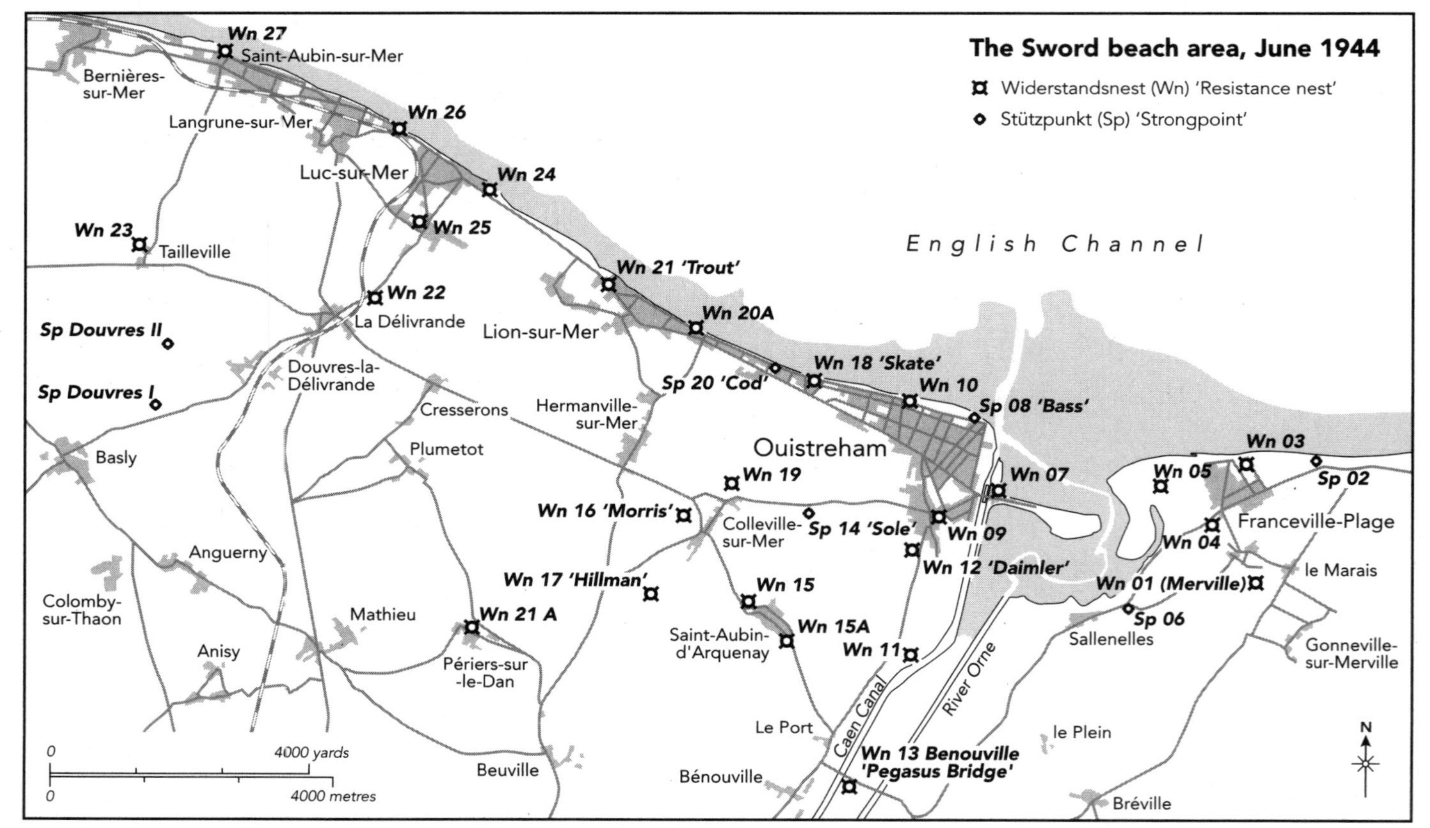
The Sword beach area, June 1944
Widerstandsnest (Wn) 'Resistance nest'
Stützpunkt (Sp) 'Strongpoint'
English Channel
Wn 27
Saint-Aubin-sur-Mer
Bernières-sur-Mer
Langrune-sur-Mer
Wn 26
Luc-sur-Mer
Wn 24
Wn 25
Wn 23
Tailleville
Wn 22
La Délivrande
Sp Douvres II
Sp Douvres I
Douvres-la-Délivrande
Lion-sur-Mer
Wn 21 'Trout'
Wn 20A
Sp 20 'Cod'
Wn 18 'Skate'
Wn 10
Sp 08 'Bass'
Hermanville-sur-Mer
Cresserons
Plumetot
Basly
Ouistreham
Wn 19
Wn 16 'Morris'
Colleville-sur-Mer
Sp 14 'Sole'
Wn 09
Wn 07
Wn 12 'Daimler'
Anguerny
Colomby-sur-Thaon
Wn 17 'Hillman'
Wn 15
Mathieu
Wn 21 A
Wn 15A
Saint-Aubin-d'Arquenay
Wn 11
Anisy
Périers-sur-le-Dan
Caen Canal
River Orne
Le Port
Wn 13 Benouville
'Pegasus Bridge'
Bénouville
Beuville
le Plein
Bréville
Sallenelles
Sp 06
Wn 01 (Merville)
Wn 04
Wn 05
Wn 03
Sp 02
Franceville-Plage
le Marais
Gonneville-sur-Merville
N
0
4000 yards
0
4000 metres

com Morris asked his driver how he was doing and got the tense response: 'All right, but – wet.' In truth, the man was up to his waist in water. Seconds later, however, the Sherman touched sand and was able to explode away its canvas flotation screen. Morris's gunner fired his first shot of the morning blind, without waiting to aim.

Tracer was flicking overhead, rockets whooshing towards the shore. A forest of barrage balloons, tethered to the bigger ships, swayed behind and above the assault vessels to impede enemy air attacks, which were mercifully absent. Most tanks grounded 350 yards out and began to crawl on their tracks towards the tideline. Crews were startled by the 'appalling flash' as they detonated the cordite rings fixed on the Sherman hulls to collapse their canvas screens.

The plan called for the DDs to land forty abreast, seven and a half minutes ahead of the two assault battalions of 8th Infantry Brigade, and also just before the two squadrons of assault engineers charged with clearing the beach obstacles; thrashing and bridging paths inland through the German mines and across their anti-tank ditches. The Hussars' A Squadron was to support the South Lancs on the right, B Squadron the East Yorks on the left, while C – equipped with conventional tanks, and landing direct from LCTs at 0815 – covered the Suffolks, who would arrive behind both. Once this vanguard had pierced the coastal defences, follow-up units, notably including the other armoured regiments of 27th Brigade, would advance inland. The men of 4 Commando would pivot left to clear Riva Bella and Ouistreham, addressing German strongpoints from their more vulnerable flank and rear, while the rest of 1st SS Brigade headed at their best pace to reinforce Gale's Airborne, via the Caen Canal bridge.

The DDs ran more than thirty minutes late. Of the forty that set forth, thirty-four reached the beach, a remarkable achievement, but from then on attrition was brutal. In the first minutes after H-Hour only five Hussar gun tanks are reckoned to have been firing effectively in the East Yorks sector, eight behind the South Lancs. The tankers' orders had warned them to shoot from the shallows until engineer 'funnies', offloading direct onto the sand from landing-craft, cleared paths through the mines. As for the mine-clearing 'Crabs', cheering sailors shouted as Lt. David Knapp led his flail troop ashore on the extreme right of Sword: 'Go to it, Tommy! Get stuck in! Give 'em one for me!' Knapp wrote: 'My sergeant roared through the water and I could see my way clearly through the smoke, straight up the beach. I forgot to blow off my waterproofing but it made no difference.' He began to flail an eight-foot path, at the operational speed of 1½ mph. His gunner fired a random round to blow the canvas muzzle cover off the 75mm gun, following up with machine-gun bursts through the tank's revolving chains. Several Teller mines exploded. Knapp was momentarily distracted by the incongruity of a grey horse galloping frenziedly across the beach.

He forged onward through the first buildings of Lion-sur-Mer; reached a meadow and halted after a hundred yards, having encountered no more mines. On the beach behind, he saw infantry coming ashore, and was bemused to realize that he and his troop had been on land twenty minutes and were still alive. 'It was obviously time for a mug of tea and we brewed up.' Knapp was uncommonly fortunate. His senior officers would have been enraged had they been privy to his decision that, having reached the appointed rendezvous, for the time being he had 'done his bit'.

Almost every other 'funny' crew experienced much rougher landings. The lead tank of 22nd Dragoons, arriving at 0726, was knocked out by a German gun straight away. The first bridge laid by an AVRE across the anti-tank ditch just beyond the beach was promptly blocked by a Hussars' tank which toppled off its side. A second gap was filled by an AVRE fascine, but the lead tank passing over this struck a mine on the south side. One Dragoons' Sherman was hit four times before finally lurching to a halt. In all, on 6 June the regiment lost fifteen of its twenty-six flails. Engineer Major Ken Ferguson, landing in the first wave of LCTs to disgorge AVRE tanks directly onto the beach, had rashly lashed a motorbike to the turret of his Sherman. A mortar bomb ignited the petrol in its tank. Ferguson shouted to the coxswain to back off and lower his ramp, flooding the deck cargo and dousing the flames. Then Ferguson drove into shallow water, followed by a bridge-carrying Sherman. This headed straight for a German position and dumped its load atop an anti-tank gun, which fell silent.

Sapper Fred Norris's 'funny' of 77 Squadron RE hit the beach at 0735. Norris cherished a grievance. In civilian life he had been a professional glider pilot but was refused an opportunity to fulfil the same role in uniform because he stuttered. Now, instead, he served as a Petard gunner in an AVRE tank, christened 'Barracuda'. His landing-craft had veered aside when its neighbour was hit by a shell and they had witnessed at close quarters its brutal overrun of a DD tank. One of his comrades was fortunate enough to survive dismounting to erect a windsock to guide in the next wave of craft – many men who quit their tanks to perform such tasks were killed within seconds. The commander of the AVRE which dumped its bridge atop a German gun climbed down from his turret to unshackle the wreckage, only to be shot. Fred Norris always thought it unjust that the man never received a medal.

A minesweeping tank advanced off the beach, flailing a path for its successors and was quickly hit, blocking the exit. Norris himself then had to dismount to clear their own Petard, but was blasted off the hull by the explosion of a German stick grenade, which badly wounded his tank commander. Norris successfully cleared the mortar and climbed back into the turret, where he found his officer losing blood fast, and barely conscious. They nonetheless lunged forward to the beach exit and rammed the stricken flail, thrusting it aside in a series of steely punches. This reflected both courage and initiative by Norris and his mates, as the Germans were firing continuously.

In the heavily-defended sectors, it took far longer than the scheduled thirty minutes to flail paths inland. AVREs were repeatedly knocked out, blocking beach exits. The Hussars' DDs suffered punishing losses: several tanks shooting cautiously from shallow water, waiting for paths off the beach to be cleared, were caught by the incoming tide after switching off their engines to save fuel. Patrick Hennessey's crew dropped their canvas screen, then began to fire while most of the Sherman's hull was still underwater. The commander called over the intercom: '75, HE – Traverse right, steady, on. 300 – white fronted house – first-floor window, centre. On. Fire!' Hennessey wrote: 'There was a puff of smoke and brick dust from the house, and we continued to engage. The shore, which had been practically deserted when we arrived, was beginning to fill up fast.'

Driver Harry Bone begged Hennessey to move up the beach, because the incoming tide was filling his compartment with water. Yet his commander hesitated: he could see no cleared path and was reluctant in its absence to expose their hull, when the wrecks of others who had done so already littered the shoreline, burning fiercely. Seconds later a wave broke over the stern of the tank, swamping the engine, and resolving his dilemma. The driver and co-driver emerged from their hatches, soaking wet and swearing horribly. They inflated the Sherman's dinghy and began to edge towards the shore, using mapboards as paddles. Within moments a German bullet punctured the dinghy and hit the co-driver in the ankle. Shouting more obscenities, the crew floundered onto the beach, dragging their wounded comrade.

Montgomery had said at St Paul's in May, 'We must time our assault so as to make things as easy as possible for the leading troops. Therefore we shall touch down so that all obstacles are dry, and so that we have thirty minutes to deal with them before the incoming tide reaches them.' In reality, almost nobody that morning got ashore with dry feet. The engineers found themselves floundering and indeed swimming to address beach obstacles which were soon awash, then became submerged. Arthur Cocks, their CO, was killed instantly, hit in the turret of his AVRE.

A scrum of Hussars, foot-soldiers and sappers milled together on the narrow band of sand, paying dearly for the privilege of leading the charge ashore. Nine of the 22nd Dragoons' flails were crippled in the first hour, becoming obstacles in the path of men, armour and landing-craft which followed. The Royal Engineers mustered a further fifty tanks including sixteen flails, eight bull-dozers and twenty-four other varieties of specialized armour. The courage of the sappers was exemplary and cost them one in five of their men who landed. German fire knocked out several tanks which were attempting to tow away beach obstacles, a task which had to be abandoned. Instead, as the tide rose, Col. Robert Urquhart and his men swam from obstacle to obstacle, simply cutting away Teller mines. One lieutenant commandeered a Sherman to ferry him across the shallow water between steel 'hedgehogs', removing explosive charges and stacking them neatly on the tank's hull until he was struck by a bullet in the shoulder.

A certain Sgt. Titley became so exasperated by snipers seeking to impede his labours disarming obstacles that he ran to the house from which Germans were firing, killed two with a Sten gun and returned to the beach escorting a prisoner who was extremely fortunate to have had his surrender accepted. In one engineer squadron on Sword that morning, four officers and twenty-one men were lost. Of its seventeen AVRE tanks three were submerged or burned out, six others temporarily immobilized. Some Royal Marine frogmen, also committed to beach clearance, abandoned their task as hopeless once the tide covered the obstacles.

The critical issue for the invaders was not the loss of men and tanks. This had been expected and, indeed, commanders anticipated much worse. The problem was that within the narrow confines of the beach, stalled or burned-out tanks blocked the advance of 'runners'. The whole story of Sword that morning was of vehicles striving under fire to open paths inland, both to speed the progress of the assault and to free space for new arrivals amid the crowding and debris on the sands. Assault engineers cleared none of the eight exits scheduled to be open by H+30. It was fifty minutes before the first lane off the beach was unblocked, and well over two hours before seven lanes became available to the hundreds of armoured and soft-skinned vehicles by then ashore. Only at 0900, almost ninety minutes after H-Hour, an eternity on such a battlefield, did the first gun tanks get past the beach and begin to move inland. Meanwhile German shelling from the east, towards Le Havre, persisted not merely all that day but for weeks, albeit in diminishing volume.

German artillery fire was heaviest at the left-hand end of the beach, where the East Yorks landed, and four of eight flails were wrecked there in the first minutes. A bulldozer received a direct hit on its engine. Two of the intended beach exits were blocked by cripples, one of them a DD which hit a mine after straying a yard off the swept path. Many tank crewmen were obliged to dismount to remove obstacles and several were hit while unprotected, including a troop leader. An NCO was killed, and his companion wounded, while addressing a Teller mine. One officer used a sandblaster to blow a gap in a six-foot-high dune, while snipers repeatedly near-missed him and German grenades burst around his tank.

The collective achievement of the 'funnies', for which Percy Hobart deserves a lion's share of the credit, was remarkable. The difficulties and losses they encountered were no more than had to be expected, as they spearheaded the British collision with the Atlantic Wall. The US Army's unwillingness to use specialized armour on its own beaches, with the exception of a few DDs and bulldozers, must have contributed significantly to the heavier losses in its landings. Hobart's supremely imaginative inspirations inflicted a trauma on the German defenders, especially the DDs rising firing from the waves, of which Rommel's intelligence had provided no inkling. Whatever setbacks the British D-Day invaders suffered throughout 6 June, which will be discussed below, it is important never to lose sight of the fundamental triumph, in which specialized armour formed a critical component. One copy of the published post-war history of the 'funnies' was touchingly inscribed – obviously by a veteran of D-Day and almost certainly for his wife – 'To Sylvia, as this is the best explanation of some of those letterless days. Love, BILL.' Of the 'letterless days' of the assault engineers and their infernal machines, 6 June was, of course, the climax.

9

The Breach

The leading infantry landed five minutes after H-Hour. A 3 Div officer wrote: 'It was inspiring to watch those LCA skippers … driving "full ahead together" for the shoreline. They spared no effort to give "their" troops a dry landing.' In this last endeavour, only a few were successful. Each man, each craft experienced a personal epic, in some cases a nightmare, in the minutes before and after spilling forth from the boats. Wilf Todd's platoon commander called to his men as the ramp dropped: 'Well, lads, it's now or never!' Ron Major from Bradford, one of Banger King's Bren-gunners, found the run-in weirdly quiet, 'but then "Ramp down!" and all hell broke loose. As we scrambled out of our craft some were hit and fell in the sea. Many more were killed as we approached the beach up to our necks in water. We were pinned down at first, then gradually we got to the beach head.' Major fired bursts from his Bren between dashes towards the road above high watermark: 'All the way, bullets had been kicking up sand inches from my face.' Just as he was taking aim, a German round hit his wrist, smashing the bones. The twenty-four-year-old, his brother a prisoner in Germany since Dunkirk, had trained for years for this moment. Yet within minutes of Major joining this first battle, his war was over.

Rationally, it matters little to a man who loses life or limb whether he falls in the first volleys of a battle or the last. But there seemed a special pathos about the fate of those who died in the water or on the lip of the sands. After all the years of training and expectation, they were within minutes or even seconds extinguished as mere victims – cannon fodder – without being conceded the chance to become protagonists. But such is the fate of most people who perish in all wars. Alf Ackroyd of B Company saw his 'mucker' Jackie Marsden take three bullets in the stomach. Marsden said: 'I am a goner … You know I am very bad.' Ackroyd said: 'I couldn't do anything for him, so I carried on up the beach.' When Lionel Roebuck's platoon jumped down from the ramp, they landed in water to the knees: 'Wrecked boats lay broadside on, dead comrades floated face down on the tide, others lay in grotesque positions on the beach. The sand dragged on our feet.'

The beach shelved relatively steeply below the seawall – little of the sweep of sand that would emerge at low tide was visible even to the first of the landing force and almost none to those who followed in the succeeding hours. A Yorkshireman sought to take cover erect, shrinking behind the steel post of a German obstacle. Banger King shouted, 'Get down, you bloody fool, get down', even as a bullet nicked the man's arm. Most of the company lay prone, until King drove them forward shouting – apparently contradictorily – 'Keep going, you bloody fools, keep going!' Hesitantly, and impelled chiefly by King's force of will, they stumbled forward. One of his men said: 'Everybody was numb, really, you didn't know what you were doing.' Pte. Jim Cartwright 'went across the beach like a hare', and he was smart. Arthur Wilson, a milkman from Bradford, silenced a German gun by lifting the steel lid of the bunker from which it was firing and dropping in a grenade. Wilson was decorated for his action – all armies strive to honour that small minority of men willing to take suicidal risks to stifle enemy resistance, because only by their examples can battles be won.

Lt. Arthur Oates of the Yorks' B Company kept a rough diary, which carries conviction because he was awarded an MC for his own role. He was not fired on as he jumped down from the landing-craft, dragging forward a lifeline to enable his overladen men to balance themselves as they waded ashore: 'MG 50 yards left – deployed and engaged – silenced after 5 minutes – "flail" burning fast and exposing centre section [of his platoon] near it – told them to move away – mortar hit them – self hit in right arm – approx. 7 others out of action. Moved with Barber up to wire, placed Bangalore … Could not blow because troops on left. Beach group bunching badly and having casualties. Blew Cortex – jumped wire … "Banger" [King] said advance – more mortars dropping both sides … M[achine]-G[un] found us … 3 Boche with white flag 20 yards ahead … "Banger" got a tank to fire and silenced MG.' The highest ambition of every Sherman gunner in those hours was to 'post a letter' – place a 75mm round through the narrow firing slit of a pillbox – and at odd moments that morning somebody accomplished this.

Lt. Reg Rutherford called for smoke as soon as he paused on the beach, but found that his platoon mortarman had been killed leaving the boat. He spotted German fire coming from a large brown house on his left and sought to respond: 'We were just putting a magazine on the Bren gun when the gunner was killed. Immediately my sergeant took over the gun … Another shot took the back sight off, and straight through his head.' The dead man had been facing disciplinary charges for breaking out of camp before embarkation, to address marriage problems which were now cruelly terminated. By the time Rutherford reached the coast road running along the beach top, he was accompanied by just eleven out of thirty-three men with whom he had landed, though most, rather than becoming casualties, had merely made the rash decision to linger on the sand.

Cpl. Bob Littlar likewise sought cover beneath the seawall until admonished by a sergeant who said sharply: 'You're not going to win this war on your own – get your men!' Lt. Hugh Bone stopped and took cover. He recalled: 'Instinctively, where we lay we hacked holes with our shovels.' This was a mistake which for some proved fatal. Lord Lovat had warned his commandos, 'If you wish to live to a ripe old age, keep moving.' About this, the brigadier was right. Bone survived, helping men to struggle with heavy wirelesses, yet others did not: 'Jerry was mortaring us pretty badly. I laid on my face for a few moments then, seeing the provost sergeant hit five yards away, I pushed over to him and shoved my field-dressing on the back of his neck.' Bone took refuge in chewing gum. He hated the stuff, but the same piece was still in his mouth twelve hours later.

Mortars are poor men's artillery, with less range and destructive power than heavy guns. The Germans nonetheless used them to formidable effect throughout 6 June. They were directing fire from carefully-chosen observation posts, notably a high concrete tower erected on the coastal front of Ouistreham. They benefited from four years' leisure, during which they had precisely registered shoreline targets. On the British side some officers, including Charles Hutchinson, CO of the East Yorks, said later that in training back in Britain too much effort had been expended on the procedures of the amphibious landing, too little on the tactics of battle. Orders for a January 1944 attack in Italy laid down precepts which were just as valid in Normandy. 'It is fatal to halt when mortared. Once you are in among the enemy's troops he will stop mortaring.' Peter Cochrane wrote of the difficulty of keeping green infantrymen moving: 'If one goes to ground under fire it requires a real effort of will to stand up again.'

Almost no personal accounts of D-Day mention its impact on the bodily functions, but there is no reason to imagine that they behaved differently among men landing in Normandy from those reported by Americans in the Pacific, who found that in conditions of extreme fear one man in five lost control of his bowels and one in ten urinated in his trousers, neither a great aid to morale in the hours that followed.

It was later estimated that the immediate German coastal positions on Sword were manned by only about 160 men, a fraction of the strength of the British force being thrown against them. But such numbers protected by thick concrete, armed with machine-guns and anti-tank weapons, supported by mortars plentifully provided with bombs, could inflict terrible injury upon flesh and blood, packed onto a small expanse of sand. The South Lancs found themselves checked by fire from the Germans' pivotal strongpoint at La Brèche, a network of twenty bunkers connected by trenches, extending over five hundred yards, much of their own sector and part of the East Yorks', codenamed by the invaders 'Cod'. This mounted 75mm and 50mm guns together with five machine-guns.

Firing points were sited with notable ingenuity: bunkers mounting anti-tank weapons, for instance, were not exposed to frontal fire from the invaders, but instead mounted gunports and slits set to defilade the beach, each opening shielded on the sea side by a massive concrete buttress. Cod fell to the invaders only after a protracted series of actions, such as that carried out by a tracked carrier in the second wave equipped with a Vickers heavy machine-gun, which charged up the beach from its landing-craft, the crew tearing away waterproofing and freeing the gun-clamp, to spray with fire some Germans in open positions, depressing the Vickers into their trench as the carrier closed in. After a brief silence fifteen survivors emerged with their hands raised. It is useful to emphasize that soldiers are encouraged to accept such surrenders, even of enemies who have minutes earlier killed their comrades, not as acts of mercy but to encourage others to abandon the fight. So it was that morning on Sword.

This sector of Cod was cleared of the enemy before 0800, but some other positions in the same network sustained resistance through the hours. Much is justly said of the courage of the invaders, but respect also seems due to the defenders, some of whom fought with dogged persistence against Allied forces wielding such conspicuous might that they could scarcely fail to terrify those manning the bunkers. They resisted with what was surely the courage of despair, especially the Russians and Ukrainians among them in Heer uniform, who knew that they were dead men walking, even if they survived the battlefield to return to their homelands.

When the South Lancs' B Company launched its own assault on Cod, Major Robert Harrison its commander was killed immediately. Battalion HQ was briefly established in the dunes, but then a bullet felled CO Richard Burbury. The colonel had come ashore carrying a hand flag in the battalion colours: intended to rally his men, it made him suicidally conspicuous. Battle schools encouraged officers to dress like their men and to arm themselves with a rifle or Sten gun rather than a revolver, so as not to be distinguishable by enemy snipers. For a man to carry a mapcase slung across his chest served to make him a magnet for bullets, since it marked him as a leader, just as did Burbury's foolish flag.

Jack Stone, his second-in-command, took over. Of the battalion's other senior officers, company commander Major John Harward was also mortally wounded in the first minutes, exploding Bangalore torpedoes under German wire, as was one of his subalterns, so that another lieutenant took command. He, too, was soon hit, leaving the company with only one officer. Lt. Bob Bell-Walker briefly assumed command of B Company, attacking the western end of Cod in classic fashion, tossing a grenade through the strongpoint's firing slit and following up with a burst of Sten-gun fire. Bell-Walker died seconds later, however, shot down from another German position.

It is extraordinary how contradictory, or plain wrong, rival perceptions by participants can be. Derrick Wormald, commanding the Hussars' A Squadron, recorded that his DD tanks experienced no enemy fire during their 'swim in'. He saw an AVRE a few yards to his left hit by a German anti-tank round just as it left its landing-craft, so that the turret 'and contents thereof' spun into the air. His own gunner engaged and silenced the position from which the anti-tank gun was firing. Then he watched the South Lancs infantry coming ashore and believed that they 'crossed the beach with very few, if any casualties' and passed inland.

Seeing no open beach exit, Wormald dismounted and walked up the sand, exploring for a possible route inland. He was astonished to behold a large stack of German mines by the roadside, waiting to be laid. However, incoming mortar and shellfire dismayed even the bold major and at 0745 he hastily remounted his tank and ordered his squadron to follow him off the beach by the exit he had identified. They advanced without loss to Hermanville, where Wormald discovered that nine Hussar tanks had been swamped and that the South Lancs had in reality suffered significantly – not least by the loss of Col. Burbury, who chanced to be his own cousin.

During the Commandos' training, Col. Peter Young admonished a young subaltern who faltered, saying: 'Terry, officers do not notice rain, cold, heat, bullets, shells or fear.' Relatively few junior leaders quite fulfilled Young's heroic mantra. The best to which they could aspire was identified by a platoon commander: 'To feign a casual and cheerful optimism, to create the illusion of normality and make it seem as if there was nothing in the least strange about the outrageous things one was asked to do.'

(Top) The first view of SWORD for many invaders and (inset) the cover of Guy Hattu's vivid memoir of his experiences as a commando, one of the first Frenchmen to land.

(Below) Advancing through Ouistreham.

(Above) A typical SWORD scene in the first minutes after landing, with men huddled under German fire.

(Left) 'Banger' King and (below) infantry move inland behind a Sherman.

Aerial view showing the chaos of armoured vehicles that built up on the shoreline through the morning.

Tanks crowding the shoreline, as seen from an LCT.

(Right) Hussars' tanks in the shallows and (left) medics tending a casualty in the shelter of a disabled AVRE Petard.

Men of K.P. Smith's brigade headquarters group flounder ashore, to spend the rest of the day in sodden discomfort, as did thousands of their comrades.

(Above) A famous image of commandos disembarking – Lovat is the isolated figure on the right in the water – with piper Bill Millin's back view nearest the camera and (below) the beach as it looked when the tide receded and the shoreline became less perilous.

(Top) Paras deploy before the hulk of a glider fortunate enough to have landed intact and (below) Commandos move up from the beach with a 'scissors' bridge behind.

Harward's company was able to press on towards the brigade's assembly point at Hermanville a mile inland, along with the battalion headquarters group. The South Lancs' overall losses on the beach were not heavy, by the standards of Normandy. But too many of their men took cover under fire within a few yards of the incoming tide, as did their American counterparts on Omaha. A 3 Div colonel had repeatedly warned his men at their final briefing before embarkation not to bunch in fours and fives: 'If a shell comes down it will hit all five of you instead of the one wretched, unfortunate person who happens to be there.' But the human instinct to huddle was too strong for many men to heed the warning. Officers suffered disproportionate casualties, as they attempted to drive their men on. Generals exercised no influence upon events on the Normandy beaches early that morning. Everything hinged upon junior leaders and the willingness of their soldiers to follow them. Majors, captains, lieutenants were small cogs in armies, yet on D-Day they became immensely important people. In the absence of reliable wireless communications, in the chaos that had always been anticipated in the wake of H-Hour, the success or failure of countless strands in the vast Overlord design depended upon the energy and courage of these young men.

In elite units, NCOs and indeed private soldiers often forged forward on their own initiative, as happened in 9 Para's attack on the Merville Battery, even if the officers at their head fell. In 3 Division throughout 6 June, however, again and again leaders died because they were obliged to expose themselves to get their men to move. Three officers of the South Lancs who, back in Scotland, had served as instructors at the divisional battle school, perished on the beach. It was asking too much of some of their novice warriors, hurled into the first action of their lives, to defy logic and keep moving under fire, when all their instincts urged them to cling to cover.

Engineer Major Kenneth Ferguson said: 'I was angry at people not getting off the beaches as fast as they could and getting away. People tended to hang around too much.' The generals were naive, in failing to anticipate the grogginess of most of the tens of thousands who waded ashore, weakened by seasickness. Finlay Campbell recalled that his legs continued to feel 'wobbly' for two days after he stumbled onto the sand. How could this sensation fail to diminish many men's spirit in their first battle, immediately upon quitting the boats?

German fire continued sweeping the beach, taking a steady toll of those unprotected by armour. The East Yorks Pte. Harold Isherwood saw a shell land among a cluster of officers, causing limbs and torsos to be 'blown high into the air'. Wilf Todd suddenly felt hungry as he sheltered in a crater. He ate some chocolate and offered a piece to his section commander who said crossly, 'What a bloody silly time to be eating chocolate!' Dennis Hallam had been impressed by their 'battle inoculation training' with live ammunition, but felt that nothing prepared him for the real sights of Sword, especially his first corpse. Men especially recoiled from the sight of wounded or dead men who were caught beneath tank tracks, forcing portions of their intestines through their faces. In all, of 460 men of the East Yorks who landed that morning, before dark sixty other ranks were killed and 137 wounded. The youngest was eighteen-year-old Arthur Blackmore, the oldest thirty-eight-year-old Eric Elliott.

Beachmaster Neville Gill of 3rd Recce Regiment landed nineteen minutes behind the lead infantry. Orders specified that he and his group should hitch a lift back to England once the shore was secure. Gill, nervous that soldiers quitting the battlefield might be taken for deserters, had secured a letter signed by Crocker, 1 Corps' commander, confirming their right to passage. He was a thirty-one-year-old Newcastle solicitor, while his deputy Captain Ivor

Stevens was a publican's son from Bradford-on-Avon. By chance both men had been at Dunkirk, holding humbler ranks.

Gill was furious to find that his landing-craft skipper, a Royal Marine, had offloaded them in chest-deep water and the wrong place. He saw infantrymen crouching or lying inert in the shallows instead of pressing on. Once on the beach they met a crowd of German prisoners whom they ignored as none of their business. Then Stevens, huge and strong, saw Gill fall and lie motionless. 'What's happened?' he demanded. Gill responded: 'Steve, I can't move. Where did it get me?' The younger man found a jagged wound in Gill's back, behind his shoulders. Knowing that the major's D-Day was over almost before it had begun, he said, 'I'd better take the corps commander's letter.' A bullet had broken Gill's spine. He would spend a year in a plaster cast, and eventually died from the wound. Stevens reached his appointed beach exit and spent the rest of the day directing traffic through it. The calm control exercised by the beachmasters 'had to be seen to be believed', according to an eyewitness. They issued orders to the men landing in their areas – most often: 'Move! Move! Move!' – through clusters of tannoy speakers, erected under fire on low pylons. Some landing-craft, seeing the shells and mortar bombs still bursting on the beach, circled unhappily offshore, causing one beachmaster to shout into his microphone towards their skippers: 'Get off that bloody merry-go-round and come and fight this war!'

'What a reception!!!' wrote George Appleton, commanding another Beach Group. For months the major had been amazingly sanguine about D-Day. Now his landing-craft took aboard so much water he thought he would never reach land. 'Shells, mortars, small arms fire – more opposition than I had expected.' Within minutes ashore his naval liaison officer and one of his platoon commanders were killed, his own jeep wrecked by fire.

Captain Hugh Collinson, an FOO for the South Lancs, started the day feeling prosperous, because the previous evening he had won ten shillings and tenpence playing bridge with the purser of his ship. He was now, however, anticipating worse things: 'It *was* rough, and I knew we were in for an unpleasant run-in to the beach.' Yet when he climbed on deck, in the face of the majestic spectacle, 'I was so lost in admiration that I had almost forgotten that this was not an exercise until brought back to reality by a few bullets overhead.' He jumped down into waist-deep water and ran to the shelter of a knocked-out tank. When he led his team in another forward bound, he heard the whine of a shell, shouted to the others 'Get down!' and dropped flat himself. After the explosion something hit his side and he felt a frightening wetness. There was no blood, however, and he understood that his water-bottle had been punctured by shrapnel.

'Then I saw something much worse. My best signaller, a chap called Harrison from Preston, was lying in a rather peculiar attitude and I saw that he had been killed outright.' Harrison had survived landings in North Africa, Sicily, Italy. 'He was only twenty-one.' They had been dropped three hundred yards east of their intended landing-place, opposite a German strongpoint, which was still firing. He witnessed Colonel Burbury exposing himself for a moment, then falling shot. 'I was lying on that beach for one and a half hours, not just sunbathing …' As the tide rose, Collinson's jeep was drowned in six feet of water. When his surviving signallers belatedly achieved wireless contact with HMS *Virago*, he ran to ask the South Lancs if they could use some fire support: 'They said they did not want anything at present, thank you.' Collinson's counterpart FOO with the East Yorks, Doug Webb, suffered matching misfortunes. A bullet hit his operator's boot as he landed, causing the man to collapse in the water, ruining the wireless. His jeep, too, was submerged.

Two Luftwaffe FW190 fighters made a single pass across the beach, machine-gunning as they roared overhead. This was an isolated air attack, of which there was no significant repetition until next day three Heinkels bombed British positions in Lion-sur-Mer. But its consequence was to make naval gunners at sea ever more trigger-happy, for which some RAF supply-dropping Dakotas, approaching the Orne estuary and 6th Airborne's perimeter, paid the price: one ditched in the Channel, two aborted their missions with severe damage.

All the landing-craft carrying the gunners' self-propelled howitzers touched the beach together and lowered their ramps exactly on schedule, causing a foxhunter among their officers fancifully to liken them to 'a pack of hounds with their noses in the trough'. As soon as the guns were offloaded, they began to fire inland from the surf, the sea washing over their tracks. At H+30 the first six-pounder anti-tank gun got ashore and started engaging the German positions that remained active. Fire from Cod was not finally suppressed until 1000.

As the ramp of Ron Lane's landing-craft banged down, he revved his tracked carrier forward, 'and we were in France'. He was shocked to find the beach so narrow, as the tide surged ever higher, but found the terrain model which they had studied before embarkation a big help in making sense of the shore as they lurched upward and onward. His sergeant, craning to see where they were heading, said: 'Pull in by the wall.'

A red spot appeared on the NCO's forehead and he collapsed on top of Lane. For a few seconds he gibbered and waved his arms, then slumped and fell silent. The other men dismounted and dragged him out of the vehicle. The dead man's helmet fell off, exposing his brain. They left him by the roadside and drove on. Lane thought: 'This is a good start!' German mortar rounds began to fall around them. Yet this boyish-looking twenty-three-year-old Londoner, who had joined up in 1940, was reassured that, despite years of worrying about how he would behave in battle, he felt calmer than expected. 'When it actually came to it you didn't have to worry – the training takes over and you just find yourself doing what needs to be done. I found that I reacted to every situation and just did it.'

A young officer, seconds after disembarking, realized he had left behind his vital mapcase. He ran back up the gangway of the LCI, dashed into the wardroom just as there was a loud explosion and a gaping hole opened in the side of the vessel. He gazed through it for a moment, beholding a stranded boat and burning tank, then grabbed the mapcase and ran back onto the shore. There was now a considerable chaos of wrecked landing-craft either beached or drifting burning offshore. A US Coastguard cutter rescued five men from a sea ablaze after their craft was stricken, a deed which inspired gratitude and admiration among the many witnesses. Second wave infantry were shocked by the floating corpses in the oil-black water, debris bobbing. Some still clung to illusions, however. 'Look, they're having to swim,' said a soldier gazing on face-down corpses, before he realized his mistake.

The general story of the first hour of the landings on Sword was of the Hussars' DD tanks doing their best to suppress the defences, while the engineers were granted nothing like the time window that Montgomery had promised them to clear beach obstacles before the tide rose. A few weeks after D-Day, a meticulous intelligence analysis was made of how closely the reality of the defences had matched expectations and also of how effective or otherwise German weapons had proved. This report estimated that 10–20 per cent of the defensive positions had been disabled or destroyed by pre-landing bombardment. Shortages of personnel had caused 15–25 per cent of the defenders' mortars and machine-guns to be unmanned. German artillery and 81mm mortars had been the most effective weapons in inflicting casualties, accounting for far heavier British losses than did machine-guns and rifles. Each enemy anti-tank gun was reckoned to have knocked out an average of three British armoured vehicles before itself being destroyed. While no mines were laid on the sand, these were spread densely in the dunes beyond the beach and were responsible for many of the delays in moving inland, especially those of vehicles.

The East Yorks' Hugh Bone was sent back to the beach from the battalion's assembly area, just inland, to round up stragglers: 'Under the side of a tank that had been hit I saw a bunch of my people and I bawled at them to get up and get moving, since they were doing no good where they were … I felt a little callous when I found that nearly all of them had been hit and some were dead.'

At intervals through the day the sun broke through the cloudy skies. An officer wrote: 'The effect was that the prepared, sensitive minds of the men were exposed to a series of flashlight photographs that were developed on the spot and printed indelibly.' Such images included some that were startlingly beautiful, even lyrical, amid the rural scenes behind the beach and seaside buildings. Some men digging in spared a moment's thought for the devastation of so much seaside prettiness. Driver Bill Scull, wielding a pick in somebody's garden, mused: 'They must have been lovely houses one time, but now they were all ruined by bombs and shells.' On the eastern flank lay a strip of marshland, reaching back five hundred yards and impassable by vehicles. Beyond were orchards, hedged green cornfields, tall poplars and elms, which almost hid the next village, Hermanville, from the sea. One road linked it to the coast, running from the extreme right of the White beach sector.

The men who landed on Sword faced heavier German fire than did those who went ashore at Utah or Gold, but less heavy than faced the invaders at Omaha and Juno. The biggest German guns at Le Havre made a serious mistake, by concentrating their fire towards the battleship *Warspite*, on which they failed to score a hit all day, instead of focusing everything on the beach, the decisive battleground. The tactical analysts later concluded that it had taken the assault wave fifty minutes to neutralize the coastal defences on Sword, against fifty-five minutes on Gold and one and a half to two and a half hours on Juno. The mopping-up phase was reckoned to have taken three hours on Gold, slightly less on Juno and Sword. The first tracked vehicle got off Sword after 105 minutes, while it was four hours before a wheeled vehicle moved inland, against two and a half hours on Juno, five hours on Gold. As for casualties, there were thought to have been 413 on Gold, 805 on Juno, 630 on Sword. A third of all British and Canadian D-Day losses were suffered by men in the initial assault waves. Of 369 armoured vehicles that landed on Sword before nightfall, thirty-six were wrecked by enemy action, as distinct from many more which merely threw tracks or were drowned by the tide.

The personal narratives quoted above are misleading: every man noticed, and was often shocked by, those who were hit – suffered wounding or death within his line of sight. Nobody, however, troubled to record the much larger number who survived; who scrambled unscathed off the beach. The important truth of the early hours was that enough of the first invaders lived and advanced inland to secure the vital British foothold. Everything was taking longer than the planners had intended. But who could have expected anything else, as unblooded British troops sought to breach Hitler's Atlantic Wall, two years in the making?

10

Green Berets

1 'THE GRANDEUR OF THE SPECTACLE'

When the commandos began to land on Sword, in successive waves between thirty minutes and two hours behind 8th Brigade, German fire seemed scarcely abated from what it had been at H-Hour. Moreover, the tide was pushing many incoming vessels eastwards, some of them significantly off-track. The two rear rifle companies of the East Yorks had been slow to board their boats and thus reached the beach twenty minutes late, behind the first of Lovat's units – 4 Commando with two French troops attached – which at 0750 approached the shore in LCIs, holding line abreast. They passed a tank landing-craft, retiring empty, in which the helmsman wore a bandage around his head but gave them a cheerful victory sign. A commando officer is alleged to have boomed through a loudhailer to the Kieffer contingent from a nearby landing-craft: '*Messieurs les français, tirez les premiers!*' In truth, only chance caused the French commandos' big vessel to touch ahead of the smaller LCAs, and there is doubt whether the invitation to fire first was ever issued. But the moment and the words are such cherished elements of the Kieffer commandos' legend – echoing an alleged episode at the Battle of Blenheim in 1704 – that it must be permitted to remain in the record.

The strangest aspect of 1st Special Service Brigade's participation in the invasion was that it represented the antithesis of everything for which they had spent four years training and preparing. They were an elite raiding force created to strike pinpoint targets in enemy-held territory, paddling canoes, scaling cliffs and crossing mountains to kill Germans and sabotage installations, before withdrawing to raid another day. On 6 June, by contrast, they were deployed as light infantry, thrown against the enemy at the start of a campaign in which they would from then on fight as a fringe component of a vast army, obliged to stay in almost continuous action until the Nazis were vanquished. Whereas 3 Division's entire existence since 1940 had been directed towards this moment, Lord Lovat's brigade had until lately been thinking of other things. Three of its four units were now charged with making haste for the Caen Canal bridge, forging the first link in the chain between the beach and the 6th Airborne perimeter. For this mission, their speed of movement, seeking to brush aside opposition, was more important than any other skill acquired on the hills above Achnacarry.

The first green berets to land were meanwhile to address the town of Ouistreham. Philippe Kieffer's two troops exulted in their symbolic role as the foremost Frenchmen participating in the liberation of their homeland. Guy Hattu wrote: 'As we filed down the gangways our eyes devoured the grandeur of the spectacle, or rather the spectacle imposed itself upon us – brutal, irresistible, something never seen before and never to be seen again. There were boats that had hit mines, craft returning to sea, debris drifting on the shoreline, shells exploding, the sand stained with blood, human voices, the whistle of bullets – an extraordinary din. Did we take in all this immediately, or did the memory of the images return to us later?'

An explosion caused warrant officer Hubert Faure to cough blood from the effects of blast, and he lost his beret and rifle when he collapsed into the shallows. The French troops' padre, René de Naurois, assumed the worst and administered the last rites. Yet after a time Faure recovered and fought on through the day. As Kieffer's own landing-craft touched: 'The sea seemed to rise in a rumble of thunder: mortars, the whistle of shells – everything seemed concentrated towards us. Like lightning the gangways were thrown down. A first group dashed onto the beach but before the second flung themselves forward a 75mm shell tore away its ramp with a scream of metal and wood.' Deprived of the gangway, the commandos jumped with their packs into six feet of water, then floundered ashore.

Guy Hattu again: 'A kind of obsession with the task to be fulfilled made us forget the danger. I believe that nobody had time to be afraid. For the moment it was simply a question for each of us of reaching dry land.' Twenty-four-year-old Robert Piage, whose mother lived in Ouistreham, threw himself into water that proved chest-high. He had advanced ten yards up the beach when a mortar bomb exploded, killing his *copain* – closest mate – and riddling him with fragments of which he carried twenty-two in his body to the grave: 'I began to cry. Not out of sorrow for myself, nor because of my wounds, but at the great joy that I felt at being back on French soil.' Not for long: he slept that night in an English hospital.

Once ashore some commandos sought to wade back into the sea and drag out the wounded, a gesture checked by an officer who shouted: 'That's what the medics are for.' They crossed the beach, a sergeant cutting wire, passed through a supposed minefield towards their designated assembly point. A British commando observed wonderingly that among his comrades the French were conspicuously the happiest – queuing to pass through the gap in the German wire 'as if it was a pay parade'. Corporal Alf Ackroyd of the Yorkshires said, 'When the commandos landed behind us we were still pinned down on the beach. They came out in a rugby scrum and stormed over the wire and got through.' In truth, most of the Yorkshires were by then moving inland, but a significant rump, like Ackroyd, still clung to precarious refuges on the beach.

Once on the lateral road to Ouistreham – the Avenue de Lion some two hundred yards beyond the tideline – the French commandos dumped their rucksacks and embarked upon their assigned task. The planners had flinched from committing men to land frontally before the powerful defences of the town. Instead, towards 0900 4 Commando pivoted eastward, to approach its strongpoints from the flank or rear, suppress these, then clear the road through to the Caen Canal. In similar fashion at the opposite end of Sword, 4th Special Service Brigade's 41 Royal Marine Commando was tasked to fight its way through Lion and Luc-sur-Mer.

The men of 4 Commando advanced east under sporadic fire, sustaining a trickle of casualties. Hattu wrote: 'Nothing in war ever happens the way one expects – at least, not in the details. Everything is left to personal initiative and the commandos have plenty of it. In spite of the losses, somebody else takes on any job for which a comrade is missing.' As the commandos moved into the town, supported by two Hussars' DD Shermans, whose commanders acted on their own inclination and against orders, they came under increasingly heavy mortar and machine-gun fire. They glimpsed ahead some helmeted heads and fired towards them, then realized that these were civilians, who dashed forward and seized them in passionate embrace. The welcoming locals said: 'We've been waiting for you for four years', and wept with joy. Hattu marvelled: 'So it's true! We are in France … We find ourselves almost incapable of speech. We have to remind these people that the zip of bullets is not fairground noise.' As they neared the centre of Ouistreham they swung north off the road, successive French and British troops advancing more or less simultaneously on three parallel axes, to approach the German coastal strongpoints from the rear.

Elsewhere the commandos who had landed on the right of the French met heavy fire as they approached the beach, which in the last hundred yards of the sea passage crippled five boats out of their twenty-two with armour-piercing rounds. Alan Semmence watched fascinated as machine-gun bullets struck the water 'like pebbles being thrown in'. Finlay Campbell's recent twenty-first birthday present, a fountain pen, fell unused into the Channel. Terry Skelly was celebrating his twentieth birthday on 6 June. He wrote: 'I was just starting down the port ramp when our craft gave a lurch as it was severely hit … depositing me in five feet of water. I was rolled over and over underwater until I came to rest against the body of a man jammed against a beach obstacle … I could clearly see his dead face with his eyes open and read his East Yorks titles and see his 3 Div shoulder flashes. I pulled myself to my feet and started for the beach with water up to my chest … The clutter was amazing compared with our well-ordered landings on exercises in the UK … I was amazed to see a lot of soldiers huddled at the top of the beach apparently stopped by one strand of barbed wire … The assault brigade were paying a terrible price for not getting off the beach quickly enough.'

This was unjust to many of the Yorkshire and Lancashire men ahead of them, but reflects the misapprehensions and tribal jealousies which afflict all armies in battle: it is common to read men's accounts of neighbouring units taking to flight, for instance, but rare to read admissions that one's own did so. Cpl. Peter Masters, a Viennese Jew now attached to 3 Commando, landed over-burdened: 'Nobody dashed ashore – we staggered. With one hand I carried my gun, with the other I held the rope rail down the ramp and with the third hand I carried my bicycle. I did not know enough to be really frightened.' Masters, like Skelly, was astonished to see infantrymen 'sitting around here and there, not doing anything in particular', in one case digging a foxhole in the water.

Few men could be spared to escort surrendered Germans to the rear: the forward troops merely disarmed them and gestured towards the beach. Alf Ackroyd saw one of these men, obviously in desperate haste to escape from the battlefield, run up the gangway of a landing-craft to meet a commando carrying a bicycle, coming down. Lovat's man swung around and with his free hand delivered an uppercut which propelled the prisoner into the sea. Some surrendered Germans were shot, by men at the very precipice edge of tension, excitement and terror, trained and conditioned for years to kill people clad in field grey.

Just before Capt. Kenneth Wright disembarked with 4 Commando, he and his troop were stunned by the explosion of a mortar bomb, causing them to fall on top of each other in a jumble of men, arms and equipment. He himself was clawed by steel fragments and bloodied, but a naval officer shouted: 'This is where you get off!' Some of those hit were too badly wounded to move, yet Wright waded fifty yards to the shore: 'The beach by now was covered with men. They were lying down in batches in some places to avoid overcrowding round the exits. Some were sitting up, most of them were trotting or walking across the sand to the dunes. There were a good many casualties, the worst of all being the poor chaps who had been hit in the water and were trying to drag themselves in faster than the tide was rising.' In increasing pain from his wounds, Wright somehow stumbled to a house in which he collapsed onto a large feather bed, 'and that was the end of my participation in the invasion'. He later lay for twenty hours on a stretcher under the sky, before being evacuated.

Etienne Webb was bowman of an LCA on the extreme left of the assault. A beach obstacle tore open the bottom of his craft, one of dozens to founder. He swam ashore, then thought, 'What in the bloody hell am I going to do now?' Transformed from a player into a mere spectator, he strove to take in 'bugles sounding, men dashing around, the commandos coming in and just moving off the beach as if it was a Sunday afternoon, chatting and mumbling away at whatever they were going to go through to do their little bit of stuff'. A beachmaster told Webb and his sodden mates to 'keep out of trouble and we will get you off'. He was evacuated in an empty landing-craft at 1100.

Peter Young's vessel lost speed just off the beach, causing 3 Commando's colonel to demand impatiently of her young skipper, 'What are you waiting for?' The lieutenant replied: 'There are still five minutes to go.' Young said: 'I don't think anyone will mind if we're five minutes early on D-Day.' The naval officer assented: 'Then in we go.' Bill Bidmead's craft was hit: 'I found myself under a pile of chaps and their 90 lb rucksacks.' The first man down the ramp, his pal Frankie Ives, was almost cut in half by machine-gun fire. Bidmead, limp with seasickness, plunged into water that immersed him up to his neck: 'I had a vision of being drowned before I made the beach.' He saw several wounded men dragged underwater by the weight of their burdens. Once on the sand, and moving inland, he was bemused by the sight of so many figures lying prone. Why did they not get up? Then he understood.

Captain Ryan Price's craft, carrying four thousand gallons of fuel, burst into roaring flames, so that he and his comrades were obliged to swim the last yards to the beach. Meanwhile skipper Rupert Curtis, whose LCI carried Lord Lovat, said, 'I'm going in', gunned his engines and bumped over the shallows: '"Stand by with the ramps!" Four [seamen] sprang to gangplanks. "Lower away there!" … That eruption of twelve hundred men covered the sand in record time.' Lovat got ashore at 0840 with his personal piper close behind. Twenty-one-year-old Bill Millin had initially baulked at performing during the landing, citing War Office regulations that relegated pipers on battlefields to the rear areas. His brigadier responded cleverly: 'Ah, but that's the *English* War Office. You and I are both Scottish, and that doesn't apply.' Thus the notes of 'Highland Laddie' wailed across the sands of Sword. Lovat wrote: 'The smoky foreground was not inviting. The rising tide slopped round bodies with tin hats that bobbed grotesquely in the waves. Wounded men, kept afloat by life jackets, clung to stranded impediments. Barely clear of the creeping tide, soldiers lay with heads down, pinned to the sand. Half-way up the beach, others dug themselves into what amounted to a certain death-trap.'

The monstrous injustice of war dictated that some units, commandos and 3 Div alike, got ashore almost without loss, and even without getting very wet, while others were harrowed, mauled, half-drowned. The colonel of 4 Commando, Robert Dawson, was hit in the leg in the first moments after disembarking, while his men suffered forty casualties. Ignoring his wound, and another which he received later, the colonel insisted on retaining command for the rest of the morning. When 3 Commando landed, one of its landing-craft took a direct hit, removing twenty men from its strength for some hours, though most rejoined later. Its CO was wounded and evacuated. David Colley, a Catholic officer not long out of school at Downside, was shot through the heart. 'Ginger' Cunningham, a medic who was the smallest man in the Commando, was hit in the leg. As he stumbled, uttering a flood of obscenities, he was seized and carried up the beach by a huge comrade. Cunningham expostulated ungratefully to his rescuer: 'To think they could miss a big bugger like you, those f---ing Germans, and then f---ing well choose to pick on me!'

Most men made land unscathed, however, tearing off the waterproof bandages and condoms protecting their weapons. To the embarrassment of Harry Drew, the drum magazine of his tommy gun fell into the sea, so that he invaded France disarmed. Derek Mills-Roberts' 6 Commando came ashore led by Captain Alan Pyman, who retained the lead for most of the day. The colonel said later: 'The landing was a soldier's battle, with the total confusion which favours spirited assault, and it was soon over.' They cleared the sand in eleven minutes, raced off the beach, then regrouped among irrigation ditches inland. Ryan Price and his troop, having lost their own arms when their landing-craft was wrecked, snatched up the rifles of dead East Yorkshiremen. Lovat later poured forth bile upon the infantrymen of 8th Brigade: 'Hopelessly slow to advance … A poor showing in the last rehearsal was faithfully repeated on the battlefield … We passed through them, leaving platoons scrabbling in the sand where the shelling hit hardest, digging holes which would be drowned when the tide returned.' Commando Knyvet Carr, known to his comrades as 'Muscles', stormed with grenades a pillbox which Lovat claimed to have been 'supposedly the responsibility of the East Yorks'.

All this was nonsense. Most of the Yorkshiremen were already pressing on inland, and every man who landed that morning was improvising. Moreover while Lovat was right that it was folly to pause in the beach area, he was mistaken to suppose that none of his own men did so. A commando wrote: 'It seemed like hours before we got moving … There were those lying there that just didn't make it.' He gazed at the landing-craft on fire, some sailors still clinging to doubtful shelter behind their wheelhouses. He thrust aside an infantryman who had frozen behind his Bren gun, apparently traumatized. Later in the day Lt. Ted Williams of the 1st Norfolks raised a comradely hand as he passed a cluster of Lovat's men whom he glimpsed brewing up in a dell beyond the beach road. Seconds later, he was appalled to see them sprawled in death after a mortar bomb landed in their midst.

On Sword and immediately beyond at mid-morning crowded a medley of men of many units. The scheduled order for the first waves was:

H-7.5 (minutes) A & B Squadrons 13/18 Hussars' DDs
H-Hour (0725) 77 & 79 Assault Squadrons Royal Engineers, C & D companies South Lancs, A & B East Yorks
H+20 South Lancs & East Yorks supporting rifle companies
H+30 4 Commando
H+45 C Squadron Hussars & first priority vehicles
H+60 1 Suffolks
H+75 6 & 41 Commandos (inc. Lord Lovat)
H+75 76 Field Regiment RA (105mm SP howitzers)
H+105 45 & 3 Commandos, 33 Field Regiment RA
H+120 Second priority vehicles & stores

As we have seen, several of these units arrived late, and as the morning advanced the disembarkation of follow-up units became seriously delayed. But nobody should have expected anything else. The real achievement was that most of the men supposed to land on Sword got past the beach alive, while the defences were progressively ground down. Only movement inland could check incoming artillery and mortar rounds from German positions miles to the south, east and west, which continued to trouble the beach for hours after local small arms fire had been suppressed.

The 'indescribable noise' was signaller Norman Barker's first impression of Sword, after landing an hour late: 'It was all incredible and fascinating and … my main feeling was curiosity and amazement, surrounded by hundreds of ships and people and "things". I was not frightened – rather foolishly the opposite. The whole is unbelievable unless it has been lived in.' Tolstoy's Pierre Bezukhov had experienced the same sensation at Borodino, and Keith Douglas in the desert – that in a man's first action curiosity could be as powerful a driver as fear: 'I observed these battles partly as an exhibition – that is to say I went through them like a visitor from the country going to a great show, or like a child in a factory – a child sees the brightness and efficiency of steel machines and endless belts slapping round and round, without caring or knowing what it's all there for.' Later, when a soldier better understood the significance of the deadly threats on the battlefield, all that changed: fascination was supplanted by an educated apprehension; sometimes a raw terror.

As the bedraggled crew of Patrick Hennessey's swamped Sherman huddled on the beach alongside the commandos, another Hussars' tank drove by. Its commander shouted down 'Can't stop!' but threw them a can of soup. The men were gratefully sharing this when an irate Royal Engineer captain ran by and lambasted the commander: 'Get up Corporal! This is no way to win the Second Front!' The shamefaced Hussars scrambled off the sands and delivered to medics the wounded member of their crew, whose spirits rose wonderfully on being told that he would be 'returning to Blighty as a wounded D-Day hero'. As for the other dismounted tankers, nobody wanted them. When they reported themselves to a stressed naval beachmaster, he dismissed them with the injunction 'Get off my bloody beach!'

Alan Richardson's landing-craft downed its ramp with a mighty splash, enabling five engineers' jeeps to plough ashore. But, with the boat's Oerlikon guns in action against a beach villa that was still held by the Germans, when they asked the beachmaster for hands to offload their huge load of ammunition, he shrugged … and refused to allow prisoners to do the work. In despair, the craft's captain pulled off the beach, to await the next high tide. When they finally began their offload, they were bewildered to hear the saxophones of Glenn Miller's 'Moonlight Serenade' blaring from their neighbouring LCT's broadcast system: 'Romance and death were strangely coupled in that brief moment.' Their propeller shafts were damaged by submerged wreckage as they backed away from the shore, obliging them to lash the LCT to another craft to get back to Sussex: 'We made our way home across eighty miles of water like a couple of drunks arm in arm returning from the village pub.'

Twenty-year-old Royal Marine Cameron Badenoch stood up in the turret of his Centaur 95mm self-propelled howitzer which started firing blind from its LCT. Once down the ramp, however, bullets zipping and pinging against the hull made him hastily retire below and close his hatch. They crossed the sand dunes ahead of the commandos whom they were briefed to support, before suffering an ignominious clutch burn-out, immobilizing the gun. They continued to fire blind, but their FOO was wounded landing with Lovat's men, and thus for a time the Centaur troop could achieve little useful.

By 1000, most unwounded foot-soldiers of all the initial assault units were off Sword and moving inland, leaving behind stragglers and a throng of engineers, gunners, Beach Group personnel, medics and – above all – vehicles of all kinds and especially tanks. The armour was crowded onto the narrow stretch of sand above the tideline, struggling to manoeuvre past wrecked Shermans and Churchills, and to find a path southwards. Each wave of arriving landing-craft was succeeded by another, as soon as offloaded vessels went astern and cleared a beaching space. A few tanks were already in action, notably the Centaurs and DDs supporting

4 Commando in the streets of Ouistreham. Most, however, were stalled in the beach area, long after the schedule demanded that they be pushing inland to spearhead the drive for Caen. Sherman crews had been repeatedly warned to avoid making abrupt turns on the sand and shingle, but some drivers did so anyway. Their tanks promptly threw tracks, immobilizing them for hours.

Inland, infantry units confronted by German strongpoints were reluctant to advance to storm them without the armoured support they expected; had been promised. Moreover wireless communications were patchy between foot-soldiers, tank units and rear headquarters. Many frustrated operators were heard in the course of the day, repeating into handsets the desperate mantra 'Report my signal. Report my signal', and receiving no response. At mid-morning a steady stream of infantry, drawn from two brigades and six regiments, had advanced inland from Sword. Many then stopped, however. Almost all the men and vehicles that subsequently made it off the sand experienced checks, sometimes of minutes but often of hours, while opposition ahead was suppressed, new orders were sought, traffic jams cleared in narrow village streets, or because commanding officers failed to drive on their units with sufficient urgency.

Those who discovered that they appeared to be going nowhere in a hurry adopted the usual recourse of British soldiers in such circumstances by brewing up, an activity sometimes terminated in a deluge of mortar bombs ordained by distant, watchful German eyes behind field-glasses. It was a contradiction of those miles of Normandy inland from the beaches that in some places a man had no field of vision – no sight of potential threats – for more than thirty yards, surrounded by houses and trees, while across other areas – rolling expanses of corn or pasture – friend or foe could see for miles, and mandate devastation.

2 RACING FOR THE BRIDGES

Only the commandos pushed on at speed, though not fast enough to satisfy the demands of Montgomery. Those fighting their way through the streets of Ouistreham continued to gain ground and take losses. The rest of Lovat's brigade meanwhile hastened across country towards the Caen Canal bridge, crossing a tram line, then trudging in long files over waterlogged ground, under intermittent German fire. Peter Young wrote: 'We trot down the inland side of the dunes and hurl ourselves over a wire fence. A shell smacks into the soft ground behind us, and something like the kick of a mule hits me on the right shoulder-blade. "That was a near one," shouted RSM Stenhouse. "Near one be damned, it hit me!"' Young was lucky, however – he had been struck by a clod of earth thrown up by the explosion, not by a bullet or shell fragment. Progress slowed as the commandos floundered in marshland and leaped clumsily across deep, slimy drainage ditches. The mud diminished the killing power of German shells and mortar bombs landing close by, but within the ensuing hour or two caused almost every man of Lovat's units to become soaked below the waist, and considerably filthy.

Emlyn Jones wrote: 'There was no cover … Shells and mortars came raining down … we had trouble with snipers.' A bulldozer lurched up the road, bypassing them. Jones shouted to its driver that the area ahead had not been cleared but the man pressed on, insisting that he had his orders. A few minutes later they passed him again, stopped by a bullet in the head. Lovat, marching with the brigade headquarters group, commandeered some prisoners to carry explosives. Encountering 'a windy officer' smoking a pipe in a shellhole, the clan chief claimed to have 'kicked him into action'.

Maj. Pat Porteous, who had won a VC two years earlier at Dieppe, commanded a troop of 4 Commando charged with destroying a coastal battery and its fire-control centre, close to the Caen Canal and just east of where the French troops were engaged. He lost a quarter of his men getting over the seawall, then raced for their objective covered by smoke grenades. To the chagrin of Porteous and his men, they found that the German guns had been redeployed inland a few days earlier: only telephone poles protruded from the coastal battery which men had just died for. One commando fell when a German grenade exploded beside him as he tried to climb the tower from which the defenders were directing fire. The invaders lobbed a PIAT anti-tank bomb at it, without effect. It was too tall for a flamethrower to reach the occupants of the upper storeys. Eventually the commandos were ordered to leave the tower for others to mop up, and hasten south in the wake of the rest of the brigade, towards the Caen Canal bridge. Astonishingly, the Germans in the tower lay unnoticed for three days, until they startled nearby British troops by emerging to offer their surrender.

The commandos, bent under the weight of huge rucksacks, 'looked like a lot of snails going home'. The biggest men were charged with carrying the heaviest weapons. A mortar of 4 Commando was hauled behind the lead troops on a trek cart drawn by Donkin, father of many children and almost forty years old, and Craig, a tough Ayrshire miner who died that day. Even for the strongest and fittest of Lovat's men, the five-mile march to the bridges was a back-breaking business.

A Frenchman ran out of a farmhouse crying out in despair, 'My wife has been wounded! Is there a doctor?' Then a mortar bomb exploded, knocking several commandos to the earth. They rose to see the Frenchman's head rolling down the road. During a halt in the advance, they noticed a field of strawberries by the roadside and some men began to pick them. A commando wrote, 'The poor little French farmer came to me and said: "For four years the Germans were here and they never ate one!"'

In Ouistreham, the French commandos continued fighting to clear the town. The least costly method of advancing in an urban area is by so-called 'mouseholing', moving from house to house by blasting a passage through successive adjoining walls. Yet Kieffer's men recoiled from such slow and destructive tactics, instead moving up the streets. Guy Hattu recorded in the present tense: 'Centaur tanks appear, and one of them stops behind our lead elements. As they head for the casino an enthusiastic group of civilians appears. One of them cries to his neighbour to fetch some Calvados.' Hattu was presented with a bottle which was passed from hand to hand.

The casino – or rather, its old foundations rebuilt by the Germans into a formidable strongpoint – was protected by wire and an anti-tank obstacle. As the commandos worked cautiously towards it, 'a magnificent figure with a huge moustache of an unmistakably Gallic type, wearing a helmet, dashes towards them and announces that he will lead the column and show them the defences. He cries out warnings that the houses are full of "*Boche*". They advance with two sections hugging opposite sides of the street, demanding "Give me rifle! I went all through the last war! *Ah, ces salauds de Boches!*"'

The commandos' local guide, probably Marcel Lefevre, insisted they follow his directions. 'Turn right at the first cross-roads!' The man was 'radiant with excitement, insistent on staying at front of the column'. For a week Kieffer's men had studied photos of the streets of Ouistreham, but bombardment had changed the town's appearance. Their guide pointed out a machine-gun post, and the commandos positioned a Bren gun to cover their movements as they approached the heart of the enemy positions. They were astonished to glimpse Germans moving in the open on a hummock beside an old water tower, only a hundred yards away. The commandos swept them with fire, then dashed forward: a stream of defenders emerged, hands in the air. The more fastidious among the conquerors complained that many of the surrendered enemy, especially Russians, 'stank to high heaven'.

Guy Hattu ran up the stairs of a house and found that from a rear window he had a view of Germans in the casino firing on the landing-craft and the beach. He called forward a man with a sniper rifle, but to Hattu's dismay the enemy spotted them. An anti-tank round smashed into the house, hitting the marksman in the chest. Hattu recoiled from the sight of what was left, 'his big eyes staring emptily, his body hideously mangled'. Wire entanglements protected the approach to the casino, and with their Bangalores ruined by immersion in the sea, the commandos embarked upon a protracted exchange of fire with the Germans around the strongpoint. Soon their own mortar bombs and PIAT rounds were gone. Bullets ricocheted off buildings and trees. They had no means to call in fire, because their wireless had been drowned during the landing.

A German sniper picked off a twenty-year-old who was sent forward to reconnoitre. Hattu felt a stab of grief. 'He had the face of a young girl, had escaped from France over the Pyrenees two years earlier; then spent months in a Spanish prison before reaching England and joining Kieffer.' Their medic, a Paris psychiatrist who had likewise broken out of a prison, ran forward, checked the corpse and signalled to the padre, René de Naurois, that he was dead, then himself fell, fatally hit in the back. The French troops were paying a heavy price for their reckless courage and tactical carelessness.

They had to have a tank. Hubert Faure ran back in search of Kieffer, met a Royal Marine Centaur howitzer, and explained to its commander that they were stuck. Amid a burst of cheering, Faure led the steel monster crawling up the street towards them. The first rounds from the Centaur sent a German 37mm gun spinning into the air. The commandos' local guide with the huge moustache, his exuberance undiminished by the exchanges of fire and the losses, said to Guy Hattu: 'For an Englishman you speak French pretty well', which prompted a surge of laughter.

Then they were ordered to break off the fight, leaving others to finish off the casino, from which firing had stopped since the Centaur addressed it. Civilians were everywhere emerging onto the streets, and the commandos distributed cigarettes, sweets, chocolate. Faure, Hattu and their group sat down in a garden, awaiting the others. A gendarme expressed fears this was only a raid; that they would be retiring once more to England. If so, the man said, he wanted to leave with them. They reassured him: the invaders were there to stay. They prepared to follow the rest of Lovat's brigade, south towards the Caen Canal bridge and the Airborne perimeter.

Keith Wakelam, a twenty-two-year-old commando signaller, had volunteered to go ashore with the spearhead in a mood of despair provoked by consciousness that his marriage to Beryl was a failure: 'I had expected too much of her. She was a fun-loving party-goer and I was serious, jealous and demanding.' He and his party cleared the beach after ploughing through the shallows in their jeep, but the vehicle kept stalling, until they poured petrol down its air intake. Wakelam noticed that Jimmy, his nineteen-year-old set operator, was shivering with terror from head to foot. The teenager was a medical category B2 with flat feet, 'so he shouldn't have been on this except that he was a very good operator and they were in short supply'. They spent the balance of D-Day transmitting unit position reports to HMS *Largs* and to England.

The commandos moving south 'under a leaden sun' were warned to stay off road verges because they were probably mined. They found themselves repeatedly called upon to halt, usually so some pocket of resistance ahead could be reconnoitred or suppressed. Each time the tired men sat down, it was ever harder to move again. There was a steady trickle of casualties, inflicted by invisible enemies firing from treelines. Terry Skelly received a message that a badly wounded comrade wanted to see him – it was Roland Coffin, with whom he had served back in 1940, now shot in the stomach. 'I squatted by his stretcher, gave him a cigarette and chatted to him until he lapsed into unconsciousness. The medical staff said he had little chance of survival, and had given him enough morphia so that he felt no pain.' Coffin died while being carried back to the beach.

Just before Colleville-sur-Orne, around 1130, 6 Commando encountered a pillbox that was swiftly captured with the aid of a flamethrower, which Mills-Roberts' men had been chafing for an opportunity to use in action. They overran an artillery position manned, to their surprise, by Italians. This was a sister battery to one just captured in Ouistreham and its gunners eagerly surrendered. Arrived in the pretty village, the road to the bridges veered left, through Saint-Aubin-d'Arquenay, where local people proffered cider and Calvados. They were briefly strafed by Allied fighter-bombers, which killed only cattle. Every invading soldier that morning supposed that every church held a sniper, and many bullets and tank rounds were fired at unoffending towers which turned out to be empty. Lovat's men were advancing towards the bridges in roughly parallel columns – 6 Commando leading, followed by Lovat and his brigade headquarters; then 45 RM; then

3 Commando, with 4 Commando lingering behind to conclude its battle in Ouistreham. They were separated by several hundred yards; began to see in the fields discarded parachutes of many colours, which meant they must be getting close to the Airborne.

Sixty cyclist commandos rode their machines up the last stages of the road to the hamlet of Le Port, just short of the bridges. They dismounted and deployed only when one of their number was shot down. 'The ground was completely open,' observed Terry Skelly, 'with no cover between us and Bénouville about two km slightly downhill on our front.' Lovat wrote: 'The rest was plain sailing all the way … We met only token resistance from poor-quality troops.' When they finally approached Bénouville, just beyond the Caen Canal, local people warned them the Germans, who still held most of the village, had executed two gendarmes whom they believed were assisting the Allies. The commandos were abruptly ordered to take up positions to meet an expected counter-attack. This never came but halted the advance for almost half an hour. That morning both armies were full of fears, ultimately better-founded on the German side. 'Our advance seemed to get slower and slower as the leading Commando ran into stronger opposition and the trickle of walking wounded making their way back got bigger,' wrote Skelly. They could see Caen ahead: 'It looked a pleasant honey colour in the sunlight – a peaceful cathedral city.'

At Notre-Dame du Port, a lanky corporal stood over a fifteen-year-old Austrian from Graz, whom he had just shot with his Bren gun. The NCO asked interpreter Peter Masters, an exile from Sudetenland, 'How do you say "I'm sorry" in German? '*Es tut mir leid* or *Verzeihung*.' The corporal, who was killed next day, leaned over and said, '*Verzeihung*.' He explained to Masters that he had never shot anyone before. Masters tried to interrogate another prisoner and found he did not speak German. The man said he was Obergrenadier Johann Kramarzyk, a farmer from Ratibor, Poland. Brigadier Lovat himself intervened, asking in French, '*Où sont les canons?*' Kramarzyk looked blank, though it was obvious he understood. He had no idea where the German artillery was firing from. Lovat chanced upon a small party of Marines from 41 Commando, sheltering in a ditch, deeply dejected after finding themselves lost and leaderless: 'The soldiers were boys who looked absurdly young and only lacked for leadership … I swore foolishly at the unfortunate castaways – an error, for cursing never helped a frightened soldier.'

Commando Bill Bidmead was shocked by witnessing 'many different acts of murder carried out … I saw Jerry Grave confronted by a German in a white shirt with his hands up, whom Jerry emptied a Bren magazine into.' There is no excuse for such conduct, save to say that it is part of every army, in every battle, in every war. The men who landed on Sword on 6 June had been trained and conditioned for years to kill Germans. By H-Hour they were hair-triggered in their eagerness to fulfil this purpose. Moreover, many of them went ashore expecting that they themselves were destined to die, some of whom indeed perished. Finally, many of the Germans who offered themselves for surrender had been firing for hours on the invaders before abandoning resistance, and had killed British soldiers. By the confused and confusing code that governs such things, understood by experienced warriors, they thus forfeited their right to mercy. What is remarkable is not how many aspiring PoWs were shot on 6 June, but how many had their surrenders accepted.

While Terry Skelly waited to cross John Howard's bridge into the Airborne perimeter, he washed and shaved with slightly salty water from the canal in his messtin; changed into his best battledress and polished his boots. 'I felt much better and shared a mug of tea with my batman.'

The arrival of 1st Special Service Brigade at the bridges was an incomparable piece of theatre which became one of the most celebrated of D-Day, chiefly because Lord Lovat was accompanied by Bill Millin his piper, who played 'Lochanside' as they crossed the Orne. Every man who was there, or heard of it, not to mention their commanders, celebrated the junction of 6th Airborne with the first invaders arriving from the sea. This took place some time after 1300 – an hour behind the planners' schedule rather than the two minutes of Lovat legend. The men of 6 and 3 Commandos, led by Captain Alan Pyman who was killed a few hours later, hastened across the bridges, which still attracted periodic German fire, despite a scornful rebuke from Lovat to the wise and windy: 'Don't run! Walk.' By the time 4 Commando crossed, however, the Germans had woken up to this significant British movement, and one of its officers fell, shot in the head. When French commando Guy Hattu met men of 7 Para, he thought them 'almost dead with fatigue'. He himself and his comrades felt 'almost too tired to speak'. Though he had eaten nothing since dawn, he experienced no hunger. He sat down at Écardes crossroads, talking to a wounded man awaiting evacuation and 'revelling in the sound of the stream and scent of the meadow. There is a sudden prodigious calm, and I realise that I have been in France for eight hours. It is then, and not before, that for the first time I feel assured that, after so many years of absence, I have rediscovered my country … We are at home.' Although exact timings are elusive, the French of 4 Commando, last of Lovat's units to cross the bridges, probably did not arrive there until around 1530.

A man who was dispatched back to the beach on some messenger task which reflected the inadequacy of wireless communications met a convoy of trucks moving south up the road. A major of the Royal Engineers leaned out of the leading vehicle and demanded to know if the Orne and Caen Canal bridges still stood. Yes, they did. The sapper explained that his transport carried the wherewithal to lay Bailey bridges if the crossings were destroyed. The infantryman urged him to move cautiously because the area was still unsafe. The engineer party reached the western approach, just short of Bénouville, unscathed. Through the days that followed, the engineers laboured furiously to prepare their Baileys to be laid across the canal or the river if German artillery or air attack wrecked the crossing. They went happily unneeded, however. The structure captured by John Howard and his men survived for years, to be rechristened and enter the history books as Pegasus Bridge.

By mid-afternoon, Lovat's entire brigade had crossed into the Airborne perimeter, which it was now their task to reinforce. The clan chief reported to Richard Gale, to receive orders for their deployment. The encounter gave little pleasure to either man. Lovat wrote that Gale 'at first blush, struck me as vain and egotistical, with a hectoring manner and a loud voice. I don't think he liked my peculiarities, either.' Lovat asserted that Gale was 'jealous of green berets', and had not forgotten a boxing match in England at which an Irish commando had felled a big Airborne NCO. 'It was clear the general expected blind obedience from subordinates', which Lovat was the last man to offer.

This sort of childish carping would not deserve rehearsal eighty years later, but for the fact that it seems extraordinary that such a man as Lovat could have been permitted to indulge it on the battlefield in Normandy. He bitterly resented the fact that 'his' Commandos, equivalent in strength only to three infantry battalions, were now to be deployed to shore up the left flank of the Airborne perimeter, south of the canal and river bridge, which seemed an inglorious subsidiary role. Yet in Lovat's defence, the respect and affection he inspired among his men deserve emphasis. 'He seemed a man perfectly at ease,' said one. The ability to generate confidence – as on 6 June several of 3 Div's senior officers failed to do – is a precious asset on a battlefield. Lovat's arrogance exasperated many people, both then and later, but his courage and charisma were beyond dispute.

At Gale's direction, most of the commandos marched northwards in the direction of the coast, to support the paratroopers holding scattered positions somewhat short of Merville – Otway and 9 Para were precariously posted at Hauger. Some Canadian parachutists in Varaville, on meeting the new arrivals, gave them their cigarettes, because they supposed that they themselves would be on their way back to England within hours. This was a fantasy soon dispelled.

'At the six-mile post', in Lovat's words – two-thirds of the way from the bridges to the extremity of Gale's rough perimeter, just short of Le Plein – 'I called a halt. It was a bad decision.' A German mortar stonk descended on the column, obviously directed by an observer, and several men were wounded. Nicol Gray's cyclists of 45 Commando headed for nearby Sallenelles, while Mills-Roberts' men fought a fierce little battle with Germans in Le Plein. His 6 Commando entered Bréville without meeting opposition, but then immediately found itself in trouble – nobody had noticed a German artillery battery posted two hundred yards away. Mills-Roberts' unit was heavily punished and eventually obliged to pull back, having lost twenty-one of a hundred men in one troop. Likewise 45 Commando was expelled from Sallenelles. Yet Lovat's men occupied positions on high ground, where they were reinforced at evening by the exhausted 4 Commando. Otway's men of 9 Para were able to withdraw a distance, joining up with the rest of Gale's formation. Peter Young's force had meanwhile been dispatched to reinforce the defence of Ranville.

Although some local people gave exuberant welcomes to the invaders, others did not. Commando Ray Hatton said: 'The civilian population seemed not to like us somehow, because they had got friendly with the Germans … The Normans seemed to be annoyed with us … We upset their routine.' Hatton and other like-minded young Englishmen were insensitive to what the invasion meant to tens of thousands of French people: mortal peril; the possible or even likely destruction of their homes and livelihoods; the extinction of their families. Around three thousand French people were killed by the D-Day air and sea bombardments, about the same number as Allied combatants who perished. Some Normans suffered terribly for aiding the invaders. The Vermighen family sheltered twenty-two British and Canadian paratroopers in their farm until 11 June. When the Germans reoccupied the area, most of these were captured. Two young Frenchmen hiding with them were shot, as were all the male Vermighens and two of their workers. The farm was burned.

The commandos had accomplished as much on 6 June as could possibly have been expected from troops who were even more lightly-armed than the Airborne. There was simply not enough weight in the British punch east of the Orne that day to secure the ground north to the sea, which would remain disputed for weeks ahead. After 1st Special Service Brigade passed the bridges, responsibility for holding Bénouville and Le Port rested until evening in the hands of Pine-Coffin's 7 Para.

Lovat's men had achieved one of the celebrated feats of D-Day, the first meeting between Gale's paratroopers and the invaders from the sea. If their brigadier's bombast won him few friends outside the commando 'family', the speed of his units' advance inland fulfilled Montgomery's aspirations more effectively than did some of the line infantry units that day.

11

Gale's Force

Even as the men of 3 Div and Lovat's commandos stormed Sword beach then moved inland, Richard Gale's six battalions of paratroopers were striving to create a defensible perimeter, consolidate their foothold on the east bank of the Orne and resist counter-attacks. A stream of men who had been dropped wide rejoined their units or, in some cases, perished while attempting to do so. The lofty Brigadier James 'Speedy' Hill, famous on foot for his length of stride, commandeered a bicycle, on which he rode to report belatedly to Gale at 1230. A sergeant-major of 7 Para was led through the German lines by a French girl, wearing her brother's civilian clothes and riding his bike. Glider pilot Major Jim Lyne spent three days leading six men forty-five miles across France, fighting two actions en route, before reaching Ranville. Commando liaison officer David Haig Thomas, who had climbed Winchester Cathedral a month earlier, was misdropped in the Orne swamps together with Ryder his batman. He was thirty-five, old for such extreme adventures, and leading a small party up a road towards Ranville when caught by a burst of German fire; killed instantly. His companions crawled, ran, hid and sometimes swam for two days before reaching the British lines, where Ryder delivered to comrades his officer's personal weapon – a cosh made from a walrus flipper bone, presented to

Haig Thomas by Eskimos during his pre-war career as an explorer.

That evening 6th Airborne was due to be reinforced by its third brigade, two battalions landing by glider, with another arriving by sea. Men of 13 Para, at Ranville, busied themselves tearing out 'Rommel's asparagus' – anti-glider poles – in the fields where many of the incoming Horsas and Hamilcars were to land. Meanwhile it was a difficult dilemma for Gale and his brigadiers to determine the prudent limits of their perimeter. It was vital to control as much as possible of the high ground, with views for miles across to Sword and beyond. A string of villages – for instance, Le Plein, Hauger, Bréville and Sallenelles – were disputed with the Germans not only on 6 June but for weeks afterwards. If 6th Airborne Division overreached itself – attempted to bite off more than it could chew, or rather defend – its lightly-armed men were vulnerable to German forces which were gaining strength all the time, and supported by some armoured vehicles including old French tanks. A battlegroup of panzergrenadiers from 21 Pz also intervened against the paratroopers, but fortunately for the British its Mk IV tanks reached the battlefield only late in the day.

Gale himself had little information about what many of his men were doing, because radio contacts were erratic. The good news was that some displayed notable initiative and imagination, causing trouble and indeed inflicting death on the enemy wherever they met him. The bad news was that many units still lacked heavy weapons, including Vickers guns and mortars, which had gone missing in the night drop.

An hour before dawn Pine-Coffin's 7 Para was attacked from three sides, in its positions west of the captured canal and river bridges, around Le Port and Bénouville. B Company was 'being pecked at almost all the time by parties of company size', in the words of their historian. In Bénouville the French occupants of some houses shouted from their upper windows to warn the British of nearby enemy activity. Capt. John Sim wrote: 'When dawn broke there was little movement to be seen. The men sat motionless in their trenches, alert with their weapons. In front a farmer was seen leading his horse and cart.' Then two German self-propelled guns began to fire on them, to which Sim and his men lacked means to respond. After suffering several casualties, he felt obliged to withdraw a distance, until later in the morning a British six-pounder arrived to support them, which knocked out both enemy guns.

As the light grew M. and Mme Georges Gondrée, owners of the café on the west side, emerged from the cellar in which they had spent a night of terror with their two children. They heard voices that sounded as if they might be English. Mme Gondrée burst into tears on beholding the paratroopers, and by noon had kissed so many that her face was blackened with accumulated camouflage face cream. Georges Gondrée disappeared into his garden and dug up ninety-eight bottles of champagne, which he had hidden through the occupation, in anticipation of this moment. By evening most of it had gone, and the café became 7 Para's medical aid post.

The British defenders of the bridges found themselves impeded by civilians who sought to cross, sometimes under fire. At the Ox & Bucks' aid post between the canal and the river, German rounds zipped overhead, causing a nervous medical orderly to draw his pistol, which went off. The bullet thudded into the ground beside the head of David Wood, prostrate on a stretcher incapable of movement, without diminishing his discomfort. As the bombardment from the sea intensified, and the navy's aiming points shifted audibly inland, John Howard and his men knew the assault troops must be storming Sword beach. '[We] kept our fingers crossed for those poor buggers … I was very pleased to be where I was, and not with the seaborne chaps.'

Small incidents punctuated the early morning at the bridges: two terrified Italians in civilian clothes, forced labourers for the Germans – 'miserable little men, very hungry', in Howard's words – were flushed out of the undergrowth in which they had been hiding. The major gave them some biscuits from his ration pack then, much to the mirth of the Airborne soldiers, acceded to their request to be allowed to resume their appointed task of erecting anti-glider poles. They feared the wrath of their all-powerful masters on the Germans' reappearance, which they assumed was inevitable. Shortly after 0900, Gale and Hugh Kindersley, commanding 6th Air Landing Brigade, arrived together, delighting the men by their stolid cheerfulness. The general told Howard's contingent: 'Good show, chaps', which their overnight assault assuredly had been.

Even as the two senior officers disappeared to consult with Pine-Coffin, directing the little battle west of the bridges, two German gunboats came into view on the canal, heading south from the sea towards Caen. One of Howard's corporals unleashed a PIAT bomb at the leader. This exploded inside its wheelhouse, causing the boat to swerve into the bank, where it stuck, blocking the canal. Members of the crew scrambled ashore from the stern, hands upraised and shouting, '*Kamerad! Kamerad!*' Only its captain, a Nazi teenager who spoke fluent English, remained defiant: he assured his captors they would soon be expelled from French shores. He was frogmarched to the PoW cage at Ranville, still shouting insults and threats. The second gunboat fled back towards the sea.

Soon afterwards the only Luftwaffe assault on the bridge took place, when a Focke-Wulf 190 dropped a bomb which clanged against the ironwork, then fell into the canal without exploding.

The invaders agreed that the pilot's courage and proficiency deserved a more successful outcome, grateful as they were that this had been denied. Ever since midnight, all the luck in the locality had gone with the British, and in daylight it continued to do so.

Through the morning of 6 June the Germans sustained pressure on the western end of the canal bridge in the hamlets of Le Port and Bénouville, inflicting on 7 Para a steady stream of losses. The Château de Bénouville maternity hospital came under fire for the ensuing fifty-one days: eighteen children were born there in the first fortnight after D-Day, some of them in the medieval chapter beneath the house. Nonetheless, some officers felt the enemy did not concentrate against 7 Para the weight of effort which the importance of the bridges deserved. 'The Germans never knew what strength we had,' said Major Nigel Taylor, who for much of the day commanded his company in the village from a stretcher, having been wounded early on. 'They never really launched an all-out attack … Plenty of fire, yes, and Very lights, but no men or bayonets. We expected it every time things brewed up, but it never came.'

The losses of 7 Para – sixty dead and wounded by nightfall – were painful even so. The Regimental Aid Post came under fire. The Germans were driven back, but Captain Parry, the battalion's beloved Welsh padre, a little man with crinkly red hair known to the men as 'Pissy Percy the Parachuting Parson', was killed. A few hours earlier he had presided over a service at Fairford during which they sang 'Onward, Christian Soldiers'. Even as the padre fell, his brother Major Allen Parry was paddling his soapbox car behind the rest of 9 Para, after their eventful night at Merville.

BBC correspondent Chester Wilmot commanded admiration for his imperturbability, puffing at a big pipe, and 'always to be found where things were at their stickiest', according to Richard

Todd. A certain Corporal Tom Killeen, a good Catholic Irishman, achieved fame by attempting to blast Germans out of the Norman church tower in Le Port with a PIAT, then telling Wilmot who broadcast his words to the world: 'When I got to the church door I looked up and, och! I was sorry to see what I had done to a wee house of God.'

Many men who were wounded or who died as a result of bullet wounds were listed as 'shot by a sniper'. There was a belief that the Germans employed scores of deadly marksmen, peering through telescopic sights from no man's land in search of 'Tommies' who exposed themselves. In truth, each German infantry unit, like its British and American counterparts, had only a small dedicated sniper section. Many of those who fell after being struck by a single bullet were killed by enemy riflemen who merely got lucky, or became chance victims of some of the millions of rounds flying through the air a yard or two above Normandy, on 6 June and later. It was remarkable how seldom most infantrymen – as distinct from machine-gunners – fired their weapons; and notable, when they did so, how seldom they hit what they aimed at. But almost every bullet travelled a mile or more, sometimes inflicting injury or death far from its firer's rifle muzzle.

John Howard's men were unamused when Brigadier Poett ordered an Ox & Bucks platoon into Bénouville to reinforce 7 Para. They felt they had done their bit at the bridges and deserved a break. They spent much of the morning exchanging fire with invisible Germans, a frustrating experience. By midday, however, enough of 7 Para's absent men had joined the battalion for the Ox & Bucks contingent to be pulled back. They were tired and yearned to be allowed to go home, as some naively expected. Howard had set off for Normandy with a strength of 181 officers and men, of whom two were already dead, fourteen wounded and thirty missing. They did not yet grasp that the battle, and their part in it, had scarcely begun. Howard said of the days that followed: 'The biggest problem I had was keeping up the morale of the troops, because we had always got the impression that we would be withdrawn to come back and refit in the UK for another airborne operation.' D Company was a highly-trained elite, but in the days and weeks ahead it suffered its share of casualties diagnosed with battle exhaustion, and of self-inflicted wounds.

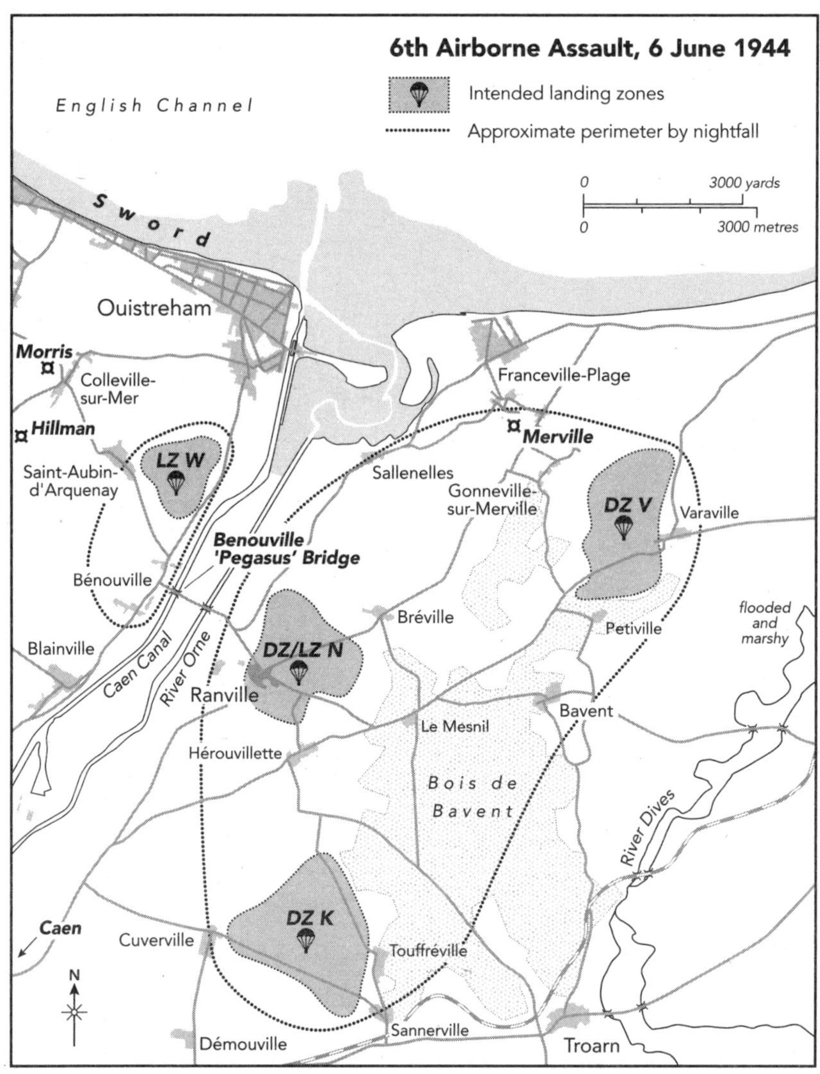

The village of Le Bas de Ranville, on high ground just east of the Orne and on the south side of Gale's perimeter, was occupied and held by 13 Para. Some two miles south-east of the bridges, at the edge of the large woodland of the Bois de Bavent, 8 Para deployed. Though much depleted by absentees – they were less than two hundred strong – at first they were not much troubled in their positions by the enemy. Yet their colonel, twenty-nine-year-old Alastair Pearson, one of the most aggressive British paratroop leaders of the war, was incapable of passivity. Born in Glasgow, where he worked in a bakery before the war, he had served in France in 1940, then enjoyed a meteoric rise up the Parachute Regiment, interrupted only by a demotion after a riotous carouse in a local garrison town. He fought in Tunisia and Sicily, and by D-Day already held three DSOs and a Military Cross. Minutes after landing in Normandy he was hit in the hand, but ignored this wound for the rest of the day while he led fighting patrols ranging far beyond 8 Para's perimeter, designed to confuse and disrupt the Germans wherever he found them.

A highlight of Pearson's private war occurred when he saw a Dakota crash, and set about rescuing its survivors, which involved commandeering a dinghy and paddling across the Dives. His men, awaiting his return, were alarmed by the sound of an approaching vehicle, then discovered it was a farmcart containing eight British wounded, of which the reluctant horse between the shafts was being dragged forward by their colonel. That evening he had the bullet in his hand removed, continuing in command of his battalion through the coming weeks. Pearson was a conspicuous example of the eager warrior and also an unusual one, because he survived. He received a fourth DSO for his doings in Normandy.

All through the day, a steady flow of misdropped paratroopers found their way to the division's rendezvous, many of them after hair-raising adventures. The sights and sounds of battle were still new to most. Stretcher-bearer Albert Gregory never forgot passing the kennels of a big château at Hérouvillette where lay strewn the bodies of several Alsatian dogs shot by one army or the other. In the course of Brigadier James Hill's D-Day odyssey his eye fell on a leg unattached to a body which he found to have belonged to the mortar officer of 9 Para, for whom he had secured a commission only a few months earlier. Now, this young man had fallen victim to a misdirected Allied fighter-bomber strike.

Richard Gale's principal difficulty, which persisted through the week to come, was that in the centre of his division's northern positions, the village of Bréville was occupied by determined Germans, with fields of fire that empowered them to inflict losses on 6th Airborne and the commandos who reinforced them. Elsewhere, however, the fighting after daybreak on 6 June was less ferocious than on the ensuing days, as German strength built up and their commanders' understanding grew of the importance of the British foothold east of the Orne. It remains extraordinary that, beyond the bomb attack on 6 June by a lone FW190, neither the Luftwaffe nor German artillery seriously addressed destruction of the bridges linking Gale's formation with 3 Div's perimeter.

Accounts of 9 Para's D-Day experience often conclude at the moment of its success at Merville. Pte. Sid Capon and more than a few of his mates had dropped into France under the delusion, shared with their comrades at the bridges, that they 'would only be spending forty-eight hours before the airlift to a hero's welcome back in Blighty with the beer and the birds for the asking'. Now they stood around chatting, laughing, watching German shells landing on the battery behind them, as if they had completed an exercise and were awaiting transport home. Otway sprang to his feet and shouted at an NCO: 'Get those stupid bastards out of it and tell them to take cover!' The commanding officer was respected but not liked by many of his men, yet now they felt sympathy for him in his obvious despondency. Capon said to his mate Eric Bedford: 'Do you know something, Eric? I haven't seen that poor bastard – beg your pardon, I mean my colonel – smile once since we left the Old Country.'

Otway's orders called for him to link up with the rest of 6th Airborne, further south, but many Germans lay between. The wounded who could not walk had to be left in a nearby château. One of them said: 'We didn't feel too happy, then.' The remains of the battalion started to move south-westwards, fighting a brisk action in the hamlet of Hauger. Seeing Germans in strength ahead, Otway led them to the Château d'Amfreville and its surrounding farm buildings. There they deployed and over the next few hours exchanged intermittent fire with the enemy. Dennis Slade, who had become unit adjutant, found a sewing machine with which he hastily stitched up his battledress trousers, torn from crotch to ankle in his landing. A German officer, one of the prisoners from the Merville whom they confined in the château's tennis court, protested fiercely under the incoming fire that it was his captors' duty to keep them safe. Otway dismissed him brusquely. Nonetheless their predicament appeared grim. At 0930 Otway said disconsolately to one of his officers, Paul Greenway: 'Paul, I don't see much point in going on. We might have to surrender eventually.' Greenway said: 'Don't you bloody well do that. Don't you bloody well think of doing it. You're the commanding officer of the 9th battalion and don't you bloody well forget it!'

Later that day the Germans reoccupied the Merville Battery and there were reports of guns firing from it, albeit ineffectually. The outrageous Lovat, some of whose commandos were on their way to relieve 9 Para, wrote: 'Otway's paratroopers up front seemed to have lost the upper hand. I had orders to bail him out

… it seemed the initiative was passing to the enemy … Enemy pressure was suddenly becoming dangerous … I could field no more of Gale's dropped catches.' The reality, down the east bank of the Orne on the afternoon of D-Day, was that Airborne forces lacking mobility and heavy weapons were striving to close up and create defensible positions after the inevitable chaos of the drop. For all Lovat's disdain for Otway's battalion, he and his own green berets performed no D-Day feat remotely comparable with the storming of the Merville Battery. In the weeks that followed, the commandos displayed high courage and determination, but no more than did Gale's men.

Late on 6 June, Otway contrived a few hours' sleep and awoke feeling better. There is little doubt, however, that he suffered some kind of nervous collapse which was understandable thanks to the stresses he had borne and continued to bear. He wrote to his wife Stella a few days later, lamenting the deaths of so many officers whom she had met during the preceding months in Berkshire: 'Peters, that tall chap who came into the "Chequers" at Newbury with his wife – Tom Halliburton, the little Scotsman who helped you decorate the Christmas tree – Mike Dowling, that ugly-looking but pleasant-faced Irishman from the Ulster Rifles who came to the 9th battalion with me, and Eddie Charlton' – the last his second-in-command. Some of the four hundred men who were missing when 9 Para charged the Merville Battery would rejoin in the following days, but many did not. The survivors eventually linked up with 6th Airborne's perimeter, however soon afterwards Otway was caught within yards of an exploding enemy shell, prompting his medical evacuation to England. He was never again fit to serve in action.

* * *

By far the most important development on the east bank of the Orne during the morning of 6 June was the concentration of 21st Panzer Division to launch a full-scale armoured thrust against the scattered units of 6th Airborne. Such an onslaught would likely have spelled the doom of Gale's force. At dawn Seventh Army was thoroughly aware of the scale of the British parachute landings. It then nonetheless reported that there was still no sign of assaults from the sea. At 0700 21 Pz was placed under the orders of LXXXIV Corps, explicitly to address Gale's formation. Although the beach assaults started thirty minutes later, at first nothing was done to shift the axis of 21st Panzer's planned commitment against the paras.

The ninety-nine tanks of the only German armoured formation to be launched against the Anglo-American invaders on D-Day received belated orders to move from their leaguer south of Caen only at 0800. A comedy of confusion followed, which did much service to the British cause and infinite harm to the German one. One panzergrenadier battlegroup under Major Hans von Luck was by then already in action against Gale's troops, as was a grenadier regiment of the 716th Division. The armoured battalions, however, were much delayed and significantly mauled by RAF Typhoon fighter-bomber attacks, which destroyed six panzers and forced the rest to abandon road movement in favour of a slower advance across country, with hundred-metre intervals between tanks. On the way north from Falaise, Werner Kortenhaus looked down on Caen and 'all I could see was a huge black cloud, as though oil had been burnt. At that point I realized for the first time that I was at war.'

Around noon the tanks began to concentrate at Escoville, immediately south of Gale's precarious cluster of forces – it did not then constitute a coherent perimeter. If the German division had gone on to fulfil the purpose decreed by its commander, the chunky little Gen. Edgar Feuchtinger, and assaulted 6th Airborne, it is likely the bridgehead east of the Orne could have been wiped out. Gale had only a handful of anti-tank guns to fight off Mk IV panzers. Moreover, the Germans could assuredly have regained possession of the bridges seized by John Howard, a mere three miles from Escoville.

Instead of this scenario unfolding, however, German orders were changed. The initial perception that 6th Airborne represented the most serious threat was supplanted by a tardy realization that the parachute landings were subordinate to the principal seaborne assault, the outcome of which was supposed by German commanders in Normandy to be still hanging in the balance. At noon Gen. Friedrich Dollmann of Seventh Army deluded himself that the Omaha landing had failed. The Germans, starved of reliable intelligence from the coastal positions, believed there could still be everything to play for, if 21 Pz was thrown into the battle at the decisive point – west of the Orne, against 3 Division.

Thus only one tank company of 22 Panzer Regiment was left on the eastern flank to support Major Hans von Luck's 21 Panzergrenadiers, while most of Feuchtinger's formation was ordered to switch axis, to attack 3 Division's advance from the sea. It quickly became clear that the Allied bombing had wrought such havoc upon Caen that most of the tanks could not move west by the most direct route. One battlegroup bypassed the city on the northern side through Colombelles, while the rest instead made a long detour around its southern outskirts, impeded by debris and French refugees.

This was the worst possible succession of command decisions. If the German armour had been ordered to move at 0445 when von Rundstedt called 12 SS Pz and Panzer Lehr to readiness, or even at 0800, directly north from Falaise against the Sword seaborne landings, the tanks would have crossed a start line for an attack on 3 Div before mid-morning and smashed into the British forces dispersed around the beachhead long before Rennie's tanks and anti-tank guns were deployed to meet them. Even if a perimeter could have been held around Sword, the division would have suffered gravely.

As it was, however, the change of German objective at noon spared Gale's battalions from a blow that might have been as fatal to them as was the panzer counter-attack on 1st Airborne at Arnhem three months later. In the meantime 3 Div escaped attack until late afternoon, when large forces of tanks and anti-tank guns were ashore, and available for deployment against the panzers. Gale's men faced heavy German assaults in the days following the landings, but not on 6 June, when their main opposition came from a ragtag of local units, albeit armed with some heavy weapons such as 6th Airborne still lacked.

The first elements of the 2nd Warwicks arrived at the Caen Canal bridge at 2130 that evening. Montgomery's staff officer David Belchem wrote sourly later: 'Regrettably it was not until towards the end of the day that 3 Division finally relieved 6 Airborne at the Benouville bridge.' Pine-Coffin's 7 Para, which had held its bridgehead for seventeen hours, was allowed a brief respite before moving east to support the defence of Ranville. Its new HQ was just north of the village church, while its companies dug in to the south-east. 'Ranville looked like a ghost village,' according to a paratrooper, 'exactly like the ones we used to practice on back in England.' Richard Todd wrote: 'It was plain we could not expect a restful night. The sounds and flickering lights of battle came from the entire southern and eastern perimeter of the divisional area, some three miles square.' They were mortared constantly. Todd struggled to do his share of the digging, a vital preoccupation of every unit of Gale's division, because he was still much troubled by the skinned hand he had sustained in the drop.

One small achievement that evening was the rescue of 9 Para's wounded from the Merville assault. They had spent a grim, lonely day lying in an empty house, twice very frightened when USAAF bombs fell close to them, shaking plaster off the wall. Once an orderly went to a nearby cottage and asked if he might pick some strawberries for the casualties, some of whom were very hungry. 'A woman was very rude to him and slammed the door in his face. Perhaps she thought we weren't going to stay in France.' At last, around 1700, deliverance came. Their padre, John Gwinnett, had landed far from the battalion's appointed dropping zone and made his way to 5 Brigade's headquarters at Le Mesnil hours after the Merville battle. Determined to rejoin Otway's band, he somehow secured the services of a little Morris pick-up truck, German booty from 1940, together with a driver. They hastened three miles across country, through an area still full of Germans, retrieved three casualties from 9 Para's temporary aid post, and returned them to Le Mesnil. Astoundingly, having completed this journey once, the padre and driver repeated it, recovering among others Captain Hal Hudson, who was expected to die, and 'Twinkletoes' – little Alan Jefferson. On the second journey – by this time in darkness – they almost collided with a German half-track but were checked in the nick of time by French civilians, who shouted a warning. Gwinnett represented a fine example of the best of the invasion army's men of God, and helps to explain why such padres were beloved by their units.

By the evening of D-Day, the Germans' best opportunity for extinguishing 6th Airborne – while its units were still scattered and off balance, lacking heavy weapons and above all cut off from the rest of Crocker's Corps – had passed. It was a slow business, reinforcing the perimeter, getting tanks across the bridges, moving ammunition and heavy weapons eastwards to replace expenditure and stuff lost in the drop. Every unit in the British Airborne perimeter would come under German shellfire for weeks. But once their lifeline to the west was secured, only a major commitment of German forces might have undone Gale's division, and the enemy had too many other priorities to send his most powerful formations against 6th Airborne. The landings, and subsequent weeks of battle, would be written into the history of parachute operations as the most successful British skydrop of the war. At the outset it had been a shambles, though somewhat less so than the landings of the US 82nd and 101st Airborne. But like the Americans in the west, Gale's paratroopers in the east had secured a flank of the Great Invasion, and incidentally sown confusion in the ranks of the enemy, and especially of his highest commanders.

12

'They Were Advancing Very Slowly'

Operation Neptune – the Normandy landings from the sea – had now become Overlord, the struggle for North-West Europe that would continue through dust, mud and blood until May 1945. Lovat's commandos enjoyed the good fortune of being able to march inland from the beach to the Caen Canal while meeting only light opposition, which its eager warriors overcame in quick time. Lovat attributed this success to the speed and tactical skill of their advance, and perhaps he was right. But for many hours after the clan chieftain met John Howard and passed on eastwards, significant pockets of resistance held out in the wake of 1st Special Service Brigade, with important consequences for the British advance towards Caen.

The afternoon of 6 June became, for a few thousand men inland from Sword, one of the most eventful and testing of their lives, crowded with experiences such as no live-fire exercise had prepared them for. Units of 3 Div took hours to overcome German strongpoints, while 1st Norfolks were mauled, merely seeking to bypass them. Because the losses suffered by the infantry in the course of these actions were relatively modest, critics have since deplored the units' sluggishness. To both officers and men at the sharp end, however, most of them newcomers to battle, the difficulties appeared daunting. Moreover, brave men paid with their lives for the limitations of some less bold comrades.

The challenge for every attack is to sustain momentum. To that end, on Sword the D-Day planners committed 8th Infantry Brigade to break the crust of the German defences, accepting that it would thus exhaust – even possibly extinguish – itself. Afterwards, once inland the 185th and 9th brigades would pass through the survivors to take the lead, revitalizing the drive for Caen. By mid-morning, according to Rennie's plan for fulfilling Montgomery's vision, six infantry battalions supported by two armoured regiments – over a hundred tanks – together with at least two self-propelled howitzer units should be advancing towards the city, which the vanguard might approach by early afternoon. Yet the commandos, who had moved as fast as any foot-soldiers could, reached the canal and Orne bridges only at 1300, and these were a mere four miles inland from Sword, whereas Caen was nearer ten. D-Day laid bare a problem that would dog British forces throughout the Normandy campaign – lack of an armoured personnel-carrier such as both the Germans and Americans had, to speed infantry advances.

Following experience of earlier amphibious landings in the Mediterranean, Allied commanders should have been more sensitive to the condition of their men, even those spared an ordeal by fire on the beach: they needed time to regain their landlegs after hours bucketing in landing-craft. Montgomery himself, writing of his preparations as a corps commander to meet an expected German invasion of Britain in 1940, said: 'After a sea crossing, troops would not feel too well and would be suffering from reaction.' The majority of D-Day invaders in 1944, as they waded through the shallows and then stumbled or even tottered up the sand, were shaken and disorientated. They were obliged to fight for the rest of the day weighted by waterlogged battledress and webbing, a depressant even for fit young men. By mid-morning it

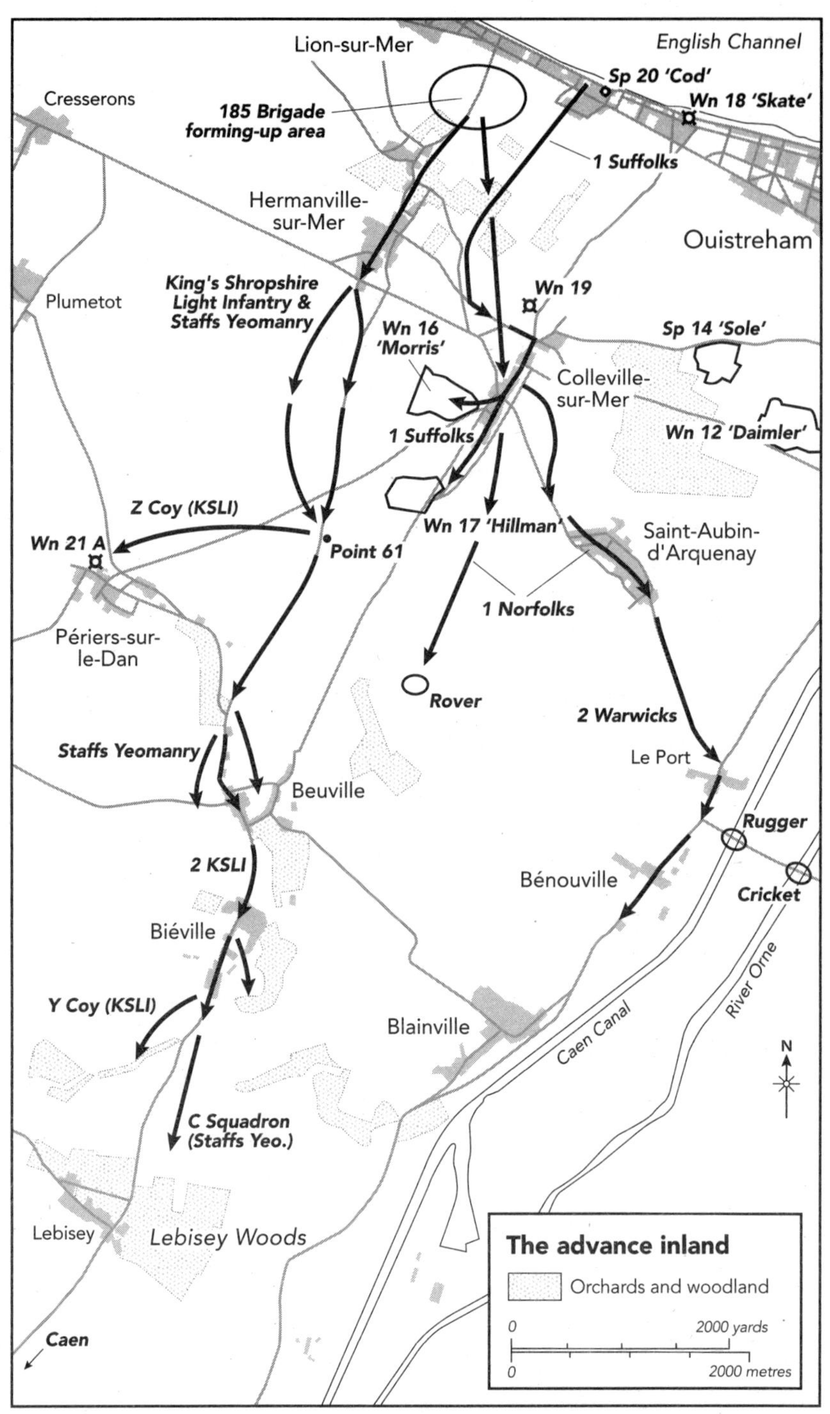

English Channel
Lion-sur-Mer
Sp 20 'Cod'
Wn 18 'Skate'
Cresserons
185 Brigade forming-up area
1 Suffolks
Hermanville-sur-Mer
Ouistreham
King's Shropshire Light Infantry & Staffs Yeomanry
Plumetot
Wn 19
Wn 16 'Morris'
Sp 14 'Sole'
Colleville-sur-Mer
Wn 12 'Daimler'
1 Suffolks
Z Coy (KSLI)
Wn 17 'Hillman'
Saint-Aubin-d'Arquenay
Wn 21 A
Point 61
1 Norfolks
Périers-sur-le-Dan
Rover
2 Warwicks
Staffs Yeomanry
Le Port
Beuville
Rugger
2 KSLI
Bénouville
Cricket
Biéville
River Orne
Y Coy (KSLI)
Caen Canal
Blainville
N
C Squadron (Staffs Yeo.)
Lebisey
Lebisey Woods
Caen
The advance inland
Orchards and woodland
0
2000 yards
0
2000 metres

was plain that every unit was moving inland more slowly than Montgomery's timetable demanded.

The two battalions of 8th Brigade which had landed first, the East Yorks and South Lancs, were well clear of the sea, albeit somewhat depleted. A gunner officer reported: 'We came into action about a hundred yards in front of [an infantry battalion, probably the South Lancs], who were lying in the ditch beside the lateral road [above the coast] and did not seem inclined to move forward. No doubt they had had a nasty time on the beach.' The Brigade war diary reported that the South Lancs 'made satisfactory progress' and were beyond the dunes by 0810. But the battalion had lost its colonel and three of four rifle company commanders. It is not surprising the men were rattled by such a blooding and indeed the unit accomplished little more that day, as they dug in just south of Hermanville, perhaps nettled by the local civilian who shouted to them, '*Vive Les Américains!*' Only their right flank company became thereafter significantly engaged with Germans, in local skirmishes in and south of Lion-sur Mer.

The South Lancs should have had the support of an entire Hussars' squadron, but after the dramas at sea and on the beach only five of its DDs now accompanied that of Major Derrick Wormald, just a week married but scarcely honeymooning in Normandy. Beyond the tanks wrecked by enemy fire, nine stood 'drowned' in the shallows, like that of Patrick Hennessey. The infantry decided that rather than themselves seek to overcome the enemy in Lion, they would await 41 RM Commando, the unit earmarked to clear the western coastal villages and link up with 46 RM Commando, which had landed with the Canadians five miles away on Juno beach.

The brigade's third battalion, 1st Suffolks, reached its assembly point almost unscathed, having come ashore an hour behind the vanguard. It suffered one significant mishap, however: a mortar bomb exploded in the midst of its accompanying naval bombardment observer's party. He himself was killed and almost all his comrades were wounded. For the remainder of the day, the battalion had no access to warship gunfire support. The Suffolks' critical mission, before surrendering the baton to others to lead the advance on Caen, was to clear two German strongpoints a mile or two inland, codenamed Morris and Hillman, each formed of a complex of bunkers and trenches.

The East Yorks were committed to seize two other enemy positions nearer the coast, Sole and Daimler. As they moved south-east, enemy shelling slackened. They halted beside a hedgerow, started to dig in, were ordered to advance again, across a field strewn with dead animals. A woman in a long black skirt, to which a small child clung, made no sign of greeting, merely gazed blankly on their passing. Who could be surprised by the incomprehension of such shockingly blitzed civilians? Meanwhile Pte. Lionel Roebuck's mate Tabby Barker returned from escorting some prisoners towards the rear and expressed guilt that he had handed them over to French commandos. He said he was not sanguine about the PoWs' prospects of longevity.

Their colonel, Charles Hutchinson, sent his pioneers to reconnoitre the road to Colleville, a mile ahead. Nineteen-year-old Wilf Todd found himself being mortared. 'How I wished I was back home!' he later wrote to his wife. 'I kept thinking I would waken up and find it all a bad dream but it was real enough.' The rest of the battalion then advanced, meeting a few German stragglers and occasional snipers, together with Commando walking wounded, heading towards evacuation. As the long files of infantry moved up a sunken lane an exploding mortar bomb fragment wounded their colonel, breaking his arm and forcing his retirement from the field. Through pain, frustration, exasperation, Hutchinson thought he heard a German voice giving fire orders, and directed

Bren-gunners to spray the trees from which the calls seemed to come.

Around noon, under intermittent enemy fire the battalion deployed to assault Sole, situated midway between Ouistreham and Saint-Aubin-d'Arquenay. Tank crews of the Hussars, who played a supporting role, applauded the 'great dash' shown by the East Yorks at this strongpoint known to the Germans as WN14, a chain of three pillboxes protected by wire, behind which was the headquarters of the 1/716th Infantry. Yet, to the bewilderment of the attackers, there was no battle. After the first display of British firepower, a motley array of Ukrainians and Germans surrendered without the East Yorks losing a man. Wilf Todd 'thanked God that he had spared me and quite suddenly I felt tired of everything. I realized what the men must feel like who have been abroad years.'

After a delay of around two hours while prisoners were marshalled and expressions of relief exchanged, the battalion moved on inland towards their main objective, Daimler, still expecting the worst. Men set down their heavy packs and deployed to cross an open field, with self-propelled howitzers firing a twenty-minute barrage in support. They dropped to a crawl as they approached a start line fifty yards short of the German wire, then leaped up and dashed forward covered by the Bren-gunners – or rather, half the company did so. Lionel Roebuck later remarked on the absence without leave of more than a few of his comrades. After later experiences in Normandy, an officer said he learned to be content if he himself, his platoon commanders, sergeants and perhaps half a dozen other men reached the objective at the immediate conclusion of an attack, allowing the rest to trickle forward to join them during the ensuing twenty minutes.

The East Yorks closed in on Daimler around 1700, five hours after their attack on Sole, which lay less than a mile behind them to the west. The length of the interval between the two attacks is puzzling, especially when Sole had fallen so easily. Ahead they saw bunkers covered by machine-guns posted in pillboxes, which opened fire. A steel fragment struck the chest of an officer who, on finding himself shocked but unbloodied, flicked aside the sliver of hot metal and dashed on. Roebuck ran to a pillbox with a primed grenade in his hand, tossed it through the entrance. In the wake of the explosion, he found it to be an unoccupied office, containing only a table and chairs. He smashed a picture of Hitler on the wall and snatched some fountain pens, before emerging again into cloudy sunlight.

The Germans were still firing, and 13 platoon's subaltern, a Rhodesian, dropped wounded; 'he had fallen over on his left side with his back arched up, writhing, straining and twisting to try and ease away from the pain of the wound in his buttock. He said he'd be okay', and told his men to leave him. Roebuck tried to turn an abandoned enemy 20mm gun on the surviving bunker; failed to make it fire; pressed on to the main position, where he saw his mate Micky Riley drop dead. Their company commander ran into the enemy bunker firing a Sten gun, just as his batman dropped a grenade down its ventilation shaft, giving the captain a noisy shock.

From there the position's defenders once again folded remarkably quickly, though the British force was small. Alf Ackroyd said: 'We should have attacked these positions with a company, but as far as I was concerned we were attacking it more or less as a section.' His mate killed one German and two surrendered, 'and as they went back the rest of the platoon came up to us and we carried on and took this giant earthen bunker … We shouted to get people to come out, and eventually we got a white flag on the end of a stick.' There was a brief interruption when some East Yorks fired on the emerging enemy, who bolted back inside. But at last the defenders were persuaded that they might yield and survive. One man fell on his knees pleading not to be shot, 'which was very sort of distressing, in its own way'.

A procession of Germans – or rather, East Europeans in Heer uniforms – surrendered, more than seventy in all. One of them enquired quizzically in English: 'Only a raid, hey?' Every nearby Yorkshireman chorused decisively: 'This is the invasion!' Lionel Roebuck seized a bottle of red wine as his share of booty, and though it tasted extremely nasty, he savoured a draught. By 1800 in the infantry record, 1900 according to the Hussars' war diary, the East Yorks had secured this last of their D-Day objectives, and set about digging in around Saint-Aubin-d'Arquenay. Since dawn the battalion had lost five officers and sixty men killed; four and 137 wounded; three missing and probably dead. This was a stiff price, but the battalion had performed more than its duty, at the tip of the British spear.

Long before the East Yorks cleared Sole, the three battalions of 185th Brigade – Norfolks, Warwicks and Shropshires – came ashore wet though in tolerably good order. The KSLI war diary recorded crossly 'NOT an easy landing'. To its men's chagrin, their private cigarette supply was drowned. Though enemy small arms fire was almost extinguished, armour and vehicles were still moving hesitantly. A sapper officer disembarked with the infantry, then walked up the beach to investigate the traffic jams: 'Things began to move, terribly slowly it seemed to me; occasionally over the din of the shelling I heard the unmistakable "whoomph" of a mine going off and a stretcher passed me with a badly wounded man with his face knocked about ... We drove off the beach in a column that was still bonnet to tail. The movement was very short-lived, for soon there was another inexplicable hold-up.'

A hundred yards inland, a sergeant-major of the Norfolks stepped politely aside onto a verge to allow a Sherman to pass, triggering a schu-mine which removed his foot. Major Humphrey Wilson, exploring the route to the battalion's assembly area a thousand yards ahead, asked a Hussars' tank commander, who appeared to be unemployed, to test the path by leading the way, which the officer obligingly did. Some incoming mortar rounds exploded behind them, but Wilson's recce party reached its destination, a little orchard, without incident, and the battalion followed not long after. Col. Jack Maurice of the Shropshires applauded Lt. Harry Jones's apparent insouciance amid incoming shellfire, when this was his first time in action. He asked the young officer how he avoided ducking when everybody did: 'I replied that I had been a schoolboy in Swansea when the town was savagely blitzed for three days and nights, and I reckoned I knew which of the bombs, and now shells, were meant for me.' Their progress through Hermanville, its main street crowded with enthusiastic French people, was 'almost triumphant'.

By 1100 all three of 185th Brigade's units were mustered inland, 1st Norfolks on the left, 2nd KSLI in the centre, Warwicks on the right. Each time a shell passed over and Norfolks sought cover, a sergeant shouted, 'On your feet – that one landed a mile away!' Their officers waited impatiently to be ordered forward on the dash for Caen. Men's spirits rose as word was passed around that the canal and Orne bridges were secured – up ahead, things seemed to be going right. They felt a small sense of achievement that they had passed over the ground displayed on their initial invasion coastal map. They now replaced this in their mapcases with the second, showing the area further inland.

Montgomery once said: 'A brigadier is the most lonely man in the division. In all other formations there is someone of about his own age whom he can become friendly with, but in a brigade he is probably older and entirely alone.' K.P. Smith's officers were underwhelmed by their brigadier, who had yet to see ground action in the current war. He was forty-five and a desperately troubled man throughout his brief time in Normandy. Gunner officer Robin Dunn wrote scornfully later: 'He [Smith] was haunted by the idea that, if the brigade pushed too boldly inland, 21st Panzer would come round our right flank and cut us off from the beaches.' During 'Leapyear', one of the last big 3 Div exercises before D-Day, Smith sought to counter this threat by diverting his battalions up the left flank, with the result that they lost each other. Tom Rennie, the divisional commander, said reproachfully: 'You won't let this happen on The Day, will you K.P.?' Dunn, a witness to the episode, observed later: '[Rennie] should have sacked him then and there.' As it was, however, on 6 June Smith was still commanding 185th Brigade, now facing the real-time challenge of moving fast towards Caen. Moreover in justice to the brigadier, the threat to the British right flank, with its yawning gap between 3 Div and the Canadians, was far from negligible, and would indeed materialise.

The Shropshires, in the centre, were supposed to advance fast, riding on the tanks of the Staffordshire Yeomanry. These had got ashore in good order at 1030 but subsequently been obliged to linger interminably, awaiting access to a road inland. Clearance of the sands, wrote Norman Scarfe, 'proved to be about the hardest and most heart-breaking job of the invasion'. The war diary of the Staffords described 'a terrible jam on the beach where no organization appeared to be operating and no marked exits were to be seen. The majority of our tanks remained stationary for approximately 1 hour … and even after leaving the beach, vehicles remained head-to-tail for long periods on the only available routes.'

Jim Eadie, the regiment's CO, decided to bypass the agreed assembly area and push straight on to a crossroads south of

Hermanville, to make up some lost time. The afternoon was nonetheless well-advanced before the Staffords were ready to join the battle. Gunner Robin Dunn, who led his own regiment of self-propelled howitzers racing forward, was contemptuous of the Yeomanry's alleged over-caution in refusing to drive outside white-taped mine-swept paths behind the beach, but several tanks which attempted to do so were rewarded with tracks blown off.

Meanwhile the Warwicks began to move south, but found themselves being fired upon by Germans on their right flank, around Lion and Cresserons. Their colonel proposed pivoting to attack these positions, but K.P. Smith hesitated. He inclined to think that his infantry battalions should wait for the tanks to arrive, and anyway avoid collision with the Germans to westwards: the commander of a Beach Group was killed reconnoitring that extremity of Sword. Scarfe wrote: 'Over on this right flank it was early apparent that the enemy was far stronger and more active than he was expected to be.' The coastal defences west of Lion were manned by only around eighty enemy troops, but throughout the day – and especially when they were reinforced by a battery of self-propelled guns – these men showed themselves relatively energetic.

The Royal Marines of 41 Commando trickled piecemeal into Lion-sur-Mer to join the advance, after being disembarked further east than had been intended. There were brief celebrations with the locals in the town square, and only desultory enemy fire – French people said the Germans had evacuated the eastern end of Lion earlier that morning. They found a company of the South Lancs already ensconced: the infantry had halted on meeting fire from strongpoint Trout and from other enemy positions further inland. Clearing Lion had been appointed as 41's job, and few Lancashiremen were ambitious to usurp it. Men settled down to remove boots and don dry socks, clean weapons and brew up.

Around 1020, still lacking several of their officers, the commandos started to probe west towards the Canadians' Juno beach.

They had some tank support. A sapper officer had assumed command of Fred Norris's AVRE, after its commander was killed. He was now ordered to move into Lion-sur-Mer, accompanied by two other engineer tanks. Not far down the beach, however, a 50mm gun mounted in Trout opened fire. Its first shot blew the visor into the face of their Churchill's driver, killing him. A second armour-piercing round entered the tank through the smoke-mortar bin, setting it on fire. They all bailed out. Their new commander was shot as he did so, and Norris was temporarily stunned by the blast of a grenade. The dismounted sapper sheltered against the hull of the wrecked AVRE while the battle continued to rage around him.

A wounded commando sergeant screamed for water and Norris clambered onto a surviving tank to beg a waterbottle. He had descended and was succouring the Marine when this AVRE, too, was knocked out, as was a third engineer tank nearby. Norris dragged the wounded NCO into shelter and armed himself with the man's tommy gun. A few minutes later, he was among a new wave of commandos who overran the enemy position which had done the killing. Norris found himself accepting the surrender of a German officer. He received the Military Medal for his endeavours that morning, and was assigned to join the crew of yet another tank. Norris's story is a fine corrective for those who suppose that engineers merely build bridges. His post-war memoir does not record whether his experiences had any influence upon the stutter which had hampered his earlier army career.

The fighting in Lion-sur-Mer cost a steady stream of casualties as well as tanks. The South Lancs pulled back east after being heavily mortared. Germans were firing from houses on the approaches to Trout, and tank crews that became dismounted suffered grievously. Wirelesses were subject to chronic malfunction, and the commando officers – like most of their infantry counterparts that day – were obliged to send runners to deliver messages, at mortal risk. Shells from a battery of 150mm self-propelled guns advancing north from Cresserons also began to fall on the commando positions in Lion.

A stalemate developed, which in the afternoon seemed liable to be broken to the Germans' advantage: they launched a counter-attack, apparently supported by tanks – in reality, the self-propelled guns. In the event, this advance ran out of steam: the enemy troops were unenthusiastic middle-aged men of 736th Regiment. From offshore the Polish destroyer *Slazak* fired almost a thousand 4.7-inch rounds, in support of 41 Commando. The Marines afterwards said that they could not have held onto their positions in Lion-sur-Mer without the warship's aid.

The commandos and a few South Lancs were left exchanging fire with the enemy, who clung stubbornly to this coastal gap between Sword and Juno. Lord Lovat, characteristically, attributed the rebuff to the feebleness of the Royal Marines, who suffered 140 casualties on 6 June including twenty-six killed. In reality, the British forces on that flank simply lacked weight to overcome relatively strong German defences. Strategically, Trout was unimportant to the 'big picture', since it was not blocking the way to anywhere urgently required by the invaders.

What mattered was the thrust inland, which continued even as the little battle for Lion was taking place. Some three miles to the south-west the Suffolks were conducting painfully protracted battles for their D-Day objectives. The battalion's orders called for its men to clear the village of Colleville; then to consolidate on a ridge to the south, from which they were to assault Morris and Hillman. These were the last important deeply-dug German positions in the Sword sector. Once beyond them, the invaders would chiefly be called upon to engage mobile forces, 21st Panzer

Division foremost among them. The Suffolks arrived from the beach at their assembly area expecting trees to provide some cover. Instead they found the woodland felled, the ground barren and exposed. They moved on, in the nick of time. Mortaring started: their advance had been observed by German eyes. A Hussars' officer appeared, to report that a squadron was on its way to support the infantry but had been delayed by the traffic chaos in the rear. Meanwhile a captain of the Suffolks was dispatched south-eastwards to establish communication with Gale's paratroopers. Harry Elliott eventually returned, weary and not a little shaken, having fulfilled his mission only after a nine-mile round-trip across Norman countryside, much of it still disputed. He described his experience as 'rather like walking across the front of the butts at Bisley [ranges] during a rapid fire practice'.

The Suffolks prepared for their assaults on the German strongpoints in the usual fashion, telling off a party of officers and specialists as LOBs – 'left out of battle' men, spared so that they would be available to take over key duties if those participating in the assault were killed. They met five Canadian paratroopers who had been dropped in the wrong place, then bombed by the Americans. The Canadians wanted to fight, and joined D Company. They all set off in long files, choosing a route through fields where cattle were grazing and thus where there were obviously no mines.

Information reaching senior officers about the several simultaneous battles taking place behind Sword was patchy and often inaccurate. Around 1200 K.P. Smith was told that Colleville was being cleared without much trouble – the commandos had already marched that way and disposed of such enemy as they met on their passage. C Company of the Suffolks nonetheless conducted its own systematic advance through the village's hundred-odd dwellings, supported by a squadron of the Hussars, to ensure no enemy remained. This was completed with the loss of a signaller who fell to a single lonely shot, its firer never located. The Suffolks relieved the commandos of some prisoners, who turned out to be Polish. Major Boycott met the mayor, M. Lenaud, who proffered Calvados and information. A trooper of the Hussars, far from observing local rejoicing, noted 'the bewildered and haunted expressions of the few inhabitants left in the village'.

Col. Dick Goodwin greeted Lord Lovat, 'looking as if he was out for a country walk'. The colonel was surprised by the bravado of Lovat's men, wearing their green berets under fire. Lovat described steel helmets contemptuously as 'useless impedimenta of a bygone age'. He was wrong. On raids berets made sense, because helmets were clumsy and attackers were unlikely to face artillery or mortars. On a big battlefield, however, steel headgear offered some precious protection against steel fragments, and 1st SS Brigade's braggadocio gesture on D-Day cost some lives.

K.P. Smith of 185th Brigade kept his unit colonels waiting at their agreed rendezvous before he arrived after noon to issue new orders. That day some men who used personal initiative were killed for their pains, but others prospered. Notable among the latter were the men and self-propelled guns of the brigade's supporting gunners, 7th Field Regiment, which roared past Hermanville crossroads, having bypassed the beach traffic jams by ignoring German signs warning of minefields, and likewise British engineers' white tapes reinforced by a furious sapper officer who scolded the gunners for acting irresponsibly. The 7th's 105mm howitzers deployed just south of the village, and at noon their CO Nigel Tapp told Smith he had everything ready to support his brigade's advance up the British right flank. The brigadier remained uneasy, however. He had heard reports that enemy tanks were manoeuvring in front of Caen, and that the Canadians on Juno were having a bad time.

On his own initiative he now switched his brigade's main axis of advance to the left. When Robin Dunn heard that Smith intended to send the rest of his force – the Warwicks and Norfolks – up the eastern route, the impatient gunner officer, a veteran of North Africa, muttered, 'Oh God! This is exercise Leapyear over again!' Tom Rennie had rebuked Smith for doing the same thing on the Scottish exercise area, precipitating dispersal of the brigade. Dunn ever afterwards blamed Smith – and also Rennie, who allegedly failed to grip the situation – for the manner in which the advance towards Caen petered out that afternoon. At a moment when there were still eight hours of daylight left, he heard the brigadier instruct Hugh Bellamy, CO of the Norfolks, to make 'Rover', the battalion's concentration point five miles short of Caen, its final objective for the day. In the event, the leading Norfolks reached 'Rover' at 1700, but were not fully consolidated on the position, with a gunner FOO on site, until two hours later.

Smith held back the Shropshires at Hermanville for an hour, waiting for the Staffordshires' tanks. The men, bemused by the long hangabout, brewed up and exchanged jokes 'about the clean sheets we'd get in Caen that night'. At 1130 Jack Maurice, their CO, borrowed a bicycle to ride back to the beach, where he discovered the Yeomanry stuck in a jam; going nowhere in a hurry. On returning to Hermanville and reporting to the brigadier, he was belatedly ordered to start his battalion marching towards Caen via Beuville, some three miles ahead, and west of the Germans manning the Hillman strongpoint: hopefully the Staffordshires would soon catch them up. Maurice was not much dismayed that his men were to be denied a ride on the tanks. From the moment the idea was mooted, he anticipated that such a tactic could prove suicidal if the advance met enemy automatic weapons, as it inevitably did.

When the Shropshires set forth at 1230, an hour behind the divisional timetable, they were initially fortunate. Though they came under fire from pockets of Germans, they suffered few casualties. Pte. Bill Hollyhead, a wireless-operator accompanying W Company commander Guy Thornycroft, placed his own feet carefully in the footprints of his officer's size twelve boots, in hopes of thus diminishing the chances of stepping on a mine. This was a green battalion, however. On hearing enemy fire directed towards them for the first time, the men threw themselves to the ground. Corporal Bob Littlar said, 'I was so scared I got down on my hands and knees, and then onto my stomach.' Robert Rylands admitted: 'The company was a little uneasy, halted uncertainly on this straight road.'

Jack Maurice was unimpressed by his men's conduct. He was thirty-nine, a doctor's son educated at Marlborough, a bachelor who served briefly in France in 1939–40, and suffered chronic poor health which did nothing to diminish his courage. That afternoon he merely continued to march up the road, fingering the chinstrap of his helmet in a characteristic gesture, and apparently indifferent to the enemy's bullets. His example shamed his men into rising from cover and pressing on. They decided, according to an officer eyewitness: 'Well – if he's all right I suppose I shall be too.' Lt. Harry Jones saw German infantry in the distance ahead, hastily boarding lorries to pull back. He snatched a Bren gun from one of his platoon and sprayed fire liberally in the enemy's direction.

They began to take casualties from sporadic shell and machine-gun fire, the latter from enemy hidden in the standing corn. The files of infantrymen now spread themselves out in line abreast, 'advancing rather like a row of beaters through the crops', taking occasional prisoners. The leading tanks of the Staffordshire Yeomanry caught up. Their war diary recorded: 'The CO [Eadie] appreciated that the ridge in the vicinity of Pt. 61' – Périers – 'was vital to us and ordered C Squadron to seize it forthwith. They galloped for it and shortly after reported it clear of the enemy.' Then the advance started to be shelled from a German position just beyond the ridge.

An infantryman elsewhere wrote of the impact on a soldier's imagination of facing an incoming barrage while making an attack: 'I could feel the exact spot in the small of my defenceless back … where the pointed nose of the shell would pierce skin and gristle and bone and explode the charge that would make me feel as if I had a splitting headache all over for a fiftieth of a second before I was spread minutely over the earth and hung up in trees. I held my breath and tried to press deeper into the earth and tensed every muscle as though by sheer willpower I could abate the force of that disintegrating shock, cheat death, defy God (O God have mercy on me please, please, *please* dear God, don't let me die).'

Out on the Shropshires' right flank, Shermans of the Staffords' B Squadron, commanded by Major George Turner, experienced brutal shocks from the impact of armour-piercing shells, such as would be reprised again and again until the last day of the war: metal melted, fuel ignited, then as a tank commander observed, 'silver rivulets of molten aluminium pour from the engine like tears'. Blazing rubber generated black smoke. Survivors in the hulls, if still capable of movement, knew they had at best ten seconds in which to escape incineration. On D-Day they began to learn why panzer crews dubbed the Sherman 'the Tommy-cooker'. In Normandy a British or American tank was knocked out in return for an average expenditure of just 1.6 enemy shells, while a German Panther needed to be hit with 2.55 rounds, a Tiger with 4.2.

The colonels of the Shropshires and Staffords agreed the German battery firing on them from the west – 122mms sited just north of the hamlet of Périers-sur-le-Dan – must be silenced, which meant overrun by infantry. The battalion's war diary observed that the battery was 'holding up the tanks and dominating our main axis'. At 1425 Jack Maurice detached Peter Wheelock's Z Company from its line of march to attack these guns, which were booty captured from the Russians, now manned by East Europeans under German officers and NCOs.

Wheelock was reckoned an army high-flier, courageous and clever. For the rest of the day he and his men fought a lonely private battle, with the Staffordshires' B Squadron in support. In this painfully protracted action, every time British shells drove the enemy gunners away from their weapons, they returned as soon as fire abated. Major Wheelock's first infantry attack got under way at 1600, but amid the rattle of small arms from enemies well protected by wire and trenches, it made slow progress: for long periods the company was pinned down. The assault on the battery caused the Shropshires' rifle strength for the advance on Caen to be diminished by a quarter – a serious loss – but Col. Maurice's view was that the German guns could not be left to fire at will on other units moving up behind them.

Further east, Hillman overlooked the cornfields through which the Norfolks were now intended to advance. K.P. Smith at first told this battalion to wait outside Colleville until the Suffolks had fulfilled their own appointed task, that of suppressing the enemy guns shooting from Hillman. The narrow streets of the village, and orchards beyond, were soon crowded with vehicles and infantrymen of several units, mingling with civilians eager to celebrate. Moreover just to the west of Colleville stood strongpoint Morris with its four 105mm guns, like so much other German artillery in Normandy made by Czechs at Skoda in 1916, and now emplaced in bunkers.

Morris came before Hillman. The function of such German bastions, constructed with enormous expenditure of concrete and

French labour, was to disrupt the invaders' advance; buy time for the panzer counter-attack which was to sweep the British back into the sea. The air and naval bombardments had made almost no impact on the bunkers. The USAAF had been scheduled to strike both positions that morning, but the Hillman aircraft aborted when it became clear they would be obliged to bomb from 15,000 feet through heavy cloud, guided only by radar aiming-devices. Six Flying Fortresses bombed Morris, merely detonating a few mines. It remained to be seen if this racket had sapped the spirit of their defenders.

B Company made its preparations to storm the battery while Nigel Tapp's howitzers registered targets. Major Philip Papillon of D Company, scanning the position through binoculars, told his colonel, Dick Goodwin, that he could see nothing moving: the Germans within the defences were not firing. Goodwin ordered the attack to start, but to be wary lest some unpleasant enemy surprise was waiting. The major had crawled forward and was lying prone, pushing five-foot lengths of Bangalore torpedo under the German wire, when a white flag appeared on the strongpoint. Soldiers emerged, their hands in the air, to be received by bewildered Suffolks. Sixty-seven enemy defenders surrendered and were escorted to the rear by four infantrymen, delighted by their own salvation, having anticipated that the attack on Morris would probably be the end of them. Soon German fire from the south-east began to descend on the captured position, but this did no harm to the Suffolks, who took shelter in the abandoned enemy bunkers.

Then it was time for Hillman, a thousand yards further south and uphill, regimental headquarters of the 736th Grenadier Regiment. Here were twenty concrete bunkers with mechanical ventilation, dug deep into Norman soil, linked by trenches and covered by seven machine-gun posts, protected by a double-wired and mined perimeter extending six hundred yards by four hundred, sited on rising ground, approached up a narrow, deeply embanked and wooded track from Colleville. Its commander, Col. Ludwig Krug, was an Austrian-born engineer who came from a dynasty of soldiers. His son Hans was serving with the Wehrmacht in Italy.

Krug was not a man to be cowed by enemy artillery barrages: he had served in World War I. Since first light he had enjoyed a grandstand view of the entire coast below and the crowded sea beyond, together with clear fields of fire for his own guns for six hundred yards in all directions. The colonel was in no doubt that this was *Der Tag* for the Allies, and that he and his men would play a pivotal role in deciding its outcome in their sector. He was in phone communication with 716th Division headquarters in Caen, and had been told of the importance of holding out. Krug was disgusted by the abrupt surrender of Morris and determined the 170 men now manning Hillman, including at least one company of East Europeans or former PoWs, together with stragglers from other positions, should do better.

Before the colonel retired into the deep bunker from which he would direct the defence, he watched the files of British infantry approaching from the beach; a few tanks in the distance, surging and plunging across his front. Hillman boasted heavy steel cupolas protruding three feet above the ground, some of them transported from the old 1940 French Maginot defensive line. The machine-guns mounted within their embrasures could harrow attackers while the men manning them were almost impervious to British infantry weapons unless a shot penetrated the narrow firing slits. Whatever might be the doubts of the defenders about their prospects of long lives, for the here and now they were directed by a determined professional, and could claw infantry seeking to approach or bypass their positions.

The Suffolks advancing towards Hillman came under German fire straight away, taking casualties – seven members of one platoon were wounded by a single shell. They met a Canadian paratroop officer with a sergeant who had broken his arm in the overnight drop. These two led Col. Goodwin to a point where he could see the enemy bunkers 150 yards distant, across a field of standing green corn. Goodwin ordered half his men to deliver the assault, with two platoons covering their flank. B Company, fresh from accepting the surrender of Morris, was held in reserve. Major Geoff Ryley, a former Liverpool schoolmaster now commanding A Company, crept forward to reconnoitre for the attack, a protracted process.

The Suffolks' mortars were deployed. An officer of 76 Field Regiment set about registering his guns on the German positions, amid worsening wireless communications: with so many British sets operating in a few square miles of France, nets were becoming confused. Moreover, while 105mm howitzers were immensely useful for laying smoke and keeping down the heads of German troops in open positions, they could make no impact on enemies inside concrete bunkers.

It was now early afternoon. The timetable for pushing towards Caen was slipping ever further behind. If Montgomery had witnessed the little drama unfolding beyond Colleville, he would have fumed that the Suffolks' preparations, as measured as if they were conducting an exercise at home, were eating into the precious diminishing daylight for 3rd Division to reach its objectives. At 1310, shortly after the commandos on their left reached the Caen Canal bridge, Col. Goodwin issued the radio codeword 'Grab', for the artillery and mortars to start their bombardment, delivering high explosives for five minutes followed by smoke for a further three. A breaching platoon crept up a sunken track to the outer wire of Hillman, then pushed forward the Bangalores that had proved happily unneeded at Morris, their jointed sections reaching fifteen feet under the entanglements. The explosions blew a path through which Lt. Mike Russell led a party to the inner wire. Here he placed more Bangalores but when he twisted their igniter, nothing happened. He was obliged to crawl back a hundred yards to secure a second igniter; creep forward again; then successfully blow a gap. Thereafter he found himself fifty

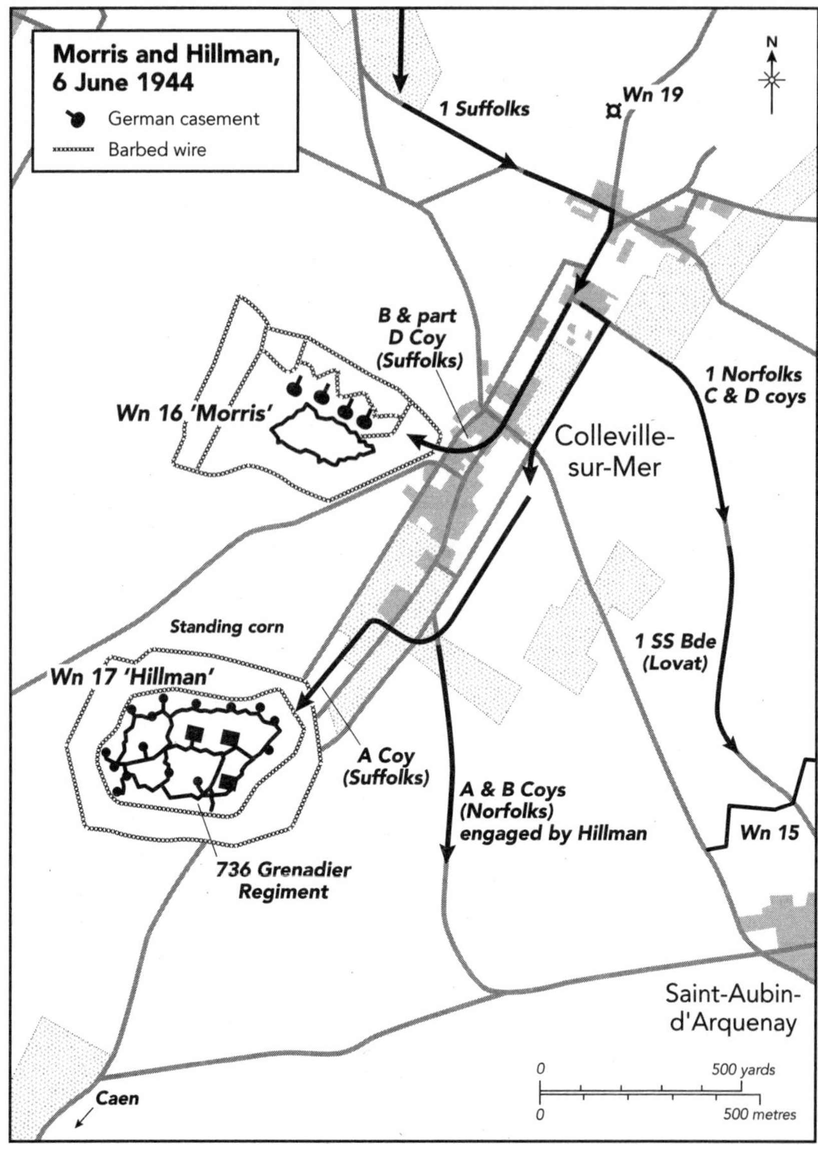

yards short of the nearest enemy cupola, from which machine-gun fire began to sweep the approaches.

This was to be no Morris walkover. The defenders of Hillman were led by committed officers who knew they held strong positions. Russell's piercing of the German wire had been painfully protracted, as now was the British infantry advance. The leading platoon of A Company, led by Lt. Sandy Powell, crawled through the gaps in the entanglements under intense fire from the cupola, which killed Corporal Jones. Powell called forward his platoon anti-tank weapon, the crude British PIAT which was far inferior to its German counterpart, the Panzerfaust. Its projectile was propelled by a heavy spring. The firer laid a bomb on its loading tray, pressed his trigger and – given luck and iron nerve to expose himself to fire and aim carefully and skilfully – catapulted the charge up to fifty yards, with a fair chance of disabling a tank. But concrete and heavy steel were almost impervious to such a weapon. The first bomb failed to dent the German cupola, or silence its gun. The PIAT firer recocked his spring and reloaded, a strenuous and cumbersome process; then fired again, with the same result. Displaying extraordinary persistence, himself still being shot at, the firer did the same a third time – with no more success.

The lieutenant now dispatched a man to the rear to report that his platoon was stuck. The runner was shot down. A second was sent, who reached Geoff Ryley, A Company's commander. The British guns and mortars unleashed more smoke and high explosives to shield the advance of another platoon, this time led by Ryley himself. When a German machine-gun again opened fire, only four men continued to move forward – Ryley, two of his subalterns Powell and Trevor Tooley, together with Corporal Stares. A well-meaning Pioneer urged the company commander: 'Keep your arse down, sir!'

In this, their first battle, an impressive number of British officers showed themselves willing, and even eager, to set an example to their men. A company commander in another unit of 3 Div said of that day: 'The atmosphere ... should be appreciated. Troops were immensely fit, morale was terrific ... but for nearly all it was their first time in battle apart from a few who had been at Dunkirk. There was a desire to "Seek Glory" ... There was the doctrine of "getting on", "taking risks" and "staking a claim". There was real determination to succeed or die in the attempt. The atmosphere was heroic.'

In Normandy, wrote a young platoon commander, 'I began to appreciate how vital is grip – grip on oneself, grip on one's soldiers and grip on the situation ... Most men react nervously to real battle conditions. Discipline and regimental pride are supports but, in decisive moments of great danger, the grip of the leader on the led is paramount ... If you do not dominate events, your enemy will.' In the Suffolks' advance on Hillman, several officers and NCOs displayed notable courage. This was matched by a few of their men, of whom more below. But much of A Company stuck. Some of the Suffolks were 'old sweats' – long servicemen who had not seen action since 1940, if at all. It seems a fair surmise that, after surviving so long in the King's uniform, such men flinched from accepting suicidal risks, such as their officers appeared willing to take. The Suffolks' other ranks on 6 June did not accept heavy casualties. Their leaders suffered severely, however, as they attempted to overcome the enemy, with embarrassingly little support.

From deep inside Hillman, one of the Germans watched them through a periscope. 'They were advancing very slowly,' said Hans Sauer, 'very cautiously. One advances, stops, waits. Another advances. They seemed extremely cautious, looking everywhere before moving forwards as much as a metre.' Major Ryley and his three companions penetrated 150 yards into the German perimeter, and even took some prisoners – a significant achievement – but the attackers were too few to make a decisive breakthrough. Powell crawled back to the wire, and it is not hard to imagine the scene, as he sought to induce the rest of A Company to follow him forward. Eventually, however, he was obliged to scramble once more into Hillman followed only by Sgt. Lankester and two men. When they reached the place where the lieutenant had left the others, they found Tooley and Stares mortally wounded, Ryley dead, the latter leaving a widow and two small children. Powell and his men retired through the wire. He himself was awarded a Military Cross for his fine effort at Hillman, but was killed before he could receive it. At 1500 3 Div's war diary recorded, with surprising complacency: 'The battle continued as planned.' Yet at precisely that time, failure of the Suffolks' initial assault on Hillman was reported.

The little battle merits attention because it represented a key episode in the British Army's D-Day struggle. Montgomery had demanded speed, speed, speed in making the advance inland, yet every stage of the Hillman attack unfolded at a crawl – often literally. It is plausible that had the men of the Suffolks been willing to follow their notably courageous officers in a sacrificial advance, Hillman could have been taken relatively quickly. The only realistic means of quickly overrunning the position was for a body of attackers to charge it head on, swamping the enemy's fire and accepting casualties in the fashion of 9 Para at the Merville Battery. It is an interesting speculation what might have transpired had at least one of Lovat's Commandos been diverted to take Hillman, obviously a formidable threat. They were shock troops, unafraid of losses. It is highly likely that a quick, fierce assault could have succeeded – but at brutal cost in casualties. It is a matter of opinion whether such a price would have been worth paying to accelerate the advance on Caen, though surely not to make it possible to secure the city on 6 June. But the Suffolks were not prepared to adopt such almost suicidal tactics. It will be argued below that critics like Chester Wilmot were mistaken to claim that this failure adversely affected the subsequent course of the entire Normandy campaign. But we do know that, by mid-afternoon, senior officers clustering in Colleville, and indeed those of the Suffolks, were dismayed and frustrated by what had happened, or not happened, thus far.

Col. Goodwin watched the debacle unfold and decided that only tanks could break the stalemate. C Squadron of the 13th/18th Hussars was now at hand, but a witness of many armoured assaults wrote wryly: 'Tanks do not rush forward … They advance hesitatingly, like diffident fat boys coming across the floor at a party to ask for the next dance, stopping at the slightest excuse, going back, then coming on again, and always apparently seeking the longest way round. When they do have to cross a plain they postpone the evil moment as long as possible … When they follow a road, they zigzag in a series of tangents. They are timid creatures.' Tank crews seldom fired their guns while on the move, and even more rarely hit a target when they did so.

One of the Hussars' Sherman Fireflies, armed with a heavy 17-pdr gun, advanced to the German outer wire and fired at the cupola from which a machine-gun had achieved such devastation – again, without effect. Then an entire troop of tanks attempted to advance up the left flank, across the open cornfields between Hillman and Saint-Aubin-d'Arquenay, only to lose two of their number to fire from the strongpoint. One, though crippled, was able to pull back to safety. Its driver was 'badly smashed up', according to a comrade, and the co-driver Cpl. Pickles took over. With the intercom out of action the Sherman's commander, Sgt. Haygarth, bravely clambered from his turret and lay prostrate behind it, shouting instructions down the driver's hatch. Thus they successfully retreated three hundred yards under fire, until back in cover. The Sherman carrying the forward observer of 76 Field Regiment was also hit, so that wireless communication with his gunners was lost.

Col. Goodwin ordered Captain Perry, who had taken over A Company from the dead Ryley, to pull back his men while the artillery delivered another concentration on Hillman. At 1615, more than three hours after the first attack started and an hour after its failure was recognized, the colonel also instructed engineer Lt. Arthur Heal to clear enough mines in the path of the attackers to enable tanks to get through. Heal urged calling for flails, but this was bound to take many minutes if not hours. The sapper himself probed forward, uncertainly protected by smoke laid by grenade-throwing riflemen. He found four rows of British-made mines – obviously booty from 1940 – set at five-yard intervals. He began to blast a path through them, detonating a succession of charges under covering fire from Mike Russell. This process took a further hour, during which the infantry remained inert.

It is hard to overstate the confusion by now prevailing a mile northwards in the main street of Colleville, where senior officers conferred among columns of halted tanks and vehicles, while infantry lay and squatted wherever they could find resting places. Two companies of the Norfolks were scattered in the surrounding orchards and gardens, waiting for Hillman to be silenced so that they could continue to advance. Another battalion, 2 Warwicks, was close behind. Smith ordered them, also, to stay put until the situation in Saint-Aubin-d'Arquenay was clarified.

Even after years of training, it could be hard for men to reconcile themselves to the brutal imperatives of battle. One 27th Brigade officer found his Sherman confronted by a high wall and wasted precious minutes manoeuvring to get around it. He said later: 'With hindsight I realise we should have gone up to the wall and pushed it over, but we had never had much built-up area training nor guessed we could use our tanks in such a way.' They would soon accustom themselves to unleashing casual destruction, but not on their first day in action.

Although Hillman still held out, it was finally decided the Norfolks must start moving south anyway, bypassing the German position. They were told not to get involved in the Suffolks' battle; instead to hasten on towards Caen. Had the Norfolks or K.P. Smith known it, they could have avoided exposing themselves to fire from Hillman, by bearing a little further east, through the village of Saint-Aubin-d'Arquenay. But somebody told them – wrongly – that it was still held by the enemy; there were even rumours the Germans had regained control of the canal and river bridges beyond. Thus the Norfolks' two leading companies adopted a course across country within easy range of Hillman's automatic weapons. Moving off very late, at 1500, within a quarter of a mile they began to face fire.

When the first men fell, the rest sought cover, and spent the ensuing two and a half hours making painfully slow progress. One described seeing a company cook behind him fall dead with a bullet in the neck: 'That was the day I first saw the red poppies of France in the cornfields ... My nose was stuck right among them. They reminded me of the hell and horrors of the 1914 war which my father had talked about so often.' Col. Hugh Bellamy's personal liaison officer dashed away in a little Weasel tracked vehicle to report to K.P. Smith that the Norfolks had run into trouble: 'News filtered in ... none of it very good.' Bellamy ordered his two follow-up companies to adopt a more circuitous route south, which they did, without encountering opposition.

The two leading companies stayed stuck, however. Geoff Duncan said: 'Crawling through the corn on one's belly with all the gear we were carrying was a punishing experience, the sweat poured down my face and I thought to myself, what the hell am I doing here? Why hadn't I joined the Royal Artillery like my elder brother? I was dirty, hungry and tired to the point of exhaustion. It seemed like an eternity before the supporting armour arrived. I was mightily glad to see the last of that field, but several brave lads were lying still and silent in that wavering sea of corn.' Duncan was shocked by the evidence of carnage they encountered – knocked-out vehicles, dead Germans and Suffolks. He was horrified by one corpse which a tank had run over, but 'it was unbelievable how quickly one gets hardened to the sight of death and accepted it with very little emotion except when it was one of your own particular friends'.

Norfolks medic L/Cpl. Ted Seaman said afterwards: 'We had a hell of a baptism … we had so many wounded and killed I was the only stretcher-bearer left.' This was an exaggeration, but of his mates in A Company, one was killed and two badly wounded. Seaman especially recalled one man stumbling back despite his own leg being broken, leaning on the shoulder of another casualty. The Norfolks were ordered to concentrate for the night at a wooded position codenamed Rover, on a slight rise between Beuville and the Orne, a mile south of Hillman. They reached it that evening to find a lonely farm which they later dubbed Norfolk House, because it played a prominent part in the battalion's fortunes during the days which followed.

On 6 June, the Norfolks lost twenty-one dead or fatally injured, with wounded in proportion. This was a modest toll in the grand scheme of the war, but a shocking one for novices, and a heavier 'butcher's bill' than the Suffolks incurred while directly assaulting Hillman. At 1700 Gen. Rennie appeared at Smith's headquarters in

Colleville, where he was exasperated to hear that the Warwicks were still in the orchards outside the village, waiting for the Hillman battle to end. The general told Smith to get them moving immediately, through Saint-Aubin-d'Arquenay. The brigadier protested that it was still in German hands. Nonsense, said Rennie. He himself had just driven through it in a jeep. The Warwicks were then launched on their final move of the day, to relieve 7 Para protecting the bridge link with 6th Airborne. Rennie told Goodwin of the Suffolks that Hillman must – absolutely must – be taken by nightfall, because of the near-certainty of a German counter-attack in the morning. Goodwin promised he would achieve this.

The commander of 8 Brigade, Edward 'Copper' Cass, now also arrived. Chester Wilmot later wrote scornfully: 'Some time was lost while the brigade commander was deciding what to do.' Goodwin asked Cass to summon flails. These arrived, however only after Arthur Heal had already blasted a tank path. Major Charles Boycott, commanding the Suffolks' C Company which had performed the formal clearance of Colleville after the commandos passed through it, never forgot the chaos of men and vehicles now in the village: 'Everybody cursed us: "Why the hell don't you get on with it?" My CO had a lot of hard things said about him. It was quite wrong.'

A criticism made of the battle schools which most officers and men had attended before D-Day was that they promoted deference to timed artillery programmes; prevented junior leaders from spontaneously exploiting opportunities. Only 1 per cent of shells of all nationalities landed in an enemy entrenchment. Thus it was never realistic to hope that supporting artillery fire would destroy dug-in defenders – it could aspire only temporarily to stun them and dull their reactions. Many attacking British infantry battalions on 6 June and thereafter lingered for ten, fifteen minutes after their own bombardment stopped, before rising from their start lines to advance against a strongpoint. This was fatal, because it gave defenders time to emerge from bunkers and dugouts and man weapons to receive them.

A subaltern wrote: 'No solo parts were written into the score, nor was there scope for small groups of performers in this mammoth ballet of machines ... I do not underestimate the influence that the Somme had on the British military psyche. Far too much time had been spent fitting the infantry and armoured junior leaders into the "big picture" and too little had been spent training them and stimulating their imagination, initiative and individual resourcefulness to probe, draw conclusions, infiltrate and exploit weakness in the enemy's dispositions.' Brigadier Smith requested more tank support for the Hillman assault, and the Staffordshires' Jim Eadie complied by dispatching his B Squadron. Alastair Spencer-Nairn, its commander, was reporting to Goodwin and preparing to support the Suffolks' next attack when word came over the radio: 21st Panzer Division was advancing from the south, threatening the British western flank. Every tank of the Staffordshires was immediately needed to stop them. The regiment was ordered to forgo any role in the Hillman attack and instead deploy against the advancing German armour. Smith lost his armoured reinforcement.

Many men discovered that day what no amount of training had prepared them for: the physical demands of infantry action were enormous – moving far and fast while carrying heavy burdens, keeping going with scant rest, reacting instantly to unexpected peril. Those over thirty, and progressively more so with the years, struggled to keep up, as indeed did colonels of that age. Some older soldiers possessed an emotional maturity absent from teenagers in uniform, but comrades often nicknamed them 'uncle' or 'grandad'. The mid-twenties was probably the best age for an infantryman.

At early evening the Suffolks were still preparing for the next assault on Hillman. Their colonel, Dick Goodwin, called in yet another five-minute bombardment before the attack, then the Hussars' tanks advanced up the minefield path cleared by Arthur Heal. Abruptly, however, the lead tank stopped. The nearest infantry section commander, Corporal Bob Lawson, demanded to be told why. The Sherman driver responded that he could not advance over a dead British soldier. A farcical and furious exchange followed, under German fire, before the infantry pressed on, dodging from shell hole to shell hole as a machine-gun continued to fire from the cupola that had thwarted the battalion all day. Lawson and a private named James 'Tich' Hunter were within twenty yards of it when a German soldier emerged from a nearby trench with his hands up, and was unsurprisingly shot. Then Hunter, with the sort of manic courage which men occasionally display in desperate situations, stood up and walked steadily towards the cupola, firing his heavy Bren gun from the hip. Lawson glimpsed a German rifle raised, from which a bullet grazed Hunter. He nonetheless reached the cupola and its surrounding trenches, to find them now occupied only by the dead of both sides.

Lawson and Hunter pushed grenades down the ventilation shaft of the nearest bunker and after the explosions were rewarded by a succession of Germans emerging to surrender, a feat for which Hunter later received a DCM. The Hussars' tanks rolled forward, crushing the German wire entanglements. Clouds of black smoke eddied from a cache of blazing petrol cans beside a bunker. From the Sherman turrets commanders tossed down grenades upon fleeing defenders. A Hussar gazed in revulsion at a German corpse draped grotesquely over the barrel of a wrecked anti-tank gun. The squadron commander, an Anglo-Irish baronet named Sir Delaval Cotter, had served as a horsed cavalry officer in

India before the war, and had hitherto not left England since Dunkirk. Now his tank crashed into an unseen pit, throwing a track. The baronet, it emerged, had plunged into the German officers' latrine.

Infantrymen occupied most of Hillman's trenches. As the light began to fail, some bunkers remained in German hands, but enemy fire had become muted. The Suffolks withdrew from the perimeter overnight, which was fortunate, because only minutes after they pulled back, the defenders called in renewed mortar and artillery fire. At dusk Goodwin's D Company achieved a small success when its sergeant-major spotted movement at a farm named Beauvais, 250 yards to the south. A platoon advanced cautiously, on the way disposing of two snipers encountered in a cornfield. As they approached Beauvais, Germans emerged with their hands up, two officers and forty-eight men – by no means all the defenders of Normandy that day were as determined as those manning Hillman. Company commander Philip Papillon then ordered the platoon to pull back, herding the prisoners in front of them, just before the Germans began to mortar Beauvais.

At midnight Colonel Krug, the officer commanding Hillman, telephoned Gen. Wilhelm Richter in Caen to report, with some slight but understandable exaggeration: 'The enemy is on top of my bunker. I have no means of resisting them and no means of communicating with them. What shall I do?' His divisional commander said: 'I can give you no more orders. You must make your own decision now … Goodbye.' When the British again warily approached Hillman at first light on 7 June, they were greeted with silence from its firing positions, then at 0645 were bemused by the sudden appearance of Krug himself from beneath the earth, offering surrender – nobody had hitherto pinpointed the German command bunker. He was accompanied by two other officers and seventy men. There was some surprise that the colonel himself chose to carry two suitcases, rather than permit others to do such heavy lifting. Krug's batman later confided to his captors their commander chose to be visibly laden, so that he would not be obliged to suffer the indignity of putting up his hands. In captivity, Col. Krug was much troubled about whether he had done his duty as a soldier before surrendering, saying to a fellow officer and overheard by British eavesdroppers: 'I wonder whether I shall be blamed for that – whether they will say that I should have fought to the death. [Our orders state] everyone who surrenders a strongpoint will be sentenced to death.' Krug was spared such a fate by ultimate German defeat.

On 6 June the Suffolks had lost seven men killed and twenty-five wounded, with some further casualties among their supporting engineers and tank crews. This was such a relatively small toll that critics unleashed considerable abuse on the battalion. The Australian war correspondent Chester Wilmot, in his later epic history of the campaign *The Struggle for Europe*, deplored what he described as 'the gravest shortcoming of the British army: the reluctance of commanders at all levels to call upon their troops to press on regardless of losses, even in operations which were likely to shorten the war and thus save casualties in the long run'. The 1st Suffolks, Wilmot said, made hesitant progress capturing Colleville, Morris and Hillman, 'yet the area of its early operations was not resolutely defended'.

Wilmot lamented 'the absence of drive on the part of two of the three leading battalions [of 8th Brigade]' – the South Lancs and Suffolks – on advancing inland from Sword. He emphasized the degree to which much of the pre-D-Day planning, training and above all psychological conditioning had focused on the first step of the invasion – securing a successful lodgement on the shore. Yet this task, claimed Wilmot, 'was much less terrible, much less costly than they had expected. The assault was almost an anticlimax after all they had been told and all they had imagined. Many of them were through the beach defences almost before they realized it and, having got through, their inclination was to dig in, consolidate, and defend what they had gained against the counter-attack which would surely come in great strength now that the coastal crust had been so quickly cracked.'

Wilmot characterized 3 Div's commander, Rennie, as 'a dogged and able Scot who had served with great distinction in the 51st Highland Division ... but by temperament he was not inclined to spur [his officers] into quick development of any early advantage'. The commander of 8 Brigade Brigadier Edward Cass was 'stolid to the point of being ponderous, a "bulldog type" who would get a grip and hang on, but was ill-cast for the role of pursuit. His troops tended to take their cue from his own measured gait ... In assault exercises they had shown the same tendency to dig in prematurely.' Wilmot explicitly criticized the South Lancs, having easily occupied Hermanville, for taking up positions immediately south of that village instead of hastening on to their further objective, the Périers rise, two miles beyond, which was intended as the jump-off point for 185th Brigade's advance on Caen.

We shall consider below how far these criticisms were, or were not, merited, but Wilmot's judgements were deemed by his huge early readership, barely a decade after these events, to carry special weight, because the author himself had been a near-eyewitness – present on the battlefield only a few miles away, with Gale and 6th Airborne. It is plausible that his remarks were influenced by the views of red-bereted officers, as tribally sceptical of the battlefield performance of 'craphats' – non-paratroopers – as were Lovat and his commandos.

There is an obvious contrast between the speedy storming of the Merville Battery by men of 9 Para, at high cost in casualties, and the protracted resistance at Hillman against the Suffolks. The former represented an elite of the British Army, trained and conditioned to the highest pitch, while the Suffolks were a county regiment, not expected to indulge heroics. As described above, four of their leaders died displaying the highest courage in attempting to penetrate the German defence, almost unsupported by their men, judging from the respective casualties among officers and other ranks.

A day or two later, wounded commando Terry Skelly lay in an English hospital beside an officer who told Skelly his grandfather and father had commanded the same battalion as himself, to which he had been posted after returning from the Mediterranean. On his first day in action in Normandy, 'he found that his soldiers wouldn't follow him and the other officers and senior NCOs into an attack, and he had been hit. He did not seem to be very badly wounded but one morning I woke to find that … he had died in the night. I think he died of shame.' That colonel to whom Skelly referred had nothing to do with the Suffolks or Hillman. But the story emphasizes an important aspect of battlefield experience, which is seldom if ever admitted in unit war diaries: it was by no means assured that when an officer embarked upon an attack, his men would rise from the ground and follow him. David French has written of wartime British soldiers: 'They would not offer unquestioning obedience … a quality that senior officers believed was indispensable if troops were to be called on to endure heavy losses without flinching.'

As observed already, the British Army's battle schools had conditioned commanders and men alike to expect to advance slowly, behind heavy artillery barrages. The American historian Williamson Murray has written in his study of wartime operational methods: 'A serious weakness in the Allies' preparations for the invasion lay at the tactical level. British and Canadian troops had had four years to prepare themselves for Normandy; not all units did a good job. At lower levels British troops possessed no common doctrine; as a result, training rarely reached a high level of consistency or effectiveness. Even basic infantry tactics displayed considerable problems. The British relied on little more than a straightforward rush and the hope that their artillery had already smashed the Germans to bits.' A contemporary British commander might have observed that the same criticism could be levelled at American formations. It is nonetheless true that, in many of Montgomery's infantry units, tactical skills were limited.

Nobody will ever know the full truth about events on Hillman, because it was in no one's interest to detail in writing what went wrong for the Suffolks. They themselves attributed some of the difficulties to the loss of their naval forward observer during the landing, so that they were unable to call in warship guns. There is nothing to suggest, however, that the presence of the FOB would have changed much: Hillman's bunkers were impervious to naval gunfire.

An obvious point is that everything took too long: much time was spent, indeed wasted, merely contemplating the German position and wondering what to do next. A bigger factor was that the garrison of Hillman, led by a determined German officer, mounted a stauncher defence than had the enemies manning Sole, Daimler, Morris. For Hillman to have been stormed as fast in daylight as had been the Merville Battery in darkness would have required the deaths of many Suffolks. On that first day in France, relatively few of 3 Div's rank and file had conditioned themselves, or been conditioned by their commanders, to shed their own blood prodigally, to spare that of others later.

13

In the Beachhead

While twenty local battles were unfolding inland – to their actors, somewhat as if deadly little plays were being performed simultaneously in a cluster of neighbourhood theatres at Bénouville, Bréville, Ranville, Hauger, Daimler, Hillman, Lion-sur-Mer and suchlike – on Sword beach offloadings of troops, vehicles, fuel and munitions continued. These were still under sporadic enemy shellfire, but eased by the receding of the tide and overrunning of almost all the German coastal strongpoints save Trout. From mid-morning onwards many landing-craft milled and circled offshore, awaiting permission to unload. So severe had become the congestion that at noon beachings were halted for thirty minutes to give the beachmasters a breathing space. Sapper vehicles and equipment were especially severely delayed, some of them arriving days late. Columns of tanks and vehicles stretched inland in all directions, stalled for reasons undiscernible by those in the rear. Infantry units continued to get ashore; most pressed onwards. Even stragglers moved off the sand once they realized that lingering held no promise of security, since enemy batteries east of the Orne and towards Caen continued to harass Sword.

The beach was shelled and mortared with such accuracy that commanders decided the enemy must be ranging on the barrage balloons floating tethered to their cables above anchored ships. In truth, German gunners merely profited from having enjoyed years in which to register on coastal targets, together with continued possession of observation posts from which they could monitor every movement and telephone to batteries miles distant. The gas bags were nonetheless cut free to drift far and high into the sky. Even windsock markers were pulled down.

The units of 9 Brigade got ashore slowly, between noon and 1300. Lord Lovat was not the only man who landed with a piper that day – the Borderers also played themselves onto the beach. James Cunningham, their brigadier, wrote: 'There were far more bullets flying about than I had expected … [And] we were on a far narrower front.' Oerlikon guns on the boats rattled intermittently at presumed enemy firing positions. Some troops were so slow to disembark that the falling tide stranded their vessels, worsening congestion. Crew members from one such boat armed themselves and went ashore, supposedly to hunt for snipers.

Cunningham established his headquarters at the western end of Lion-sur-Mer, where he was bewildered to come under shellfire – he had assumed that 41 Commando would long since have cleared the village. He then walked the mile back to Hermanville, where under a wall beside an orchard he was astonished to meet not only Gen. Rennie, who had landed at 1030, but also John Crocker. Cunningham said: 'I've never before been beaten into action by both my divisional and corps commanders!', which sparked laughter. He was much less amused, however, to be told that his brigade's anticipated dash for Caen was 'off'. Instead one of the infantry battalions – 2nd Lincolns – was to adopt a defensive position on the western flank while 1st KOSB swung eastward towards Saint-Aubin-d'Arquenay and 2nd Royal Ulster Rifles advanced to dig in on the Périers ridge. In short, the brigade was to be committed piecemeal, to shore up perceived weak places in the British perimeter, in anticipation of German counter-attacks.

It was then somewhat after 1300, and from that moment any realistic hope was gone – if it had ever existed – of capturing Caen on D-Day. Cunningham said, 'This was disappointing as 9 Brigade had their run down the right flank [towards Caen] all buttoned up.' But he declined afterwards to second-guess his divisional commander's decision: 'It cannot be emphasized too strongly that they [Rennie and Crocker] were on the spot to make the decision – it must have been a very hard order to give, knowing what it entailed.'

Cunningham left the generals and set off to issue the new orders to his units. As he and his command group walked back towards his temporary headquarters, a cluster of mortar bombs descended upon them, killing one member of the staff and wounding another six, including the brigadier himself. This shambles – 'a severe blow,' acknowledged the war diary – decapitated 9th Brigade. Cunningham's second-in-command Col. Dennis Orr was sent for, but took hours to arrive because he was then at the canal bridge liaising with 6th Airborne. 'The result,' wrote Cunningham later, 'was a long hiatus when the Brigade should have been moving and nothing happened.' Here was yet another illustration of the consequences of the feeble infantry wireless communications. These made it necessary to deliver many messages by runner, or by requesting gunners or armoured regiments to relay them on their more powerful and effective vehicle-mounted sets. Though 9th Infantry Brigade participated in the D-Day invasion, it contributed nothing to the fight that day beyond the fact of its presence in France.

Some defenders fought on with the stubbornness of despair, especially if they were under the eye of determined German officers. Poles and other East Europeans wearing Heer uniforms in Normandy recognized how small were their chances of ever again seeing their homes. They had enlisted, willingly or no, in the army of the losers, the doomed – indeed, the damned. Although since dawn hundreds of prisoners had been taken on Sword and inland, it was not easy for a man wearing a coalscuttle helmet to surrender with much confidence in his own future.

A small party of the East Riding Yeomanry was put ashore with the infantry, to post directional signs for the regiment, which was earmarked to support 9 Brigade's advance. However the ERY's shipping was held offshore by the beachmasters for seventy-five minutes, delaying the tanks' disembarkation until German artillery fire had been somewhat suppressed and some wrecked vehicles were towed aside. This authorized pause was extraordinary because the East Ridings' fifty-four Shermans were a vital component of Montgomery's plan for the heavyweight dash for Caen, and well Rennie and his staff knew this. The likely explanation is that by then it had become obvious to senior officers that 3 Div had no chance of reaching the city that day. The issue was now simply that of how far towards Caen the spearhead units might push.

Even when cleared to discharge, one LCT skipper carrying East Riding tanks proved hesitant about doing so. Another vessel hit a German beach obstacle, obliging it to withdraw offshore, where its Shermans were transferred onto Rhino rafts, a protracted and cumbersome process. A half-track containing a squadron's entire inventory of tools and specialist equipment plunged into seven feet of water, to be lost forever. One troop was deposited on the wrong beach. Much of the regiment finally got ashore at 1415, to face further delays. Within moments of clearing the sand, one tank hit a mine and threw a track. Most of the East Ridings reached their assembly area at 1440, where a squadron-leader was heard saying to a subaltern over the radio: 'For Christ's sake, Peter, don't you realize this isn't an exercise?!' The troop leader in the case had not yet ordered his crews to load their guns. Still in some confusion, the young man climbed onto the major's tank in search of enlightenment and was promptly wounded in the back by a mortar fragment. Before nightfall he was evacuated to an English hospital, nursing embarrassment if not humiliation.

The regiment achieved nothing in the ensuing hours, and its brigadier descended upon the East Ridings' assembly area, 'urging us to move forward more aggressively'. It was hard for anyone on foot, even Erroll Prior-Palmer, to communicate with armoured crews until, later in the campaign, intercom handsets were fitted to the back of tank hulls. Climbing onto a turret to shout into a commander's ear above the roar of the engine was effective but not infrequently fatal to those who exposed themselves. PP's temper was not improved when the subaltern whose tank he ascended failed to recognize the brigadier. The young man seems to have urged this trespasser to go away.

Yet it was one thing for Prior-Palmer to urge the East Ridings to get on with it, another to decide what they were supposed to do. The regiment was earmarked to provide support for 9th Brigade but after its brigadier was wounded, nobody could be found to get the infantry moving. The East Ridings' historian wrote that the regiment 'had great difficulty in finding out what if any plan they were meant to carry out … After some hours' delay orders began to filter through.' It reflects very poorly on Rennie and his divisional staff that they failed to take a grip after 9th Brigade's headquarters was knocked out. Even if the infantry battalions remained inert, the tanks could have been invaluable anywhere in the Sword beachhead. As it was, the East Ridings lingered through hours in which they could have advanced to support the KSLI heading for Caen, or assisted the Suffolks at the suppression of Hillman, or joined the Staffords in meeting 21st Panzer, or even driven the few cross-country miles to provide precious armoured support to 6th Airborne Division. Instead, thanks to failure at the top, through that afternoon of huge tension, strategic importance and drama, fifty-odd tanks did absolutely nothing.

One squadron of the ERY began to advance only at 1920 that evening, while the rest stayed in their assembly area. This detachment briefly engaged a German self-propelled gun, which knocked out a Sherman and killed two of its crew before itself being dispatched. At 2015 the Yorkshiremen were told to withdraw to an overnight position just south of Colleville. Their war diary noted with misplaced complacency: 'Fortunately no replenishment [of fuel or ammunition] was needed as none of the tanks had moved far or been heavily engaged.' It added that the regiment enjoyed a 'quiet, undisturbed night'. This would be the end of an anticlimactic D-Day for the East Ridings, though for reasons that were not their own fault.

Elsewhere around the beachhead, at 1500 an AVRE squadron from 5 Assault Regiment was ordered to capture the Caen Canal lock gates east of Ouistreham, which nobody had got around to clearing in the initial commando advance through the town. Their commander asked for the aid of infantry, considered indispensable to every armoured attack, only to be told that none was available. Ten AVREs thus advanced unsupported upon the canal approaches. They were fortunate enough to succeed in this perilous foray, blasting concrete blockhouses in their path. The German defenders blew up the bridge above the lock gates but thereafter surrendered. The AVRE squadron took five officers and fifty-one men prisoner, Sapper Bean triumphantly collecting twenty of these at the point of his Bren gun.

On the sands, through the afternoon, order was established where chaos and delay had prevailed at mid-morning. Beachmasters secured control of the offload while military police began to assume responsibility for directing the movements of vehicles inland. At home or in rear areas, 'redcaps' were detested as enforcers of regulations and prohibitions. On the battlefield, however, they directed traffic – sought to disentangle under-fire tanks and vehicles clogging narrow roads – with a courage and proficiency that enforced respect and gratitude.

With three artillery field regiments ashore, self-propelled howitzers were supporting the infantry ahead. Their commanders nonetheless reported that for long periods of 6 June, nobody called upon their firepower, because the infantry were not immediately engaged with the enemy. David Belchem of Montgomery's staff also criticized Rennie's units for making inadequate use of available air power. The RAF's fighter-bombers of 2nd TAF carried out a hundred strikes in the Sword sector on 6 June, and struck some devastating blows against German formations heading for the battlefield, especially 21 Pz. However, '[3rd] Division had made few calls on the air forces for direct support, which was of course a mistake', according to Belchem. Much of this latter problem derived from the absence of forward air controllers with the leading units, such as had been the norm in the Mediterranean. In Normandy, the art of using 'cab-rank' air support had to be relearned apparently from scratch, and was not available on 6 June. This was ultimately the responsibility – the fault – of the chronically incompetent Sir Trafford Leigh-Mallory, air supremo for the invasion.

Most of the invaders' specialized technology worked well, but some did not. The lowered bow gangways down which men disembarked from the big LSIs proved vulnerable both to enemy fire and the tidal swell. When the gangways in the vessel carrying the Suffolks' headquarters company failed, sailors dropped scrambling nets from the sides into the shallows, which the heavily-laden soldiers flatly refused to descend. There was no one to order them to do so, since the battalion's second-in-command was prostrate with seasickness, and for some minutes disorder prevailed. The soldiers were eventually cajoled ashore, very late, from another landing-ship. Meanwhile AVRE Petard mortar rounds were prone to explode in their barrels if the big 'dustbin' charges were hit by a bullet, as happened to more than one tank in Lion-sur-Mer. Above all, British voice wireless communications showed themselves wretchedly inadequate.

The inspiration of 9th Brigade's Cunningham to issue the assault battalions with giant waders, to wear over their boots and equipment, was a flop – indeed a dangerous and potentially fatal one. Most were discarded before landing, and men who wore the waders found them flooding in deep water, threatening to drown their wearers. Corporal Bob Littlar of the Shropshires drew a clasp knife and hastily slashed open the waders of several men in obvious peril.

Some glider pilots who had landed in Normandy on the morning of the 6th stayed to fight alongside the Airborne. However, when the Commandos arrived at the Caen Canal bridge those who had flown the Ox & Bucks decided, not unreasonably, that they had 'done their bit', and opted to go home. One of them wrote: 'We took our leave of Major Howard and his men, then walked along the road to Ouistreham.' For a time they lay down in a field of cabbages and snatched such fitful sleep as was permitted by the thunder of *Warspite*'s fifteen-inch guns. Having reached the beach safely, they waded out to a vessel which had just offloaded its men and begged a ride home, presenting its captain with an authorization for their repatriation, issued before they took off. They landed at Newhaven two days later.

Lt. Arthur Oates of the East Yorks, left behind by his battalion after being hit, was increasingly troubled by his wounded arm, which was swelling: '[I] felt very weak ... went into Ouistreham, patrolled the town and left some money in Church ... Had wound bandaged and ate sandwiches.' Terry Skelly was also wounded, but in no condition to move. A nearby German casualty gazed at him for some time before observing, '*England kaput*', 'to which I replied, not very originally, "*Nein, Deutschland kaput*".'

Many men who found themselves out of a direct line of enemy fire brewed up. Among special items that had been issued to British and Canadian troops before landing, self-heating soup cans, with central chemical filaments ignited by a burning cigarette, became immensely popular, and formed many men's first meals in France. It was soon after decided that the soup, developed by Heinz and ICI, was prohibitively expensive to produce. On 6 June, however, for a significant number of those who landed on Sword the soup provided their first – and, for a few, final – meal. French urchins begged for chocolate or cigarettes and, when denied, said 'Fuck off, Tommy!'

They started to find booby traps. A 'clot of a sergeant', in the words of a driver with him, picked up a pistol in a German bunker, causing the entire interior to catch fire, and the trespassers to flee. As two hundred German prisoners crowded aboard an emptied tank landing-ship now headed back to England, the chief bosun's mate marvelled disgustedly at a Wehrmacht officer wearing 'boots so highly polished that he looked more like he had come from the Ritz than from a battlefield'.

Every familiar function of humankind takes a soldier on a battlefield four times as long as the same task at home, whether cooking a meal then cleaning a messtin; defecating after creating a hole in which to do so; dressing and undressing when he was fortunate enough to be able to do so; and, above all, digging. Men spent vastly more time excavating slit trenches and shelters than ever they did fighting. It required perhaps four or five hours of intense labour to make a hole deep enough to provide shelter from bombardment.

The historian of 6th Airborne wrote of its men: 'They learned the first and most important lesson of all in the first 24 hours [in Normandy]; that he who would survive on a modern battlefield must dig and dig again; and that cover from view … was not enough when fighting an enemy as skilled as were the Germans in the use of mortars and machine-guns.' Aerial photographs of the battlefield soon showed the entire Allied perimeter pockmarked with burrows, such as a million moles or rabbits might have contrived. The worst thing, however, was that even as a hole became at last habitable, within days or more likely hours a man would be moved on, to do the whole thing all over again.

By mid-afternoon, though the foremost British forces advancing from the sea were well inland – Lovat's commandos across the bridges and deployed with 6th Airborne, the Shropshires forging southwards towards Caen – behind them other units were still addressing the extensive archipelago of German resistance nests: in the west at Lion-sur-Mer and Luc-sur-Mer, in the centre at Daimler and Hillman, in the east at Ouistreham and the canal locks. Between outbursts of fierce action, there were protracted local silences as units organized themselves for attacks, commanders briefed subordinates or strove through binoculars to discern the seriousness of enemy threats ahead in fields and woods of which the innocent and even idyllic appearance belied the potential menace.

Those who led the way into unknown or contested territory, whether on foot or in vehicles, deserve respect and indeed admiration. Again and again the point man, often an officer or NCO, was shot down, or the lead tank knocked out. Moreover, information about the enemy reaching senior officers continued to be vague and often plain wrong. As late as the morning of 7 June, Second Army's commander Sir Miles Dempsey noted: 'The situation of 3 Div north of Caen and 6 Airborne east of the two rivers is still rather obscure.' Twelve hours earlier, there was even more confusion. The critical reality was that the British moving inland from Sword had broken the German crust at relatively low cost in casualties but were advancing hesitantly, a consequence of poor communications and cautious leadership. Lord Lovat was entitled to take credit for the speed with which his men had reached the bridges, contrasted with the falterings of some of those who followed.

14

The End of the Road to Caen

The loneliest members of 3 Div in the late afternoon of 6 June were the leading companies of the Shropshires, 2nd KSLI, marching doggedly towards the city of Caen, its tall industrial chimneys clearly visible as they ascended the summits of switchback hills before descending into shallow valleys, most of them wooded and thus potentially threatening. 'The KSLI battalion group will assault and capture CAEN,' asserted the 185th Brigade operation order imperiously and unrealistically before the landing. The Shropshires had assumed, back in England, that they would be advancing against the German army in step with the other two battalions of their brigade, the Norfolks and Warwicks. Both were, however, miles behind. The battalion had armoured support only from C Squadron of the Staffordshire Yeomanry, which was about to experience some of the busiest hours of a battlefield career that had begun seventeen months earlier at El Alamein in the faraway Egyptian desert. As for the infantrymen, though they had suffered significant losses from shelling and long-range machine-gun fire as they moved inland past Périers, in an officer's words, 'the men were in good heart and out for revenge'.

They encountered that afternoon the dilemma which would persist until the last day of the war: Who rightfully went first in such an advance? Infantry or armour? Sherman crews with hatches closed were almost blind – periscopes were no substitutes for plain view. They were also incapable of hearing noise beyond that of their own engines. The tanks were therefore highly vulnerable at close range to enemy foot-soldiers with Panzerfaust anti-tank weapons. Indeed, armoured crews rode and fought in a curious isolation from the ground. Commanders most often stood up in their turrets, clinging to the hatch sides amid the lurching, lunging motion, craning for a sight of the enemy, at mortal risk to themselves from small arms. Several times as the advance approached woodland, the tank squadron's commander Pat Griffin asked for some infantrymen to check treelines for hidden anti-tank guns before his Shermans moved within range.

On foot, the men of the Shropshires' point section knew that there was nothing save deceptively idyllic fields, woods and golden farmhouses between themselves and elements of the German army, which were invisibly hastening to meet them. At every step, apparent tranquillity might be shattered by enemy fire, knowledge which promoted a sensible wariness. The Shropshires had done little training with tanks, or for street-fighting in villages. Later operational research showed that a British infantry unit in NW Europe, seeking to advance in the face of light opposition, moved an average four to five hundred yards an hour in daylight and substantially less at night. It was impressive how far the Shropshires progressed that afternoon, in the face of spasms of enemy fire that cost the British time, as they were intended to.

They crossed open farmland up a long slope south-west of Hillman, X Company leading, and at 1330 crested the Périers ridge – Point 61 on their maps. Slightly downhill and off to their right lay the hamlet of Périers-sur-le-Dan. On the road between themselves and Caen stood the successive villages of Beuville, Biéville and Lebisey, set in closer country, ideal for defenders. On the gentle descent just past Périers at 1400 they passed its church and

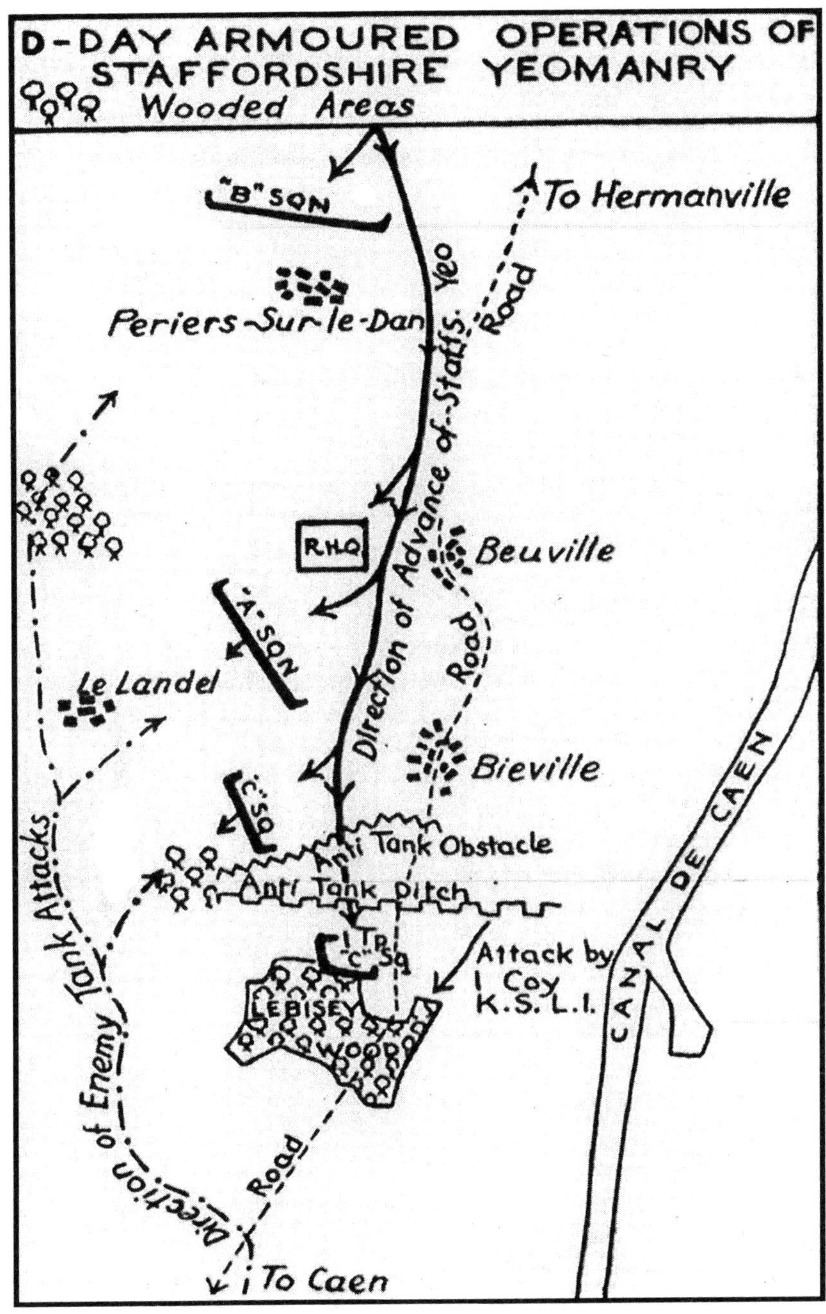

This sketch was made either by or under the guidance of a Staffordshire Yeomanry witness, and thus is almost certainly accurate

an abandoned German half-track. Platoon commander Lionel Murray was bemused by the incongruity that 'on our left half-a-dozen cows munched placidly'. Out on their right C Squadron of the Staffordshires for some reason remained unscathed as its tanks moved southwards, while a few minutes behind them B Squadron under George Turner found itself ambushed and mauled. A German gun – identified as an 88mm as was almost every tank-killing weapon which the Allies met in Normandy but was more likely a self-propelled 75mm of 21 Pz – opened fire. Then began five minutes of shock and horror for the Staffords. The first German shell hit a tank which blew up. The troop leader, twenty-three-year-old Lt. Douglas Alexander, drove forward to try to help, only to have his own tank hit. He jumped down and ran to the blazing Sherman, dragging one man from the turret. He was attempting to rescue a second casualty when the tank was hit again, killing him. The regiment's medical officer, Kerry Harper, raced forward in a White half-track and tried to load aboard one of the wounded men but his own vehicle was struck by a shell, causing it to explode. Harper was blown clear though his orderly suffered a broken leg, and the regiment's medical stores vanished in flames.

In quick succession two Dragoons' fascine-carrying tanks, accompanying the Yeomanry, together with their artillery FOO's Sherman were hit. Here was an example of the extraordinary rate of attrition that a skilled gunlayer on either side could achieve, against armour on the move in the open. There were some moments of alarm and confusion before the Staffords steadied in positions where they commanded a long field of fire but were themselves less conspicuous. At last they pinpointed and then destroyed the enemy gun that had harrowed them. Afterwards they halted by Point 61 to give support to the Shropshires' Z Company, attacking the German battery towards Périers.

C Squadron was meanwhile still moving south, having escaped such punishment. The KSLI's other companies, advancing with one of the gunners' tracked howitzers in immediate support, came under fire from Beuville. A handful of German defenders, mostly riflemen, sought to delay the British advance and, in the words of Capt. Robert Rylands, 'delay us they did … The civilians refused to evacuate themselves and at that stage we were too soft-hearted to shell their homes, a proceeding which might have expedited the whole advance considerably.' The two companies parted to pincer the little village from both sides, Lt. Murray leading W Company amid German shellfire from the west. This inflicted 'severe casualties' on Murray's platoon, as did the enemy's riflemen. Harry Jones saw a stick grenade explode between the legs of a man who died instantly. Jones was suddenly called on to rescue Guy Thornycroft, his own company commander, from shelter behind a wall, where he was trapped by enemy fire. The subaltern achieved this with the aid of smoke grenades, tossed ahead by his men.

Major Arthur Slatter, a thirty-six-year-old pre-war regular commissioned from the ranks, thereafter marched impatiently and unwisely up the main street, only to be hit and severely wounded in the arm. Jones shouted for a stretcher-bearer and led his platoon forward, 'continually sniped at'. A namesake, Pte. Arthur Jones, was shot dead 'as, curiously enough, he had told his friends he was going to be', in the dry words of Robert Rylands. When the infantry told the crew of their accompanying howitzer that there was a sniper in the belfry of the church, the gunners obligingly put a shot into the tower, causing the bells to clang wildly. Lt. Murray believed he saw a German woman sniper, in camouflage clothing, taken prisoner: 'She seemed not the slightest perturbed when finally brought out.'

That afternoon, as everywhere in the beachhead, every enemy rifleman was classified as a sniper, which was often a misnomer:

rather, a surprising number of defenders showed themselves marksmen. Moreover the Shropshires afterwards acknowledged that they had too carelessly advanced up the village street in full view, instead of moving circumspectly. In the days and weeks that followed, those who survived became progressively more wary and skilled at reducing exposure and risk. On 6 June, however, they paid a price for their greenness, for which some compensated by displaying courage, or at least a boldness founded upon ignorance.

Having driven out the German defenders in Beuville, they moved on half a mile to Biéville, the next hamlet, which they reached at 1545. Y Company rushed the château where they found an uneaten stew cooling on the table; took a handful of not unhappy prisoners; then lingered to mop up. X Company carried out a series of right-flanking movements, completing each one by pushing back into the village, at the cost of a steady trickle of losses. Mme Germaine Barette, a trained nurse who lived with an invalid daughter, showed herself fearless under fire, aiding British wounded and treating them in her home. The Shropshires subsequently testified that she was a notably good-looking woman and that she saved several men's lives. A mate told Bob Littlar that he noticed how many of the battalion's officers and NCOs were being picked off – the Germans were identifying leaders. An institutional error of the wartime British Army was that NCOs' white chevrons of rank were visible at long distances on the battlefield. Both men whipped out knives and cut off the stripes sewn on the arms of their battledress, never again to wear them in Normandy. The tanks reached Biéville without loss and 'after a certain amount of confused fighting', both villages were reported clear. Part of the 'confused fighting' was that a Stafford was wounded when a Sherman came under unexpected small arms fire. Its crew was out of the tank, tending to this casualty, when they found themselves

Commandos during an action on the approach to the Caen Canal bridge.

GERMANS: (top) Oppeln-Bronikowski and Marcks. (Centre) Feuchtinger, 21 Pz's commander, inspecting troops. (Below) Von Luck with battlegroup officers during the action and (right) Richter, commanding the 716th Infantry Division defending SWORD.

(Top) A mortar crew in action and (above) a Mk. IV tank of 21 Pz. (Right) Col. Ludwig Krug, commander of Hillman.

(Left) 'Tich' Hunter and (right) Dick Goodwin, CO of the Suffolks. (Below) One of the 105mm howitzers supporting the assaults inland.

(Top) Tanks of the Staffordshire Yeomanry in action on 6 June with (inset) Jim Eadie their CO. (Below) One of many pauses during the advance inland.

(Top left) Richard Todd, on the right of photo, with a comrade in Normandy and (right) Huw Wheldon. (Below left) Gunner Robin Dunn receives an MC from Montgomery and (below right) tank commander Patrick Hennessey and the Shropshires' Peter Steel, killed while leading his company up the road to Caen on the evening of 6 June.

Portly and brilliant BBC correspondent Chester Wilmot
in Normandy with French commandos.

Ron Major of the East Yorkshires on a casualty evacuation train back in England. His features reflect the exultation of having become a 'D-Day hero' who was now safely out of it.

surrounded by German soldiers, who took them prisoner. When the enemy were driven back, the abandoned Firefly was recovered intact by the somewhat mystified British, who recorded its crew as 'Missing'.

It was now 1630. The Suffolks were still struggling at Hillman, and the East Yorks had not yet started their attack on Daimler. Maurice decided that X Company had done enough for the moment, and ordered Y to take over the lead. Its men were commanded by a regular officer named Peter Steel, born in Chile, married with a baby daughter. He was distinguished by angular features, protruding ears and conspicuous courage. Back in England, he had become friendly with Jim Eadie and his wife, surely because of their shared South American connection. For Steel, like nearly all his men, this was the first day in action.

Two miles behind and to the right, they could hear Peter Wheelock's men engaged with the enemy 122mm battery north of Périers village. From two miles to their left came the sounds of sporadic firing in Bénouville, where 7 Para was still skirmishing with panzergrenadiers. Little over a mile ahead the Shropshires could see the Lebisey ridge, principal high ground feature before Caen, topped by a wood with the village of its name lying invisible beyond. This corner of Normandy was to become the scene of boundless British bloodletting in the days and weeks ahead. On that afternoon of the 6th, however, the weary men of the KSLI felt themselves tantalizingly close to the old city, focus of every D-Day ambition of their army commander. Lionel Murray nonetheless observed that 'our numbers had shrunk rather alarmingly'.

In the valley below Lebisey Wood, Lt. Michael Bellamy reconnoitred forward, exploring a wooded, almost dry riverbed which ran wide across the British line of advance. Before the invasion, briefing documents for 27th Armoured Brigade had clearly identified this obstacle: 'A wooded ravine of considerable depth runs in an easterly direction from inc. wood 044730 to junction with Caen Canal.' The Germans had been excavating this into a major anti-tank ditch, which ran several hundred yards to the east of the road but was still uncompleted to the west. Though there were no more German bunker networks on the road to Caen, such as 3 Div encountered earlier that day on its units' marches inland from the coast, the enemy had taken pains to ensure the way ahead continued to be beset with difficulties. Obstacles covered by fire create almost as formidable an impediment to attackers as do concrete emplacements. Moreover, two of the British tanks knocked out an hour earlier, while accompanying B Squadron, had been carrying fascines. These latter were being brought forward explicitly to create passages across anti-tank ditches. The fascines were now lost to the attackers.

The ditch seemed to represent an impassable barrier to any Sherman moving off the road – one troop of the Staffords was stopped by it, though further west two other troops found a way across or around. Without warning Lt. Bellamy found himself confronted at almost point-blank range by a German machine-gun, manned by panzergrenadiers of 21 Pz, who opened fire, wounding Bellamy in the arm and knee. He managed to make his way back with the aid of his platoon sergeant, reporting to Jack Maurice that he had identified a possible crossing-place for the Staffordshires, though it was never used.

Twenty-one-year-old Lt. Harry Jones of the Shropshires' X Company, a slight figure just five feet five inches tall, was poring over a map with his company commander Guy Thornycroft and fellow platoon leaders when a shell exploded nearby. This caused a surge of guilty consciousness among the officers that by thus clustering in the open, they had broken every rule of tactical discretion: 'I looked towards the enemy and could not believe my eyes. There advancing round the corner about five hundred yards away were five or six German tanks. We hurriedly dispersed and I returned to my platoon.' Within seconds he began to hear the sound of the German tanks firing 'and was relieved also to hear our own anti-tank guns and those of the Staffordshire Yeomanry'.

It was then, and there, that everything changed – by no means unfavourably for the invaders' cause, but in a fashion which immediately checked the Shropshires. For the next important hour they lost their accompanying tanks, and thus halted their own advance. Across the wireless net of the armour came urgent orders to redeploy. The panzers seen by Jones and his comrades, from 5 Company of 22 Pz Regt, were the first earnest of sixty of their kind which now posed the foremost threat offered by the German army on D-Day to the Sword beachhead and the scattered invasion forces within it. The absolute priority of every British tank and anti-tank weapon within reach had to be to throw back and, if possible, destroy the enemy's armour. The very word panzer had become, since 1939, steeped in menace for the soldiers of Britain and America. To be sure, the Allies had learned in North Africa, Sicily, Italy that neither Rommel nor Hitler's tanks were invincible. But every man of the Staffordshires and Shropshires knew that in the late afternoon of 6 June they faced a trial by battle, with huge implications for the Sword beachhead and, indeed, for the entire invasion.

Gen. Edgar Feuchtinger's armoured units had begun to concentrate on the Lebisey ridge, north and slightly west of Caen, an hour or so earlier. Beyond their losses to RAF Typhoons, a significant number of tanks had broken down on the march, as always befell tracked vehicles of every nationality. Confusion in the German command was exemplified by the dispirited demeanour of Maj. Gen. Wilhelm Richter, the local infantry commander. He bemoaned the dissolution by fire of his 716th Division and avowed that he had little idea where most of his men were. At 1500 corps commander Gen. Erich Marcks arrived from his headquarters at Saint-Lô, in a rage about the delays that had been imposed first by failure to get the tanks moving before dawn; then by the long limbo before they were placed under his control, as area field commander; and finally by the time taken to bring the formation onto the battlefield. It was Marcks' fifty-third birthday, and like a good many others in Normandy that day he had less than a week left to live. Now, as commander of LXXXIV Corps, he famously told Col. Hermann von Oppeln-Bronikowski, the former Olympic equestrian gold medallist who commanded 22 Pz Regiment: 'Oppeln, the future of Germany may well rest on your shoulders. If you don't throw the British back into the sea, we've lost the war.'

Bronikowski, forty-five years old and an immensely experienced panzer commander who wore the Knight's Cross, was flawed like many German officers at that stage of the war by an extravagant enthusiasm for alcohol. A month earlier Rommel had called at his quarters early one morning to find the colonel visibly the worse for wear, having slept in his tunic. The field-marshal rebuked Bronikowski and his comrades, apparently jesting but obviously in deadly earnest, as idle swabs. He demanded: 'What happens if the enemy lands before 8.30?!' The colonel replied in kind: 'Catastrophe!' Rommel laughed. Now, however, the colonel had nothing to laugh about: he bore a huge responsibility, in circumstances that were almost entirely unfavourable to his regiment – a brigade, in a British formation.

At 1620, fourteen hours after 21 Pz had first been alerted to British landings, the bespectacled Marcks, a man of notable courage despite the absence of a leg left behind in Russia, personally led forward one of three columns, headed on roughly parallel northern axes across open country – ground they knew well, because they had trained across it. A battalion of panzergrenadiers under Col. Josef Rauch was ordered to drive straight for the sea at Luc-sur-Mer, supported by some self-propelled guns, while Oppeln himself led the other two columns. He dispatched one company directly northwards on the road to Biéville while the others, further west, prepared to swing right in company groups, to smash into the exposed flank of the British forces advancing upon Caen. The German dispositions were extraordinary. In defiance of all accepted tactical principles, Rauch's column advanced without tanks, and those of Oppeln and Major Wilhelm von Gottberg without accompanying infantry, most of which seem to have remained on the high ground, digging in around Lebisey village. Essentially, Marcks appears to have launched an almost mindless lunge against 3 Division's beachhead, and 21 Pz received the punishment that such a clumsy attack invited.

The British flank was no longer exposed. Stuart light tanks of the Staffordshires' reconnaissance squadron, moving on the right of the Shropshires, saw the panzers emerge from the trees of the Lebisey ridge and advance towards Biéville. Most of the Staffords' C Squadron and the Shropshires' anti-tank guns were deployed close at hand. The troops of Lt. Lionel Knight and Lt. Arthur Winterhalder had already found a way across the anti-tank ditch and were thus on the same southern side as the panzers.

Knight, a former regular NCO who had been at Dunkirk and in the desert, may have learned on the wireless net that his closest friend, Douglas Alexander, had been killed two hours earlier at Point 61. Now, however, as lead troop commander of the Staffordshires he had too much to think about, on his immediate front, to reflect on the dead. He found the trees on the rising ground held 'by only a few very frightened and disorganized enemy infantry', who had obviously just taken up positions. There followed an episode as surely confusing for C Squadron as it seems to posterity. He called urgently on the radio net for infantry to sweep their onward path – no sane tank officer moved unprotected through woodland. These proved slow to materialize: only one section eventually reached the tanks' position. The Shropshires' Y Company was away on the east side of the Caen road, several hundred yards to Knight's left. Then a panzer shell hit Winterhalder's Sherman, killing him though not knocking out the tank. Winterhalder's driver stayed calm and succeeded in reversing back down the slope. Though only twenty-one, Winterhalder was a veteran of North Africa who left behind a widow, Violet, and an unborn daughter. The rest of his troop appears to have retired behind the ditch, though the records do not make this clear.

When Bob Littlar saw the six-pounders unlimber beside a farmhouse and prepare to fire, he said to his neighbour, 'Trouble coming up, mate!' and so there was. B Squadron was three miles south, on the Périers ridge, supporting Z Company in its private battle for the 122mm gun battery. Jim Eadie the Staffords' CO requested, and secured, the immediate recall from the Hillman action of A Squadron, to fill the gap between the two, south-west of Beuville, where they arrived 'just in time to take up battle positions', in the words of the regiment's war diary.

The British armoured officers who deployed to meet the 21st Panzer column showed tactical skill honed over years in the desert, and at battle schools since. When the Staffordshires first went to the Middle East in 1940, they were still a cavalry unit which sailed with its own horses. The men of Eadie's own squadron were known as 'the Burton boys' because so many of its Yeomen came from Burton-upon-Trent. In four years of war, he had risen to command the regiment, becoming the first Territorial to do so. He was intimately familiar with panzer tactics.

Eadie anticipated back in England the likelihood of an enemy armoured counter-attack through the gap between the British and

Canadians. Germans on every battlefield were keenly observant. They often spotted, and sought to exploit, weaknesses and thus opportunities. What they did not recognize on 6 June, however, is that the British confronting them were not only ready and waiting, but also exceptionally well-armed – one troop of each of the Staffordshires' squadrons were battle-experienced veterans manning Sherman Fireflies, which mounted seventeen-pounder guns, their barrels as long as telegraph poles, rather than the usual lighter 75mms.

Eadie's three squadrons contrived to fight with remarkable coherence, achieved across the wireless net – the colonel posted himself just west of Beuville, between his tank groups. Again and again through three years of desert war in North Africa, British armour had been punished for tactical clumsiness – recklessly exposing itself to German guns. Now the boot was on the other foot. It was the Germans' turn to take a beating, at the hands of adversaries who showed themselves more skilful. Eadie had written to his adored wife before embarkation: 'There is no flush of excitement within me, such as one gets at one's first battle, just a steady resolve to do my best as long as my strength shall last … I know experience counts, and I hope mine can stand others in good stead.' It did.

Around 1620 as thirteen Panzer IVs approached the ravine, which posed as much of an obstacle to them as to the Shermans which had earlier sought to advance the other way, British shells lashed down into them. At least two panzers were destroyed by the Staffords' Sgt. Billings and two more by the KSLI's six-pounder anti-tank guns. German responsive fire cost Rayner Walker, a Shropshires' gunner, an arm. He was carried back to Mme Barette's house in the village, where a tourniquet was successfully applied. Harry Jones later saw the severed limb lying grotesquely by the roadside 'with its hand pointing towards the sky … I had an irresistible urge to pick up the arm and shake the hand of the sergeant with whom I had trained and got to know well.' Billings' Sherman was then hit by a high-explosive shell and set on fire, but when the crew bailed out they found that only equipment on the outside of the hull was ablaze. They were able to douse the flames and clamber up once more into the fighting compartment.

The panzers on the Biéville road recoiled west into the woodland on the ridge. When they reappeared out on the British right, moving fast to reach the end of the anti-tank ditch, two troops of the Staffordshires' A Squadron, a mile from C, caught up with them just east of the Château Le Landel and inflicted more carnage from a range of six hundred yards: 'Two were K.O.d' in the laconic phrase of the war diary. It was textbook stuff. As in every clash between tank and tank, a loader's dexterity was vital because outcomes were often determined by the speed with which a second round could be dispatched, and then a third, before the enemy could pinpoint the firer and respond. The gunner's eye never left his telescopic sight while the loader ejected a spent case, rammed home a new shell, closed the breech then called 'Gun ready!' and banged the gunner's shoulder.

A tank driver recorded: 'With every round fired clouds of dust obscure the driving compartment and … two feet above my hatch the goggles jump on my nose and I experience the sensation of being hit on the head with a mallet. The roar of the tank's engine is drowned by louder noises so that its behaviour had to be gauged by the instrument panel, yet I am loath to take my eyes for an instant from periscope or visor … To all five of us the intercom, our lifeline, relays a bedlam of orders, distortions and cries from another world.' It was relentlessly tiring, manipulating dual clutches to manoeuvre a heavy steel oven by braking its tracks, amid a babble of intercom instructions from the commander, with wireless mush in between, and every crewman's body jolting and lurching against unyielding metal. When enemy shells burst nearby, the sound of the detonations echoed around the turret.

Tank commander Sgt. Leslie Joyce was a typical member of the Yeomanry, one of five children of a worker on the High Park estate of Lord Dartmouth, who had personally raised a troop in 1939, with which his own son Lord Lewisham was killed in the desert. Now Joyce's gunner destroyed three panzers out of a total of at least ten knocked out by the Staffords, one of them that of battalion commander Wilhelm von Gottberg, another commanded by Oppeln-Bronikowski himself, before the surviving Mk IVs again turned away, accepting repulse.

It deserves emphasis that this action was fought by British soldiers who had spent the previous night wallowing at sea, before experiencing the exhausting demands, delays, frustrations of their beach landing. An officer of the KSLI had mused as he boarded his landing-craft the previous day, 'It was another world into which we were to step', and so indeed it proved. Many of the tank crews were young and fit, though regimental commander Jim Eadie, at forty-four, was a decade older than most officers fulfilling such a role. But there could not fail to be a sense of unreality for the Staffords, finding themselves locked in a tank battle in France five hours after crossing Sword beach. It seems astonishing that they responded so well when already tired men, facing a stunning shock of war.

Three Fireflies and one 75mm Sherman of B Squadron on the Périers ridge settled hull down, scarcely visible to the advancing panzers, alongside the M10 Wolverine self-propelled guns of 20 Anti-Tank Regiment. They commanded a field of fire extending more than a mile across open cornfields which they knew the Germans must cross. Behind the guns, crews enjoyed a view far downhill to the crowded sea. When Oppeln's panzers made one further attempt to drive east, they met the same fate as their comrades a few minutes earlier: at a range of 1,200 yards three more Mk IVs were destroyed, for the loss of one M10 and two Shermans. The Germans afterwards lamented the inferior penetration of their tank shells at long range, compared with that of the British. German Tigers and Panthers, which outgunned Montgomery's armour, would soon enter the Normandy battlefield, but on 6 June 21st Panzer lacked such firepower.

Elsewhere the column initially led by Gen. Marcks, who peeled off after a few miles to resume his corps command role, was able to drive directly north, unchallenged, led by a motorcyclist and accompanied by lorried panzergrenadiers, eventually to reach the coast some time after 1900, perhaps as late as 2000. Its panzergrenadiers and handful of self-propelled guns, commanded by Col. Josef Rauch, were unable to achieve anything when it did so, however, unsupported by 22 Panzer Regiment. Oppeln-Bronikowski withdrew his battered and diminished force to form a defensive line on the Lebisey ridge. Werner Kortenhaus wrote later: 'The one and only chance on D-Day' – for German arms, against Sword beach – 'had been lost. Never again was there to be such an opportunity.' The Germans paid rueful tribute to the skill and effectiveness of the British response to their advance.

The Staffords had played the decisive role in throwing back 21st Panzer's counter-attack. It was a fine performance, arguably the best of the day by any Sword unit, surely assisted by the fact that the Yeomanry was among the most experienced armoured regiments to land on D-Day, and had seen more war than most crews of 21 Pz. Eadie already wore one DSO, awarded for his leadership in the Mediterranean, and was now to receive a second for his performance on 6 June. He wrote to his wife: 'My chaps did very well indeed and quite lived up to my expectations of them. It is very different from the desert but our experience stood us in good stead.'

Sometimes in this book British tactical limitations are highlighted, but between Lebisey and the Périers ridge on 6 June the invaders' tank crews and gunners showed the highest professionalism. Once, twice, three times the Germans attempted flank advances, and on each occasion they were clawed and forced to retire. That night the battlegroup which had reached the sea was obliged to beat a retreat, to join the rest of 22 Panzer Regiment on the Lebisey ridge. Though reliable numbers are elusive, by the end of 6 June 21 Pz's tank strength was reduced by more than half, to around fifty Mk IVs and SP guns.

After the Germans retreated the Shropshires' X Company's war diary recorded the episode in a surprisingly juvenile spirit of enthusiasm, writing that its men had 'witnessed a most exciting battle between our anti-tank guns and a Hun tank attack'. A fault of almost all movies about the Second World War is that warriors are played on screen by actors who are much older – often in their forties – than were most 1939–45 soldiers. Only a handful of the men below the Lebisey ridge were more than thirty, and many were a decade younger, even if the stress of battle soon caused many to age in appearance far beyond their years. Few Normandy war diaries would much longer find any battle 'exciting'.

Once the threat to the British flank had been repulsed at 1730 the Shropshires, who had been obliged to halt until their own supporting tanks had seen off the panzers, resumed the advance from Biéville towards Lebisey, followed by a single troop of the Staffordshires – the rest of the squadron were way out on their right. As evening descended and the light began to dwindle, one of the Staffords' accompanying troops, No. 4, became bogged in the anti-tank ditch, and the rest proved unable to cross it. They gave supporting fire to the Shropshires' Y Company, but were stuck several hundred yards behind, on the eastern side of the

Caen road. The anti-tank ditch had achieved pretty much what its German constructors intended. Save during the drama of 21st Panzer's eruption, C Squadron's tanks spent most of the afternoon and evening probing hesitantly, and with repeated checks, delays and false moves, for ways over and past the deep ravine. As was asserted by the witness to armoured behaviour who was quoted earlier, 'tanks are timid creatures' – for good reasons.

Y Company advanced uphill towards the trees on Lebisey ridge 'in perfect formation, absolutely opened up like a textbook field day', with just one Sherman behind, firing tracer in support. Then concealed German automatic weapons began firing from what the Shropshires dubbed 'Square Wood', in Bob Littlar's words 'a terrible place'. Pte. Norman Millward said: 'We were going up and there was a Jerry machine-gun hidden by some bushes. Major Steel just rushed it with his revolver … and was shot, of course.' His men sought cover. The Germans had a perfect observation position on a high water tower. Lt. Tom Gwilliam nonetheless said stubbornly, 'We must try to take the high ground.' He crawled further uphill until he reached a cattle trough perhaps forty yards from Lebisey Wood. There he told his wireless-operator to remain in its shelter while himself moving beyond. Within seconds there came a new burst of fire and he collapsed, shot in the stomach. Almost miraculously Gwilliam's platoon sergeant contrived to drag his officer back behind a bank running down the sunken lane towards Biéville. There stretcher-bearers reached them and bore him to the rear. Gwilliam, who had advanced further towards Caen than any other British soldier that day, survived.

Y Company, however, was stuck in positions where its men, hugging cover, became visible to Germans concealed in the trees every time they attempted to move. Bob Littlar, back down the hill and behind the anti-tank ditch with X Company, said: 'It was all a bit of a shambles.' He heard a tank officer saying that from his high turret vantage point he had just seen some forty Germans approaching a house three thousand yards out on their right. Littlar thought: 'Pray God don't let's go after them; leave them where they are.' Jack Maurice, the battalion CO, decided – surely rightly – that his men had exhausted their powers. He had earlier planned a full-scale assault on Lebisey before nightfall, but in the absence of the brigade's two other infantry battalions, he 'now decided not to attack that night', saying: 'I think we have come far enough today.' The Brigade war diary recorded that Maurice was considerably troubled by the warning overheard by Littlar, of a substantial German force working around the Shropshires' flank. He reported to Smith, according to the war diary, that 'a party of enemy was in the process of encircling them … [He] considered that to commit his two available companies (already considerably depleted by casualties) into this extensive and obscure objective [Lebisey Wood] … would be running the risk of defeat in detail. The brigade commander agreed to the withdrawal of the company from Lebisey.'

Wireless communication had become exasperatingly erratic, but at last the colonel succeeded in passing an order to Steel's second-in-command: Captain Richard Dane was to hold his position until the light had gone – which involved a long lingering in Y Company's uncomfortable position below the trees. But delay was more prudent than a withdrawal downhill, in daylight across open ground under fire. The company duly exploited darkness to pull back to Biéville, a movement successfully completed only at 2315.

Captain Robert Rylands of W Company said: 'We were a little apprehensive about a possible armoured counter-attack, but were not unpleased with ourselves: we had penetrated about six miles as the crow flies; our casualties were slighter than expected; and we were further south than any other Coy in the Division.' X

Company's war diary noted its own twenty-four casualties, around 20 per cent of strength, but added defiantly: 'Our spirits were high.' As the Shropshires dug in for the night in an orchard, their South African FOO Dickie Tooth arrived and fixed a fire plan to give the Germans a hot time if they attempted to counter-attack during the night – which they did not. Yet the last hours of D-Day were marked by a tragic incident. A lieutenant was sent out with an NCO to reconnoitre south of their front. When the two men returned to the Shropshires' positions, the officer called out 'Don't shoot! Mr Rees!' The jumpy defenders nonetheless opened fire, killing Dai Rees and his platoon sergeant. Bob Littlar said wearily that those responsible were 'just trigger-happy green troops, in the end'.

The battalion had that day done all that could have been asked of its men. The fact that they failed to reach Caen represented a failure of the plan and, in lesser degree, of its execution by higher commanders, not by the Shropshires. They had marched and fought almost seven miles from Sword beach, and remained three short of the city of Caen. The Staffordshires' tanks commanded by Lionel Knight which had successfully crossed the German anti-tank ditch and reached the edge of Lebisey Wood several hundred yards west of the infantry withdrew at last light, to leaguer with the rest of the regiment near Biéville. Knight vented the frustration they all felt about turning back: 'If we'd had another infantry regiment up there we could have done it.' He himself drove back with a wounded Shropshire on the back of his tank, along with a prisoner who kept crying out '*Ost! Ost!*', to explain to the uncomprehending Knight that he was a Russian.

'Many weeks of desperate fighting were to elapse before the regiment again stood on that high ground,' wrote 27th Brigade's historian sadly. Knight received an MC for his achievement in getting so far that afternoon. The experiences emphasized how vital it was for tanks and infantry to advance close enough to each other to give mutual support, such as was frustrated by the anti-tank ditch south of Biéville. If Y Company had had tanks alongside Major Steel, or if infantry had been available to keep pace with Lionel Knight's Sherman troop, the vanguard of 185th Brigade might have advanced significantly further that day. These were now mere might-have-beens, however.

A further point bears making: it was fortunate the Shropshires and Staffords advanced south down the Beuville-Biéville axis towards Caen. Had they moved towards Lebisey on a more westerly axis, they would likely have collided headlong with 21st Panzer, already concentrating on the ridge before the British cleared Biéville. In such an event, the outcome must have been a slaughter of the weak invading force. Thus there seem good reasons to believe that fortune, on the afternoon of 6 June, went with the Shropshires and Staffords, even if it did not seem that way at the time, especially to poor Peter Steel and to Sir Bernard Montgomery.

Two miles further back, the Shropshires' Z Company concluded its own battle against the artillery battery behind the Périers ridge. This persisted almost until nightfall, an action entirely isolated from that conducted by the rest of the battalion, and was interrupted for some time while the Staffordshires' supporting tanks engaged the late afternoon panzer thrust. Only at the last gasp of day did a Polish-born prisoner volunteer to show the British a way through the rear of the entanglements protecting the battery. Led by the company commander and a sergeant, they duly worked around the position and at 2200 burst through the wire, causing the gunners to take flight, leaving eight German dead. A courageous sapper NCO, though severely wounded, laid and detonated charges to destroy the German 122mm guns – it is an injustice that we do not know his name. Wheelock wrote to his father with justifiable pride: 'We did it on our own, after a long and tiring six hours.' This was the Shropshires' last action of D-Day. Z Company lost six killed including a subaltern, three missing and twenty-three wounded. Wheelock's men took ten prisoners – the rest of the German gun crews escaped. Only the next morning was the company able to rejoin the rest of the battalion at Biéville. The 2nd KSLI as a whole lost 113 officers and men killed or wounded on 6 June, most of these within a mile or two of Lebisey Wood.

Kenneth Smith of 185th Brigade wrote after the war: 'I did not expect on my race to Caen, to confront 21st Panzer Division or any other armoured division ... Information concerning the strength and dispositions of [the German] 716th Division was somewhat nebulous and what with the speed of my advance and with the expected support of the Staffordshire Yeomanry tanks, [and] 7th Field Regiment, Royal Artillery, I did not anticipate much opposition.' This apologia was naive. No intelligent commander should have expected licence to conduct a deep thrust into territory occupied and fortified by the enemy since 1940, without the best available elements of the German army intervening. All that was remarkable about events on 6 June was that 21 Pz appeared on the battlefield so late.

Gunner Robin Dunn thought the ease with which the Firefly tanks punched away the advancing German armour showed that the threat, which had haunted K.P. Smith for months despite his disingenuous explanation above, was never serious enough to warrant the cautious – indeed, in Dunn's view feeble – advance by 185th Brigade that afternoon. The major, who ended a later legal career as a Lord Justice of Appeal, argued that the British mistake on the afternoon of D-Day, characteristic of the conduct of Montgomery's formations on many occasions, was to dance to the German tune, reacting to 21st Panzer's advance, rather than making the Germans dance to theirs, as should have been possible with the larger tank force at Rennie's disposal: 'At all our briefings, we had been urged to "bash on regardless", which was precisely what Rennie and Smith did not do.' This was another way of expressing the warning of another junior officer in Normandy: 'If you do not dominate events, your enemy will.'

Dunn did not go so far as to claim that it was plausible to secure Caen on 6 June. But he urged that it should have been possible to take and hold the high ground at Lebisey, just short of the city. This is probably true. In the weeks that followed the British suffered severely from German fire unleashed from those commanding heights. Little additional haste and more energetic leadership would have been needed for elements of 185th Brigade to seize Lebisey Wood before panzergrenadiers deployed there in strength, on the evening of 6 June.

The means were not at hand, however, to sustain a more far-reaching British thrust beyond Lebisey. In Montgomery's 14 April memorandum to his army commanders, he wrote: 'The best way to interfere with the enemy concentrations and counter-measures will be to push forward fairly powerful armoured force thrusts on the afternoon of D-Day. If two such forces, each consisting of an Armoured Brigade Group, were pushed forward on each Army front ... it would be very difficult for the enemy to interfere with our build-up ... I am prepared to accept almost any risk in order to carry out these tactics. I would risk even the total loss of the armoured brigade groups.' Churchill warmly applauded such a declaration of daring, indeed bravado, but it was always rooted in fantasy. There were no British 'armoured brigade groups' on the approach to Lebisey as the light faded on 6 June – only Y Company of the KSLI and half a squadron of Staffordshires. On D-Day Erroll Prior-Palmer was able to command 27th Armoured Brigade only in name. Its three regiments were dispersed and fragmented, and for many hours after the landings this state of affairs was inescapable, because the tanks had been ordered to operate in accordance with the demands of their respective infantry brigades.

That afternoon Crocker and Rennie seem right to have fixed 3 Division's priorities upon the repulse of 21st Panzer. Moreover, even had the Yeomanry and some Shropshires reached Caen, it is wildly unlikely that they could have achieved anything. A further reflection seems important: German pusillanimity delayed 21st Panzer's wild lunge until late afternoon, when the British had been granted ample time to prepare to receive them. It would be fanciful to suggest that on the afternoon of D-Day this lone German armoured division could have undone Neptune/ Overlord, or even rolled up the Sword beachhead. But its tanks could have inflicted brutal damage on 3rd Division and 27th Armoured Brigade before they found their landlegs.

If it was a misfortune for the British that 3 Div failed to advance further south, it was a vastly larger one for the Germans that 21st Panzer's intervention came so late. Had the division been ordered to move in the early hours of 6 June, as assuredly it would have been if Rommel had been at hand to exercise command, they could have struck at the Sword perimeter before the Staffordshire Yeomanry even got off the beach, far less deployed on the Périers ridge and beyond. The 'what-ifs?' argue far more critical lost German opportunities than British ones.

15
Nightfall

1 THE BEACHHEAD SECURED

As the close of day approached in Normandy, hundreds of thousands of men of a dozen nationalities – those fortunate enough to have escaped from preoccupation with their own immediate survival – succumbed to awe about the magnitude of the event in which they had participated; its monumental historical significance. A cluster of Hussars listened in an orchard to King George VI's BBC broadcast, applauding the success of the invasion. The 13th/18th leaguered on the south side of Hermanville, diminished by the absence of many of its tanks – A Squadron was short of fourteen; B of ten; C of seven. Some of these were recovered and repaired during the days that followed, however: in armoured warfare, whoever ends a battle as master of the field secures custody of cripples.

Most of the Hussar crews had been merely 'unhorsed', to use the regiment's stubbornly sustained cavalry vernacular, but one officer and fifteen men had been killed, the same number wounded. In the leaguer they examined curiously the first German prisoner they had taken, 'a dejected and frightened spectacle', in the words of the adjutant, Julius Neave. He added: 'Of all the other impressions of the day, by far the most pronounced at the end of it was a feeling of surprise and thankfulness that we were still alive to tell the tale.' Commando signaller Finlay Campbell felt the same: 'Before I left England I had resigned myself to the fact that I would get wounded if not killed, so by midnight I was very relieved to find that I was no more than exhausted.' Jim Eadie wrote to his wife, 'In the end it was not as bad as I had pictured, and after a bad start' – obviously a reference to the long beach delay and ambush of B Squadron by a German anti-tank gun – 'we made rapid progress inland ... We had a really good shoot-out with the Hun and completely scored off him.'

The East Yorkshires dug in on the edge of a partly ploughed field near Saint-Aubin-d'Arquenay, which in daylight yielded a 'glorious panoramic view of Sword beach ... a fever of activity'. They found Normandy resistant to their light tools: an hour's labour achieved only six inches of depth, meagre protection against shot and shell. An exhausted Lionel Roebuck had just completed his own trench when a trickle, and then a stream, of the battalion's stragglers arrived. Only half of his own company, he estimated, had participated in the successful assault on Daimler. The newcomers claimed to have been pinned down or lost, as do such men after all battles. Roebuck was disgusted to be ordered to surrender his laboriously-contrived excavation to two of the late arrivals, old sweats who had served in pre-war India. He felt better when a German shell landed on the disputed trench, killing both.

Back on the beach the East Yorks' wounded colonel was preparing to board a landing-craft for evacuation to England. Charles Hutchinson chanced upon a black and white rabbit, somebody's abandoned pet. In a spasm of sentimentality, surely brought on by the violent sensations he had experienced since dawn, Hutchinson picked up the bewildered creature and carried it to England, cradled in his good arm. 'Banger' King wrote to his batman's mother: 'I cannot express too deeply my admiration for the men I have been commanding. When we landed at H-Hour they went straight over the beaches in spite of a murderous fire and in half-an-hour had cleared a gap about 200 yards wide ... through which poured the reserve companies, Commandos, and it seemed to me about half the British Army ... There can't be many men in the Allied armies who got there before your son ... You have every reason to be proud of your son and the part he has played in this damn war.'

And before the stupendous events of 6 June were concluded, the killing and destruction interrupted by a few hours of darkness, one more drama unfolded above the Sword perimeter: the descent of 6th Air Landing Brigade – Mallard Force. In the beachhead thirty-four-year-old RAF war correspondent Alan Melville wrote: 'There was a wonderful sunset that evening. I was standing at the entrance to our dugout during a lull in the shelling when the most almighty roar of aircraft brought everyone up from their holes. Two great waves came in from the sea, the first of glider-towing bombers, the second of [planes dropping parachute-borne supply containers]. They roared in majestically as though this was just one more exercise over Salisbury Plain. The bombers released and the gliders slipped down between our own position and the first rising slopes of the ridge of hills.

'The troops forgot all about the shelling and the snipers. They stood on the edge of their trenches and waved and yelled themselves silly. It was the greatest hoister of morale which anyone could have provided, and it came at precisely the right minute. I talked to some German prisoners, and the arrival of those ... aircraft seemed to have had an equally great effect on them. They said they had never imagined we possessed so many ... and that when they saw them, they knew that it was hopeless.' A soldier of the Heer said long after about his feelings on becoming a PoW:

'At first I was rather depressed, of course. I, an old soldier, a prisoner after a few hours of invasion. But when I saw the matériel behind the enemy front, I could only say "Old man, how lucky you have been!"' The air landings impacted even upon 21st Panzer's tank crews, who a few hours earlier had supposed themselves invincible. Their commanders persuaded themselves that Mallard Force was being committed as an immediate tactical response to the panzer threat to Gale's perimeter, rather than to conform to a long-fixed schedule; they thus aborted an imminent counter-attack on 6th Airborne.

This second aerial armada, following the first in the early hours of the morning, comprised 256 Horsa and Hamilcar gliders, of which one crashed on take-off and three more force-landed safely in England, following tow-rope breaks. The remainder stayed low on their passage across the sea, at five hundred feet and 130 mph, to evade German radar for as long as possible. Three Horsas and one towing aircraft crashed into the Channel, almost all their passengers and crews being lost. Yet onward and upward surged the rest of the host, until they approached Normandy to provide a spectacle which many eyewitnesses, though previously thinking themselves sated with spectacle, afterwards judged to have been the most awesome of the Day of Days.

Specially trained aircraft-identifiers had been placed aboard all the transport vessels off Sword beach, in an effort to prevent the sort of tragedy that unfolded during the Sicilian landings, where naval gunners shot down British aircraft. Yet one of these observers, George Bourne, wrote of the crews aboard his own ship, *Empire Broadsword*: 'The gunners were very keen to relieve their nervous tension by shooting at something ... especially as some of the big shells bursting in the water looked suspiciously like bombs.' As the armada delivering 6th Air Landing Brigade passed over the fleet, several anti-aircraft guns opened fire.

Then tug after tug slipped its tow, freeing the gliders to slide down into the meadows on both sides of the Orne – in residual daylight, there was little risk of missing the British perimeter, though a bouncing Horsa crushed in its path two signallers of the Warwicks. Lt. Charles Cross of John Howard's battalion of the Ox & Bucks, from which the remaining three companies arrived with the dusk fly-in, wrote: 'The landing was ghastly. Mine was the first glider down though we were not quite in the right place, and the damn thing bucketed across the very upsy-downsy field and then broke across the middle. Our immediate opposition – a machine-gun – was very effectively silenced by another glider which fetched up plumb on the trench, and a couple of Huns – quite terrified – came out with their hands up.' Gunner Donald Thomas said: 'I always remember the smell of the ground – a sweet, scented smell. After all, I had my nose in it.' Some infantrymen, over-exuberant, burst out of their gliders to spray the countryside with random fire, until calmed by veterans of a whole day's battlefield experience. A mass of multi-coloured canopies opened as planes unloaded from their bomb-doors containers of weapons, ammunition and supplies, vari-coloured to signify their contents.

All thirty heavy Hamilcars got down safely, disgorging vehicles, guns and eight Tetrarch light tanks. Some of the latter immobilized themselves within minutes of starting to move, by catching discarded parachute harnesses in their tracks. When protective darkness came, fitters burned off the offending webbing with blowtorches. One tank was briefly trapped in a crashed Hamilcar, set on fire by German shelling. Its driver started his engine and smashed a path out of the glider 'like a moth bursting from its cocoon', in the words of Chester Wilmot. Motorcyclists set off on cross-country prowls during which some, after pinpointing German concentrations, called in air strikes or gunfire from HMS *Mauritius*. A six-pounder gun was put to use against an enemy tank within minutes of being disgorged onto Norman soil. The glider pilot who had flown in the weapon became its loader and when the gunlayer was killed, he took over that role. Surgical teams established a dressing-station in Ranville with two operating theatres, which performed extraordinary feats in the days that followed, at the cost of three of its eleven officers killed, along with twenty-eight of 102 other medical personnel.

The Warwicks of Smith's 185th Brigade had been dispatched up the canalside road south from the beach, to escape the unpleasantnesses of the Hillman battle and the tank actions with 21 Pz further west. They relieved 7 Para, which had been fighting in Bénouville all day, taking over its positions. The fly-in persuaded the residual German defenders to retire from the village, but when the Warwicks sought to press on further, they encountered strong resistance. Their FOO was aboard a tank knocked out as they approached Blainville, a mile further south, and thus they lost access to artillery support. At midnight the battalion dug in, stuck on the outskirts of the latter village.

The dusk fly-in delivered an astonishing 246 gliders. Naval officer Jack D'Arcy, down on Sword beach, wrote: 'I have never felt so grateful and proud in all my life.' Huw Wheldon, one of those who landed, wrote: 'I was conscious of bursting out of the glider … The next thing I noticed … was the sight of the troops, ever sensitive to unexpected opportunity, standing on the quiet grass in the twilight relieving themselves with the absent-minded look that men assume on these occasions.'

By the time full darkness fell, Richard Gale's perimeter contained fourteen infantry units, if each Commando was counted as a battalion, together with support troops. Gale had budgeted for 20 per cent losses in the D-Day drop and initial fighting, and in reality his formation lost 17 per cent of its strength. It was a heavy toll, compared with the casualties of others, but acceptable in return for such a contribution to fulfilment of the giant purpose of Overlord. The divisional commander's foremost concern was that his formation should be able to retain its ground, amid the ferocious German counter-attacks which must come. In the ensuing days the fields and woods held by 6th Airborne, Lovat's commandos and a trickle of reinforcements from 51st Highland Division became steeped in blood. Their lines held, however, one of the decisive achievements of the Normandy campaign.

To the east enemy forces, including elements of 21 Pz, clung to positions that extended to the coast: the commandos' attempts to reach the mouth of the Orne at Franceville-Plage had to be abandoned. On the opposite flank of Sword, however, German defenders holding ground between the British and Canadians were deeply shaken by the air landings. The 21 Pz battlegroup which had closed the coast between Luc and Lion at 1900, apparently unnoticed by 41 RM Commando, retired that evening to join its main body at Lebisey. Likewise the tank company supporting Hans von Luck's battlegroup east of the Orne abandoned a belated attempt to launch a counter-attack against Gale. The German Seventh Army telephone log recorded: 'Attack by 21 Panzer Division rendered useless by heavy concentration of airborne troops.' In the hours of darkness, many other Germans in positions between Lion and Luc-sur-Mer, including the defenders of strongpoint Trout which had held out all through 6 June, likewise withdrew, deeming their positions no longer defensible. This enabled the Allies next day to close the gap between Sword and Juno beaches, against light resistance.

The historian of 3rd Division wrote: 'When the light in the sky went out that night, the men who had survived could not jump into bed, turn over, and go to sleep … For a year now all their thoughts and energies had been directed to this day … But …

though men now knew where they stood, the prospects were no less grim for being more apparent.' Rennie's formation occupied an overnight perimeter five miles deep by four wide, but its men recognized that, in the days ahead, they would be obliged to renew the struggle to press southwards towards Caen, against German forces every hour gaining in strength and now thoroughly prepared to meet them. Of the British battalions that had been most heavily engaged, 2nd KSLI had already lost 113 killed and wounded; the South Lancs 107; the East Yorks 206 – a third of its fighting strength.

As the light failed, Guy Hattu and his comrades of 4 Commando were ordered to rouse themselves for one last move. They crossed the Cabourg road, noting corpses both of Germans and men of their own brigade. In Amfreville they saw German mini-tanks, destroyed by Otway's 9 Para, and wounded horses writhing and bucking in agony, because nobody had found time to shoot them. They took up positions on high ground and summoned their last reserves of strength to dig in, with much difficulty amid the resisting earth. A farmer begged them to take milk from his cows because no one else would do so. They cooked self-heating soup: it was 'horrible, but delicious'.

Afloat off Sword at 2400 Surgeon-Lt. Graham Airth wrote: 'This has indeed been D-Day, Dawned-day, Death-day, Destruction-Day. Disappointment and Disillusion Day. I have seen men die suddenly, horribly. I have twice been very near death myself, so near that I desperately wish to forget ... Tonight we are sleeping fitfully, with our clothes on.' Men watched curiously as anti-aircraft fire from the beach decorated the sky. As darkness descended, so likewise did biting insects, of which every combatant in Normandy would feel much during the weeks to come. A paratrooper wrote irritably to his parents: 'I can't see what God had in mind when he created the [mosquito].'

The historian of 3 Div later wrote: 'D-Day seemed *very* long', but finally it drew towards a close. It should prompt reflection that in the course of this one day, 6 June 1944, those who landed in Normandy had experienced a flood of sensations, some of them horrific, such as afflict few people through whole lifetimes of peace. Some 29,000 men had landed on Sword, against 25,000 on Gold; 21,500 on Juno; 23,250 on Utah; 34,250 on Omaha. Four thousand tons of munitions and stores had also come ashore on Sword, three-quarters of the target total. By nightfall, the most serious deficiency in 3 Division's perimeter was that of medium artillery. British and Canadian planners had budgeted for 7,750 casualties across their three beaches on D-Day and actually suffered 2,515. The 3rd Division lost 957, of whom about a quarter had died. Thus on Sword the British landed five times as many men as had attacked Dieppe two years earlier, yet these suffered only a quarter of the thousand fatal casualties of the disastrous 1942 raid.

This last statistic bears emphasis. The narrative above has referred to the phenomenon that many men remembered and recorded the sights and sounds of those who fell wounded or dead, while few noted the vastly larger number who survived. The exact toll of Allied casualties on 6 June remains a focus of quibbles, but nobody questions the broad brush figure that around three thousand invaders died, an astoundingly small number given the magnitude of the task and the achievement. Given the accounts above of the Sword battles, especially that for Hillman, it may seem astonishing that an officer of the Hussars' C Squadron who participated in the latter action, Lt. Eric Smith, wrote in retrospect about D-Day as 'an historic and exciting day but one which really had not been nearly as difficult' as he and his comrades had expected. As will be discussed below, there were several days later in what became the murderous Normandy campaign when more British and American soldiers died than had perished on 6 June. To the astonishment and dismay of those who participated in D-Day, and who permitted themselves a monumental sigh of relief on discovering at nightfall that they were still alive and unwounded, much worse battlefield experiences lay ahead of them.

Wilf Todd, in an English hospital after being hit in the arm, penned a long account of his D-Day experience with the East Yorks to his wife Mary. He ended this by saying: 'I am sorry if it has bored you darling but I felt as if I must tell someone just to get it off my mind and I thought the best person would be my wife. Perhaps I will be able to sleep now dear because up to now I have dreaded going to sleep in case I dream I am back on that beach.' Your ever-loving husband Wilf.xxxxxxxxxxxxxxxxxxxxxxx.' Todd was nineteen years old.

Commander Rupert Curtis, who that morning had put Lord Lovat ashore from his LCI, in the evening steered a westerly course offshore, passing across the entire British and Canadian coastal frontage, 'a grandstand view of the invasion beaches for which many would have paid thousands … an unforgettable sight. Through the smoke and haze I could see craft after craft which had been driven onto the beach with relentless determination to give the troops as dry a landing as possible. Many of these craft were now hopelessly stranded on obstacles and I could not help feeling a sense of pride at the spirit which their officers and crews had shown … It was clear that the battle for the footholds in the British and Canadian sectors had gone well enough.' The image – the spectre – of Churchill's armed forces as bunglers and losers, forged in the earlier years of the war and epitomized by the shambolic August 1942 raid on Dieppe, was laid at last.

2 WHAT CAME AFTER

Back in Britain, the *Daily Sketch* newspaper of 7 June reported on its front page: 'FIERCE FIGHTING IN STREETS OF CAEN; FIRST WAVE ALL SET FOR LAND BATTLES; LOSS MUCH LESS THAN EXPECTED'. The main headline asserted: 'THE BEACHES ARE CLEAR. MONTGOMERY IS PLEASED.' Here was a characteristic wartime media mingling of reality and fantasy, sanitized by the blue pencil of the censor. It was true that the Allies had got ashore at acceptable cost and secured defensible positions. It was false that the invaders were in Caen. The outcome of D-Day fell significantly short of Montgomery's proclaimed ambitions and expectations, though not those of most sensible British and American commanders.

For many of the men who had landed on 6 June, it was a source of surprise, and indeed dismay, to discover that their life-threatening experiences, far from having ended with the success of the assault, were instead scarcely begun. Hugh Collinson, an artillery FOO, awoke on the morning of the 7th 'feeling very cheerful and starting to enjoy myself', after the terrors of the previous day. His sunny spirits did not last long. He was first strafed into a ditch by Luftwaffe FW190s, then a mortar bomb exploded in the midst of his team, wounding all of them. 'I lay down by the side of the road oozing blood. Stretcher-bearers appeared within ten minutes. By 9 pm I was on my way home … with a nice "Blighty one".' He added the droll reflection: '4 ¾ years training … for this.'

On that second day, 3rd Division and explicitly 185th Brigade was called upon to renew its advance on Caen, most immediately by seizing the Lebisey ridge, from which the Shropshires had been repulsed on the previous evening. Considerable anger had been relayed down from the summits of command – in fact, from Montgomery himself – about the formation's perceived failure to achieve his D-Day objectives. Now, unfortunately, instead of Rennie's units starting out the following morning in positions from which they could deliver a powerful concentrated thrust, they were dispersed within the Sword perimeter, shoring up perceived weak places – in Robin Dunn's jaundiced view, still dancing to the enemy's tune. The Lincolns of 9th Brigade were dug in just south of Lion-sur-Mer, the Borderers at Saint-Aubin and 2nd Ulsters behind the Périers ridge, in case the Germans attempted a new counter-attack on that flank, as happened late in the afternoon.

Thus only the Warwicks and Norfolks were available to renew the drive for Caen, supported by the Staffordshire Yeomanry, with the tired Shropshires in reserve. Local commanders were called upon to launch a rushed attack, during which everything possible went wrong. In the rueful words of a tank officer, 'It was discovered that the enemy had moved into [Lebisey] wood in great force.' The defending panzergrenadiers knew their ground, which offered excellent cover. They were led by officers who understood their business. The British operation was planned by K.P. Smith, almost certainly shaken by his failures the previous day, and by the harsh criticism he had received. The great Gen. Bill Slim told his officers in a wartime lecture: 'Every important battle develops to a point where there is no real control by senior commanders. Each soldier feels himself to be alone … The dominant feeling of the battlefield, gentlemen, is loneliness.'

On the morning of 7 June, Brigadier Smith was very lonely indeed. He decreed a start line which proved to be exposed to German fire, then postponed for an hour the attack and its supporting artillery barrage. This decision did not reach the leading company, which started forward at its previously appointed time and met murderous resistance. The battalion's colonel was killed when he went forward to try to salvage the situation. Then

Smith somehow convinced himself that the objective was secure, and ordered forward the Warwicks' anti-tank guns, mortars and tracked carriers to consolidate. These, too, were overwhelmed by the Germans. The battalion lost ten officers and 140 other ranks, many of them taken prisoner, together with all its heavy weapons.

When the Norfolks were ordered to make a further attempt to retrieve the situation, they too were harrowed. John Talbot, one of the gunner FOOs supporting the attack, said: 'We were pinned down all day about a hundred yards short of [Lebisey] wood and my pack [set] was the only [wireless] link with division as all the other sets failed to work!' At midnight he borrowed his colonel's jeep to take a party to retrieve his own crippled armoured vehicle from no man's land. The Staffords' attempts to support the attacking battalions were hampered by failure to get their Shermans across the ditch – the anti-tank obstacle that had caused both sides such inconvenience on the previous day – which lay between Biéville and Lebisey. By nightfall the Warwicks were reduced to a fighting strength not much above sixty men, few with weapons, while the Norfolks mustered only three hundred. K.P. Smith became lost when he himself went forward to try to discover what was happening. He spent the night hiding in a barn before escaping back to his headquarters at dawn, where one of his staff revived him with a bottle of champagne discovered in the château's cellar.

Meanwhile elsewhere in the Sword perimeter the Borderers of 9th Brigade became engaged in a chaotic battle around Le Mesnil, which ended with them making a desperate charge only to discover that they were attacking tanks of the East Riding Yeomanry. The Germans nonetheless suffered a worse day. A big new attempted counter-attack by 21 Pz and the newly arrived 12 SS Pz, the latter probably the best German armoured division in France, was broken up before it even reached its start line by devastating British artillery and naval gunfire. The 2nd Ulsters fought a savage battle near Périers to hold off SS panzergrenadiers, and by evening had repulsed them. Elsewhere the Lincolns' rifle companies were deployed piecemeal – one to Bénouville, the rest to Saint-Aubin, to reinforce other units under pressure.

The British attacks further south towards Lebisey were abandoned at last light, as were all hopes of a swift occupation of Caen. Montgomery wrote unapologetically: 'The Germans are doing everything they can to hold onto CAEN. I have decided not to have a lot of casualties by butting up against the place.' Instead of penetrating the city, he thereafter embarked upon successive attempts to envelop it from the west, which would precipitate carnage – perhaps unavoidable – that persisted into July.

The battle to defend 6th Airborne's perimeter turned cruelly attritional. John Howard's men, relieved by the Warwicks at the Caen Canal bridge, joined the rest of their newly-arrived battalion. Having suffered just sixteen casualties on D-Day, they incurred more than sixty at Escoville on 7 June. That day Huw Wheldon's 1st RUR, which had landed the previous night, pushed southwards and captured Longueval, but at a cost of sixteen killed, sixty-nine wounded and forty missing, mostly casualties of German mortars. These novices of war found it hard to come to terms with the ubiquity of death and destruction. Wheldon, who was awarded an MC for his actions, wrote in distress to his mother, 'There is waste and devastation everywhere', and likewise to his father, 'The waste is overwhelming to a chap like me, new to it – & a non-conformist conscience to boot.'

Wheldon's battalion lost in all, by the time the Normandy campaign was ended, six officers and forty-five men killed, one and thirty-three missing – mostly taken prisoner – eighteen and 385 wounded. In 6th Airborne's first month after D-Day, it lost 215 officers and 2,750 other ranks, and thereafter sustained casualties averaging three hundred a week. One of its battalions, 7 Para, lost 452 of 610 men who flew to Normandy – six officers and eighty-four men killed, two and 112 missing, twelve and 236 wounded. Richard Todd had just fourteen left of eighty mortar-men under his command on 5 June, and found himself posted to divisional headquarters, working in an outbuilding of the much-battered château where Gale and his senior officers were based.

'It would be less than honest,' wrote Todd, 'to suggest that I did not have some sense of relief to be sheltered in a stable and not charging into the holocaust.' Around Ranville 'every tree was shattered and riven by shell and mortar fire, buildings and roofs were pockmarked and the surrounding ground heavily pitted'. The Airborne Division was finally relieved on 5 September, by which time it had left behind in Normandy around 50 per cent of its strength – 821 men killed, 2,709 wounded and 927 missing, of whom half were dead and the others PoWs.

It was a reflection of the erratic fashion in which units were plunged into heavy fighting; then spared for a while; then bloodied once more, that on 7 June 1st Norfolks lost twenty killed, the same number as fell on D-Day, then only a total of eight dead until 8 July when suddenly they lost thirteen; then on 6 August another twenty-three killed, with wounded in proportion. Late in June the East Riding Yeomanry's padre approached a young officer and said: 'George, we have a job to do.' They returned to the place where one of their Shermans had been destroyed earlier in the battle, to recover the dead: 'In the front driver's seat was what remained of Trooper Smith, only his boots and the charred remains of his legs lay beneath where he had been sitting. In his seat were further charred remains of his body. It was the same for the rest of the crew. We buried what we found.' In some cases, crewmen in tanks which 'brewed up' were reduced to charcoal dwarves, no more than two feet high. Most units reported as 'missing' men whose bodies were obliterated by a direct hit, in the absence of identifiable remains for burial.

The point to be noted about the above statistics is that the majority of all casualties were incurred after D-Day: the landings seemed costly, on 6 June, to men unaccustomed to battle, but in 6th Airborne many paratroopers listed as 'missing' either rejoined their units in the hours and days that followed, or proved to have been taken prisoner. It was in the weeks which came after that Normandy became the bloodiest of Britain's 1939–45 campaigns, comparable in its scale of losses to the heaviest actions of World War I. At Third Ypres in 1917, for instance, the British Army lost a daily average of 2,324 men for 105 days. In Normandy, for eighty-three days Montgomery's forces suffered an average of 2,354 casualties. Each infantry division lost an average of 341 officers and 5,115 other ranks, equivalent to three-quarters of its rifle strength, had not this been constantly restored by replacements. An infantry battalion lost an average of thirty-six officers and 809 ORs, killed, wounded or taken prisoner. Since barely half its paper strength served in rifle companies, the most dangerous role, this means that a typical unit's fighting ranks were entirely refilled twice before the Germans in Normandy broke.

In North-West Europe just over a quarter of British officers sooner or later became casualties, compared with 19.6 per cent other ranks, these being concentrated overwhelmingly in the fighting elements of the army. On D-Day on the Sword front including 6th Airborne, one brigadier, six unit colonels and more than thirty company and squadron commanders were killed or wounded. Between June and November 1944, each month about one in three rifle company and platoon commanders became casualties, 70 per cent of these in attack and 40 per cent when in close contact with the enemy, as distinct from falling victim to long-range fire. By May 1945 just one of the 3 Div company commanders who had landed on D-Day was still alive, unwounded and in his job. Each month almost one in five rifle battalion commanders – lieutenant-colonels – became a casualty. A War Office liaison officer wrote later in the campaign that most battalions landed in Normandy with a decent corps of junior leaders, but as attrition set in, the quality markedly declined.

For the British Army, one of the surprises of the campaign was that some novice formations, 3 Div notable among them, turned into increasingly proficient warriors, while veterans brought back from the Mediterranean, especially 7th Armoured and 51st Highland divisions, proved embarrassing disappointments: they had become exhausted and risk-averse. Even after Montgomery sacked and replaced their commanders, the formations lacked drive and enthusiasm. A further problem evolved progressively, and most acute in 1945: it grew obvious to every man of Eisenhower's armies that the Allies were destined to win the war. Many soldiers displayed a very human desire to avoid finding themselves among the last to be sacrificed on the road to victory. This did not make them cowards – most were resigned to doing their duty. But they were reluctant to take risks beyond the norm – to go the extra yard to seize an enemy position. Infantry were ever more persuaded that in attack it was best to allow artillery to do the heavy lifting; then to follow tanks forward, rather than to precede them.

In July 1944, when the British Army serving under Montgomery in NW Europe attained its peak strength, fourteen British, three Canadian and one Polish division of 21st Army Group were in contact with the enemy. At that time the Americans had already twenty-three divisions in the field, and would eventually have sixty. The German army at that time boasted 237 divisions in its order of battle, albeit most of them much weaker than their Allied counterparts. The Red Army claimed 480 formations, though all were smaller than those of the British and Americans.

After the great race across France and Belgium that took place in late August 1944, after the collapse of the German armies in Normandy, everything seemed to go into slow motion. Each movement took longer than the generals hoped, especially when winter came. Insofar as anything in a war can be characterized as glamorous, D-Day on 6 June was such an event, when Eisenhower's armies and the air and naval forces shared in a vast spectacular such as the world had never seen before, and surely never would again. The invasion became the Finest Hour of the citizen soldiers of Britain, Canada and the United States. Before 6 June 1944, for three years and at stupendous cost, the Russians had borne the principal burden of challenging the legions of Hitler. After it took place, once the Western Allies had committed themselves wholeheartedly to battle against major German armies, they shared the sacrifices until the end, though not remotely on the same scale as those of the Russians. Most of the British, Canadian and American armies never matched the professional skills of the best of the German army, but there is a powerful argument that had they done so, they would have forfeited the spirit of the democracies, the doctrine of moderation rather than fanaticism, for which the struggle was being fought. They did enough to prevail with credit and honour; sufficient to fulfil the hopes and the destiny their leaders and the British people had cherished and sought since 1940.

3 SWORD'S RECKONING

In captivity Lt. Gen. Wilhelm Richter, commander of the German 716th Division in Normandy, commented on the British D-Day performance in an interview with US Army historians: 'The tactics of troops during the first landing were good and showed very good co-operation between all three British branches' forces … The attacks after the landing and push towards the south were not launched with the same power. Despite the rapid advance of numerous enemy tanks, putting German artillery out of action, the follow-up by the infantry was, in my opinion, relatively slow.'

Ronald Lewin, a distinguished war historian who served as a British gunner both in North Africa and Normandy, wrote later of the latter: 'It was pretty clear … (certainly it struck me forcibly within the limited range of experience of a regimental officer) that the standard of training of our troops for this battle in this place sometimes fell far short of perfection. Without the assured and massive support of artillery and armour, our infantry were too often disposed to be sluggish and unambitious.'

One of Montgomery's principal staff officers David Belchem, who ran 21st Army Group's Operations and Plans division, wrote harshly in 1981: 'The record of 3 British Division is the most disappointing of all the assault sectors. Having started off with commendable élan, with the rapid capture of Hermanville … progress … afterwards gave the impression of over-cautiousness … A more dynamic formation would not have dug in … which reflected the lack of training and battle experience of some of their officers.' Once the front stabilized Montgomery visited 3 Div and 'being bitterly disappointed at my not having reached Caen', in the words of K.P. Smith of 185th Brigade, 'suggested that I was on the old side and not up to the stresses which laid ahead … Thus, sad to relate, Lebisey being my Waterloo, as Napoleon was banished to St Helena, I was, metaphorically, banished to Madagascar' – to become that island's British military commander. 'Understandably, I was broken-hearted.'

During the spring a staff officer named Woodrow Wyatt had served as brigade-major under Smith. Before the invasion he was transferred to Rennie's headquarters, resisting pleas from the brigadier to remain his executive officer. Wyatt was a maverick, who soon afterwards was committed for trial by court-martial for insubordination when he formally reported to the divisional commander that one of his most senior staff officers, a regular colonel, was unfit for his post and threatened the welfare of the entire formation. Wyatt wrote of Smith's dismissal that in Normandy he learned that not all tragedies involve death. He described 'the pitiful face of [the brigadier] sitting in the back of a jeep on his way to the beachhead and a bitter journey home'. The failure of 185th Brigade on 6 June 'was a major reason for our being pinned down for so long in a narrow bridgehead … [Smith's] desolate face haunted me. Would it have made any difference if I had been at his side? Would it have given him that minute piece of extra confidence he might have needed to take risks at a moment when perhaps he fatally hesitated?'

Although Smith was indeed a weak officer, who on 6 June and thereafter proved to lack grip, drive and judgement, neither his failings nor those of other commanders were responsible for 3rd Division's failure to take Caen. It has been a folly of the British Army for much of its modern history to seek means to escape bloody and protracted attritional fighting – to unlock keys to quick victories – which against major enemies have almost invariably proved unattainable. It is doubtful there was any shortcut to the Allied defeat of the German armies in Normandy without the costly clashes which took place during June and July, progressively wearing down Hitler's legions, until in August they finally broke.

A fundamental question facing 3rd Division and its foremost units on D-Day was whether they were expected or required either by their commanders or by their country to pour blood in profusion onto the fields of Normandy, in order to fulfil historic purposes, perform great deeds. By the standards of the Three Hundred at Thermopylae, Grenville's *Revenge* amid the Spanish fleet in 1591, Wellington's squares at Waterloo, countless British battalions on the 1914–18 Western Front, many of Rennie's units in Normandy on 6 June showed themselves cautious, hesitant, slow, dilatory, fearful of loss. The relatively modest casualty figures provide incontestable evidence of this. Some individuals, mostly officers and NCOs, displayed exemplary courage and will for sacrifice, but this did not extend to the collectives, the units. It seems nonetheless mistaken thus to condemn Rennie's men. Before the first British, Canadian or American soldier landed on D-Day, it was apparent the Allies would be the victors of World War II. What availed them, then, to embrace sacrifices worthy of the last ditch, the forlorn hope, the courage of despair? On Sword beach and beyond, indeed across every invasion beach on 6 June, there was courage enough and sacrifice enough. There was merely not the courage and acceptance of self-immolation demanded by extremity and national survival.

It is hard to imagine that 3rd Division could have done much better than it did on D-Day, without embracing a military culture quite different from that of the 1944 British Army. It would have needed senior officers with Rommel's inspiration and dash, together with a suicidalist spirit such as lay far outside its doctrine and traditions. The director of military training wrote in a report composed before D-Day: 'The marvellous thing is not that young soldiers under fire for the first time get "pinned down", but that they later fight as magnificently and courageously as they have done [in the Mediterranean].' In other words, in Normandy on 6 June it was no just cause for surprise that some men of the assault battalions proved slow to advance: many who did not distinguish themselves on the beaches showed themselves doughty fighting soldiers later in the campaign.

It was David Belchem's boss, Montgomery himself, who was responsible for the most critical sin of omission in the planning for D-Day, and explicitly for Sword beach. Three months later, as 1st Airborne Division's senior officers were being briefed for the descent on Arnhem, Polish brigadier Stanislaw Sosabowski famously expostulated in protest at the 'Market Garden' plan: 'But the Germans, general … the Germans!' Arnhem was doomed from its inception by a stubborn refusal by its originators to consider how the enemy would respond to the slow-motion engagement of the British airborne formation: SS panzers were granted hours of grace in which to deploy against the paratroopers, between lunchtime when landings began and evening when the British belatedly reached the north end of the vital bridge. In the same fashion before D-Day, Montgomery and his subordinates failed to review their rashly declared expectations for what 3rd Division might reasonably achieve, even after it was confirmed that 21st Panzer had moved relatively close to Caen, within easy reach of the Sword beachhead.

On 6 June it was a crowning mercy, which the invaders had no right to expect, that the German armour proved so slow to reach the battlefield; that British tanks and anti-tank guns were granted priceless hours in which to get ashore; to move inland; deploy to meet the panzers. It was inevitable that 21 Pz's intervention should delay and, in fact, for an hour absolutely halt, the British advance on Caen, which already promised to deliver a weak punch as well as a fatally late one – just three green infantry companies and one armoured squadron.

The Potsdam Institute for Military History's multi-volume narrative, the nearest thing Germany has ever published to an official history of its own side of the war, asserts: 'The broad advance announced by Montgomery did not happen. British armoured units were not aggressive enough ... Montgomery and his staff mistakenly assumed that [21 Pz] would only be deployed once all its units were fully assembled ... Poor co-operation among the various [British] forces also weakened the momentum of the Allied offensive.'

Little of this seems valid. The problem on the road to Caen was not that the British armour was insufficiently aggressive, but that its regiments were delayed by beach issues inseparable from the friction of war and explicitly from the largest and most complex amphibious landing in history. Much of the lingering and stumbling that followed was caused by poor voice radio communications, which dogged the British Army throughout the war. Its sets' short-range performance was impeded by operating on a lower 6–9 MHz high-frequency band which required signals to propagate in so-called ground-wave mode, by hugging the surface of the earth, limiting their strength and making them chronically vulnerable to interference. Such bands were entirely appropriate for public radio broadcasting, which employed large antennae, but not for military tactical sets with short aerials. Unsurprisingly, infantry in contact with the enemy were desperately wary of exposing high protruding aerials above their positions.

This persistent communications weakness was the result of an ill-judged British pre-war procurement decision, contrasted with the German and American choice of much more efficient 28–52 MHz VHF military technology. A devastating British technical report in November 1944 asserted that tests proved US Army voice radios to be much more effective. It was too late in the war, however, to abandon the flawed British technology. On 6 June when the rapid transmission of information and orders was vital, repeated communications breakdowns hampered progress. Only the artillery and armoured units, with their bigger sets and longer aerials, were reliably in voice contact.

The Germans used mortar concentrations to deadly effect, indeed these were the most effective weapons deployed by the defenders on 6 June. Allied soldiers hated them because the bombs exploded in clusters, without warning such as was given by high-velocity artillery shells. Lobbed with astonishing precision from their launching tubes by an integral cartridge, mortar rounds flew so slowly through the air that a watchful eye on the ground sometimes glimpsed them aloft. They described an arc; attained a summit; then descended in a terrifying silence to wreak havoc upon a farmyard, a gently waving field of Norman corn, or human flesh. Commanders sought to reassure their men that the Germans used so many only because they lacked the profusion of high-velocity guns which the Allies possessed. This was true, but offered no comfort to those on the receiving end of a mortar 'stonk', as almost every invader found himself on D-Day. In Normandy mortars were responsible for more Allied casualties than any other German weapon.

On the Eastern Front, the Red Army's offensives were conducted by vast masses of men and tanks. After the war Wehrmacht veterans testified in dismay, disgust and disbelief about the manner in which, faced with a Russian assault, they mowed down a first wave of attackers, then a second, then a third, until finally they were overwhelmed by the apparently limitless men and tanks Stalin's generals could unleash, especially from 1943 onwards, without heed to casualties. No comparable weight of force was available to Montgomery and his subordinates to swamp the defences of Normandy on 6 June 1944, then thrust inland with the energy demanded by his plan. The Allies lacked access to landing-craft to convey more men to France, and explicitly to Sword. It required herculean efforts to transport the six British and American 'division slices' that initially went ashore. Whatever courage and dash 3 Div had displayed, it lacked strength to occupy Caen that day. Even had some British troops got into or through the city, they must have been isolated and crushed by German counter-attacks.

The most important point missed by the Potsdam Institute historian is that whatever mistakes were made by the British in the Sword beachhead on D-Day were dwarfed by those of the Germans. The changes of objective for 21 Pz, the only major armoured formation available for immediate commitment, were disastrous, as were the hopelessly tardy orders to get the tanks forward. Even when Rommel returned to his headquarters late on 6 June, he continued to expect further Allied landings in the Pas-de-Calais, a delusion which persisted for weeks and severely weakened the counter-invasion build-up in Normandy.

Meanwhile academic turned wartime infantryman David Hunt once observed about the Heer's overall performance in World War II: 'The preeminent German characteristic was brilliance at improvisation.' NCOs, especially, displayed astonishing initiative in almost all circumstances. Yet very little of this spirit – of the accustomed professionalism of Hitler's armed forces – was manifest in the Sword sector, or indeed anywhere else in Normandy, on 6 June. A pitiful exchange took place in a PoW camp eavesdropped by the British, when a young coastal artillery officer announced to Colonel Ludwig Krug, the man who had surrendered Hillman: 'I would like to report to you, sir, that I sunk a cruiser.' Krug said, possibly ironically: 'Heartiest congratulations.' The gunner continued: 'I am extremely proud of having achieved that before being taken prisoner.' In truth, of course, he had achieved nothing of the sort. Like a host of German soldiers and commanders in the wake of D-Day – including Col. Krug – he was simply striving desperately to make himself feel better about failure.

Most of the enemies whom 3 Div and 6th Airborne encountered were not native-born. Instead they were Poles, Ukrainians, Russians, far less skilled and committed, albeit commanded by German officers and NCOs. This was a notable piece of good fortune for the invaders. Though some of the best of the Heer and Waffen SS arrived on the battlefield in the days after 6 June, they were not manning the coastal defences when the Allies landed.

The most severe criticism that might be made of Crocker, Rennie and Smith is that they showed themselves more concerned with not losing than with striving for a decisive breakthrough. British generals had spent most of their inter-war careers in the service of an army of which the principal function was to serve as an imperial gendarmerie. Such men were chronically uneasy handling large forces on big battlefields, by comparison with their Russian, German and sometimes also American counterparts. Lt. Gen. Sir John Harding, an able officer who conducted for the War Office a September 1944 study of British higher command performance, reported: 'Many Division and Corps commanders have failed … because they were not trained for such commands.' More than a few Allied senior officers were found wanting in the early actions in North-West Europe. A procession of corps, divisional, brigade and battalion commanders were replaced, in the same fashion as was K.P. Smith, after their first or second battles. But this book has sustained the argument advanced in *Overlord* in 1984 and by many other historians since that no such coup as the seizure of Caen was achievable by the British Second Army on D-Day. Commanders on the spot had their priorities right, even if execution was clumsy.

The foremost objective for D-Day, recognized by most of its commanders albeit not by Winston Churchill, was that it should not fail to secure a defensible beachhead. This was triumphantly achieved, on Sword and across the other four landing-places. Norman Scarfe, the historian of 3rd Division, wrote: 'Our feelings were that if we did not take Caen on D-Day, we'd surely take it on D plus 1. Certainly we felt pretty disappointed and frustrated not to have got into Caen as planned on D-Day.' The overwhelming focus of their training had been on the assault, the descent upon France from the air or sea. While Montgomery, as their commander-in-chief, had spoken carelessly about expecting his tanks to push south of Caen 'to knock about a bit down there', the men who would have to perform such heroics thought of little beyond the sea, the landing zones, the beaches – their first objectives. This was natural, and right.

It was not foolish of Montgomery to set ambitious objectives for those who were to land, march and fight. It was arrogant and reckless of him, however, to allow the prime minister, and his British and American command peers, to suppose that he expected these to be fulfilled. Montgomery, in his conceit, gave a clear impression to the warlords of Britain and America that he proposed to launch a series of immediate armoured assaults through and beyond Caen, to unbalance the enemy before they knew what had hit them. This was wholly unrealistic.

After the war K.P. Smith of 185th Brigade reflected much on events in the Sword beachhead which had destroyed his career. He observed that for Caen to fall on 6 June, 8th Brigade had to suppress Morris and Hillman fairly quickly; armour had to be ashore in time fully to support 185th Brigade's drive on Caen; the Staffordshires and the 185th had to get to Caen before 21st Panzer arrived; and the British needed to meet no unexpected opposition, especially around Lebisey. 'None of these four provisos materialised and that is why Caen did not fall on D-Day.'

Though Smith's memoir, written in old age, suggests a simple soldier with little capacity for reflection, these remarks are right and just. The infantry of 3 Div and its supporting armoured units lacked weight to overcome the German opposition and achieve a decisive breakthrough on 6 June. That night they were best off where they found themselves: deployed in strength three miles short of Caen, relatively well-placed to meet the German firestorm that came during the following days. Likewise, 6th Airborne was obliged to fight for its life to hold its ground.

Maj. Ken Ferguson, an engineer who landed in the first wave that morning, had been infuriated by the spectacle of infantrymen lingering passive on the beach. He said later of D-Day: 'I suppose it could have been done better.' Well, yes, of course. The same might be said of every battle throughout history. But few thoughtful soldiers in 1944 failed to grasp the towering reality, which should dominate every modern perception of Neptune/Overlord: the Allies set out to perform the immensely difficult task of landing and sustaining huge forces on the coast of Normandy, where Hitler's legions strove to prevent them from doing so. The Allies succeeded in their purpose and the Germans failed in theirs. This was as true on Sword as on the other four beaches assaulted by the British, Canadian and American armies. Even granted the Allies' huge superiority of means, the landings remain a supreme achievement of the Western war.

This book has addressed the experience of the men who landed in upper Normandy with 3rd Division and 6th Airborne. Yet it must be appropriate to conclude by reverting to General Sir Bernard Montgomery and his personal vision for the seizure of Caen in a first glorious eruption of 'his' army – and thus he undoubtedly perceived the British and Canadian force, as their commander-in-chief – into occupied France. Cynics might say that men died on 6 June in pursuit of the fulfilment of Montgomery's impossible vision, urged upon him by Winston Churchill; that Lt. Gwilliam of the KSLI, who was badly wounded at 1730 having advanced further towards Caen than any other British officer on D-Day, was a victim of the field-marshal's hubris. Yet such a view seems mistaken.

Montgomery was Britain's most famous soldier of World War II – not necessarily the best, but far more celebrated than Slim, Alexander, Wavell. He was the only general of whom every toy shop of the author's 1950s English childhood sold toy examples, amid the serried ranks of his soldiers. This was not least because he had the good fortune to attain high command at the moment of the war in August 1942 when his army could engage the Germans in North Africa with an overwhelming superiority of men, tanks, planes, such as had previously been absent. He was certainly a winner, but he was dealt a winning hand.

His vanity and ambition were indisputable. Yet these vices are common to many career soldiers. Although historians have concluded that Montgomery was a much more limited director of armies than he perceived himself – no Marlborough or Wellington – he was a highly competent professional, of a kind of which the World War II British Army never possessed a sufficiency. In the twenty-first century the towering reality is that the D-Day plan, overwhelmingly Montgomery's personal conception, succeeded. It made a decisive contribution to the eventual Anglo-American triumph in Normandy in August.

If Operation Neptune/Overlord was set in motion by generals, however, it was carried to fruition by what in bygone centuries were characterized as 'common soldiers'. Few of the units which landed in Normandy deserve to be ranked among the great companies in the history of war – Caesar's legions or Napoleon's Old Guard. They were, instead, citizen soldiers, not many of whom aspired to be heroes. This book has sought to chronicle the transition of a portion of the British Army from the poor thing that it was in June 1940, and which much of it remained at the time of the Dieppe tragedy in August 1942, into the force that achieved a successful landing on Sword beach in June 1944, and fought on to the Elbe and victory almost a year later. Few of its men ever became eager warriors, but this makes all the more admirable the manner in which they did their duty, fulfilled their nation's purposes.

Jim Eadie, colonel of the Staffordshire Yeomanry, wrote home to his wife on 23 July 1944, when he had just learned that, to his vast relief, he was to be posted home to become chief instructor at Sandhurst: 'We must indeed if we are spared try to help with all we have got to end this madness of war. It is easy at times of stress and imminent danger to resolve to give one's all to ensure that such things shall never happen again, but it is easy to then slip into one's old mode of living when the crisis is passed. I will not do this latter. I am resolved to use what life I have left to add to the happiness of mankind and to make good to those who have suffered.' If these sentiments sound mawkish in the twenty-first century, they reflect the wholly sincere emotions of a soldier appalled by the scenes he had witnessed, the dead men whom he had known, in the course of the battle for Normandy.

The soldiers of 27th Armoured Brigade, 6th Airborne and 3rd Division, the commandos of the 1st and 4th Special Service Brigades, performed a great thing on 6 June 1944 and in the months that followed, matched by the achievements of others on Juno, Gold, Omaha, Utah. 'Those first days are going to be exhausting and probably absolutely hell,' the colonel of the Lincolns warned his men before they embarked. '[We] must have confidence that we are going to do it well, better than the other side.' And so they did. It is right that their descendants should honour their memories in this eightieth year since the Allies celebrated the ending of the Second World War.

Some Afterlives … and Deaths

George Appleton, who commanded a Beach Group on Sword, finished the war as a Lt. Col., then returned to his pre-war career as a director of an Aintree soap company. He later turned farmer, bred pedigree pigs, became high sheriff of Merseyside and had four grandchildren before dying aged ninety-two in 2005.

The outspoken Major Robin Dunn MC of 7th Field Regiment, Royal Artillery, left the army after the war and became a lawyer, finally Rt. Hon. Sir Robin Dunn, a Lord Justice of Appeal. In 1993 he published a lively memoir entitled *Sword and Wig*. He died in 2014, aged ninety-six.

After the war Col. James Eadie of the Staffordshire Yeomanry returned to his old role at what had become the Bass Brewery. He became chairman of the Brewers' Society together with many good causes such as he had promised for himself on the battlefield in July 1944. He died in 1959 aged sixty, on descending comfortably into an armchair at his home, after what he described to his family as the best day's hunting of his life. He had suffered a heart attack that followed others, and which must have owed much to the wartime stresses he had endured, when already approaching middle age.

French commando Hubert Faure fought until wounded by shrapnel and evacuated to England on 9 July 1944. He suffered further injuries on returning to the battle, when the jeep in which he was travelling collided with an Allied tank. By the end of the Normandy campaign, 140 of the 177 Kieffers had been killed or significantly wounded. Faure died in 2021, aged 106, having spent his later years as a public works engineer.

Captain Hon. Paul Greenway, who cleared mines for the assault on the Merville Battery, in 1963 inherited his father's title as Baron Greenway and died in 1975, aged fifty-eight.

Lt. Col. Dick Harrap, CO of the 13th/18th Hussars, was killed on 16 June 1944, when he drove around a corner in Normandy in his jeep, to be confronted by a German Mk IV tank.

Major John Howard, who led the glider assault on the Orne and canal bridges, returned to England with his battalion in September. One day driving a jeep, he was badly injured in a head-on collision with an American Army truck, and invalided out of the army. He spent the rest of his working life as a relatively humble civil servant, dying in 1999, aged eighty-six.

Alan Jefferson of 9 Para, wounded during the assault on the Merville Battery, married dancer Lisa Grogan and after the war pursued a successful career in the operatic world. After an apprenticeship backstage in theatre, he became director of the BBC concert orchestra and author of outspoken biographies of several leading musical figures. He had six children by three wives before his death in 2010, aged eighty-nine.

By the end of August 1944, only nine men remained in A Company of the East Yorks, of 120 who had landed on 6 June. The beloved, reckless and indiscreet Major Charles 'Banger' King won two DSOs before he and his jeep were blown up on a mine in Germany in April 1945. He was forty and had no life of which his comrades knew anything, outside his beloved regiment. By a tragic coincidence his brother was killed in Burma just ten days after himself.

Lt. Col. Jack Maurice of 2nd KSLI was killed on the night of 7 July by a chance German shell, two days before Canadian forces entered Caen, which he and his battalion had striven so manfully to achieve on 6 June.

Major Allen Parry, wounded in the Merville Battery, was evacuated to England, spent ten days in hospital, then discharged himself and rejoined 9 Para in Normandy on 18 June. He died in 1992, aged seventy-six.

Maj. Gen. Tom Rennie was wounded and evacuated on 13 June. After returning to the battlefield to command 51st Highland Division, he was killed by mortar fire in March 1945, aged forty-five, following the Rhine crossing.

Albert Richards, the war artist who jumped with 9 Para into the assault on the Merville Battery, and who afterwards painted several striking oils of the action, was likewise killed by a mine in Holland in March 1945, aged twenty-five.

For some of the actors whose roles in one of the greatest performances of the twentieth century have been recorded above, participation on D-Day proved, unsurprisingly, to have been the most noteworthy event of long lives. 'When you have had such a tremendous experience,' said Ron Lane long after, 'the usual sort of civilian life seemed to be so mundane in comparison later that it seemed unreal.' He himself lived until 2004.

Lord Lovat was badly wounded by friendly fire on 12 June 1944, and after recovery returned in 1945 to his Highland castle and 250,000-acre estate. He entered the pantheon of official British war heroes, and indeed legends, and also became involved in Conservative politics. In the film *The Longest Day* he was portrayed, somewhat implausibly, by Peter Lawford. His piper Bill Millin (1922–2010) became almost equally celebrated, and in keeping with his brigadier's feudal spirit worked on Lovat's Beaufort Castle for years after leaving the army. Lovat died in

1995, aged eighty-three, having suffered the sadness of seeing the family estates sold to pay inheritance taxes.

Lt. Lionel Murray, the Shropshires' platoon commander who led W Company through Biéville, was evacuated from Normandy three days after D-Day with severe battle exhaustion. He never returned to active service, but – now known as Len Murray – recovered to become 1973–84 general secretary of the Trades Union Congress, dying in 2004.

Col. Hermann von Oppeln-Bronikowski, the equestrian dressage gold medallist who led 22 Panzer Regiment on D-Day, finished the war commanding 20th Panzer Division. He died of a heart attack in 1966, aged sixty-seven.

Terence Otway was concussed by blast under shellfire two days after the Merville battle and deemed unfit for further active service. He later served in India and in civilian posts in the colonies. When he made post-war pilgrimages to Normandy, he sought to shoo away picnickers from the old bunkers of the Merville Battery, saying 'I don't like people eating and drinking where my men died.' Otway survived to the age of ninety-two, dying in 2006.

Alastair 'Jock' Pearson, the wild CO of 8 Para with four DSOs and an MC, in 1945 returned to civilian life and his family's bakery in Glasgow, where he became a pillar of the community and eventually lord-lieutenant of Dunbartonshire. He died in 1996, aged eighty.

Captain Ryan Price, who swam ashore on Sword with 6 Commando, resumed his pre-war career in racing, and was five times Champion National Hunt trainer. In 1962 he trained the winner of the Grand National. He died in 1986, aged seventy-four.

Brigadier K.P. Smith died in 1985, aged eighty-seven.

Richard Todd of 7 Para became a movie star, most famously playing RAF hero Guy Gibson VC in *The Dambusters*. He died in 2009, aged ninety.

Huw Wheldon of 1st RUR became a much-loved TV arts presenter and also a brilliant BBC senior executive, before dying aged sixty-nine in 1986.

The great war correspondent Chester Wilmot published in 1952 his magisterial work *The Struggle for Europe*, which set a standard for WWII campaign narratives and analysis that few historians have since matched. He died two years later, aged forty-two, when he was a passenger in a BOAC Comet I that crashed into the Mediterranean as a consequence of a catastrophic design flaw.

Captain Woodrow Wyatt escaped court-martial, instead being dispatched to a staff role in India, and after the war became a rich though controversial businessman and Labour MP, latterly a Tory peer and close confidant of prime minister Margaret Thatcher. He died in 1997, aged seventy-nine.

Rosie Boycott, daughter of Major Charles who commanded C Company of the 1st Suffolks on D-Day, said eighty years later: 'We grew up carrying our father's shame. I think my own life would have been different but for Hillman. I hated the army.' Her father was obliged to resign his commission in 1956, still a major – 'his life was upended' – and thereafter pursued a series of unsatisfactory jobs, of which the most humiliating was selling linen in Selfridges' store. He had a late renaissance when he researched and published in 1997 a biography of his Norfolk forebear Captain Boycott, who gave his name to a notorious form of public sanction. Yet Major Boycott died an unfulfilled and unhappy man, much of which his daughter traces to his D-Day experience. It is hard to see any rational cause for his sense of guilt, given the story of Hillman as recorded above, and especially since his own company played no direct role in the assault. Moreover, the chiefs of the British Army obviously did not think ill of the battalion's commanding officer in Normandy, because he died in 1986 aged seventy-eight as Lt. Gen. Sir Richard Goodwin, KCB, DSO.

Appendix

Order of Battle of the British forces which landed on Sword beach and in the Orne perimeter on 6 June 1944

I Corps – Lt. Gen. John Crocker

3rd Infantry Division – Maj. Gen. Tom Rennie

8 Infantry Brigade – Brigadier Edward Cass

1st Suffolks – Lt. Col. Richard Goodwin
A Coy Maj. Geoff Ryley *kia 6.6.44*
B Coy Maj. Dennis McCaffery
C Coy Maj. Charles Boycott
D Coy Maj. Philip Papillon *kia 28.6.44*

1st South Lancs – Lt. Col. Richard Burbury *kia 6.6.44*
A Coy Maj. John Harward *kia 6.6.44*
Replaced by Lt. Robert Pearce *wia 6.6.44*
B Coy Maj. Robert Harrison *kia 6.6.44*
Replaced by Lt. B. Walker *kia 6.6.44*
C Coy Maj. Eric Johnson
D Coy Maj. J. Egglinton *wia 6.6.44*

2nd East Yorks – Lt. Col. Charles Hutchinson *wia 6.6.44*
A Coy Maj. Charles King
B Coy Maj. S. R. Sheath
C Coy Maj. David Barrow
D Coy Maj. Robert Barber *kia 6.6.44*

185 Infantry Brigade – Brigadier Kenneth Pearce Smith

2nd Warwicks – Lt. Col. Hugh Herdon *kia 7.6.44*

1st Norfolks – Lt. Col. Hugh Bellamy

2nd KSLI – Lt. Col. Jack Maurice *kia 7.7.44*
W Coy Maj. Arthur Slatter, DCM *wia 6.6.44*
X Coy Maj. Guy Thornycroft
Y Coy Maj. Peter Steel *kia 6.6.44*
Z Coy Maj. Peter Wheelock *kia 21.7.44*

9 Infantry Brigade – Brigadier James Cunningham *wia 6.6.44*

2nd Lincolns

1st King's Own Scottish Borderers

2nd Royal Ulster Rifles

Divisional troops: 3rd Recce Regiment; 7th, 33rd and 76th Field Regiments Royal Artillery; 20th Anti-Tank Regiment RA; 92nd Light Anti-Aircraft Regiment RA; 15th, 17th, 246th, 253rd Field Park Companies Royal Engineers; 5th Beach Group – Lt. Col. Broad *kia 6.6.44*; 22nd Dragoons Assault Regiment RE – Lt. Col. Arthur Cocks *kia 6.6.44*; 2nd

Middlesex (machine-gun battalion) 5, 77 & 79 Assault Squadrons Royal Engineers

1st Special Service Brigade – Brigadier Lord Lovat
No. 3 Commando – Lt. Col. Peter Young
No. 4 Commando – Lt. Col. Robert Dawson *wia 6.6.44*
No. 6 Commando – Lt. Col. Derek Mills-Roberts
No. 45 RM Commando – Capt. Norman Ries *kia 6.6.44*

4th Special Service Brigade – Brigadier B. W. Leicester
No. 41 RM Commando – Lt. Col. T. M. Gray
No. 46 RM Commando – Lt. Col. Campbell Hardy

27th Independent Armoured Brigade – Brigadier Erroll Prior-Palmer

13th/18th Royal Hussars – Lt. Col. Richard Harrap *kia 16.6.44*
A Squadron – Maj. Derrick Wormald
B Squadron – Maj. A.A.G. Rugge-Price
C Squadron– Maj. Sir Delaval Cotter

Staffordshire Yeomanry – Lt. Col. James Eadie
A Squadron – Maj. M.A. Spencer-Nairn
B Squadron – Maj. George Turner
C Squadron – Maj. Pat Griffin

East Riding Yeomanry – Lt. Col. Tom Williamson

6th Airborne Division – Maj. Gen. Richard Gale

3rd Parachute Brigade – Brigadier James Hill
8 Para – Lt. Col. Alastair Pearson
9 Para – Lt. Col. Terence Otway
1 Canadian Para – Lt. Col. George Bradbrooke

5th Parachute Brigade – Brigadier Nigel Poett
7 Para – Lt. Col. Geoffrey Pine-Coffin
12 Para – Lt. Col. A.P. Johnson
13 Para – Lt. Col. Peter Luard

6th Airlanding Brigade – Brigadier Hugh Kindersley
2nd Ox & Bucks – Lt. Col. Michael Roberts
1st Royal Ulster Rifles – Lt. Col. Robert Carson
12th Devonshires – Lt. Col. Reginald Parker

Divisional Troops: 6th Airborne Recce; 53rd Airlanding Regt. RA; 6th Airborne Engineers

Note – Details of subordinate commanders are given only for those units prominently mentioned in the text above. Lines of communication troops such as RASC, REME and signals are also omitted.

Acknowledgements

The staff of the Imperial War Museum, National Archives and London Library were helpful as always, and I should signal a special debt to Ben Hill and Jon Baker of the Airborne Assault Museum Archives at Duxford. Julian Whippy of that excellent battlefield tour organization Battle Honours guided me through the detailed locations of Sword beach and key battlefield sites inland. I have consulted many websites, especially regimental ones such as that of the Friends of the Suffolk Regiment. The Museum of the Staffordshire Yeomanry in Stafford has also been most helpful, especially its archives trustee Nigel Maus. David Shergold's 2024 book *Critical Hours on D-Day*, largely based upon material held by the Soldiers of Shropshire Museum in Shrewsbury, brings together many personal narratives of experiences of men of 2nd KSLI during their advance on Caen, and has been invaluable in composing my own narrative. Lt. Lionel Murray of the KSLI recorded some of his experiences in a summer 1945 issue of his old school magazine, *The Wellingtonian*. The distinguished journalist Rosie Boycott kindly talked to me about the lifelong tragic impact on her father, Major Charles Boycott, of his battalion's battle for Hillman. Dr Tracy Craggs, author of a wonderfully vivid book on the East Yorks on D-Day and after, gave me valuable information about 'Banger' King. Alastair Eadie talked about his father, CO of the Staffordshire Yeomanry. His niece our family friend Sarah-Jane Shirreff has allowed me to read and quote from her grandfather Jim's moving letters to her grandmother. Simon Prior-Palmer kindly permitted me to read his draft biography of his father, Maj. Gen. Erroll.

Other dear friends Serena Sissons and Denys Blakeway, the latter maker of so many brilliant BBC TV documentaries including a few presented by me, kindly read my draft text and made some characteristically shrewd suggestions. At HarperCollins Arabella Pike, Iain Hunt and Katherine Patrick did wonderful things, as they always do. My secretary Rachel Lawrence has never failed me since 1996, and my wife Penny has never failed me ever.

References and Sources

In the references that follow, UKNA signifies material from the National Archives; IWM files held in the Imperial War Museum; AAMA the Airborne Assault Museum Archive at Duxford. SWWEC denotes the Second World War Experience Centre near Leeds. Eadie Letters indicates the collection of wartime correspondence from the CO of the Staffordshire Yeomanry to his wife, now held by his granddaughter Sarah-Jane, Lady Shirreff. The diary of Julius Neave, adjutant of the 13th/18th Royal Hussars, is widely available online, including through the Light Dragoons website.

1 Garrisoning Britain

2 'The future! There seemed no future' IWM Rex 87/39/1
2 'For the past two years the invasion' Wilson, Andrew *Flamethrower* Kimber 1984 p.11
3 'And when I prepare to die behind my gun' Douglas, Keith *The Letters* Carcanet Press 2000 p.159
4 'This division has been chosen' IWM Lane 26556
4 'War seems to be mostly hanging around' Waugh, Evelyn *Put Out More Flags* Penguin 1966 p.220
4 'Training was designed' IWM Waller 87/42/1
5 'ungrammatical English laced with infusions' Hennessey, Patrick *Young Man in a Tank* private publication 1988 p.24
5 'Eric, these bloody fools' Lincoln, John *Thank God and the Infantry* Sutton Publishing 1999 p.19

5 'Liverpudlian Royal Engineer George Duncan' IWM Duncan 01/571

5 'In the summer of 1943' Todd, Richard *Caught in the Act* Hutchinson 1986 p.143

6 'to thrive on a few encouraging words' Ellis, John *The Sharp End: The Fighting Man in World War II* Pimlico 1980 p.14

6 'that terrible, recurrent army dejection' Powell, Anthony *The Valley of Bones* Heinemann 1964 p.116

6 'Uniform does something to you' IWM Phillips 61/47/2

6 'when we did at last get our forty-eight' Lionel Birch in *Lilliput Goes to War* Hutchinson 1985 p.141

7 'very disappointed in my prowess' IWM Waller 87/42/1

7 'I was very immature and inexperienced' IWM SW Bridgen 15/22/1

7 'None of this modern hugging' IWM Reg W Blake 25023

7 'I did not like being shouted at' IWM Campbell 97/84/182

8 'two kids, a two-shillings-a-day soldier' IWM AW Griffiths 06/99/1

8 'Judy thought that if the' Dunn, Robin *Sword and Wig* Quiller 1993 p.27

9 'I've just been looking through the Compassionate file' Macksey, Kenneth *Armoured Crusader: Maj. Gen. Sir Percy Hobart* Hutchinson 1967 p.225 letter of March 1942

9 'Never doing a damn thing' Ambrose, Stephen *Pegasus Bridge June 6 1944* Simon & Schuster 1985 p.31

10 'tired, disillusioned and dispirited' Mace, Paul *Forrard: The Story of the East Riding Yeomanry* Leo Cooper 2001 p.69

11 'It kept up a spirit of harmony' Scott, Walter *Journals* 1826 18.3.26

12 'I can't get a room for you' Hill, Heywood & Anne *A Bookseller's War* Russell 1997 p.45

13 'that off duty his company commander' IWM Waller 87/42/1

13 'Thank you for your kindness' IWM CK King 93/39/1

14 'the perfect private soldier' UKNA WO205/1c 14.5.42

14 'the silly snobbishness' Wheldon, Wynn *Kicking the Bar Huw Wheldon: A Filial Biography* Unbound 2016 Wheldon letter of 15.12.40, pp.76–7

14 'he complained to his battalion chaplain' ibid. p.83

14 'In khaki men have nothing' ibid. p.74

14 'which he certainly is' ibid. p.86

15 'The proliferating responsibilities of an infantry officer' Powell p.171

15 'Well! Two pounds!' Townsend, Colin & Eileen *War Wives* Grafton 1989 p.78

16 'The qualities required by an officer' Dunn p.10

16 'Another utterly incredible appointment' Wheldon, Wynn p.90

16 'the war was merely foreign travel' Ellis, John p.53
16 'Their significance was' French, David *Raising Churchill's Army* Oxford 2000 p.70
17 'Getting involved in this army business' IWM Phillips 61/47/2
17 'The general fear was to end up' IWM D Chamberlain 18138
18 'We shall meet again' Hattu, Guy *Un matin à Ouistreham: Témoignage d'un français libre* Kindle edition letter of 13.5.41 location 842
19 'plunged himself into military servitude' ibid. letter of June 1943 location 1613
19 'It is in the front line that a Christian' ibid. location 1676
19 'I am proud of not having abandoned' ibid. location 1792
19 'The men were discontented' Wilson p.23
20 'There is apparently a lot of fighting' Fennell, Jonathan *Fighting the People's War* Cambridge 2019 p.483
20 'Rumour held that the Fort Garry' Hennessey p.49
20 'They were go-getters, those Americans' IWM JF Rex 87/39/1
21 'Darling, I am horribly homesick!' Eadie letter of 16.1.44
22 'the fidelity of nearly all wives' Townsend p.79
22 'When Jack D'Arcy went to show off' IWM J O D'Arcy 15/5/1
23 'Oh they fitted us up with Shermans' IWM Pearman 08/85/1
23 'What's it like in battle, sir?' Hennessey p.52
23 'As the war dragged on' IWM Roebuck 94/41/1
24 'It had by then dawned' IWM Wakelam 06/126/1
24 'There's a bloody war' Lewis, Jon ed. *Eye-Witness D-Day* Robinson 1994 p.13
24 'I was nineteen years old' IWM WH Bidmead PP/MCR/223
24 'John Hislop, a celebrated' Hislop, John *Anything but a Soldier* Michael Joseph 1965 *passim*
25 'He is, in some ways, most curiously' Lascelles, Alan *King's Counsellor* Weidenfeld & Nicolson 2006 p.204

2 Montgomery's Fantasy

26 'It'd better be slap-up' Wilson p.27
30 'I am not much perturbed' Douglas p.328
30 'In 1944 the war could still be regarded' Andrew Wilson *Observer* magazine July 1984
31 'It is to Monty's credit' Hamilton, Nigel *Monty: Master of the Battlefield 1942–44* Hamish Hamilton 1983 Vol. II p.550
32 'I told Monty he couldn't take Caen' ibid. p.491 quoting Pogue interview of 19.2.47

32 'you can do with a platoon' Stewart, Andrew *The Caen Controversy* 2014 p.153

34 'Try as you would, during the days of preparation' Scarfe, Norman *Assault Division: A History of the 3rd Division from the Invasion of Normandy to the Surrender of Germany* 1947 p.93

34 'D-Day was our horizon' Neave narrative on Light Dragoons website p.43

34 'We considered the repulse at Dieppe' Beevor, Antony *D-Day* Penguin 2009 p.33

37 'We crawled around on the floor' Liddell Hart Archive KCL, Wilmot notes on undated conversation with Dempsey

39 'This was the fragile reed upon which the entire campaign' D'Este, Carlo *Decision in Normandy* Collins 1983 p.78

3 Paras

42 'a real man's man, a soldier's soldier' IWM Jefferson audio 13723

44 'It was awe-inspiring gliding' Miller, Victor *Nothing is Impossible: A Glider Pilot's Story* Pen & Sword 2015 p.32

44 'yanked across the sky' Wheldon, Wynn p.110

45 'excellent, particularly in the case of 6 Airborne' Liddell Hart Archive 19924 quoted Fennell p.486

46 'Our confidence was boundless' Todd p.63

47 'We were eager. We were fit' Ambrose, Stephen *D-Day: June 6, 1944* Simon & Schuster 1994 p.24

49 'the most wonderful model' Jefferson, Alan *Assault on the Guns of Merville* 1987 p.44

50 'We ate, drank and slept the bloody battery!' ibid. p.34

50 'It was a marvellous battalion' IWM Jefferson audio 13723

51 'One sits in the middle of all this' Wheldon, Wynn p.107

51 'England indescribably lovely' April 1944 ibid. p.108

4 The Seafarers

53 'They cut samples of German' Messenger, Charles *The Commandos 1940–46* William Kimber 1985 p.250

53 'We hadn't done a thing apart from' Leslie Wright in Messenger p.250

55 'whose colonels were allegedly' Lovat, Lord *March Past* Weidenfeld & Nicolson 1978 p.286

55 'Marines felt, and usually tried not to say' The Royal Marines' *Sphere* 1973 p.101

55 'Yes, you must wear the red flannel' Lovat p.285

56 'any commando work that might be asked' Alanbrooke diaries 25.9.41 p.185 and *passim*

56 'The view inside a pill-box' Lovat p.293

57 'To the brigadier's delight, the horse' ibid. p.290

57 'I had a feeling that I had been listening' ibid. p.301

57 'When the Frenchmen began to study' Hattu location 2034

57 'We knew that in this casemate' ibid. location 2049

58 'As an ex-infantryman trained' IWM Skelly 15/15/1

58 'He had the supreme gift' Lovat p.283

59 'Cardiff-born Ray Hatton' IWM Hatton Box 10/8/1

59 'A madman … he wasn't liked' ibid.

60 'Very nice. Now start them' Hennessey p.32

60 'oldish … and of an uncertain temper' Neave p.15

61 'I would have just assumed' IWM Campbell 97/84/182

61 'the biggest test of physical and mental courage' Mace p.95

61 'I am very lucky to have such super chaps' Staffordshire Yeomanry Museum Eadie Diary 15.5.43

62 'Rather you than me, mate!' Hennessey p.42

64 'How ever did we win?' IWM Waller MSS87/42/1

66 'It's the relief, sir' Ellis, John p.255

66 'I agree with you' LHCMA Alanbrooke MSS 6/2/6 5.7.42

66 'Montgomery's operational techniques' French p.262

66 'I am tired of being dedicated' Wheldon, Wynn p.108 May 1944

67 'The average platoon includes three or four' UKNA WO231/14 Col. T N Glazebrook

67 'six gutful men who will go anywhere' UKNA WO231/14

67 'Jack Maurice' Smith, K.P. *Adventures of an Ancient Warrior in War, Peace & Revolution* p.99

68 'We were all wondering how we should react' Lincoln p.6

68 'We longed to get on with it' ibid. p.5

68 'In Charlie Chilton's battalion' IWM Chilton 06/99/1

68 'but something went wrong' Wilson p.20

69 'the entire complement of one aircraft' Todd p.160

69 'A carrier overturned' IWM Roebuck 94/41/1

69 'An unfortunate shooting accident' Scarfe p.33

71 'We toiled far into the night' IWM Rex 87/39/1

71 'A new spirit was born in the early hours' Scarfe p.23

72 'The general replied that their brigadier' Smith p.99

72 'hesitant and badly-led troops' Lovat p.295

72 'Say that word again and I'll' IWM Lane 26556

72 'I had my own doubts' Lovat p.297
73 'The chaos on the beach itself' Neave p.29

5 The Eve

74 'Monty really was a heroic figure' Hoare, J A MS *Huw Wheldon: A Public Man* p.4 quoted Wheldon pp.91–2
74 'an atmosphere of adolescent innocence' Moorehead, Alan *Eclipse* Hamish Hamilton 1945 p.87
76 'whose brilliant staff' Lewin, Ronald *Montgomery as Military Commander* Batsford 1971
76 'We have been fighting the Germans' ibid. p.87
77 'We felt that if we had to go to war' Dunn p.53
77 'I shut my eyes and turned them on my heart' Browning, Robert *Childe Roland to the Dark Tower Came*
77 'A sternly religious man' IWM GF Appleton 15/7/1
77 'I am having to call on all my reserves' Eadie letter of 20.4.44
78 'Everyone laughed when he said' Scarfe p.57
78 'It must have seemed to him' ibid. p.58
79 'One sergeant became very bolshie' IWM Jefferson audio 13723
79 'We knew that this was the last time 9 Para' ibid.
79 'a rotten sermon about death and destruction' Lovat p.303
79 '*Vous allez rentrer chez vous*' ibid. p.304
80 'I was so ashamed of myself' Eadie letter of 29.5.44
80 'I write in a world ill at ease' Eadie letter of 2.6.44
81 'They can't fool me' Mace p.109
81 'Several among us recognized the area' Hattu location 2051
81 'I have just finished packing' Wheldon, Wynn p.110
82 'and any religious book we chose' IWM Campbell 97/84/182
82 'To the disgust of some' Craggs, Tracy *D-Day: To Bremen & Beyond* BookPrinting 2023 p.46
83 'He was crafty, was Pepper' ibid. p.48
83 'The scene that greeted us was fantastic' Lewis p.59
84 'through dense streets of half-cheering' Mace p.112
84 'Portsmouth was an incredible sight' Neave p.36
84 'a grotesque gala atmosphere' Saunders, Hilary St George *The Green Beret* Michael Joseph 1949 p.235
84 'I never loved England so truly' Lovat p.297
85 'Delivered fresh blood to ships' IWM Airth 05/63/1
85 'turned each landing-craft into a sort of Noah's ark' Scarfe p.46
85 'We had been training a bit too long' IWM Davies 16/3/1

85 'The face of the Thames was choppy' IWM J F Rex 87/39/1
86 'For most of us it was a frustrating postponement' Todd p.165
86 'In that simple phrase we felt that she had said' Radcliffe, G.L.Y. *2 KSLI on D-Day* posted by *War Chronicle* as an online narrative
86 'this country that we were quitting' Hattu location 2327
87 'One's chief fear was that of being afraid' Neave p.60
87 'At last the names "in clear!"' Scarfe p.61
87 'South of Caen the going is good as far as BRETTEVILLE' UKNA WO171/845 Hussars war diary
87 'Well, fair stands the wind for …?' Douglas p.343
87 'Naval officer Alan Richardson was aboard' IWM A A Richardson 94/43/1
88 'Thereafter its captain sustained a flow of facetious' IWM H Rogers 03/14/1
88 'It never got really dark that night' Lewis p.60
88 'I prayed that night' Craggs, Tracy *An Unspectacular War: Reconstructing the History of the 2nd Battalion East Yorks in WWII* White Rose Theses Online p.118
89 'Aboard *Glenearn* a corporal of the East Yorks' ibid. p.117
89 'If anything untoward does happen to me' IWM GF Appleton 15/7/1
90 'Looking around at the other chaps' IWM Lane 26556
90 'Each of us was loaded down like a pack mule' Lincoln p.21

6 Operation Tonga

93 'We are History' Lewis p.62 from *The Times*
94 'As for the op itself, only a bloody fool' Jefferson p.53
94 'Philip Burkinshaw of 12 Para was pestered until the last moment to wear a bulletproof breastplate' Burkinshaw, P. *Alarms and Excursions* 1991
95 'It was an amazing sight' Ambrose *Pegasus Bridge* p.86
95 'See you on the bridge' ibid. p.87
95 'we staggered into the air' Wood, Alan *The Glider Soldiers* Spellmount 1992 p.262
95 'Back at Harwell, BBC correspondent' Wilmot, Chester *The Struggle for Europe* Wordsworth 1997 p.233
96 'Each aircraft, which was its own island' Jefferson p.99
97 'You've got the wrong airfield!' Wood p.261
97 'it was the battle for the foothold' D'Este p.120
98 'The gentle hiss of the slipstream' Miller p.33
99 'a God Almighty crash' AAMA Edwards personal narrative

101 'We're here, piss off and do what you're paid to do' Ambrose *Pegasus Bridge* p.92
104 'a feeling of sadness' AAMA HJ Sweeney narrative
105 'Eisenhower's deputy, Air Marshal Sir Arthur Tedder' Tedder, Lord *With Prejudice* Cassell 1966 p.549
105 'Though air chiefs later sought to excuse' see, for instance, Professor Allan Millett, *D-Day Companion* p.175
106 'here below is the white curving strand' Wilmot p.236
106 'An astonishing number of paratroopers' Todd p.170
106 'The monotonous greyness' Saunders p.166
107 'Landing in water and deep mud' AAMA Hill narrative
107 'In Lt. Jeremy Spencer's plane' Payne, Roger *Paras: Voices of the British Airborne Forces in the Second World War* Amberley 2006 Kindle edition
109 'The crew had an awfully difficult job' Lewis p.75
109 'Complete chaos seemed to reign' Saunders p.175
109 'At the sight of the motherly, middle-aged' Lewis p.77
110 'By contrast Bill Elvin and three others' AAMA Elvin narrative
110 'Warfare and tourism are less often linked' Raban, Jonathan *Father and Son* Picador 2023 p.45
110 'The welcome was astounding' Payne, Kindle edition
111 'Where the hell am I?' Lewis p.89
111 'I had but one thought, to get out' Miller p.160
113 'Troops from every formation' *Royal Engineer Journal* Vol. CVIII–CXI April–Dec 1994–95
114 '[It] was constantly dinned into us' Todd p.157
114 'The jeep, however, enmeshed' Ambrose *D-Day* p.231
115 'There seemed to be a Boche in every doorway' *Royal Engineer Journal* Vol. CVIII–CXI April–Dec 1994–95
116 'Padre Whitfield Foy' AAMA Foy narrative
117 'It is a reflection of the poor relations' James Hill letter to Lt. Col. David Benest 8.3.93
117 'just one little pocket on the end' AAMA ParaData Canadian narrative
117 'It really was the most awe-inspiring' Ambrose *D-Day* p.110
118 'Tall, lean and tough' Todd p.154
119 'the realization that we were in a bloody' AAMA Sweeney narrative
120 'The parachutists began to drift in' ibid.
121 'Here was I, a young officer' Ambrose *D-Day* p.123

7 Merville

124 'His men did not mourn him' Jefferson p.75
127 'We sat up. I realized how lucky' AAMA Smith narrative
129 'I am afraid that many were lost' Wood p.339
130 'He looked very peculiar' IWM Jefferson audio 13723
130 'You're commanding C Company!' Jefferson p.105
131 'Then he felt ashamed of himself' Golley, John *The Big Drop: The Guns of Merville June 1944* Janes 1982 p.110
134 'Have a nip' Jefferson p.109
134 'started a frightful hullaballoo' AAMA Smith narrative
135 'which we used to do in training' IWM Jefferson audio 13723
136 'A tornado of action swept into the battery' AAMA Smith narrative
137 'The whole place was an eerie mess' Jefferson p.116
137 'You're my first real wartime casualty' IWM Jefferson audio 13723
139 'There was a feeling of elation' ibid.
140 'Evidence is contradictory' see Carl Rymen's 2016 essay in the online Pegasus Archive *The Merville Gun Battery and Its Role after 9 Parachute Battalion's Attack*
140 'Why did they come' Jefferson p.147
141 'It was an enterprise as miraculous' Gale, Richard *Call to Arms* Hutchinson 1968 p.141
141 'A jolly good battle, what?!' AAMA Smith narrative
141 'The Allies would just be landing' AAMA Boardman narrative
141 'Eight captured paratroopers were summarily executed' Beevor p.55
141 'to date the greatest enemy' AAMA Lt. W Parrish narrative
141 'From our grandstand position' Todd p.173

8 Grappling the Atlantic Wall

147 'to wish I was going in there' IWM Airth 05/63/1
147 'It was rather appalling' Lewis p.93
148 'I had never seen so many ships' IWM HJ Willie 95/3/1
148 'so close you felt you could almost' Craggs *D-Day* p.77
148 'Surviving defenders told British interrogators' UKNA WO232/25 Special Tactical Study No. 30
149 'no serious damage to the defences' Fennell p.493
150 'She spent the ensuing eleven months in an English hospital' Ambrose *D-Day* p.420
151 'Many of them looked very sick and cold' https://www.lightdragoons.org.uk/documents/THE%20ASSAULT%20[1].pdf

151 'it did not go so far towards removing the purely personal sense of mortality' Scarfe p.69
152 'but few had any appetite' IWM Roebuck 94/41/1
152 'got shot of last night's meal' Craggs *D-Day* p.56
152 'Many usually tough and cheery fellows' Mace p.115
153 'Connie my dearest' IWM W Cutler 89/3/1
155 'and it was a miracle that most of us did' Hennessey p.57
160 'My sergeant roared through the water' IWM D R Knapp 62/224/1
161 'Now, instead he served as a Petard gunner' IWM Norris 14/17/1
162 'The driver and co-driver emerged' Hennessey p.58

9 The Breach

166 'It was inspiring to watch' Scarfe p.75
166 'Well, lads, it's now or never!' Craggs *D-Day* p.118
166 'but then "Ramp down!"' IWM R Major 95/23/1
167 'Alf Ackroyd of B Company saw' Craggs *D-Day* p.70
167 'Wrecked boats lay broadside on' IWM Roebuck 94/41/1
167 'Everybody was numb, really' Craggs *D-Day* p.72
167 'went across the beach like a hare' Lewis p.128
168 'MG 50 yards left – deployed and engaged' SWWEC Oates Collection
168 'We were just putting a magazine' Craggs *D-Day* p.67
169 'You're not going to win this war' BBC People's War A2524439
169 'Instinctively, where we lay we hacked holes' IWM H T Bone
169 'On the British side some officers' Renison quoted Craggs *D-Day* p.84
169 'It is fatal to halt when mortared' Ellis, John p.73
169 'If one goes to ground under fire' ibid. p.87
169 'Almost no personal accounts of D-Day mention' ibid. p.103
172 'crossed the beach with very few' Light Dragoons website Wormald journal of D-Day p.3
172 'Terry, officers do not notice rain' IWM Lt. Col. TN Skelly IWM 15/15/1
172 'To feign a casual' Craig, Norman *The Broken Plume* IWM 1982 p.75
173 'If a shell comes down it will hit all five of you' Welby-Everard of the Lincolns, Kilvert-Jones, T. *Sword Beach* p.188
174 'I was angry at people not getting off' IWM Ambrose *D-Day* p.551
174 'blown high into the air' Craggs *An Unspectacular War* p.19
174 'What a bloody silly time' ibid. p.19
174 'Dennis Hallam had been impressed' ibid. p.81, 1.10.2005 interview with Hallam
174 'The youngest was eighteen-year-old' ibid. p.35

175 'Get off that bloody merry-go-round' IWM KV Mee 11/27/1
175 'What a reception!!!' IWM Appleton 15/7/1
176 'Captain Hugh Collinson' IWM Collinson 11/3/1
177 'a pack of hounds with their noses' Dunn p.58
177 'and we were in France' IWM Lane 26556
178 'When it actually came to it' ibid.
178 'Look, they're having to swim' Craggs *D-Day* p.83
178 'A few weeks after D-Day' UKNA WO106/44472
178 'Under the side of a tank' IWM H T Bone
179 'The effect was that the prepared, sensitive minds of the men' Scarfe p.74
179 'They must have been lovely houses' IWM WS Scull 06/41/1
180 'The tactical analysts later concluded' UKNA WO106/44472

10 Green Berets

182 'Philippe Kieffer's two troops' Faure obituary 17.4.21
182 'As we filed down the gangways' Hattu location 2366
183 'I began to cry' Ambrose *D-Day* p.552
183 'A British commando observed wonderingly' ibid. p.556
183 'When the commandos landed' Craggs *An Unspectacular War* p.125 interview Ackroyd 10.2.2002
185 'like pebbles being thrown in' IWM A H Semmence 14/29/1
185 'I was just starting down' IWM Skelly 15/15/1
185 'Nobody dashed ashore' Ambrose *D-Day* p.560
186 'The beach by now was covered' ibid. p.556
187 'What in the bloody hell' ibid. p.552
187 'I found myself under a pile' IWM WH Bidmead PP/MCR/223
188 'The smoky foreground was not inviting' Lovat p.310
188 'Hopelessly slow to advance' ibid. p.313
189 'It seemed like hours' Emlyn Jones, Lewis p.121
190 'It was all incredible and fascinating' IWM NJ Barker 17/15/1
191 'I observed these battles' Douglas p.5
191 'returning to Blighty as a wounded' Hennessey pp.59–60
192 'Romance and death were strangely coupled' IWM Richardson 94/43/1
192 'Once down the ramp, however' IWM Badenoch 04/34/1
194 'There was no cover' Lewis p.135
195 'looked like a lot of snails going home' Ambrose *D-Day* p.555
196 'Give me rifle!' Hattu location 3541
198 'I had expected too much' IWM Wakelam 06/126/1
200 'The rest was plain sailing' Lovat p.318

200 'It looked a pleasant honey colour' IWM Skelly 15/15/1
202 'almost dead with fatigue' Hattu location 2590
202 'It is then, and not before' ibid. location 2613
203 'at first blush, struck me as vain' Lovat p.325
204 'The civilian population seemed not to like us' IWM Hatton 10/8/1

11 Gale's Force

207 'being pecked at almost all the time' Saunders p.163
208 '[We] kept our fingers crossed' Ambrose *D-Day* p.130
210 'They never really launched an all-out attack' AAMA Taylor narrative
210 'always to be found where things' Todd p.174
210 'The biggest problem I had' Ambrose *Pegasus Bridge* p.156
214 'Now, this young man had fallen victim to a misdirected' AAMA Hill narrative
214 'they would only be spending forty-eight hours' Golley p.125
215 'Do you know something, Eric?' ibid. p.125
215 'We didn't feel too happy, then' IWM Jefferson audio 13723
215 'Paul, I don't see much point' Golley p.137
215 'Otway's paratroopers up front' Lovat p.329
216 'Peters, that tall chap who came' Golley p.158
219 'Regrettably it was not until towards' Belchem, Maj. Gen. David *Victory in Normandy* Chatto & Windus 1981 p.110
219 'Ranville looked like a ghost village' AAMA O'Connor, Reginald *France without a Passport*
219 'It was plain we could not expect' Todd p.180
220 'A woman was very rude' IWM Jefferson audio 13723

12 'They Were Advancing Very Slowly'

223 'After a sea crossing' Montgomery, Field-Marshal Viscount *Memoirs* Collins 1958 p.74
225 'We came into action about a hundred yards' Dunn p.59
225 'The Brigade war diary reported that the South Lancs' UKNA WO171/611
225 '*Vive Les Américains!*' Fisher, Stephen *Sword Beach* Bantam 2024 p.252
227 'Lionel Roebuck later remarked on the absence' IWM Roebuck 94/41/1
227 'After later experiences in Normandy' interview with Sir Robin Dunn quoted Craggs *An Unspectacular War* p.20
228 'We should have attacked these positions' Craggs *D-Day* p.94
229 'NOT an easy landing' UKNA WO171/1325
229 'Things began to move, terribly slowly' Kilvert-Jones p.114

230 'I replied that I had been a schoolboy' Jones personal narrative, Soldiers of Shropshire website
230 'On your feet – that one landed' Lincoln p.22
231 'He [Smith] was haunted by the idea' Dunn p.54
231 'proved to be about the hardest' Scarfe p.80
231 'a terrible jam on the beach' UKNA WO171/863
232 'Over on this right flank it was early apparent' Scarfe p.89
235 'rather like walking across the front' Lummis, Eric *1 Suffolk and D-Day* Les Amis du Suffolk Regiment 1989 p.11
236 'useless impedimenta of a bygone age' Lovat p.205
237 'Dunn ever afterwards blamed' Dunn p.64
237 'From the moment the idea' Radcliffe narrative
238 'I was so scared I got down' BBC People's War A2524439
238 'Well – if he's all right I suppose' Radcliffe narrative
238 'The CO appreciated that the ridge' SY Regimental War Diary 6.6.44
239 'An infantryman elsewhere wrote of the impact' Bagnall, S. *The Attack: Reminiscences of the War* Hamish Hamilton 1947 p.161
240 'The battalion's war diary observed that' UKNA WO171/1325
246 'The atmosphere' McNish, Robin *Iron Division: History of the 3rd Division 1809–2000* HQ 3rd UK Div 2001 p.105
246 'I began to appreciate how vital' Jary, Sydney *18 Platoon* self-published 1987 p.7
246 'From deep inside Hillman' http://nvx.franceinfo.fr/leur6juin1944/hans/I
247 'The battle continued as planned' UKNA WO171/410
247 'Yet at precisely that time' UKNA WO171/611
248 'Tanks do not rush forward' Ingersoll, Ralph *The Battle is the Pay-Off* Harcourt Brace 1943 p.188
250 'That was the day I first saw' Lincoln p.25
250 'News filtered in … none of it' ibid. p.24
251 'it was unbelievable how quickly' ibid. p.25
251 'We had a hell of a baptism' ibid. p.30
252 'Some time was lost' Wilmot p.280
252 'Everybody cursed us' IWM Oral histories Boycott 18734
252 'A criticism made of the battle schools' see, for instance, Jary, *passim*
253 'This was fatal, because it gave defenders' UKNA WO232/25 Special Tactical Study No. 30
253 'No solo parts were written into the score' Jary p.19
256 'I wonder whether' Neitzel, Sönke and Welzer, Harald *Soldaten: On Fighting, Killing and Dying* Simon & Schuster 2012 p.256

256 'the gravest shortcoming of the British army' Wilmot p.561
256 'the absence of drive' ibid. p.278
256 'was much less terrible' ibid. p.278
257 'a dogged and able Scot' ibid. p.279
258 'A day or two later, wounded commando' IWM Skelly 15/15/1
258 'They would not offer unquestioning obedience' French p.14
258 'A serious weakness' Murray, Williamson *There's a War to Be Won* Harvard 2000 p.417

13 In the Beachhead

261 'The units of 9 Brigade got ashore' IWM Cunningham file P398
262 'It cannot be emphasized too strongly' McNish p.104
262 'This shambles – "a severe blow", acknowledged the war diary' UKNA WO171/616
264 'urging us to move forward more aggressively' Mace p.125
264 'had great difficulty in finding out' ibid. p.124
265 'Fortunately no replenishment' ibid. p.126
267 'Corporal Bob Littlar of the Shropshires' BBC People's War A2524439
267 'However, when the Commandos arrived' Wood p.264
267 '[I] felt very weak' SWWEC Oates
268 'clot of a sergeant' IWM WS Scull 06/41/1
268 'boots so highly polished' IWM Airth 05/63/1
269 'They learned the first and most important' Saunders p.218
269 'The situation of 3 Div north of Caen' UKNA Dempsey diary WO285/9

14 The End of the Road to Caen

271 'The KSLI battalion group will assault' UKNA WO171/702
272 'Later operational research showed that' UKNA WO291/1169 Army Operational Research Group report 17/52
274 'on our left half-a-dozen cows' Murray in Shergold, David *Critical Hours on D-Day* Shergold Press 2024 p.92
275 'seemed not the slightest perturbed' ibid. p.119
276 'Both men whipped out knives' BBC People's War Bob Littlar A2524439
276 'after a certain amount of confused fighting' Kemp, P.K. *The Staffordshire Yeomanry (QORR) in the First and Second World Wars* Gale & Polden 1950 p.140
277 'A wooded ravine of considerable depth' UKNA WO171/845
281 'Knight, a former regular NCO' IWM audio Knight 18828/3

281 'by only a few very frightened' Underhill, Major D.F. *The Staffordshire Yeomanry during World War II* Staffordshire Yeomanry Museum 1994 p.26
283 'There is no flush of excitement' Eadie letter of 2.6.44
284 'With every round fired' Ellis p.147, from *Through Mud and Blood* by B. Perrett
285 'It was another world' Radcliffe narrative
286 'My chaps did very well indeed' Eadie letter of 13.6.44
287 'witnessed a most exciting battle' UKNA WO171/1325
288 'We were going up and there was a Jerry' Shergold p.142
289 'Pray God don't let's go' Littlar interview with the Soldiers of Shropshire Museum 9.11.99, quoted Murray, Shergold p.117
289 'The Brigade war diary recorded' WO171/702
289 'We were a little apprehensive about' *War Chronicle* Rylands narrative, originally published in *KSLI Regimental Journal*
290 'Our spirits were high' NA WO171/1325
290 'just trigger-happy green troops' Littlar 1999 Soldiers of Shropshire interview
290 'Many weeks of desperate fighting' Kemp p.156
292 'We did it on our own' Wheelock letter quoted in Shergold p.103
292 'Kenneth Smith of 185th Brigade wrote' in a 27.8.82 letter to Carlo D'Este
292 'Gunner Robin Dunn thought the ease' Dunn p.64
293 'At all our briefings' ibid. p.62
293 'If you do not dominate events' Jary p.7

15 Nightfall

295 'Of all the other impressions of the day' Neave p.52
296 'Before I left England' IWM Campbell 9/84/182
296 'In the end it was not as bad' Eadie letter of 19.6.44
296 'Only half of his own company' IWM Roebuck 94/41/1
297 'There was a wonderful sunset' Holman, Gordon *Stand By to Beach!* as quoted by Lewis p.155
298 'At first I was rather depressed' ibid. p.137
299 'The landing was ghastly' IWM C T Cross quoted Lewis p.158
299 'like a moth bursting from its cocoon' Wilmot p.287
300 'I have never felt so grateful and proud' IWM D'Arcy 15/5/1 p.163
300 'I was conscious of bursting out of the glider' Wheldon, Huw *Red Berets into Normandy* Jarrold 1982 pp.15–16
302 'This has indeed been D-Day' IWM Airth 05/63/1

302 'I can't see what God had in mind' Wheldon, Wynn p.115
303 'D-Day seemed *very* long' Scarfe p.90
303 'an historic and exciting day' Light Dragoons website 'The Assault'
304 'I am sorry if it has bored you darling' Craggs *D-Day* p.121
305 'feeling very cheerful' IWM Collinson 11/3/1
306 'It was discovered that the enemy' Underhill p.26
306 'Every important battle' Hastings, Max *Nemesis* HarperCollins 2005 p.77
307 'We were pinned down all day' Lincoln p.33
308 'Wheldon, who was awarded an MC' Wheldon, Huw p.112
309 'It would be less than honest' Todd p.187
311 'A War Office liaison officer' UKNA WO252/21
313 'It was pretty clear' Lewin review of the British official history *Victory in the West* Vol. I *International Affairs* 1962 pp.422–3
313 'The record of 3 British Division' Belchem p.109
313 'being bitterly disappointed' Smith p.109
314 'Wyatt wrote of Smith's dismissal' Wyatt, Woodrow *Confessions of an Optimist* Collins 1985 p.98
315 'The marvellous thing is not' UKNA WO231/8
317 'The broad advance announced by Montgomery' Vogel, Detlef & others *Germany & the Second World War: The War in the West* Vol. VII Research Institute for Military History Potsdam 2005 translated edition Oxford 2006 p.595
317 'This persistent communications weakness' information from Dr Brian Austin, late of Liverpool University's Department of Electrical Engineering and Electronics, who has made a fascinating and authoritative study of military communications
319 'I would like to report' Neitzel and Welzer *Soldaten* p.276
319 'The preeminent German characteristic' Hunt, D. *A Don at War* London 1966 p.41
320 'Many Division and Corps commanders have failed' UKNA WO193/981 DMT tour of the Mediterranean Aug. Sept. 1944
321 'He observed that for Caen to fall' D'Este p.144
322 'I suppose it could have been done better' Ambrose *D-Day* p.551

Some Afterlives … and Deaths

327 'When you have had such a tremendous experience' IWM Lane 26556
329 'We grew up carrying our father's shame' conversation with the author 16.12.23

Bibliography

Ambrose, Stephen *D-Day: June 6, 1944* Simon & Schuster 1994

——*Pegasus Bridge June 6 1944* Simon & Schuster 1985

Anon *The Story of 79th Armoured Division* Hamburg 1945

Atkin, Ronald *Dieppe 1942: The Jubilee Disaster* Macmillan 1980

Atlantikwall.org.uk a remarkable modern website detailing every strongpoint and defensive position in Hitler's Atlantic Wall

Bagnall, Stephen *The Attack* Hamish Hamilton 1947

Beevor, Antony *D-Day* Penguin 2009

Belchem, Maj. Gen. David *Victory in Normandy* Chatto & Windus 1981

Bishop, Patrick *Operation Jubilee: Dieppe 1942* Penguin 2021

Bush, Eric *Bless Our Ship* Allen & Unwin 1958

Craggs, Tracy *An Unspectacular War: Reconstructing the History of the 2nd Battalion East Yorks in WWII* White Rose Theses Online

——*D-Day: To Bremen & Beyond* BookPrinting 2023

D'Este, Carlo *Decision in Normandy* Collins 1983

Douglas, Keith *The Letters* ed. Duncan Graham Carcanet Press 2000

Dunn, Robin *Sword and Wig* Quiller 1993

Edwards, Denis *The Devil's Own Luck* Pen & Sword 2001

Ellis, John *The Sharp End: The Fighting Man in World War II* Pimlico 1980

Ellis, Major L.F. *Victory in the West Vol. I The Battle of Normandy* HMSO 1962

Fennell, Jonathan *Fighting the People's War* Cambridge 2019

French, David *Raising Churchill's Army* Oxford 2000

Gale, Richard *Call to Arms* Hutchinson 1968

Gardiner, Juliet *Britain at War 1939–45* Headline 2004

German, David & Coogan, Chris *The Staffordshire Yeomanry* Churney Valley Books 2006

Golley, John *The Big Drop: The Guns of Merville June 1944* Janes 1982

Hamilton, Nigel *Monty: Master of the Battlefield 1942–44* Hamish Hamilton 1983

Hastings, Max *Overlord: D-Day and the Battle for Normandy 1944* Michael Joseph 1984

Hattu, Guy *Un matin à Ouistreham: Témoignage d'un français libre* Kindle edition

Hennessey, Patrick *Young Man in a Tank* private publication 1988

Howarth, David *Dawn of D-Day* Collins 1959

Jary, Sydney *18 Platoon* Sydney Jary 1987

Jefferson, Alan *Assault on the Guns of Merville* 1987

Johnson, Garry & Dunphie, Christopher *Brightly Shone the Dawn: Some Experiences of the Invasion of Normandy* Frederick Warne 1980

Kemp, P.K. *The Staffordshire Yeomanry (QORR) in the First and Second World Wars* Gale & Polden 1950

Kieffer, Philippe *Béret vert* Paris 1982

Lewis, Jon ed. *Eye-Witness D-Day* Robinson 1994

Lincoln, John *Thank God and the Infantry* Sutton Publishing 1999

Lovat, Lord *March Past* Weidenfeld & Nicolson 1978

Lummis, Eric *1 Suffolk and D-Day* Les Amis du Suffolk Regiment 1989

Mace, Paul *Forrard: The Story of the East Riding Yeomanry* Leo Cooper 2001

Macksey, Kenneth *Armoured Crusader: Maj. Gen. Sir Percy Hobart* Hutchinson 1967

McNish, Robin *Iron Division: History of the 3rd Division 1809–2000* HQ 3rd UK Div 2001

Messenger, Charles *The Commandos 1940–46* William Kimber 1985

Miller, Maj. Gen. Charles *History of the 13th/18th Royal Hussars 1922–1947* Chisman, Bradshaw 1949

Miller, Victor *Nothing Is Impossible: A Glider Pilot's Story* Pen & Sword 2015

Milton, Giles *D-Day: The Soldiers' Story* John Murray 2018

Montgomery, Field-Marshal Viscount *Memoirs* Collins 1958

Moorehead, Alan *Eclipse* Hamish Hamilton 1945

Murray, Williamson *There's a War to Be Won* Harvard 2000

Neillands, Robin *The Dieppe Raid* Aurum 2005

Neitzel, Sönke and Welzer, Harald *Soldaten: On Fighting, Killing and Dying* Simon & Schuster 2012

Payne, Roger *Paras: Voices of the British Airborne Forces in the Second World War* Amberley 2006

Penrose, Jane ed. *The D-Day Companion* Osprey 2004

Radcliffe, G.L.Y. *2 KSLI on D-Day* posted by *War Chronicle* as an online narrative

Shergold, David *Critical Hours on D-Day* Shergold Press 2024

Smith, K.P. *Adventures of an Ancient Warrior in War, Peace & Revolution*

Todd, Richard *Caught in the Act* Hutchinson 1986

Underhill, Major D.F. *The Staffordshire Yeomanry during World War II* Staffordshire Yeomanry Museum 1994

Vogel, Detlef & others *Germany & the Second World War: The War in the West* Vol. VII Research Institute for Military History Potsdam 2005 translated edition Oxford 2006
Wheldon, Huw *Red Berets into Normandy* Jarrold 1982
Wheldon, Wynn *Kicking the Bar Huw Wheldon: A Filial Biography* Unbound 2016
Wilmot, Chester *The Struggle for Europe* Wordsworth 1997
Wilson, Andrew *Flamethrower* Kimber 1984
Wood, Alan *The Glider Soldiers* Spellmount 1992
Wright, Laurence *The Wooden Sword* Elek 1967
Wyatt, Woodrow *Confessions of an Optimist* Collins 1985
Young, Peter *Storm from the Sea* 1974

Index

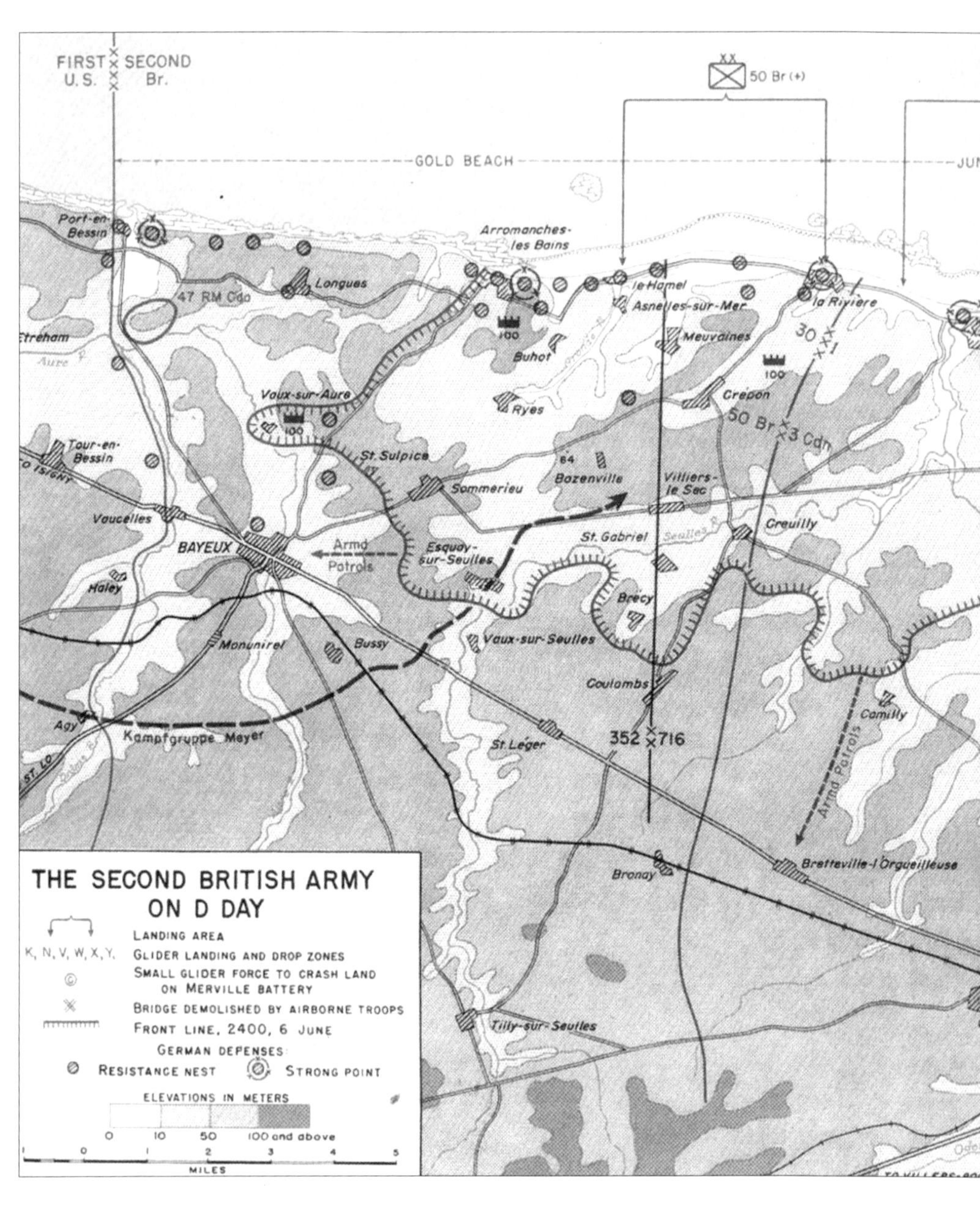

FIRST U.S.
SECOND Br.
50 Br (+)
GOLD BEACH
JUNO
Port-en-Bessin
Arromanches-les Bains
Longues
47 RM Cdo
le Hamel
Asnelles-sur-Mer
la Riviere
Etreham
Aure R.
100
Buhot
Meuvaines
30 XX I
100
Crepon
Vaux-sur-Aure
100
Ryes
50 Br 3 Cdn
Tour-en-Bessin
TO ISIGNY
St. Sulpice
64
Bazenville
Villiers-le Sec
Sommerieu
Vaucelles
St. Gabriel
Seulles R.
Creully
BAYEUX
Armd Patrols
Esquay-sur-Seulles
Haley
Brecy
Manunirel
Bussy
Vaux-sur-Seulles
Coulombs
Camilly
Agy
Kampfgruppe Meyer
St. Leger
352 716
Armd Patrols
ST. LO
Bretteville-l'Orgueilleuse
Bronay
THE SECOND BRITISH ARMY ON D DAY
LANDING AREA
K, N, V, W, X, Y, GLIDER LANDING AND DROP ZONES
SMALL GLIDER FORCE TO CRASH LAND ON MERVILLE BATTERY
BRIDGE DEMOLISHED BY AIRBORNE TROOPS
FRONT LINE, 2400, 6 JUNE
GERMAN DEFENSES
RESISTANCE NEST
STRONG POINT
ELEVATIONS IN METERS
0 10 50 100 and above
1 0 1 2 3 4 5
MILES
Tilly-sur-Seulles
Odon